China as a Twenty First Century Naval Power

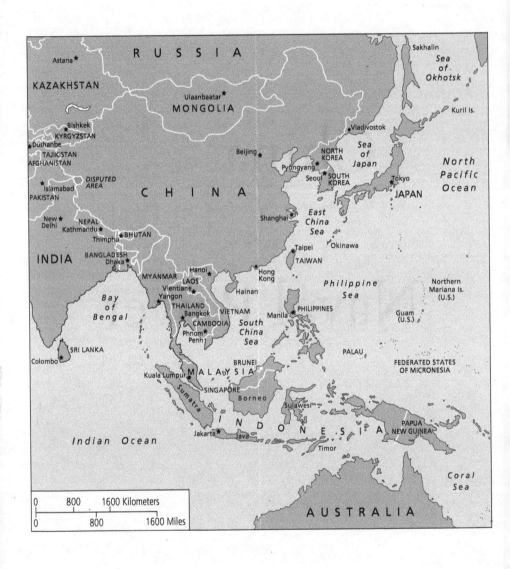

RUSSIA

Astana★

KAZAKHSTAN

Bishkek★
KYRGYZSTAN
★Dushanbe
TAJIKISTAN
AFGHANISTAN

DISPUTED
AREA

★Islamabad
PAKISTAN

New★
Delhi
NEPAL
Kathmandu★ ★BHUTAN
Thimphu

INDIA

BANGLADESH
Dhaka★

Ulaanbaatar★
MONGOLIA

Beijing★

CHINA

Shanghai★

Vladivostok

Sea
of
Japan

NORTH
KOREA
Pyongyang★
Seoul★ SOUTH
KOREA

Tokyo★
JAPAN

Sakhalin

Sea
of
Okhotsk

Kuril Is.

North
Pacific
Ocean

East
China
Sea

Taipei★
TAIWAN

Okinawa

Bay
of
Bengal

MYANMAR
Vientiane LAOS
Yangon
THAILAND
Bangkok★
CAMBODIA
Phnom
Penh

Hanoi★

VIETNAM

Hong
Kong

Hainan

South
China
Sea

Manila★

Philippine
Sea

PHILIPPINES

Northern
Mariana Is.
(U.S.)

Guam
(U.S.)

SRI LANKA
Colombo

BRUNEI

Kuala Lumpur★ MALAYSIA
★SINGAPORE

Sumatra

Borneo

Sulawesi

PALAU

FEDERATED STATES
OF MICRONESIA

Jakarta★
Java

INDONESIA

PAPUA
NEW GUINEA

Indian Ocean

Timor

Coral
Sea

AUSTRALIA

| 0 | 800 | 1600 Kilometers |
| 0 | 800 | 1600 Miles |

China as a Twenty First Century Naval Power

Theory, Practice, and Implications

Michael A. McDevitt

NAVAL INSTITUTE PRESS
ANNAPOLIS, MARYLAND

Naval Institute Press
291 Wood Road
Annapolis, MD 21402

First Naval Institute Press paperback edition published in 2023.
ISBN: 978-1-55750-113-4 (paperback)

The Library of Congress has cataloged the hardcover edition as follows:
Title: China as a twenty-first-century naval power : theory, practice, and
   implications / Michael A. McDevitt.
Description: Annapolis, MD : Naval Institute Press, [2020] | Includes
   bibliographical references and index.
Identifiers: LCCN 2020013637 (print) | LCCN 2020013638 (ebook) | ISBN
   9781682475355 (hardcover) | ISBN 9781682475447 (epub) | ISBN
   9781682475447 (pdf)
Subjects: LCSH: China. Zhongguo ren min jie fang jun. Hai jun. |
   China—Military policy. | Sea-power—China. | Military planning—China.
Classification: LCC VA633 .M39 2020 (print) | LCC VA633 (ebook) |
DDC
   359/.030951—dc23
LC record available at https://lccn.loc.gov/2020013637
LC ebook record available at https://lccn.loc.gov/2020013638

♾ Print editions meet the requirements of ANSI/NISO z39.48-1992
(Permanence of Paper).
Printed in the United States of America.

31 30 29 28 27 26 25 24 23   9 8 7 6 5 4 3 2 1
First printing

CONTENTS

ILLUSTRATIONS

PREFACE

This is a book about today's Chinese navy and how it transitioned from the baby operational steps it was taking in the 1990s to the legitimate "blue-water" force it is today. It argues that twelve years of northern Arabian antipiracy patrols, thousands of miles from China, represented the key accelerant in this rise in capability. These operations were a blue-water "laboratory" where the Chinese navy learned how to sustain warships on distant station for many weeks at a time. They overlapped with the takeoff in Chinese naval warship procurement that began just fifteen years ago. Since 2005 the People's Republic of China (PRC) has financed the building of enough warships to create the second-most-capable blue-water navy in the world.

Burdened with the awkward official name of People's Liberation Army Navy, the PLA Navy (in some sources simply PLAN) is the naval arm of the Chinese Communist Party (CCP). Although it flies the national flag, its loyalty is to the CCP, and the leaders of the PRC never let its members forget this. This party navy is a modern, well-equipped force that is numerically larger than the U.S. Navy. Yes, the PLA Navy is the largest navy in the world. This is still a bit of shock; in fact, one respected scholar argued in 2018 that China "will never become a seapower as long as it remains a vast land empire. . . . [T]he sea is so unimportant [to China] that China does not have [a] navy."[1] Technically, I suppose he is right, but if China does not have a navy, the CCP certainly does. In fact, the sea is so important to the PRC that it has its sights set on becoming a "great maritime power" with a navy that is "world-class," in the words of Xi Jinping, the general secretary of the CCP and also president of the People's Republic of China and commander in chief of China's military, the PLA.

This book is not a history of the PLA Navy; that book has already been well written, twice, by Dr. Bernard Cole. What it attempts to do is explain how the PLA Navy arrived, seemingly overnight, in its role of eminence; where it is headed in terms of growth; and what role it plays in defending China and Chinese national interests. It delves in some detail into the role the PLA Navy plays in the Chinese military's layered-defense concept. That concept the U.S. Department of Defense (DoD) characterizes as "anti-access" and "area denial" (or, as it is better known by defense experts worldwide, A2/AD). It explains how the PLA Navy fits into a joint Chinese military concept of operations aimed at keeping America's navy and air force at arm's length should conflict between the United States and China break out. The role the PLA Navy might play in denying U.S. armed forces access to the western Pacific Ocean—where America's regional allies (Japan, South Korea, the Philippines, and Thailand) all live in the shadow of China—is explored in this book.

Taiwan, also known as the Republic of China (ROC), is also in the PRC's shadow. Taiwan is an important topic in this book, because it is the East Asian friction point that could most credibly involve the United States in a war with China. Should the PRC elect to use force to "reunite" what it deems its wayward province, the PLA Navy will play a leading role. In the unlikely but possible event that Xi Jinping orders the PLA to attack, U.S. forces permanently stationed in East Asia could quickly become involved in conflict with China. That is especially true for the U.S. Seventh Fleet and Fifth Air Force, both of which are stationed on Japanese territory. The book explores the operational roles of the PLA Navy and its sister PLA services in such a conflict.

This work also aims to put the PLA Navy into the broader context of China's national goal to become a great maritime power—or, as some would have it, a "maritime great power." The PRC has developed an impressive blend of all the capabilities one would associate with maritime power. Discovering these facts is the reason I decided to write this book. I was reviewing, in connection with a research project, the text of former PRC leader Hu Jintao's 2012 tediously long "work report" to the party congress at the end of his term in office. Wading through an English version of the document, I came across a statement establishing as a national objective that China should become a "great maritime power." I was immediately struck by the audacity of such an assertion, as well as with its candor and lack of equivocation.

My curiosity was piqued. How did the leadership of the Chinese party-state think about maritime power? How did it interpret maritime power? Why did it want to become a maritime power? These questions eventually led to an eighteen-month study, which in turn eventually led to this book. It became clear over the course of my research that the Chinese Communist Party leadership has concluded that becoming a maritime power is essential to long-term national goals—goals that the current general secretary has encapsulated as the "China Dream," a so-called great rejuvenation of the Chinese state that will be accomplished by 2049.

The more my colleagues at the Center for Naval Analyses (or CNA, a research center in Arlington, Virginia, just across the Potomac River from Washington, DC) and I dug into the maritime-power goal, the clearer it became that when Hu announced this objective in 2012, China was not starting with a clean sheet of paper. This was not a "bolt out of the blue" aspiration; rather, in terms of party policy, it was the culminating point of over a decade of careful consideration of, and appreciation for, the importance of the maritime domain to China's continued development, to its security, and to its vision of its place in the world.

China's strategic circumstances have changed dramatically over the past thirty years. Since the 1990s, the dramatic growth in China's economic and security interests abroad have combined with traditional maritime-centered strategic objectives (such as unification with Taiwan and the "reclaiming" of land features in the East and South China Seas) to create a new reality that demands a focus on the maritime domain. Once Xi made maritime power an element of his "dream of the great rejuvenation of the Chinese nation," it became a forgone conclusion that becoming a great maritime power will remain a national objective.

China defines maritime power the way the world largely defines it, as a broad construct that encompasses more than naval power. What is different, however, is the Chinese emphasis on the power that having a "world-class navy" yields. Such a force is the essential prerequisite of "great" maritime power. That is why the focus of the book is the PLA Navy; it is the keystone of the entire Chinese maritime-power edifice. Beijing clearly understands and appreciates that the maritime-power equation also includes a large and effective coast guard; a world-class merchant marine and fishing fleet; a globally recognized shipbuilding capacity; and an ability to harvest or extract economically important maritime resources.

This book also dwells on another statement made before a party congress, this one by Xi Jinping. During his first work report as general secretary, to the 19th Party Congress in 2017, Xi stated he wanted the entire PRC military establishment, known as the People's Liberation Army, to be a "world-class" force by 2049 and that ongoing modernization was to be largely be completed by 2035, just fifteen years away.[2] Neither Xi nor other senior officials have defined what "world-class" means, but the phrase connotes "second to none," "top tier," or "best in the world." This work puts flesh on these bones and provides a sense of what "world-class" means for the PLA Navy.

The central role the PLA Navy plays in China's contemporary national strategy is examined. PRC strategists are obsessed with the notion that America is bent on containing China; the PLA Navy's mission includes trying to thwart any attempt at military containment, which would almost certainly capitalize on the PRC's economic dependence on maritime trade in raw materials, especially hydrocarbons. This dependence causes Beijing and the PLA Navy to be anxious that its sea lines of communication (SLOC) could be interrupted. Reading official PLA defense documents could lead one to believe the PLA Navy is suffering from a case of "SLOC anxiety." For the PLA Navy, the problem is real. It is particularly acute in the Indian Ocean where its long SLOC presents the PLA Navy with a very difficult defensive problem. A very different SLOC situation exists in the South China Sea, where since the late 1950s the PLA Navy has played a leading part in China's slow but steady accumulation of land features and their conversion into military bases. Today a network of island bases provides the PLA Navy the means to protect this thousand-nautical-mile SLOC.

In short, this book addresses the surprising growth and maturation of the PLA Navy. It is an exploration of the growth of China's navy from the perspective of the missions assigned by the party-state. It discusses why China seeks to become a maritime power; why President Xi Jinping has determined that China should possess a "world-class" navy by midcentury; and why he is pressing the entire PLA, including the navy, to have this world-class objective "largely completed" in fifteen years. Coincidently perhaps, 2035 is also when the Trump administration's goal of a 355-ship U.S. Navy is projected to be achieved.

The book concludes by exploring what a "world-class navy" might look like. We know it will be big, but will it begin to operate sizable naval task forces abroad on a routine basis as the U.S. Navy does, or will the operational focus remain regional, with only modestly sized formations active overseas? My conclusion is that it will be a force with global expeditionary capability, mimicking the United States in certain aspects in the Indian Ocean region, but that it will also maintain an overwhelming regional force reminiscent of imperial Japan's on the eve of World War II.

Finally, not so very long ago the idea that China would become a maritime power seemed absurd. Today, that preposterous idea has become reality. On June 1, 2019, DoD released an official *Indo-Pacific Strategy Report* that repeats a claim first made in the Trump administration's *National Security Strategy*, that China seeks "Indo-Pacific regional hegemony in the near term and ultimately global preeminence in the long term." This book judges that maritime predominance in the western Pacific is a credible Chinese aspiration. I am, however, dubious that China seeks global preeminence; however, if the DoD is correct, Beijing is going to need a very large navy.

A word about the appendices.

This work has two superb contributed appendices, one on the China Coast Guard and the other on China's maritime militia. They were written by America's leading experts on these subjects, Ryan D. Martinson, Dr. Andrew S. Erickson, and Conor M. Kennedy, at my request. I asked them to do this because to focus simply on the PLA Navy would produce an incomplete and unbalanced picture of the totality of China's coercive maritime power. In the East and South China Seas, the PLA Navy has largely remained over the horizon, leaving the dirty work of asserting China's maritime claims, in an often heavy-handed way, to the coast guard and the PLA-controlled maritime militia.

ACKNOWLEDGMENTS

Since leaving active duty in the U.S. Navy I have had the good fortune to remain involved in national security issues involving the United States, especially those in East Asia, through my work at CNA. I am not a sinologist, and I do not speak Chinese, but fortunately I have been in the company of many incredibly talented sinologists who do speak and read Mandarin and have taught me a great deal about China. I want to thank especially Dr. David Finkelstein, a friend and colleague for over two decades who heads CNA's large and talented China team. I am also indebted to Dr. Thomas Bickford, a scholar of note on Chinese maritime issues, who made a major contribution to our study of China's maritime-power ambitions; to Mr. Alan Burns, another member of the CNA China team who also contributed an insightful paper to the maritime ambitions study; and to Mr. James Bellaqua, whose cheerful assistance in researching Chinese-language sources is gratefully appreciated. I also need to thank Mr. Robert Murray, who over two decades ago took a chance in hiring me to initiate a program dedicated to East Asian security issues. My sincere gratitude goes also to Dr. Bernard "Bud" Cole, who provided advice and encouragement during the entirety of a project that is attempting to follow in his wake.

Finally, I wish to express my gratitude to the love of my life, my wife Edie, who has tolerated with extremely good grace and much encouragement my hours hidden away in my study working on this book. Try as I might, I have failed to arouse in her even a scintilla of interest in the Chinese navy.

CHAPTER ONE

China's Maritime Power Ambition

November 17, 2012, was an important moment in China's maritime history.[1] The approximately 2,200 senior party members attending China's 18th Party Congress heard something they had never heard from a leader of the party-state. Hu Jintao, the outgoing general secretary of the Chinese Communist Party, informed them China should become a *haiyang qiangguo*—a maritime great power.[2] This single sentence, that China "should enhance our capacity for exploiting marine resources, develop the marine economy, protect the marine ecological environment, resolutely safeguard China's maritime rights and interests, and *build China into a maritime great power*" (my emphasis), was of great significance. For the first time in China's long history, its leader had asserted that China, a traditional continental power, aspired to become a leading, perhaps *the* leading, maritime power.[3]

At the time it would have been easy to disregard this single sentence as just one more in a long list of objectives and aspirations in Hu's "end of tour" wrap-up. It was not. Party Congress work reports are accounts of the preceding five years of leadership of the party-state and also reflections of party consensus on the policy agenda for the next five years. They most certainly are not empty exercises in party jargon and rhetorical ritual.[4] Now, almost a decade after Hu's departing exhortations, Beijing's tangible actions make it quite clear that becoming a maritime great power is a very serious and well-considered strategic objective, one dictated by China's growing dependence on the high seas for defense, trade-driven economic growth, raw materials, food security (fish for protein), and the recovery of "lost" island territories.

In short, the announcement of the objective of becoming a maritime great power was not a "bolt out of the blue"; rather, it marked the culminating point of over a decade of careful Chinese consideration of, and appreciation for, the importance of the maritime domain to its continued development, its security, and its vision of its place in the world. For instance, as early as 2007 Hu asserted to a group of PLA Navy officers at a party meeting that China was a "great maritime power" and that it needed to continue to develop "blue-water" (high seas) capabilities.[5]

Later in his long presentation, Hu announced another goal directly related to the "maritime power" objective. He called for building a military that would be "commensurate with China's international standing." This statement is a broadly defined benchmark for determining how large and capable the PLA should become. As we will see, Hu's successor has elaborated on this rather vague objective and restated it more specifically as achieving a "world-class military" by 2049. Again, neither Hu's statement or his subsequently established related goals were empty rhetoric. Becoming a great maritime power and building a world-class military have been embraced as objectives and clarified by his successor, the current party general secretary, chair of the Central Military Commission (CMC), and president of the People's Republic of China (PRC), Xi Jinping. During his first work report as general secretary, to the 19th Party Congress in 2017, Xi redefined "commensurate with China's international standing" to mean "world class": "We will make it our mission to see that by 2035, the modernization of our national defense and our forces is basically completed; and that by the mid-21st century our people's armed forces have been fully transformed into *world-class forces*."[6]

While building a "world-class" military is a work in progress, there is no question that the necessary reorganization and modernization of the PLA is well under way.[7] The PLA Navy has been an especially favored beneficiary of the decisions to grow and modernize the PLA.[8]

For students of the PLA, the immediate question in the aftermath of Hu's speech was how much his chosen successor, Xi Jinping, had influenced the report and embraced its objectives. This question was answered conclusively in the China's 2012 defense white paper (DWP), which was not released until April 2013, after Xi Jinping had assumed party and national leadership.[9]

China is a major maritime as well as land country. The seas and oceans provide immense space and abundant resources for China's sustainable development, and thus are of vital importance to the people's wellbeing and China's future. It is an essential national development strategy to exploit, utilize and protect the seas and oceans, and build China into *a maritime power*. It is an important duty for the PLA to resolutely safeguard China's maritime rights and interests.[10]

In 2012 it was not entirely clear to observers what the leadership of China meant, since in Western usage "maritime power" is ambiguous. Was Beijing using it as a synonym for "sea power," a term that in the West normally relates specifically to navies? Or were they using it in its broader sense, one that includes all aspects of the maritime enterprise?

What Is a Maritime Power?

As Professor Geoffrey Till has written in his well-regarded work *Sea Power,* "maritime power" and "sea power" are often vaguely defined.[11] Ever since "sea power" entered the global security lexicon, thanks to Adm. Alfred Thayer Mahan, its precise definition and that of "maritime" power have been unclear, which results in their often being used interchangeably.[12]

In current Western discourse, "maritime power" tends to be used as an inherently broad concept, embracing all uses of the sea, both civil and military. In its widest sense, it can be defined as ability to use the sea to exert military, political, or economic power or influence. The maritime power of a state reflects sea-based military capabilities, such as ships and submarines, as well as a range of military land-based assets and space-based systems that may or may not be operated by the navy. It also includes civilian capabilities, such as a coast guard, port infrastructure, merchant shipping, fishing, and shipbuilding.[13]

A good example of a broad definition of maritime power was given during a 2003 U.S. Naval War College conference dedicated to the topic. The then-commandant of the U.S. Coast Guard said that twenty-first-century maritime power speaks to a nation's needs beyond purely military ones. It embraces the needs to preserve maritime resources, ensure safe transit and passage of cargoes and peoples by water, protect its maritime borders from intrusion, uphold its maritime sovereignty, rescue the distressed at sea, and prevent misuse of the oceans.[14] In sum, the difference between maritime power and sea power, in this view, is that "sea power" emphasizes largely the naval dimension, whereas "maritime power" connotes both the naval and civil elements of a nation's maritime capabilities.

Chinese leaders, military and civilian officials, and security analysts have consistently viewed maritime power in this fashion, as encompassing a wide range of military and civilian capabilities. In the Chinese interpretation, however, the foundation of maritime power is a strong navy, on which other very important factors rest. These latter include a large and effective coast guard, a first-class merchant marine and fishing fleet, a globally recognized shipbuilding capability, and the ability to extract economically important maritime resources.

Since 2012 it has become clear also that while China defines "maritime power" in its broadest sense, it also has concluded that its coercive elements are central to the protection and advancement of China's maritime rights and interests and that they are not limited to the navy but include the coast guard (described in appendix I) and maritime militia (appendix II). It is the coercive elements of maritime power—particularly the navy—that constitute the primary focus of this book.

What Exactly Are China's Maritime Rights and Interests?

Since the phrase "China's maritime rights and interests" first came into use in 1992, with the passage of the PRC Territorial Sea and Contiguous Zone Law, Chinese leaders have been talking about the importance of defending them.[15] Determining precisely and in practical terms what "China's maritime rights and interests" means is a frustrating undertaking. It involves coming to grips with a process of circular reasoning that permits Beijing to translate Chinese perceptions, opinions, and policy preferences into Chinese laws and regulations that cannot be questioned and are to be strictly enforced. It is hard to escape the conclusion that China's maritime rights and interests are whatever China says they are. They take precedence over customary international law, including, especially, the United Nations Convention on the Law of the Sea (UNCLOS), and are considered as having more weight than the rights and interests of neighbors.

The term is used to rationalize specific maritime measures taken to enforce domestic Chinese regulations or laws passed by the Chinese

National People's Congress. These laws and regulations "enshrine" Chinese legal "rights." China's maritime interests—its goals, ambitions, and geopolitical aims—have been absorbed into its laws. The so-called nine-dash line (9DL) in the South China Sea is an example. Here, a claim to land features drawn on a nautical chart in 1946–47 by the eventual losers of the Chinese Civil War, the Republic of China (ROC), was co-opted by Beijing into Chinese maritime law as establishing its own "historic rights" to all resources within the 9DL.[16]

Nearly every public Chinese pronouncement about maritime power invokes China's maritime rights and interests. As we have seen, Hu Jintao officially linked the formulation of "rights and interest" to China's becoming a maritime power at the 18th Party Congress. President Xi Jinping has reiterated and intensified his predecessor's call for maritime power and to that end has mobilized the state to take active "countermeasures to safeguard our nation's maritime rights and interests."[17] Essentially, China's promotion of its maritime rights and interests is an important facet of efforts to develop economically, regulate legally, and control effectively ocean areas under its claimed jurisdiction.[18]

Central elements of the "rights and interests" concept, accordingly, are protection and enforcement. The ability to protect China's maritime rights is considered essential to China's becoming a maritime power. In fall 2013, an official of the State Oceanic Administration (SOA) wrote, "The most important prerequisite for the building of a maritime power is to . . . *protect the nation's maritime rights and interests from being violated.* If our nation's core maritime interests and the basic maritime rights and interests *cannot be effectively protected, there is no way to talk about building a maritime power.*"[19]

That is, Chinese leaders treat the protection of maritime rights and interests as a *necessary condition* for becoming a maritime power. Officials, experts, media, and semi-informed citizens routinely cite it as the key component of maritime power. Simply having maritime rights and interests is not sufficient; after all, every nation that borders the sea does. For China what is essential is being able to protect them from being violated. This is what sets China apart from many of its Asian neighbors: Beijing has the capability not only to protect but also to advance its rights and interests coercively, if need be, while most of its neighbors do not.

Why Does China Want to Become a Maritime Great Power?

There is a sound strategic rationale behind China's desire to become a maritime great power; that will be addressed in a moment. In today's China, the most important reason is that "the boss" has established maritime power as a strategic objective. It is linked directly to Xi Jinping's grand strategic vision, known as the "China Dream," of achieving the rejuvenation of the Chinese nation by 2049, the hundredth anniversary of the founding of the People's Republic. Xi has embraced maritime power as an essential element of this dream, encouraging a Weltanschauung among the party and PLA that maritime power is a necessity. Once Xi linked maritime power with the China Dream, it became a foregone conclusion that as long as he is in charge this will remain a national objective. According to Xi, building maritime power "is of great and far-reaching significance for promoting sustained and healthy economic development, safeguarding national sovereignty, security and development interests, realizing the goal of completing the building of a well-off society, and subsequently realizing the great rejuvenation of the Chinese nation."[20]

At a Politburo study session in July 2013, Xi Jinping pointed out that China is at once a continental power and a maritime power and that it possesses broad maritime strategic interests.[21] These interests revolve around four primary strategic ends (objectives); first, defending China from an attack from the sea by the United States; second, making certain that China's international trade, much of it conducted by sea and on which the nation is economically dependent, is secure; third, pursuing the global political and security interests that China's global economic interests have created; and fourth, recovering sovereignty over its claimed maritime territory—especially Taiwan. To accomplish all of these strategic objectives requires a mix of maritime capabilities: a shipbuilding industry, a large Chinese-flagged merchant marine, a capable coast guard, and most of all a large navy able to deal effectively with the threat of "containment," defend China's sovereignty in the maritime domain (which includes Taiwan), and protect China's maritime trade and overseas interests.

China's economic growth over the past thirty years has provided the means to accomplish these ends. China's industrial and technical capability allows it to manufacture the basic sinews of maritime power—

steel, shipyards, ships of every sort, advanced shipboard weapons and combat systems—necessary to make becoming a great maritime power a realistic ambition.

Exploring China's "Strategic Ends"
Protecting China from Attack from the Sea

As far-fetched as it might seem that any nation would launch a surprise attack on China—with its secure retaliatory inventory of nuclear weapons and its impressive and growing conventional military—PLA strategists do not overlook that possibility. Its primary competitor, the United States, has demonstrated since early in the twentieth century the ability to sail across vast oceans and then employ decisive military power against nations in Eurasia and the Middle East. It also has formal defense treaties with Japan, South Korea, and the Philippines, arrangements that could bring the full force of American power into East Asia if those allies were attacked. Thus, it is not a surprise that strategists at the Academy of Military Sciences (AMS) could write:

> The danger of war in the maritime, air, space, and/or cyber domains is escalating. The threat of war in the east is more serious than the threat of war in the west, the threat of war from the sea exceeds that of the threat of war from the land . . . the probability of military [use for] rights protection abroad, and even limited operational actions is increasing. The most serious threat of war is from a formidable enemy to initiate a war with our country through a surprise attack with [the] purpose of destroying our country's ability to wage war. . . . The most likely threat of war is *limited military conflicts from the maritime direction*.[22]

It is important to note that AMS authors think that a large-scale, high-intensity defensive war involving "hegemonic" countries (read: the United States) that seek to stop China's "peaceful rise" would be dangerous but is of low probability. The PLA's main mission in defense of China is "to contain, prevent, and resist possible attacks from the maritime direction, especially large-scale, high-intensity intermediate- and long-range precision strikes, to ensure the security of the homeland" (more about this in the next chapters).[23]

The center of gravity of China's economy is along its eastern seaboard, where the great economic centers of Guangzhou, Hong Kong, Fujian, Shanghai, and the greater Bohai Gulf region are all susceptible to attack from the sea. This vulnerability has historical resonance with the leadership of China, and any discussion of why Beijing is focused on securing the nation's maritime approaches must start with nineteenth- and twentieth-century history.

Ironically, given that China is the now the world's largest trading nation, its "Century of Humiliation" (1840–1949) was triggered by a trade dispute. The desire of English merchant traders to sell ever larger quantities of opium was the proximate cause. China's emperor was the impediment; he was attempting to curtail the scourge of opium addiction that was sweeping China. In truth what was happening was that the British wanted unlimited access to Chinese markets and China's imperial court did not want to grant it. China did not want trade to increase. Humiliation began when Great Britain's Royal Navy was able to brush aside imperial China's pathetic maritime defenses; the antiquated forts and sailing junks that protected its main ports were overrun and captured during the First Opium War (1840–42). This was the opening salvo in a hundred-odd years of disaster for China. A series of short, "limited" maritime conflicts—the Arrow War (Second Opium War), the Sino-French naval war, the Sino-Japanese War, the Boxer Rebellion—resulted in more defeats and ever increasing losses of Chinese sovereignty, primarily to the British but to the Americans close behind, then the French, and soon the Russians, Japanese, and Germans.

All these states were able to impose unequal treaties that permitted Westerners to gain access to China, carve off pieces of the Chinese Empire (northern Vietnam, Korea, parts of Siberia, and Manchuria), take over crucial parts of its government, proselytize its people, and eventually, in the case of Japan, invade and attempt to conquer China in an unlimited war (1937–45).[24] Xi's work report to the 19th Party Congress in October 2017 recalled this history: "With a history of more than 5,000 years, our nation created a splendid civilization[,] . . . became one of the world's great nations. But with the Opium War of 1840, China was plunged into the darkness of domestic turmoil and foreign aggression; its people[,] ravaged by war, saw their homeland torn apart and lived in poverty and despair."[25]

Significantly for today's Chinese commentators, the foreign militaries that humiliated imperial China came mainly by sea. In 2013 the AMS textbook *The Science of Military Strategy* gave a threat assessment that would have been valid 170 years earlier: "Today and for a long time to come, our country's . . . national security is threatened mainly from the sea, [and accordingly] the focal point of military struggle is mainly in the sea."[26]

Contributing to China's Economic Growth and Defending Interests Abroad

Expansion of trade has played a critical role in China's economic growth over the four decades since the CCP's decision to open China's economy to trade and investment. China moved from hundredth in terms of world trade in 1978 to the world's largest trading nation in 2013, when it supplanted the United States.[27] It is worth recalling that in October 1992 Jiang Zemin, then general secretary, specifically called for China to "open up more international markets, diversify our trading partners and develop an export-oriented economy. We should expand export trade, change the export product mix and export high grade commodities of good quality."[28] China has done all that. It has become fully integrated into the globalized economy, as a consequence of two events in particular. First, in 2001 China became a member of the World Trade Organization (WTO); second, soon after, China adopted a "go-out" strategy, based on encouraging its state-owned enterprises to invest and expand overseas. The result was the rapid expansion of China's economic presence around the world.[29]

The growth of trade as a pillar of China's economy raised sensitivity to potential vulnerabilities of sea-lanes well beyond China's "near seas." As long ago as 1993 China became a net importer of oil, and by late 2017 it had become the world's largest importer of crude oil, again overtaking the United States; by then China was importing 8.4 million barrels of crude daily—about 85 percent of it arriving by tanker.[30] Crude oil is by far China's largest import by dollar value, but the remainder of China's top ten imports are also raw materials needed for its economy (iron ore, copper, plastics, coal, etc.) or are food products (soybeans, cereals, vegetable oil) to feed its people and livestock.[31] On the other side of the ledger, China has been the world's largest exporter since 2009. Given that (according to the London-based International Chamber of Shipping) approximately 90 percent of world trade travels by sea and that China is the world's largest trading nation, it is safe to conclude that somewhere between 80 and 90 percent of China's total trade travels by sea. This means the health of China's economy requires a secure maritime environment in which its trade can continue to flow uninterruptedly. This means, in turn, that the SLOCs to and from China must be protected. The upshot of all this is that China today is suffering from what I characterize as a bad case of "SLOC anxiety."

Well before Hu Jintao's 2012 announcement, the leaderships of China and the PLA were both concerned about sea-lane security.[32] This concern became most obvious in 2008, when for the first time China decided to send two warships and a large oiler thousand miles away to the northern Arabian Sea to participate in a sustained operational mission. That is, it opted to join the global "crusade" against Somali piracy. Beijing had been embarrassed a year earlier when Somali pirates had hijacked a Chinese fishing boat and the only thing China had been able to do was to "assess" the situation and hope for help. But in October 2008 the United Nations Security Council adopted Resolution 1838 calling on nations whose vessels routinely traveled through the area to apply military force to repress piracy, and by December China was ready to act.[33] Little wonder—in 2008 there were 111 pirate attacks, including forty-two successful hijackings.[34]

A central theme of this book is the impact of anxiety regarding SLOCs on the development of a Chinese navy capable of operating anywhere in the world. In chapter 3, the "accelerant" effect of the multinational antipiracy effort on the operational development of the PLA Navy will be detailed. At this point it is enough to say these operations seem to have heightened awareness in Beijing that its SLOC security issue involves more than pirates in the Gulf of Aden. Official manifestation of this broadened anxiety is found in the 2015 defense white paper, *China's Military Strategy*: "With the growth of China's national interests, its national security is more vulnerable to international and regional turmoil, terrorism, piracy, serious natural disasters and epidemics, and the security of overseas interests concerning energy and resources, strategic sea lines of communication (SLOCs), as well as institutions, personnel and assets abroad, *has become an imminent issue.*"[35]

Beyond trade and sea-lanes it is important to recognize the emphasis that China is placing on what it calls the "blue economy." Over the past fifteen years the importance of the ocean to China's overall economy has become a major element in Beijing's overall economic planning. To that end Beijing has formulated a comprehensive national ocean-development strategy and has now codified it in China's five-year-planning process. Ocean development first appeared in the twelfth five-year Plan for National and Social Development (2011–15), under the rubric of the "ocean economy" as a key part of national development.[36] In April 2012 Premier Wen Jiabao highlighted this new focus: "In the 12th Five-Year Plan period we specifically opened up and elaborated on the concept 'promote ocean economic development' and put forward a 'formulate and implement ocean development strategy.' This is a great change in our country's strategic thinking."[37]

The ocean economy is closely related to China's anxiety over "food security," even the possibility of scarcity. Large tracts of land can no longer be farmed because of pollution, forcing China to become a net importer of grain and corn. China's drive for economic growth has also greatly damaged its offshore waters, where contaminated runoff and overfishing have reduced fish stocks significantly. The fishing industry has accordingly been pressed to operate farther from China to meet increased demand for protein in the Chinese diet. As a result, China has the world's largest fleet of fishing vessels capable of operating globally. This fleet is growing in numbers (currently around 2,700) and is playing a growing role in assuring China's food security.[38] In recent years, the notion of "blue granary[,] or marine based food security" has become a domestically popular concept for achieving that goal.[39]

Regional and Global Security Interests: Starting with Taiwan

The crucial economic reliance on the sea might have been enough in itself to make the Chinese Communist Party decide to take the historically remarkable step of deciding that China must become a maritime power, but in fact it was not the only factor. With the collapse of the Soviet Union in 1991 China's fundamental security interests became centered on the maritime domain, especially since, operationally, Taiwan was a maritime problem.

China has unresolved maritime sovereignty, maritime entitlement, and demarcation disputes with all of its maritime neighbors. The most serious of these is reasserting de facto sovereignty over Taiwan and ending the existence of the Republic of China. China wants this "unification" of the mainland and Taiwan to occur peacefully and to that end has offered the concept of "one country" (i.e., China) and "two systems" (democratic Taiwan and communist China).[40] However, Taiwan's almost thirty years of democratic governance has created a new generation of Taiwanese who want nothing to do with the heavy hand of Xi Jinping–style Communist Party control.[41] Beijing reluctantly recognizes that the people of Taiwan are not eager to cede their independence and de facto sovereignty to communist Beijing. Accordingly, the mainland has not renounced the possibility of using force either to deter a unilateral move toward de jure independence or to compel reunification militarily. In 1993 China's high command, the CMC, made Taiwan its focal point for strategy, planning, and procurement—what the PLA calls "the main strategic direction."[42]

In fact, a military solution to the Taiwan question was a credible contingency since 1949, when the ROC government fled there; Beijing immediately recognized that capturing the island might be the only way to reunite the two. However, the opportunity quickly passed: since 1950, the U.S. military has stood in the way, sometimes literally, as when the Truman administration directed the Seventh Fleet into the Taiwan Strait.[43] The option once again became realistic in 1991, when the collapse of the Soviet Union removed the threat of ground attack from the north and left the PLA able to concentrate its planning and procurement on its maritime frontier, with Taiwan the top priority. This is why Jiang Zemin laid down in 1993 that "the focal point of military struggle is to prevent a major incident of Taiwan independence from occurring."[44] In the hierarchy of maritime-oriented threats, *Science of Military Strategy* places a large-scale, high-intensity "antisecession" conflict over Taiwanese independence second to only a surprise attack to destroy China's ability to wage war.

In 1996, Beijing, worried that Taiwan's President Lee Teng-hui was inching toward independence, attempted to influence the March 1997 presidential election by conducting large-scale exercises opposite Taiwan and firing ballistic missiles to within twenty to thirty miles of Taiwan's two main ports, Keelung and Kaohsiung. After much deliberation, Washington decided to respond with a show of naval strength. Two aircraft carrier battle groups were ordered to stand by near Taiwan in case the PRC used the exercises as a cover for an actual attack.

In the end no confrontation took place, and despite subsequent journalistic claims, no U.S. warships sailed through the Taiwan Strait during the crisis. The PLA's clumsy attempt to intimidate Taiwanese voters failed dismally; Lee Teng-hui won handily. For China's leadership, the lessons were clear: the PLA exercises had inadvertently drawn Washington into a more explicit commitment to Taiwan's defense, and the United States had demonstrated it could send warships to the vicinity with impunity.[45] From now on the PLA would have to assume that Washington would militarily intervene if Beijing decided to use force to accomplish reunification. Any doubts as to whether Washington would interfere in what Beijing considered (and still considers) a domestic matter had been removed. PLA war planners now had to factor into any operation to take over Taiwan how to stop the U.S. military from thwarting it. This new requirement eventually led the PLA to a concept of operations that the Pentagon has named "anti-access/area denial," or A2/AD, intended to keep reinforcements from Hawaii or the continental United States from interfering (as will be discussed in detail in chapter 5).

The importance of Taiwan to the CCP as a matter of national sovereignty and territorial integrity is well known. A statement by Xi Jinping in his 19th Party Congress address makes it crystal clear:

We will resolutely uphold national sovereignty and territorial integrity and will never tolerate a repeat of the historical tragedy of a divided country. All activities of splitting the motherland will be resolutely opposed by all the Chinese people. We have firm will, full confidence, and sufficient capability to defeat any form of Taiwan independence secession plot. We will never allow any person, any organization, or any political party to split any part of the Chinese territory from China at any time or in any form.[46]

But in the quest for reunification not just mainland irredentism, but also the island of Taiwan is in itself of great geostrategic importance to the PRC. As the 2005 edition of the *Science of Military Strategy* explained,

Taiwan is located in the southeast of our sea area and is in the middle of the islands surrounding our coastline. It is in the key area of sea routes of the Pacific Ocean and is thus crowned as "the key to the southeast coastal area of China," and "the fence to the seven provinces in the center of China." The sea routes from the East China Sea to the South China Sea, from Northeast Asia to Southeast Asia, as well as the route from the West Pacific to the Middle East, Europe and Asia pass here.

It is where we can breach the chain of islands surrounding us in the West Pacific to the vast area of the Pacific, as well as a strategic key area and sea barrier for defense and offense. If Taiwan should be alienated from the mainland, not only our natural maritime defense system would lose its depth, opening a sea gateway to outside forces, but also a large area of water territory would fall into the hands of others. What's more, our line of foreign trade and transportation[,] which is vital to China's opening up and economic development[,] will be exposed to the surveillance and threats of separatists and enemy forces and China will forever be locked to the west side of the first chain of islands in the West Pacific.[47]

This remarkable assessment makes clear the centrality of Taiwan to China's maritime strategic interests. Virtually all of China's eastern seaboard is geographically "contained" by what is termed the "first island chain," running from the main islands of Japan southward along the Ryukyu Islands to Taiwan and then through the Philippines. Not coincidently, Japan and the Philippines are U.S. treaty allies; for its part, the ROC has an implied American defense commitment because of the Taiwan Relations Act. The Chinese strategic perspective is clear: the island chain is effectively a barrier around the Yellow, East China, and South China Seas, constraining China's access to the Pacific Ocean. China wants to control these virtually enclosed seas to keep them from becoming avenues of attack on China proper and, at the same, to prevent denial of Chinese access to the high seas in peace or war. Control of Taiwan would solve this geostrategic problem. Beijing is also painfully aware that all of its major ports can be reached by sea only via the South China or East China Sea.

Taiwan is not China's only island-sovereignty dispute with its neighbors. It is embroiled with Japan in the East China Sea over the Senkaku/Diaoyu Islands and in the South China Sea with Vietnam, the Philippines, Brunei, and Malaysia about overlapping claims in the Paracel and Spratly Island chains. The PRC's turning tiny specks of land in the Spratly chain, some underwater at high tide, into major island bases has received global notice and has been interpreted by many as foreshadowing how the PRC would behave to its neighbors if it achieved regional military primacy. These island-fortification activities will be explored later in the book, but for the moment the important point is that Beijing sees them as justified as part of regaining control of islands and land features that it firmly believes have historically been Chinese territory.

The Twenty-First-Century Maritime Silk Road: Yet Another Rationale for Maritime Power

Directly related to China's overwhelming dependence on seaborne commerce is the twenty-first-century "Maritime Silk Road" announced by Xi Jinping in Jakarta, Indonesia, in October 2013. Xi spun that vision as a maritime companion piece to his earlier-announced "Silk Road Economic Belt" across the Eurasian landmass linking China to Europe, the routes to be created by a comprehensive "Belt and Road Initiative" (BRI). The BRI is Xi's Jinping's signature strategic and economic objective. The strategic aim is to connect Eurasian, Middle Eastern, and East African nations in a vast global trading network, enabled by Chinese loans, financing, or direct investment for trade-related infrastructure development. China is to be the center of this network—that is, in the case of maritime trade, all sea-lanes are to lead to China. The MSR is the BRI's maritime component.[48] In truth, the Maritime Silk Road has long existed, known more prosaically as China's traditional SLOCs to Europe. The route, by whatever name, runs from China through the South China Sea to the Strait of Malacca, then westward across the Indian Ocean, then northward, grazing East Africa, to the Red Sea and the Suez Canal, and finally into the Mediterranean. Significantly, this sea-lane is also the route that oil from the Persian Gulf travels to China. The BRI is closely associated with the China Dream, his objective of making China the equal of the greatest nations.[49]

To these ends China has mobilized its political, diplomatic, intellectual, economic, and financial resources, as well as the PLA in general and the navy in particular. As we shall see, the Maritime Silk Road vision, China's intention to become a maritime great power, announced just eleven months before, are closely linked, self-reinforcing ambitions. Perhaps the most startling evidence of the symbiotic relationship between the two was the establishment of China's first overseas base, in Djibouti.[50]

Assisting Chinese Citizens in Danger Abroad

China has more citizens living outside the country than does any other nation in the world. Many currently live in very dangerous countries in South Asia and Africa. As Lt. Gen. Liu Jixian, former commandant of AMS, wrote in *People's Daily* in February 2018, "With the development of the Belt and Road Initiative, massive personnel, resources and property are expanding to other countries and some countries are facing problems like war and terrorism," the implication being that China has no choice but to protect its assets in volatile regions. This perception is not new; even before the BRI took shape Beijing recognized as one of its most challenging maritime issues the protection of the burgeoning communities of Chinese workers overseas. China has already had to evacuate its citizens from Libya, in 2011, and from Yemen, in 2015.[51] In fact, by 2015 the DWP was fretting about overseas interests and people, warning that collectively they "had become an imminent issue."[52]

Final Thoughts: Xi Has His Foot on the Gas Pedal

Maritime power and the China Dream are inextricably linked. On one hand, the China Dream encapsulates China's long-standing national aspiration to become powerful and prosperous; on the other, the steady expansion of China's "comprehensive national power" is how the dream is eventually to be realized.

According to Xi's timetable, "the Dream" is to come true by the hundredth anniversary of the establishment of the People's Republic of China, in 2049. Importantly, the Dream includes the development of a military commensurate to great power; indeed, given Xi's formulation it would be impossible to accomplish the Dream without a powerful military, especially a navy, inasmuch as so much of China's wealth generation rests on imported natural resources and export of finished goods. According to Dr. James Mulvenon of Defense Group, Inc., "At the strategic level, he [Xi] linked the 'realization of the Chinese dream' to 'the dream of strengthening the military forces.' For Xi a powerful PLA is a necessity for achieving 'the Dream.'"[53]

Xi's October 2018 work report to the 19th Party Congress took three and a half hours to deliver and set the party's agenda for the next five years. He did not specifically repeat the object of becoming a great maritime power, already well in motion. It is already established policy.

Nor did he repeat the objective of a military befitting China's international standing. Instead, he raised that bar: "[T]he military should make an all-out effort to become a world-class armed force by 2050."[54] "World class" connotes being "second to none," being "top tier," even the "best in the world."[55] Most significantly, he established an accelerated deadline for military modernization. With a clear sense of urgency, Xi declared that "we will step up efforts to build China into a strong maritime country." He then explicitly outlined what "stepping up efforts" actually meant: "We will make it our mission to see that by 2035, the modernization of our national defense and our forces is basically completed; and that by the mid-21st century our people's armed forces have been fully transformed into world-class forces."[56]

Since his 19th Party Congress speech Xi has continued to reinforce the urgency of the task. Xi watched a May 2018 South China Sea naval review from the flying bridge of a new destroyer (wearing a trendy camouflage uniform). His message reminded the ten thousand or so sailors on over fifty ships and submarines "that the task of building up the strength of the people's navy has never been so urgent."[57]

As will be seen in succeeding chapters, the buildup of the navy has been most impressive. China will by 2020 be the second-most-capable navy in the world, at least in terms of ships and installed combat systems. How these ships actually will be employed is uncertain. They are already a regular presence in the western Indian Ocean—indeed, all along the Indian Ocean littoral. Will the PLA Navy, as its blue-water capability continues to expand, begin to routinely operate sizable naval task forces as the U.S. Navy does, or will its operational focus remain regional, sending only modestly sized formations abroad? This question is still open: China's newest and most outwardly impressive guided-missile destroyers (DDGs) and its fledgling aircraft carrier(s) have yet to deploy for sustained periods. Also open is the fundamental question of the effectiveness of their mainly Chinese-designed weapons systems.

Finally, though questions remain regarding the capability of their crews, twelve years of seven-month antipiracy deployments to the

Arabian Sea suggest that the crews (and their ships) perform at a high level. This is not to say, however, that the PLA Navy has been immune to persistent criticism from Xi and other senior CMC members that overall PLA training must improve and become more realistic. The PLA Navy itself worries about crew training and performance in combat. It is not permitted to be overconfident on the strength of its decade of operations halfway around the world: Xi himself continues to harp on realistic training.[58] All these questions will be addressed throughout this work.

CHAPTER TWO

Getting Started

Learning How to Operate Abroad

This chapter will survey the step-by-step process by which the PLA Navy developed the ships and the basic skills necessary for it to evolve from the coastal defense force of the Mao Tse-tung years to a navy with a burgeoning global expeditionary capability by the end of the second decade of the twenty-first century.[1] This transition began in 1975, when Mao, at a meeting of the Central Military Commission, directed the development of a modern (oceanic) navy. He did so probably in response to the growth of the Soviet navy and its influence in Vietnam, not because he anticipated that China would become an economic superpower.[2]

Today, some forty-five years later, the PLA Navy has mastered many of the operational skills necessary to deploy and sustain surface combatants, amphibious ships, submarines, and support ships on distant stations for long periods of time. It has been a quick study, thanks (in my judgment) to over a decade of continuous antipiracy deployments to the Arabian Gulf. These deployments have been a real-world "blue-water operations laboratory." For the past twelve years they have given the PLA Navy an opportunity to observe the day-to-day operations of the world's great navies and absorb best practices for its own use. These operations have been the single most important factor in the present sophistication and professional competence of the PLA Navy. How it had come to have the skill and confidence in 2008 to "sign on" to United Nations antipiracy SLOC-protection missions when the opportunity arose is where this chapter begins.

Distant-Seas Operations: Getting Started

The PLA Navy has gradually been building the skills necessary
to operate beyond the first island chain since 1980. The PRC had
overcome the slowdown in the development of intercontinental ballistic
missiles (ICBMs) caused by the Cultural Revolution and was ready to
conduct a full-range test of its DF-5. The target area selected for the test
was in the South Pacific Ocean, open waters bounded by the Gilbert
Islands (a major portion of the nation of Kiribati), the Solomons, Fiji,
and Vanuatu (New Hebrides). Here was an operational opportunity
for the PLA Navy. It assembled an eighteen-ship task force, including
instrumentation ships to monitor the ICBM flight and warships to
escort them and retrieve the dummy warhead. One of the test missiles
failed, but the other reached the target area. The task force recovered its
dummy warhead some 4,300 nautical miles from the launch site.[3]

It was another five years before the PLA Navy was deemed ready to
go abroad for an exercise with another navy. Its first planned interaction
with a foreign navy took place in November 1985, when a small task
force made the navy's first foray into the Indian Ocean and visited
Pakistan, Sri Lanka, and Bangladesh. But this trip did not start a trend.
The PLA Navy's cadet training ship *Zheng He* made distant cruises,
but otherwise Beijing did not routinely begin sending warships abroad
until 1994. Then began a decade-long pattern that saw an average of one
engagement activity with a foreign navy every year. At the time, many
Western observers adopted patronizing attitudes toward these fledgling
steps.[4] For example, in the late 1980s a senior active-duty American
naval officer characterized the PLA Navy to me as a "junkyard" navy,
woefully amateurish. In retrospect, however, it seems clear that the PLA
Navy was carefully planning each long-range deployment and then
absorbing the lessons—lessons that largely revolved around logistics and
communications.

These early voyages (see table 1) established a systematic approach
toward improvement. The PLA Navy had to keep ships on long voyages
refueled, deal with equipment breakdowns, make fresh food available,
and so on. These problems were manageable in the early stages because
the ships were simply proceeding from "point A" to "point B," not conducting multiday operations between port visits. Meeting the logistical
demands of ships in transit is a matter simply of adequately provisioning

them for relatively short durations and arranging periodic refuelings at sea. Sustaining ships that remain at sea on station is a very different matter, but these early excursions were an important start to the learning process.

PLA Navy Warship Voyages Abroad: 1985–1999

A close examination of table 1 and the ships involved allows some inferences to be drawn. By the 1990s the Luda-class destroyer was obsolete compared to the destroyers of the world's leading maritime powers, but it was the first modern warship class to be designed and built in China (although its combat systems were a mix of foreign equipment).[5] The last

Table 1. PLA Navy Warship Voyages Abroad: 1985–1999

Year	Destination	PLA Navy Ships Involved
Nov. 1985	Pakistan, Sri Lanka, Bangladesh	Luda-class DDG *Hefei* (Type 051D) and replenishment ship
May 1994	Russia (Vladivostok)	Luda II–class DDG *Zhuhai* (Type 051G), Jiangwei-class FF *Huainan*, plus tender
Aug. 1995	Indonesia	Luda II–class DDG *Zhuhai*, Jiangwei-class FF *Huainan*, and replenishment ship
July 1996	North Korea	Luhu-class DDG *Harbin* (Type 052A) and Luda II–class DDG *Xining* (Type 051D)
July 1996	Russia (Vladivostok)	Luhu-class DDG *Harbin*
Feb. 1997	United States (Hawaii, San Diego), Mexico, Peru, Chile	Luhu-class DDG *Harbin*, Luda II–class DDG *Zhuhai*, and replenishment ship *Nancang* (subsequently renamed *Qinghaihu*)
Feb. 1997	Thailand, Malaysia, Philippines	Luhu-class DDG *Qingdao* (Type 052A), Jiangwei-class FF *Tongqing*
Apr. 1998	New Zealand, Australia, Philippines	Luhu-class DDG *Qingdao*, replenishment ship *Nancang*

Source: Office of Naval Intelligence [ONI], *China's Navy 2007* (Washington, DC: Office of the Chief of Naval Operations, 2007), 114. (Lists PLA Navy ship visits abroad between 1985 and 2006.)

ship of the Luda class, *Zhuhai*, commissioned in late 1991, was to participate in the most challenging voyage the PLA Navy made during the decade—the 1997 deployment to the United States and South America. In that cruise, an important lesson was learned—that the Luda class was not suitable for long-range, sustained operations. During the transit to Hawaii the task force ran into ten consecutive days of heavy weather and had a great deal of difficulty getting the 3,700-ton *Zhuhai* refueled in the high seas.[6] That will have been a training and seamanship issue, since destroyers of considerably less displacement had been routinely refueling at sea in all kinds of weather since World War II.[7] Still, *Zhuhai* was very small compared to the mid-1990s state-of-the-art DDGs worldwide. For example, the U.S. destroyers then, of the *Spruance* and *Arleigh Burke* classes, displaced approximately 8,000 tons and 8,400 tons, respectively.

In the mid-1990s the PLA Navy simply did not have many modern, hence more reliable, destroyers or frigates. It is important to note that none of the ships that made the overseas deployments listed in table 1 are involved in today's antipiracy operations. In fact, many are now out of commission. They have been supplanted by larger, helicopter-capable destroyers and frigates better suited for extended operations. Soon after they were commissioned, the Luhu-class units CNS (for Chinese Navy Ship) *Harbin* and *Qingdao*, commissioned in 1994 and 1995, respectively, were assigned to the longest-range operations. They were the newest and most capable DDGs the PLA Navy had at the time.[8]

Among the more valuable lessons learned during this period of operations, in addition to the seamanship required, was the need for ships with better sea-keeping characteristics (which normally means larger, fin-stabilized vessels), with greater fuel and freshwater capacity, and with reliable gas-turbine or diesel propulsion. These are all seen in the PLA Navy ships currently conducting antipiracy patrols—all but one of which have been commissioned since 2004.

The PLA Navy Begins to Hit Its Stride (2000–2008)

The PLA Navy essentially developed its global "sea legs" over the past twenty years. The twenty-first century can be divided into pre-antipiracy (2000–2008) and post-antipiracy (December 2008 to today) periods, because once the PLA Navy began to conduct antipiracy operations its entire approach to distant operations changed.

The new century marked an increase in the tempo of overseas deployments. Not only did the frequency increase to an average of two per year, but the deployments themselves became much more ambitious in terms of the variety of countries visited. Whereas during the 1990s four of the PLA Navy's international voyages were to the Russian Far East or North Korea, within easy steaming distance and inside the first island chain, during the 2000s it began to make its presence felt globally. The Chinese continued to deploy their newest ships, very soon after their postcommissioning shakedown training. Table 2 shows, for instance, that *Qingdao*, a new Type 052 DDG of 4,800 tons, was kept very active on high-profile deployments, as was the newly commissioned *Shenzhen* (1999), the only ship of the Luhai class (Type 051B). At 6,100 tons *Shenzhen* when delivered was the largest Chinese-designed-and-built destroyer, but destroyer design was moving at such a pace that neither the Luhai nor the first Type 052 was put into series production. Instead, two even newer classes appeared; this was a period of "build a little and test a little," as China searched for "best of breed" destroyer designs. The PLA Navy finally settled on the 7,000-ton (Type 052C) and 7,500-ton (052D) DDGs, which began to appear in 2005.[9]

It is worth noting that the four Russian-built *Sovremenny*-class destroyers the PLA Navy purchased between 1999 and 2006 never made appearances internationally, neither on single-ship "showing the flag" deployments of table 2 nor later during the antipiracy patrols. Aside from their not being Chinese designed or built, one reason for not employing them internationally may have been engineering-plant unreliability. During the Cold War there were persistent rumors that the pressure-fired boilers the Soviets adopted for this class were very difficult to maintain and prone to frequent breakdowns (as were those the U.S. Navy had). All four ships have started or soon will begin major midlife upgrades replacing the older Russian combat systems with new Chinese ones—another indication of how far China has come in modern warship development.[10]

Strikingly, the same ships keep showing up as distant-waters deployers, illustrating how small an inventory of modern, reliable seagoing destroyers and frigates the PLA Navy had just eighteen years ago. The situation changed markedly after 2006, when new destroyers and frigates began to enter service in numbers.

PLA Navy Overseas Deployments: 2000–2008

The point of going into detail about overseas warship deployments during the first seven years of the twenty-first century is to show how the PLA Navy developed global operational experience. In these years it was able to show the flag in every continent save Antarctica. PLA Navy headquarters, and presumably the Central Military Commission, were obviously confident that their ships and men would be up to the demands of long overseas missions, that there would be no national embarrassments. To the contrary, Beijing was very eager to show off its destroyers and frigates soon after they entered service.

A learning experience that stands out was the 2002 circumnavigation of the world by CNS *Qingdao* and the oiler *Taicang*—a PLA Navy first.[11] But it was not the first time a Chinese warship had done so; that achievement was accomplished in 1911, when the Chinese warship *Haiqi*, a 4,300-ton, English-built armored cruiser, steamed around the world flying the "golden dragon" flag of imperial China. (It visited New York City, and the embarked flag officer called on President W. H. Taft.)[12]

Qingdao suffered a major engineering casualty in the Mediterranean. One of its diesel main engines (the ship depends upon a combined diesel-engine-and-gas-turbine arrangement for propulsion) failed. The ship's company was not able to accomplish repairs; technical representatives from the German manufacturer had be transported to the ship.[13] (This should not necessarily be seen as evidence of poor training; such "tech reps" are flown to deployed U.S. Navy ships on occasion.)

In the end, this 123-day voyage covered thirty-two thousand nautical miles. Interaction along the way with the navies of host countries was limited to simple passing exercises (PASSEXes) in the South Pacific with the French and the Peruvians. Nonetheless, it was an important milestone in a decade of firsts for the PLA Navy.

2007: An Important Year

As table 2 reveals, 2007 was particularly significant in the growth in seamanship and material readiness of the PLA Navy. In terms of overseas deployments and exercise participation, that year was important not only for what the PLA Navy actually did but, in hindsight, for how its successes that year prepared it to take advantage of the opportunity that arose the next year. In 2008 the PLA Navy would be ready to

Table 2. PLA Navy Overseas Deployments: 2000–2008

Year	Destination	PLA Navy Ships Involved
July 2000	Malaysia, Tanzania, South Africa	Luhai-class DDG *Shenzhen** (Type 051B), replenishment ship *Nancang*
Aug. 2000	United States (Hawaii, Seattle), Canada	Luhu-class DDG *Qingdao* (Type 052A), replenishment ship *Taicang* (subsequently renamed *Poyanghu*)
May 2001	India, Pakistan	Luhu-class DDG *Harbin* (Type 052), replenishment ship *Taicang*
Aug. 2001	France, Italy, Germany, United Kingdom	Luhai-class DDG *Shenzhen*, replenishment ship *Fengcang*
Sept. 2001	Australia, New Zealand	Jiangwei-class FF *Yichang**, replenishment ship *Taicang*
Nov. 2001	Vietnam	Jiangwei-class FF *Yulin** (later renamed *Huludao*)
May 2002	South Korea	Jiangwei-class FFs *Jiaxing** and *Lianyungang**
May 2002	Singapore, Egypt, Turkey, Greece, Portugal, Brazil, Ecuador, Peru (around-the-world deployment)	Luhu-class DDG *Qingdao*, replenishment ship *Taicang*
Oct. 2003	Brunei, Singapore, Guam	Luhai-class DDG *Shenzhen*, replenishment ship *Qinghaihu*
Nov. 2003	New Zealand	Jiangwei II–class FF *Yichang*, replenishment ship *Taicang*
Nov. 2005	Pakistan, India, Thailand	Luhai-class DDG *Shenzhen*, multiproduct replenishment ship *Weishanhu** (new *Fuchi*-class Type 903)
Aug. 2006	United States, Canada, Philippines	Luhu-class DDG *Qingdao*, replenishment ship *Hongzehu*
Mar. 2007	Pakistan (multinational exercise Aman 07)	Jiangwei II–class FFs *Lianyungang* and *Sanming*
Aug./Sept. 2007	Russia, United Kingdom, Spain, France	Luyang I–class DDG *Guangzhou** (Type 052B) and replenishment ship *Weishanhu*
Oct. 2007	Australia, New Zealand	Luhu-class DDG *Harbin* (Type 052) and replenishment ship *Hongzehu*
Nov. 2007	Japan	Luhai-class DDG *Shenzhen* (Type 051B)

* Recently commissioned / new class

Sources: ONI, *China's Navy 2007*, 114; Information Office of the State Council of the People's Republic of China, *China's National Defense in 2008*, Beijing, January 2009, http://www.fas.org/programs/ssp/nukes/2008DefenseWhitePaper_Jan2009.pdf.

advance along the blue-water learning curve, by agreeing to participate in a far-seas mission that would involve several months of operations under way.

In March 2007 the PLA Navy participated in its first multinational maritime exercise, known as Aman (Peace) 07. The Pakistani navy organized this major effort, which involved twenty-seven countries, eight of which sent ships. The focuses were antipiracy, terrorism, and illegal uses of the sea in general. The PLA Navy dispatched to Aman 07 two Jiangwei II (Type 053H3)–class frigates, not coincidently the type that China subsequently built for Pakistan.[14] The highlight for the PLA Navy came during the four-day at-sea phase, when it was put in charge of a two-hour search-and-rescue exercise involving twelve ships from all eight countries. This meant that the PLA Navy had to design the exercise scenario, coordinate the positioning of ships, and promulgate a plan that included communications procedures. Reportedly, this was the first time the Chinese navy had led and coordinated a multinational drill of this scale—another confidence-building first.[15]

Two months later, Singapore held its annual International Maritime Defence Exposition (IMDEX), immediately followed by the Western Pacific Naval Symposium (WPNS), which had an at-sea exercise phase. The PLA Navy sent the Jiangwei II–class frigate *Xiangfan*. Participation in both IMDEX and WPNS was another first for the PLA Navy.[16] Reportedly, the experience enhanced the PLA Navy's ability to operate in multilateral venues, such as the later antipiracy mission. Active participation in WPNS specifically was an important professional step for the PLA Navy. That Australian navy–sponsored event, which began in 1988 to promote naval professionalism, maritime understanding, and naval cooperation in the western Pacific and places attendees under the gaze of many regional navies.[17]

The third important event in 2007 was the August deployment of the new Luyang I (Type 052B)–class destroyer *Guangzhou* and a *Fuchi*-class multiproduct replenishment (or what the U.S. Navy would call a fast combat support) ship (AOE) on an eighty-seven-day deployment to the Baltic and Western Europe. The deployment was a tangible gesture of appreciation by Beijing for Moscow's having designated 2007 as "The Year of China." The message for Russian hosts, as well as other international observers, was that the PLA Navy could operate globally. The first port of call was St. Petersburg, which marked another PLA Navy first—its first deployment to the Baltic. Interestingly, the two ships steamed nonstop from China to St. Petersburg, a thirty-day transit through the Indian Ocean, Red Sea, Suez Canal, Mediterranean, English Channel, North Sea, and the Baltic.

This deployment of the 6,500-ton *Guangzhou* and the 25,000-ton replenishment oiler, or AOR, *Weishanhu* (Type 903) was a "coming out party" of sorts for the PLA Navy. Both ships are handsome in appearance, and although the Type 052B significantly lagged the state-of-the-art, Aegis-equipped DDGs active at the time in the U.S., Japanese, and South Korean navies, its hull form and propulsion plant gave the PLA Navy a good platform on which to build. Over the next few years it relatively quickly worked its DDG force into the top ranks, with the Type 052C/D and as of 2019 the Type 055, equipped with phased-array radar and vertical-launch surface-to-air missiles (SAMs).

After leaving Russia to return home, the task force conducted a trio of bilateral exercises with, successively, the Royal Navy off Portsmouth, the Spanish navy off Cadiz, and the French navy off Toulon, in each case a search-and-rescue exercise. The aircraft carrier *Ark Royal* participated in the Royal Navy's bilateral event, another PLA Navy first—an exercise with an aircraft carrier. In each exercise, the Chinese replenishment ship simulated a ship in distress; the participants were to locate it, then coordinate rescue teams to board and deal with whatever situation the scenario specified. Each of the major events was followed by formation exercises, helicopter landing practice on one another's ships, and flashing-light and semaphore drills.[18]

The final major PLA Navy deployment in 2007 was in October, to Australia and New Zealand. The destroyer *Harbin* made its first out-of-area deployment since 2001, along with the replenishment ship *Hongzehu*. The at-sea phase of this deployment involved another first—the first multinational search-and-rescue exercise with these countries. It did not go smoothly, because either the Australian or the New Zealand ship (the press account is not clear) did not get under way on time, and then rough weather in the Tasman Sea forced the curtailment of a portion of the exercise program. Nonetheless, this was another example of the PLA Navy's willingness to engage with navies with a strong sense of professionalism and well-honed seamanship skills.[19]

To be sure, in 2007 the PLA Navy limited itself to search-and-rescue exercises (the phrase "one-trick pony" comes to mind), but subsequent developments imply that it had been a watershed year in terms of building confidence in its senior leadership. The PLA Navy could operate in company with several of the great navies of the world—the U.S., the British, French, Spanish, and Australian—with self-confidence and without fear of embarrassment.

Interestingly, however, in 2008 the PLA Navy was not "out and about" as it had been since the start of the new century. Only in December did this change, and dramatically, when two of the PLA Navy's newest DDGs, *Wuhan* (Type 052B) and *Haikou* (Type 052C), supported by the reliable *Weishanhu*, departed on the service's first antipiracy mission. This task group, like all of the succeeding ones, was under the command of an embarked PLA Navy rear admiral.

Antipiracy Patrols: A Blue-Water Navy Laboratory (2008–Present)

It is not clear what occasioned the deployment "pause" in 2008; it likely had something to do with the debate in the United Nations (UN) on Somalia and the dramatic increase in piracy in nearby waters of the Gulf of Aden and the northern Arabian Sea. Beijing may have been waiting to see if the UN would authorize an international naval response; if it did, Beijing did not want to have committed capable ships to other operations before the CMC reached a final decision on participation. In a surprise to many, the UN did in fact opt for decisive action, passing UN Resolution 1816 on June 2, 2008, which authorized international action against Somali pirates and permitted "hot pursuit" of pirates into Somali territorial waters.[20]

The UN having acted, the PLA Navy could focus on careful preparation to join the multinational antipiracy effort already under way. It is easy to forget now, twelve years on, that having signed on to the antipiracy mission, China was risking a political setback if it could not sustain the open-ended commitment of ships—a matter very different from showing up once or twice.

By January 2009, more than a dozen nations had already sent ships to patrol the Gulf of Aden/Horn of Africa region. A number of these elected to include their warships in U.S. Fifth Fleet–organized Combined Task

Force 151 (CTF 151), created specifically to deal with piracy. China, as did Japan, Russia, India, and Malaysia, eschewed direct CTF 151 involvement; their ships were to operate under national tasking. At the time, on any given day, an average of fourteen naval vessels were patrolling the Gulf of Aden. The PLA Navy was joining them at an opportune time; as it turned out, its ships were present at the creation of a coordinated effort. The participating forces recognized that a comprehensive operational approach was essential for optimal stationing of forces and helicopter safety of flight. Many helicopter-equipped warships were present but there was no single "air boss" to coordinate flight schedules and establish basic safety guidelines.

The initial PLA Navy concept of operations was to "safeguard and provide security for Chinese vessels and personnel sailing through the region."[21] That soon changed, and China began to escort all comers transiting a designated sea-lane through the Gulf of Aden known as the Internationally Recognized Transit Corridor (IRTC). China also eventually agreed to help escort UN World Food Program merchant ships en route to Mogadishu, Somalia, over a different route. Although the PLA Navy did not join any of the maritime coalitions that were represented, it realized that exchanging information via radio, especially for deconfliction of helicopter operations, required some level of tactical coordination, as well an overarching appreciation of what was going on throughout the Gulf of Aden. Tactics were sorted out at the operational level, while broader, area-wide coordination was normalized by means of the "Shared Awareness and Deconfliction," or SHADE, arrangement. Under the auspices of Fifth Fleet, all interested parties met periodically in Bahrain in a forum, or "facilitating venue."[22] As a result of the SHADE process, China, India, and Japan in early 2012 finally agreed to coordinate their escorted convoys through the IRTC, each country being the "reference nation" for three months on a rotational basis. In June 2012 it was announced that South Korea would join these three countries.[23]

The PLA Navy's antipiracy mission has been a dramatic "accelerant" in the development of the PLA Navy into a genuine global force. To quote a telling observation:

On patrol operations in a water area side-by-side with navies from the European Union, NATO, Russia, India, Japan, the Republic of Korea and other countries, the Chinese naval fleet gained rare opportunities to learn advanced maritime experiences from their foreign counterparts. . . . This has helped the country's navy, which has long been deployed along its own coast, gradually get used to using a variety of modern ways and means to communicate with foreign fleets, creating a new type of cooperation model.[24]

The twelve years of continuous operations at the farthest reaches of the Indian Ocean that have now elapsed have given the PLA Navy an opportunity to hone its skills and learn what conducting sustained blue-water operations really entails. For the Chinese, dispatching ships to a distant location to operate there for months at a time was a new experience, with new challenges. At the most fundamental level, such deployments effectively "untether" ships from their regular home ports, long-familiar support facilities, normal chains of command—and, of course, the crews from their families.

Antipiracy operations are obviously not high-end (i.e., high in technology, tempo, and lethality) combat, but for the PLA Navy they represent the first time since the 1988 shootout with Vietnam in the South China Sea in which the use of lethal force is a real possibility. In an interview on the second anniversary of his service's involvement, the PLA Navy commander, Adm. Wu Shengli, claimed, with forgivable hyperbole, that "open ocean escorts are actual combat-oriented operations that test the Navy's ability to perform missions and tasks." Beginning with the fifth rotation, he went on to say, significant numbers of officers and men were making second deployments to the Gulf of Aden.[25] He asserted, accurately, that these operations were testing the navy's ability in ways it had never been before.

Since these deployments are, at this writing, in the thirty-third rotation, it is not useful to detail each task force. It can, however, be noted that of the fifty-eight warships that over the past twelve years have deployed to the northern Arabian Sea, forty-three have been guided-missile frigates (FFGs) of Type 054/054A. This very successful design entered service in 2008, the year antipiracy operations began. They began to be assigned to these distant cruises very soon after commissioning and shakedown training. These frigates are PLA Navy workhorses, delivered at a rate of three to four per year and soon afterward assigned to antipiracy. Nevertheless, the second in the class, CNS *Xuzhou* (FFG 530), has made only three antipiracy deployments in almost ten years of service—a figure low enough to suggest how fast the PLA Navy has been able to ramp up deployable warship strength.

In contrast to the Type 054A frigates, the PLA Navy destroyer force as a whole has so far made only fifteen antipiracy deployments, but one of these involved the newest class at the time, the Type 052C. The first of that class commissioned in 2005 and made the very first PLA Navy antipiracy deployment, in what was a good test of an entirely new combat system—its phased-array, electronically scanned radar, similar in concept to the U.S. Navy's Aegis. Four of the six Type 052C DDGs have demonstrated their capability for extended far-seas deployment; in fact, one of them, CNS *Haikou* (DDG 171), has made three so far. Destroyers of all of the earlier classes of "modern" PLA Navy DDGs (defined as Types 051B, 052A, and 052B but excluding, again, the four Russian imports) have also made these deployments, as have the first three of the 23,000-ton amphibious LPDs of Type 071.

Keeping these deployers refueled and replenished with food and consumables turned out to be more of a challenge than apparently had been anticipated. For the first six years of antipiracy operations, the PLA Navy's only two modern multiproduct replenishment ships, the 20,000-ton *Fuchi*-class AOEs, were pushed hard. They would each be on station over two rotations (about eight to nine months), return to home port, then deploy again after less than half a year for another eight or nine months.[26] For example, CNS *Qiandaohu* (AOE 886) was featured in a *Renmin Haijun* article as having already made, in the six years it had been in commission, thirteen overseas deployments: "They established 10 firsts with regard to things such as distant sea, nighttime replenishment of three vessels abreast, entering the waters of the Red Sea for the first time for escort operations, and carrying out replenishment drills *with foreign military vessels for the first time*, thus filling in numerous blanks for our Navy with regard to carrying out logistical support during non-war military actions."[27]

The experience that crews gathered was invaluable to the PLA Navy in terms of operations, ship design, training, and most importantly, logistical support to the fleet. The fact that these two ships had to make back-to-back deployments for three years does, however, suggest that the PLA Navy had previously failed to understand the importance of large multiproduct ships in sustained distant operations. Once feedback from early antipiracy patrols made this clear, the PLA Navy reacted very quickly (as is detailed in chapter 3). By 2013, newly commissioned ships were entering the rotation; today there are nine *Fuchi*-class, as well as two new, larger multiproduct replenishment ships (Type 901) in commission. The latter two are seemingly intended to operate with China's new aircraft carrier groups (again, see chapter 3). The rapid expansion of its at-sea replenishment force is clear evidence that China has learned well how much deployed naval task groups depend on underway replenishment. It also indicates how quickly its shipbuilding industry can respond to an emerging requirement.

An interesting interview with Mr. Zhang Wende, the chief designer of the *Fuchi*-class AOEs, sheds some light on why the PLA was caught short when antipiracy patrols began. He suggests that the cost of building ships the size of the *Fuchi* class was a factor in initially limiting the class to two ships, as was wanting to learn how well these ships would do in actual operations—again, a "build a little, test a little" approach characteristic of Chinese warship procurement at the time.[28] After all, the PLA Navy had for two decades made single-ship flag-showing visits around the world with just an accompanying oiler; multiproduct ships would have been useful but not essential. However, multiproduct replenishment ships are certainly essential if one aspires to an expeditionary navy. Ten years ago, experienced naval experts argued that should the PLA Navy intend to incorporate distant-seas operations into its normal modus operandi, the first indication would be the building of more multiproduct replenishment ships.[29] The PLA Navy has now done exactly that: today it has eleven ships in commission that can fill that role, which is simply one more piece of evidence that distant-sea operations are going to be routine.

The PLA Navy Learning Curve
Logistics

Its first antipiracy deployment taught the PLA Navy many lessons—most importantly, that omitting periodic port visits for fresh food and liberty for the sailors was a mistake. The first task group sent only its replenishment ship into Aden, and only for water, fuel, and food; the two destroyers never left station. While that maximized on-station time, the absence of fresh food became a health issue, and the fact that no one could go ashore on liberty had a negative impact on morale.[30]

A *China Daily* article written in the summer of 2009 by a researcher at the PLA Navy Naval Academy made the point: "China's navy should make bigger efforts to shorten its material and armament supply cycle to guarantee its success, and if necessary, set up some coastal refuel and maintenance stations. Good quality fresh food supplies constitute an indispensable component for a country's naval servicemen to keep up robust and enduring fighting capability. . . . [F]resh vegetables and fruits are still things that are desperately needed . . . on long voyages."[31]

The need for a reliable place the PLA Navy could use for logistical and morale purposes was obvious, and by the second deployment its ships had begun to call routinely at Salalah, Oman, a major transshipment point with good facilities, including a secure port area. The commanding officer of *Weishanhu* explained that the main reason for selecting Salalah was "to further explore and perfect the way [i.e., technique] of large-batch comprehensive replenishment on [a] commercialized model, relying on foreign commercial ports so as to accumulate experience for the PLA Navy in carrying out oceanic logistics during military operations other than war."[32] What would later become China's first overseas base, Djibouti, was also visited for "replenishment and recuperation" in the early days of antipiracy operations.

There was a commotion in the China-watching community in January 2010, when PLA Navy rear admiral Yin Zhou suggested that China needed to establish a permanent base in the Gulf of Aden, because resupply and maintaining the task group off Somalia without such a base was "challenging."[33] Rear Admiral Yin's view was disavowed by Beijing, where spokesmen pointed out that Chinese shipping companies could perform the task perfectly well.[34] Formalizing logistical arrangements and procedures that relied on Chinese commercial entities was in itself a major step. It was also logical: China's state-owned enterprises, with offices and facilities already in place, represented a de facto logistics network.

Of course, as it turned out, Admiral Yin was correct; the Chinese base at Djibouti was formally opened on August 1, 2017, the ninetieth anniversary of the founding of the PLA, with a flag-raising ceremony, a military

parade, and Djibouti's defense minister in attendance.[35] Asked about the
seeming dramatic departure from China's traditional antibase rhetoric,
China's foreign minister replied that the intent was to fulfill international
obligations to protect shipping: "We are willing to, in accordance with
objective needs, responding to the wishes of host nations and in regions
where China's *interests are concentrated*, try out the construction of some
infrastructure facilities and support facilities; I believe that this is not only
fair and reasonable but also accords with international practice."[36]

In the years between Yin's recommendation and the opening of the
base at Djibouti, the PLA Navy did learn how to work with state-owned
enterprises like China Ocean Shipping (Group) Company (COSCO) for
such logistical support as they could provide. In the early days, according
to one *Renmin Haijun (People's Navy)* article, every time food and materials needed to be purchased locally the requirement had to go through
five entities: navy headquarters in Beijing, the Ministry of Transport, the
Chinese shipping company main office, the Chinese shipping company
in West Asia, and the local distributor. The process normally required
more than twenty days.[37] (No wonder Admiral Yin wanted a base.) As
the same article goes on to say, "emergency foreign purchase plan was
instituted allowing the task group commander to directly purchase from
a Chinese shipping company in West Asia, cutting the advance time to
two days." By 2016 a navy lesson-learned report could state, "The Chinese
PLA Navy has established a command coordination mechanism with
the Ministry of Foreign Affairs, the Ministry of Transport, COSCO
and some other agencies and companies to conduct close coordination
between each other."[38]

Command and Control

Finally, and most importantly for both the senior command staff and
the force itself, the PLA Navy has learned how to command a naval
force operating almost halfway around the world from its "home" theater
command structure. What the PLA Navy eventually settled on, after an
initial clumsy structure brought operational complaints, was a dedicated
twenty-four-hour command center at PLA Navy headquarters in Beijing
that worked directly with the commander of the antipiracy task group.
The PLA Navy describes the arrangement as "unified command and
control of escort operations . . . a two-level flat command link from Navy

headquarters to escort task groups to achieve continuous, real-time and effective command."[39]

PLA Navy headquarters has also established a command-level coordination with the Ministry of Foreign Affairs, the Ministry of Transport, COSCO, and other agencies and companies for handling emergent situations.[40]

In input to the Contact Group on Piracy off the Coast of Somalia for Capturing Lessons Learned, the PLA Navy provided examples of the "two-level flat structure" in action. It appears that PLA Navy headquarters in Beijing makes the initial decision as to whether the task group should get involved and that if headquarters decides to act it is up to the task group command to carry out the operational and tactical details.

Dealing with the Miserable Weather of the Northern Arabian Sea

In the same input to the Contact Group, the PLA Navy commented that the "bad weather and severe environment of the area of responsibility . . . constitutes another challenge. Our task forces are exposed for long period of time at harsh environment of high temperature, high salinity and high humidity. In addition, the sand dust and monsoon period also pose negative effect[s] upon the safe operation of equipment and personnel safety as well."[41]

Having made two deployments to the northern Arabian Sea, I can testify to the accuracy of this assessment.

Major Engineering Repair

In May 2010 the PLA Navy achieved another first: the flagship of the fifth (rotation) escort task group had to put into Djibouti because its port main gas-turbine engine had suffered a major casualty and needed to be replaced. Drawing on its experience of 2002, when CNS *Qingdao* had a diesel engine casualty in the Mediterranean, the navy organized a military air transport resupply, using the Military Transportation Department of the Navy Logistics Department. Once again the bureaucracy was tortuous, involving the Beijing Military Region and the Main Administration of the Civil Air Fleet, and also the General Administration of Customs to get the new engine through Djibouti customs.[42] The stakes were high: the fifth task group had a very ambitious port-visit agenda to carry out when relieved by the incoming sixth task group.

Longer Deployments and Naval Diplomacy

Once the PLA Navy proved to itself it could logistically support extended, distant-seas deployments of three-ship task groups, it began to take advantage of them for duties other than protecting ships from pirates. Headquarters began dispatching them on naval diplomacy visits, to "show the flag" around the Indian Ocean littoral and into the Mediterranean Sea. These "taskings" lengthened task-group deployments considerably. The first task group's deployment lasted a modest 124 days, the third's 158 days, and the fifth's an impressive 192 days.[43] (Over the years since the duration seems to have stabilized at approximately 210 days.) In any event, by the fifth iteration PLA Navy headquarters had made naval diplomacy a major task of the deployed units. The fifth task group transited the Red Sea and Suez Canal and made port calls in Egypt, Greece, and Italy, conducting modest exercises with two Italian frigates in the Gulf of Taranto.[44]

This was the beginning of a new operational template. At this writing, whenever a replacement task group (two warships and an AOR) leaves its Chinese home port, it sails directly to the northern Arabian Sea to replace the on-station group and begin four months of dedicated antipiracy operations.

The task group that it relieves departs for about two months of naval diplomatic activity before arriving home. In its notional deployment of seven months it has steamed between 100,000 to 120,000 nautical miles. Each task group is assigned a different set of ports to visit, so that collectively the PLA Navy manages to show the flag throughout the Indian Ocean, Mediterranean, the coasts of both West and East Africa, Australia, New Zealand, and Oceania. For example, during 2016–18 one task force visited Algeria, Tunisia, Morocco, and South Africa; another visited the states of Ghana, Cameroon, Gabon, and Spain; yet another Pakistan, Sri Lanka, Bangladesh, India, Thailand, and Cambodia; and finally one went to Madagascar, Australia, New Zealand, and Vanuatu.

In each stop, lasting three to five days, the task force senior officers call formally on high-level local and sometimes national officials; the admiral in command of the task group hosts an evening reception on the flagship for local notables; the ships hold "open houses," in which local civilians are able to visit for tours; the crews conduct cross-deck training and sports competitions with the host navy; if appropriate, crew members visit schools, and the crew tours local attractions. It is not clear whether the sailors are given what Western navies would consider normal "liberty," free to sightsee on their own. The ships are made to feel welcome by a group of local "expat" Chinese rounded up by the embassy to greet them with great enthusiasm, including banners and flags. When the task group leaves, it often conducts short exercises with the host navy.

The PLA Navy's naval diplomacy is well thought out, each operation carefully planned to show off its new, well-kept ships and well-disciplined sailors and to permit senior-level interactions in countries in which Beijing has economic and diplomatic interests. Nothing especially remarkable here—most great navies do these things. The PLA Navy just seems to be doing them extremely well.[45]

Realistic Exercises

The PLA Navy realized that specialized and realistic training was necessary for the contingency that an escort might actually have to retake a captured ship (which happened in April 2017) or use small arms and helicopters to chase away potential pirates.[46] It was not until several rotations had taken place that articles began to appear describing how the escort task group practiced boarding and "taking down" a captured ship, simulated by one of its own ships. For example, shortly after arriving and assuming responsibility, the tenth escort task group conducted such an exercise (which was widely publicized in China, because it took place on the third anniversary of the antipiracy mission).[47]

Looking After Chinese Citizens in Dangerous Places

The security of overseas Chinese is a problem for Beijing. Starting with the 2011 evacuation from Libya, which involved detaching a frigate from antipiracy duties, and the kidnapping by rebels in January 2012 of twenty-nine Chinese road construction workers in the border region of Sudan. the evacuation or protection of nationals working abroad has taken on greater immediacy. Total numbers are vague, but in 2014 Premier Li Keqiang was quoted as saying, "The number of outbound Chinese is expected to exceed 100 million this year." He also made the point that "the job of protecting overseas citizens is a serious one."[48]

In Africa, approximately one-third of the one million or so Chinese citizens were contract workers, while the balance were independent migrants and entrepreneurs, many of whom are in the violent and potentially volatile regions of Africa and the Middle East.[49] This was best illustrated in 2015, when the PLA Navy promptly and professionally evacuated hundreds of Chinese and foreign nationals from Yemen, transporting them from Aden to Djibouti.[50]

Implications for the Future

On January 11, 2012, Adm. Wu Shengli held what the *PLA Daily* called a "symposium" to conduct a comprehensive review of achievements and lessons learned in the antipiracy mission and discussions on "promoting reform and innovation in escort work."[51] Unfortunately, the proceedings are not publicly available—understandably, since such after-action events inevitably directly or indirectly address shortcomings or mistakes and as a result are sensitive if not classified. Understandable or not, this is of course the basic problem in assessing what the PLA Navy has learned during exercises or real-world operations. We do know that a month earlier, in December 2011, Wu presented a "commemorative badge" during a ceremony marking the third anniversary of the antipiracy mission.[52] The accolades for the navy were well deserved then and remain so today.

The antipiracy operations have demonstrated the leading role the PLA Navy now plays in looking after Chinese interests abroad. China's security interests are geographically global, well beyond the western Pacific. They involve more than simply defending China from attack on its eastern seaboard. Chapter 3 discusses "offshore waters defense," which is essentially a wartime defensive concept, not particularly relevant for operations beyond the western Pacific during either peace or war. What the PLA Navy has learned in the context of antipiracy operations is how to think globally about wartime operations in defense of the nation's maritime interests. It has had over twelve years to think about this possibility in a peacetime context and face the planning challenge of how it might be accomplished in wartime.

Eleven years ago, a *Military Science* article author argued that the PLA Navy needed to be able to "protect strategic SLOCs and preserve freedom of movement on the high seas. Distant-seas capabilities include maritime patrols, surface and subsurface operational capabilities, island and reef offensive/defensive operational capabilities, seaboard assault capabilities, at-sea operations command, and comprehensive support capabilities."[53] The PLA Navy has mastered many of these skills and has laid a foundation for all of them. The article listed the interests to be defended under the concept of "distant or far seas" as energy assets in the Persian Gulf, Africa, and Latin America; SLOCs between China and the Middle East; more than 2,400 Chinese fishing vessels operating on the distant seas and off the waters of forty nations; ocean resources in international waters; and the security of overseas Chinese.[54]

Conclusion

While the PLA Navy made global transits long before the antipiracy deployments began, the last twelve years of these operations have had a major, transformative impact. If China expects its navy to take the lead in defending its global interests, it is fundamental that the navy learn how to do that—in effect, to become an expeditionary navy. The experience gained by the commanding officers of the warships involved and, especially, by the embarked flag officers, who learned how to exercise command of an afloat task force in a dynamic, tactical real-world environment, has been invaluable to the maturation and professionalism of the Chinese navy. Thanks to the well-conceived use of the same ships, once off antipiracy station, to visit countries throughout the Indian Ocean and Mediterranean Sea, officers found themselves on the front line of Chinese naval diplomacy throughout the much of the world—perhaps becoming in the process a more "worldly" cohort of officers.

One result of twelve years of far-seas deployments is that the PLA Navy has developed a still-expanding cadre of then relatively junior flag officers, ship commanding officers, junior officers, and sailors who have been exposed to major overseas deployments. While on station they interacted on a regular basis to the best navies in the world. According to the PLA vice commander, Vice Adm. Qui Yanpeng, as of April 2019 the PLA Navy antipiracy task forces had involved some twenty-seven thousand officers and sailors.[55] This is a large experience pool to draw upon when forming crews for the many new ships entering the force.

Although it has not had to use air-defense systems in combat, the PLA Navy has undoubtedly learned important lessons regarding its electronic combat systems' reliability and performance in the often harsh, hot, and dusty environment of the northern Arabian Sea. Detection capabilities and sustained intership data linking were challenged, and problems of mutual electronic interference with sister ships were encountered. Chinese crews have also undoubtedly taken advantage of the presence of a whole host of warships from around the world to record their electronic fingerprints.

On balance, the antipiracy operations have permitted the PLA Navy to learn what mix of propulsion, size, and combat suite for its surface warships is best for distant, deployed operations. Such missions have reinforced the basic rationale behind the PLA Navy's apparent decision to build a modestly sized aircraft carrier force. These years of operating alone in waters where the airspace is dominated by the either the United States or India has reemphasized the importance of air cover for distant operations that could involve combat. Finally, the value of shipborne helicopters has been confirmed by antipiracy operations, in which the PLA Navy task forces have made very good use of them as scouts and to scare off apparent pirate boats.[56] The PLA Navy has also learned the more mundane but crucially important lessons of ship design, material reliability, and logistical support for distant-seas operations, all lessons absolutely essential to the effective operation of an expeditionary navy.

The PLA Navy has learned the strengths, weaknesses, and maintenance shortcomings that its surface combatants, amphibious ships, support ships, and periodically submarines reveal when deployed and sustained on distant stations for long periods of time. When it comes to offshore defense—the PLA Navy's wartime strategy to defend China, addressed in the next chapter—the submarine force and fixed-wing naval air force play significant roles. When not at war—which is to say virtually all of the time—it is China's surface warships, including aircraft carriers, that are the most useful. The PLA Navy, while not overlooking its mission to defend China itself, will continue to deploy, day in and day out, surface warships that provide the nation capabilities in diplomacy, peacetime presence, sea-lane protection, crisis response, and, in its near seas, deterrence.

CHAPTER THREE

The PLA Navy Becomes a "Blue-Water" Navy

This is the first time that [China] has conducted naval exercises in the Mediterranean Sea. It is a new challenge for the Chinese Navy. It also showed that [China] is expanding its national interests and security interests to waters further away from China. People should get used to seeing China's warships out in the sea.

XINHUA, MAY 12, 2015

The PRC has never issued something entitled a "maritime strategy," but all the elements of a strategy have been addressed in official documents and statements:[1] a clear national objective of becoming a maritime power has been established, all the essential constituent elements of maritime power are being addressed, a target date for accomplishment of the overall objective has been set (at 2049), an earlier target date (2035) established for the navy has been set, and the intended mission that these forces are intended to accomplish has also been identified (it will be addressed in this and later chapters). Finally, tangible activity in all aspects of the maritime enterprise has been under way since well before Hu Jintao announced the goal of becoming a maritime great power in 2012.

In fact, the concrete evidence of progress is overwhelming: new consolidated shipyards; modernized or new ports, harbors, and naval bases; new ships for commercial and government service launched at a remarkable pace; schools established for civilian mariners; expanded fishing fleets;

deepwater drilling platforms constructed and deployed; an aggressive
deep submergence program under way; Arctic-capable icebreakers under
development; an aggressive maritime science and technology program
ongoing; and so on. The PRC is approaching the "great maritime power"
objective comprehensively and with the full backing of the CCP, especially Xi himself.[2]

The CCP recognizes that a powerful navy is ultimately what provides credibility to any claim of maritime greatness and that a crucial
element of any nation's maritime strategy is explicitly identifying the
missions its navy is to accomplish. This was done, publicly, in the PLA's
2015 defense white paper, *China's Military Strategy*, which is explicitly
dedicated to explaining China's overall military strategy. As MIT's Dr.
Taylor Fravel, a leading American expert on China's overall military
strategy, has argued, what China calls its "military strategic guidelines"
should be considered its national military strategy (NMS). The latest
strategic guidelines, with the formulation of winning "informatized
local wars," were adopted in 2014. *China's Military Strategy* was issued
the following year, effectively a confirmation of a new NMS, and is
assumed by Fravel to be an almost complete open-source explanation
of the strategy.[3] In it the maritime domain received considerable attention. The PLA Navy's mission set was explained with a curious cir-
cumlocution "a modern maritime military force structure" for the word
navy: "It is necessary for China to develop a *modern maritime military
force structure* commensurate with its national security and development
interests, safeguard its national sovereignty and maritime rights and
interests, protect the security of strategic SLOCs and overseas interests,
and participate in international maritime cooperation, *so as to provide
strategic support for building itself into a maritime power.*"[4]

While one can imagine a Chinese army colonel charged with draft-
ing the white paper deciding to characterize the navy as a "maritime
military force structure," the basic missions the paper lays out are clearly
described and are strategically sensible for China:

- Safeguard national sovereignty
- Safeguard China's maritime rights and interests
- Protect the security of strategic SLOCs and overseas interests
- Participate in international maritime cooperation.

In fact, it is no surprise that the PRC expects its navy to do these things: they are exactly what the navies of other major trading nations have historically been charged to accomplish. However, every other major naval power that has attempted to relate the structure and size of its forces to their assigned missions has publicly made clear how many ships it required. Building warships is expensive and involves seeking funds from legislative bodies, which means publicly specifying what a government intends to buy. (As a recent example, the United States, in its National Defense Authorization Act of 2018, established in law its goal of a 355-ship fleet.) China, uniquely, has yet to reveal how large a navy it seeks to build to execute this naval mission set; such details remain state secrets.[5]

Importantly, the navy that Beijing eventually controls will be, it is expected, powerful enough to act as the foundational element of China's maritime power—this is what "providing strategic support" for the nation's maritime enterprise means. In short, Beijing's overall maritime power ambitions will depend, one way or another, on a strong PLA Navy. Xi Jinping routinely emphasizes in his speeches to the military that a goal for China is to have powerful armed forces and to build the PLA "into *the* first-class armed force in the world."[6]

Protection Missions in the Far Seas

China's Military Strategy publicly acknowledged that the PLA Navy has a blue-water mission that is not defined by island chains or specific bodies of water. It did this by introducing "open seas protection" as a planning objective. That is, the Chinese navy is going to broaden systematically its operational capabilities beyond those associated with defending China proper to the level needed to conduct blue-water operations. According to the 2015 DWP, "In line with the strategic requirement of offshore waters defense and open seas protection, the PLA Navy will gradually shift its *focus* from 'offshore waters defense' *to the combination of 'offshore waters defense' with 'open seas protection,'* and build a combined, multifunctional and efficient marine combat force structure."[7]

This chapter explores the "open seas protection" mission and the naval capabilities the China has built to accomplish it. Thankfully, the 2019 DWP's English version renders "open seas protection" as "protection missions in the far seas."[8] This is a far more precise characterization of what the PLA Navy is expected to be able to do, in that it identifies "protection" as a specific mission. The phrase is based on the Chinese word *yuanhai*, translatable as either "open seas" or "far seas," or, in some English sources "blue water." (I will use "open seas" and "blue water" interchangeably, since in the context of operating warships globally they mean the same thing.) So during peacetime, "protection missions in the far seas" means defending Chinese interests and citizens overseas, by, for instance, showing the flag (naval diplomacy), protecting Chinese sea-lanes (antipiracy deployments), evacuating citizens from trouble spots, rendering humanitarian assistance, responding to natural disasters, and exercising with navies anywhere in the world. It also implies a requirement in times of conflict to defend China's most vital sea-lanes from interdiction. "Protection missions in the far seas" are not limited to peacetime; after all, Xi Jinping frequently reminds the PLA that its raison d'être is to "win wars."

China's Military Strategy is relatively transparent in its anxiety regarding China's sea-lanes—an anxiety that is explored in detail later in this chapter. *China's Military Strategy*, reinforced since its issuance by PLA Navy activity, strongly suggests that dealing with threats to the sea-lanes is the most important of the Chinese navy's overseas missions, because sea-lanes are the veins and arteries that keep China's economic heart pumping. In practice, China has been doing this since December 2008—this is what chasing pirates away from China's merchant ships is all about. To be clear, SLOC protection is not exclusively a far-seas mission, however; China also has very important sea-lanes to protect in the South China and East China Seas.

Importantly, despite its indications that the PLA Navy is shifting its focus to blue-water operations, there is no suggestion in *China's Military Strategy* of projecting power to influence events ashore; "protection missions in the far seas" are cast in a strictly defensive setting. But it would be a mistake to conclude that China is not considering power projection or "expeditionary" missions. China's economic interests are worldwide, and with these economic interests come political, and potentially, security ones that could, and probably eventually will, depend upon offshore shows of strength (what used to be called "gunboat" diplomacy) or in extreme cases, the use of force. Five centuries ago, China was very good at this indeed. Well before Westerners sailed the Indian Ocean, China's Admiral Zheng He was projecting power and conducting expeditionary operations in waters very close to China's current sea-lanes. The last of his seven expeditions took place over sixty years before the first voyage of Portugal's Vasco da Gama to the Indian Ocean in 1497.[9]

The maxim of paying close attention to another's military capability because political intentions can change in an instant applies to China's navy. It is undeniable that a good deal of China's impressive warship building has focused on ships that are designed, and demonstrably well suited, for blue-water operations. They are also unmistakably equipped to project power (in the form of land-attack cruise missiles, modest-scale amphibious assaults, or limited carrier-based aircraft strikes) should the need arise.

Taken literally, the DWP passage above makes protecting overseas interests and sea-lanes as important to China's leadership as defending the nation itself. The navy is expected to "gradually shift" its focus to include not only the direct defense of China in the western Pacific but also the defense of China's interests abroad. One of the PLA Navy's four main missions is to "protect the security of strategic SLOCs and overseas interests," and that mission is predicted to grow, if "gradually," in importance. That means that China's top military leadership does not anticipate any diminution in the country's global economic and political interests. To the contrary, these interests will expand, undoubtedly in connection with the twenty-first-century Maritime Silk Road. The maritime portion of Xi Jinping's signature strategic project, the BRI, is for all practical purposes a sea-lane, embracing the ports and related infrastructure that enable trade (see chapter 1).

With the defense white paper's very public revelation, made credible by the warships the PLA Navy continues to commission, the CCP has signaled to the world that its navy (and it is a *party* navy) is going to become a global force to be reckoned with. At the least, only with a very large navy would it be possible to execute the sea-lane protection mission. In addition, of course, a large, globally capable fleet is also a prerequisite to the stature of a maritime leading power with a "world-class navy."

The Genesis of the Blue-Water Navy

The "gradual shift in focus" referred to in the DWP can be best followed by tracking the building of warships capable of sustained blue-water operations. The introduction of truly blue-water-capable warships began to accelerate seriously in 2004 and has continued unabated. This is not to say that the PLA Navy did not have before that a handful of ships that could undertake blue-water voyages; it did, as discussed in the previous chapter. But since 2004 the PLA Navy has commissioned or launched around 131 warships (as of July 2020) that by virtue of their size and multimission combat capabilities can be considered blue-water capable. These ships include China's two aircraft carriers, some thirty-six modern DDGs equipped with Aegis-like combat systems, eleven large replenishment ships, eight nuclear-powered attack submarines, and nine large amphibious ships.[10] Over the same timeframe China has also commissioned around 160 ships that for reasons of their size, sustainment capacity, or sea-keeping characteristics are best suited for operations in China's near seas.[11]

The strategic calculus of overseas interests, China's maritime power ambition, and the political importance to President Xi of the Maritime Silk Road has resulted in budgetary plenty for the PLA Navy. The service is likely to continue to enjoy such largesse, because becoming a "world-class" blue-water navy will require a richer mix of high-end ships (i.e., of maximal combat capability) than China currently has afloat, perhaps twice as many. The other PLA services, especially the air force, have also been directed to develop overseas expeditionary capabilities—a directive they probably welcome, having undoubtedly have noticed the amount of money flowing to the navy.[12]

One other point is worth mention. Prior to 2015, China defense white papers referred to "far seas" activities within the context of "MOOTW," surely one of the world's worst acronyms—"military operations other than war," or more plainly, *peacetime* operations.[13] In short, China's overseas naval activities were cast only in a peacetime setting. But, with *China's Military Strategy* the enumeration of peacetime MOOTW missions no longer includes any reference to the sea-lanes on which China relies. These are addressed in separate sections within the context of "protection" as an "imminent concern"; the implication is that thinking about far-seas operations has shifted from conceptually framing those them as strictly peacetime, to taking into account more broadly the need to protect ships traveling on "strategic SLOCs" in wartime. This has obvious long-term implications for PLA Navy's force structure: first, such a mission along sea-lanes that stretch for thousands of miles is no trivial problem; and second, getting merchant cargoes safely across the Indian

Ocean will drive requirements for bases and a substantial mix of ships, aircraft, and submarines.

The SLOC Fixation

The antipiracy patrols seem to have heightened awareness in Beijing that its SLOC concerns are broader than the "Malacca dilemma," a phrase purportedly coined to characterize the vulnerability of ships entering or exiting the choke point created by the narrow Malacca and Singapore Straits.[14] A decade's worth of operations in the shadow of India and of getting to know the U.S. Navy's Fifth Fleet, which operates in the northern Arabian Sea and Persian Gulf, brought home to Beijing the vulnerability of its entire Indian Ocean sea-lane, especially the nexus in the northern Arabian Sea (i.e., of the vital Straits of Hormuz and the Bab el Mandeb). Beijing's tankers ply a very long (11,000 nautical miles, or nm) sea-lane carrying oil either from the Gulf of Guinea off West Africa around the Cape of Good Hope or from the Persian Gulf across the Indian Ocean to China (6,900 nm). Its exports are carried in huge container ships that travel nearly the same sea-lanes in reverse to deliver Chinese goods to Africa, the Middle East, and Europe (Shanghai to Piraeus, Greece, is 8,950 nm) via the Red Sea and Suez Canal. In the discussion of China's "National Security Situation," a heading in the DWP *China's Military Strategy*, put it clearly: "With the growth of China's national interests . . . the security of overseas interests concerning energy and resources, strategic sea lines of communication (SLOCs), as well as institutions, personnel and assets abroad, has become an *imminent issue*."[15]

Why Are China's Sea-Lanes an "Imminent Issue"?

The last serious attempts to interrupt sea-lanes of communications were made during World War II. The best known of these efforts resulted in the "Battle of the Atlantic," which pitted German U-boats (submarines) against merchant convoys carrying men, food, and war materials from North America to Great Britain. The Nazi objective was to stop this flow by attacking the ships with an ever-increasing number of submarines whose deployment and positioning was centrally controlled ashore. Germany failed in the end, but not before over 3,400 Allied ships had been sunk and thousands of mariners lost at sea in a multiyear struggle that involved hundreds of warships both protecting convoys and taking the offensive by seeking out U-boats. Thousands of aircraft were also involved, and they were essential to the defeat of the U-boat threat.[16]

More relevant to China's anxieties is that in Asia the largely American effort in that war to cut Japan's sea-lanes was successful. The United States, from the first day of the war, declared "unrestricted submarine warfare" against the empire of Japan and by the end of 1944 had, by a combination of submarines, land-based aircraft, and aircraft-delivered mines, essentially curtailed Japanese shipping bringing oil and other resources, like tin and bauxite, to Japan from Southeast Asia. The Japanese ships used the very same South China Sea SLOCs that China is anxious about today.

During the Cold War, the U.S. Navy worried that the very large Soviet submarine force would do what the German navy had failed to accomplish: halt reinforcements to Europe in response to a Red Army attack across the inter-German border. The Soviets certainly had the capability. In 1983, for example, the Soviet Navy had over 350 submarines of all classes in commission.[17] In light of this threat, it is not surprising that roughly a third of the Cold War U.S. Navy was accounted for by ships and aircraft whose primary mission was antisubmarine warfare (ASW).[18] When the Soviet Union self-liquidated in December 1991, the threat to America's sea-lanes ended.[19] But for Japan the large PLA Navy submarine fleet kept alive in the minds of Japanese naval strategists its experience with cut sea-lanes in World War II. As a result, the primary mission for the Japan Maritime Self-Defense Force was, and remains to this day, ASW.[20]

It is fair to ask: Does it make sense today for Chinese strategists to worry about waging an ASW campaign against an American or Indian effort to interrupt shipping destined for China? More to the point, is it credible that two nuclear-weapons-armed antagonists could fight an extended all-out war at sea without escalation to nuclear use? Apparently Beijing thinks so—its entire military strategy is based upon implementing an "active defense" strategy and adjusting its "preparations for military struggle (PMS)" to the focus of "winning informationized *local* wars, highlighting *maritime military struggle* and *maritime PMS*."[21]

The second central question with which China's strategic community, which prides itself on "scientific planning," has to wrestle is what it would require in terms of ships, submarines, and aircraft to win such a campaign. In a war against India, it would be very difficult to overcome New Delhi's advantage of geography, potentially commanding the Indian Ocean's east–west sea-lanes. China might try to offset this advantage by initiating a two-front campaign, possibly three fronts if Pakistan becomes involved. One front would be on India's disputed northern frontier with China; on a second front, Chinese submarines deployed to the western Indian Ocean could turn the tables and attack Delhi's oil SLOCs. Since 2014 PLA Navy submarines have been conducting periodic deployments to the Arabian Sea, likely to remind India of its own SLOC vulnerability problem; the PLA base in Djibouti could play an important role here. Meanwhile, China could seek to offset India's geographic advantage also through evasive routing, directing its ships across the Indian Ocean well south, out of range of most Indian aircraft. Predicting how such a conflict could play out would require analytic resources beyond what this author can bring to bear, but assuredly both the Indian military and the PLA are thinking though how this possibility might unfold.

India, then, presents problems enough. What if China's fight is with the United States? While the United States does not have the geographic advantages of India, it does have well-developed airfields on Diego Garcia, which it leases from the United Kingdom. That island is almost exactly in the middle of the Indian Ocean, ideal for maritime-patrol aircraft and long-range bombers. The United States also has the advantages of a large nuclear-powered attack submarine force, an effective global maritime surveillance capability, a numbered fleet command (the Fifth Fleet) with units stationed in and around the Persian Gulf, and another numbered fleet (the Seventh) assigned responsibilities for the eastern Indian Ocean and western Pacific. The PLA Navy would find actually countering this threat a major task, one that would take several overseas bases in countries that probably would not be eager to be caught in the middle. It would also require quite a few ships and aircraft. The military implausibility of Chinese success aside, until recently a conflict that would involve an all-out campaign against China's shipping did not seem politically very likely. However, the current downward trajectory of U.S.-China relations, triggered by trade and economic issues within the context of a sustained geostrategic competition for position, power, and influence, especially in Asia, suggests that the prospect of a campaign at sea to halt China's trade cannot easily be brushed aside.

Despite the obvious difficulties broadly outlined and implied earlier in the book, historical campaigns to isolate trade-dependent nations in war and preparations (in the Cold War, for example) for one suggest that an anti-SLOC campaign against China is possible. As a result the PLA Navy has taken a forward-leaning planning and resource-allocation approach. Rather than declaring that protecting its SLOCs from interdiction is too hard, *China's Military Strategy* suggests that China is trying to deal with their vulnerability. Finally, any doubts that China might have had about that vulnerability have long since been removed by Western analysts who argue that the best way to fight China would involve "distant blockade." Perhaps the most influential exposition of this concept was formulated by a well-known military strategist and retired Marine colonel on the staff of the U.S. National Defense University, T. X. Hammes. The goal of this concept, which he labels "offshore control," he describes as intercepting Chinese maritime exports, as well as imports of oil and other essential raw materials, at a great distance from China—well beyond the reach of its shore-based air and missile forces.[22] Arguably, the rapid buildup of China's blue-water capabilities can be considered a riposte, intentional or not, to this sort of thinking.

Readers should not assume that the Chinese are anxious about their sea-lanes only beyond the first island chain. That would be incorrect. The South China Sea is addressed in detail in a separate chapter, but to avoid misunderstanding it is necessary to point out at this point that all shipping that crosses the Indian Ocean—either from the Persian Gulf, East Africa, West Africa (the Gulf of Guinea), or Western Australia—passes through one of the major Indonesian straits (Malacca or Lombok, most likely) and then (the vast majority of it) through the South China Sea into the East China Sea and on to Chinese ports. The PLA Navy's blue-water capabilities are very relevant to operations in the South and East China Seas; accordingly, it is important to recognize what the PLA and PLA Navy are doing to bolster SLOC protection capabilities in the near seas.

Building a Blue-Water Navy

China does not absolutely need a "far seas capable" surface navy for "counterintervention" in the maritime approaches, but it absolutely does need one if it hopes to be "world class" and accomplish the missions associated with open-seas protection.[23] Blue-water operations require more emphasis on building surface ships than land-based aircraft and submarines. That PLA Navy submarine deployments to the Indian Ocean have become regular indicates that senior PLA Navy officers also appreciate the worth of submarines capable of sustained operations abroad. Submarines bring great value to both SLOC protection (sinking enemy warships) and interdiction of enemy SLOCs. Using submarines for these sorts of distant missions, places a premium on nuclear-powered attack submarines (SSNs) and modern AIP-equipped conventional submarines.

A navy that operates in distant seas must be able to defend itself there, where it can no longer depend on an air force or rocket force for protection. Unless it has a well-equipped ally willing to provide this sort of support, the PLA Navy must bring its own defense with it. That in turn means large, multimission destroyers, frigates with helicopter facilities, improved antisubmarine systems, and air defenses. Destroyers with long-range surface-to-air missiles can accomplish the latter where the land-based air threat is limited, but most of China's most important SLOCs—for instance, in the northern Arabian Sea and Gulf of Aden—face a substantial potential air threat from either India or the Fifth Fleet.

The Aircraft Carrier Force

The need for organic air cover was a very important factor in China's decision to begin building an aircraft carrier force.[24] China's first carrier, CNS *Liaoning* (CV 16), is a Soviet-designed, *Kuznetsov*-class ship purchased partially complete from Ukraine in 1998, purportedly to become a floating casino and tourist attraction. Over the succeeding fourteen years construction was completed in China. The ship was commissioned on September 2012, in Dalian.[25] Since that time it has served as a platform to train Chinese naval aviators in arrested landings and ski-jump takeoffs. *Liaoning* has no catapults; its jets launch under their own power off a ski-jump-like ramp on the bow. Training pilots to launch and "recover" on board perforce includes learning how to operate the "airport" and to integrate an air wing and ship into a fighting unit. The ship was initially declared combat ready in November 2016. That was misleading: it meant only that the ship itself was ready for operations after a long maintenance period.

A declaration of this sort happens every time *Liaoning* comes out of the shipyard after major work. In the latest and perhaps the most important development, in April 2019 the ship's executive officer (XO) said during a CCTV interview that "the *Liaoning* is shifting from a training and test ship to a combat ship. I believe this process is going faster and faster, and we will achieve our goal very soon." He also said that during this latest shipyard maintenance period *Liaoning* had received upgraded arresting cables and arresting nets, improved anti-jamming capabilities, and an enlarged flight control tower. Finally, he indicated that the propulsion and ship's electrical systems "are now more stable and efficient." This is a telling insight: trying to launch or recover aircraft on an aircraft carrier with unreliable—that is, unpredictable—propulsion and electrical power is a nightmare. The XO claimed that "these changes will definitely help us make the best of the ship, improve our training protocols and boost our combat capability even further."[26]

All of these improvements will certainly help, but the most important aspect of combat capability for an aircraft carrier is a smoothly functioning ship/air wing team and proficient air crew. These areas are still "works in progress." For instance, the official Chinese press announced in May 2018 that night landings had been successfully conducted, calling that a "huge leap toward gaining full combat capability."[27] In short, it was almost seven years after commissioning before the PLA Navy felt

China's first aircraft carrier, *Liaoning* (CV 16), under way in the South China Sea with four escorting DDGs in close stations to accommodate a group photo. China Military, *January 3, 2017, http://eng.chinamil.com.cn/*

comfortable enough to qualify its carrier pilots for night operations. The main implication would seem to be that the PLA Navy is following a very patient, step-by-step approach, carefully mastering the skill (and art) of operating an aircraft carrier at sea.[28] Patience and the long view were reinforced, perhaps inadvertently, in the article cited above, which also quoted a senior researcher at the PLA Navy Naval Equipment Research Center as asserting that the value of *Liaoning* as China's first carrier "will be very clear in a decade or two."[29]

Meanwhile, the PLA Navy commissioned its second carrier, named *Shandong* (CV 17), in December 2019. It is a near sister ship to *Liaoning* and is Chinese built from the keel up. Chinese designers have made improvements to the *Liaoning* design most visibly in the superstructure, which will accommodate the latest Chinese active electronically scanned array (AESA), or active phased-array radar (APAR). One must assume that they also paid close attention to building a reliable propulsion and electrical power plant. The ship will also be around twelve feet longer than *Liaoning*, which will increase displacement by about five thousand tons and probably provide enough additional room to increase the size of the air wing.[30] Finally, beginning in January 2018 press reports indicate that China is building a third carrier, a Type 002, that will be much larger than either *Liaoning* or *Shandong*, somewhere around 85,000 tons. Significantly, the Type 002 will reportedly abandon the ski jump and instead employ a catapult launching system.[31] This ship will probably not make an appearance until 2023, but when it does, it will be able to embark an air wing with a fixed-wing airborne early warning (AEW) aircraft that could also act as an airborne command post for tactical fighter sorties—provided, of course, that the PLA Navy can design and field such an aircraft by the time the ship is ready.

The air wing is, of course, the reason for having an aircraft carrier. Details of *Liaoning*'s air wing remain vague, probably because the PLA Navy is experimenting.[32] Informed speculation suggests the notional air wing will include twenty-four J-15 fighters, four to six ASW helicopters, four helicopters dedicated to AEW (i.e., putting an air-search radar in the sky), and two helicopters dedicated to pilot rescue.[33] Meanwhile, the weight penalties and thus ordnance restrictions imposed by ski jumps do not prevent the first two carriers from launching jets with air-to-air weapons to provide future task forces with air cover. All indications are that around 2020–22, the PLA Navy will have at least two carriers available for "distant seas" operations.

A word about the J-15 fighter nicknamed "Flying Shark" is in order. After more than six years of flying from *Liaoning*, it is apparently proving less than satisfactory. It is a derivative design, based on a partially completed Russian Sukhoi Su-33 that China obtained from Ukraine. The airframe is of Russian design, while the avionics, radar, flight control, and weapons systems are from China's J-11B (itself a Chinese version of the Sukhoi Su-27). The airframe, then, is an old design, and at thirty-three tons the J-15 is very heavy for a carrier aircraft, especially one that has to launch without the advantage of a catapult. Reportedly, it is difficult to control when in a low-speed landing profile and two, perhaps four, have crashed. Further, open sources suggest that as of 2018 not enough J-15s had been built to equip two air wings; it seems that only twenty-four have been delivered to the PLA Naval Air Force. There is also a J-15 variant modified (strengthened) for experiments with both a land-based steam catapult and an electromagnetic (EMALS) catapult.[34]

The upshots are that PLAN Naval Aviation is considering a new carrier-based strike fighter and that unless more J-15s are produced, it

A Shenyang J-15 Flying Shark about to land on deck of the carrier *Liaoning*. This sort of arrested landing is similar to U.S., French, and Indian aircraft-carrier procedures. *Li Tang, eng.chinamil.com.cn/*

A Flying Shark takes off. *Liaoning* is not equipped with a catapult launching system, which only the U.S. and French navies use. *Liaoning* relies on a ski jump at the forward end of the flight deck to launch jets into the air from a standing start. The ramp compensates for the low takeoff speed as compared to catapult launch. There must be enough wind along the flight deck to provide adequate lift for the thirty-three-ton J-15. *Liaoning* does this by heading into the wind to launch and recover or by creating its own "relative wind" by steaming at high speed. *Li Tang, eng.chinamil.com.cn/*

is willing to settle for undersized air wings for its two carriers while it develops one.[35] Having made major investments in a carrier force, it would be foolish for the PLA Navy to put up with a suboptimal fighter unless it has no choice. It was four decades ago, in 1986, that Adm. Liu Huaqing (1916–2011), often dubbed "the father of China's aircraft carrier," argued the need for carrier-based airpower, because "from the standpoint of our strategic mission of safeguarding the country's maritime interests, including the recovery of the Nansha [Spratly Islands], and the reunification of Taiwan, the Navy should develop aircraft carriers."[36] Since that time the PLA Navy focused first on convincing itself, then on convincing the CMC that operating aircraft carriers was a practical ambition and that the Navy could actually do it. Implicitly, getting the ship was a higher priority than the aircraft. Now, after seven years of operational testing, any hesitations regarding the wisdom of funding a "serious" carrier force seem to have been overcome. Now, the PLA Navy seems to finally be turning its investment to creating a combat-credible aviation component for that force to fly.

Becoming a Member of the Twenty-First-Century Destroyer Club

Until 2004, China approached its destroyer force as a two-decade-long research-and-development project. This has cursed Western observers, stuck with using NATO terminology, with having to keep track of the difference between Luda, Luhai, Luhu, Luzhou, and Luyang classes of destroyers. (The discussion below focuses on the Luyang II and III variants, which I will distinguish as the Type 052C, for Luyang II, and the Type 052D, the Luyang III.) It appears the basic challenge China's designers were trying to solve by "building a little, testing a little" was to find a hull form and propulsion plant that, combined, would produce a ship suitable for distant operations: one that had the volume to accommodate the fuel, food, and fresh water needed for long endurance, a helicopter hangar, magazines with a substantial number of missiles, and the necessary radar and electronics. A concomitant challenge was to develop a Chinese-manufactured combat system for that hull. The PLA Navy became "self-sufficient" through a combination of reverse-engineering combat systems components from France, Russia, Italy, and the United Kingdom, licensed production deals, and indigenous Chinese development.

Chinese builders finally delivered in Types 052C and D a design that the PLA Navy really likes. Starting with CNS *Lanzhou* (DDG 170), commissioned in 2005, the PLA Navy has in commission or is building thirty of these ships, six of Type 052C and twenty-four of Type 052D (as of January 2020). Both variants have roughly the same hull—length of 510–515 feet, full-load displacement of 7,000–7,500 tons, and combined gas-turbine and diesel propulsion. They are handsome warships, with clean hull forms and superstructures that reduce their radar cross section. On paper their combat capability is impressive.

Unlike China's earlier DDGs, with their Russian, French, and Chinese suites, the Type 052 initiated the use of primarily Chinese systems. The Type 052C in particular was a jump into the "big leagues" in terms of air defense, with a new combat system and the HHQ-9 surface-to-air missile, range fifty-four nautical miles. In the Type 052C, for the first time, the PLA Navy had a ship that could both credibly defend itself and contribute to the air defense of a group. Both variants are also armed with potent (162-nm range) antiship cruise missiles.[37]

In 1983 the U.S. Navy introduced Aegis, a computer-based command-and-control combat sytem built around a powerful radar that, not limited by a physically rotating antenna, could search and track simultaneously. This capability, mated with a vertical missile launching system, permitted nearly simultaneous engagement of many air threats. Over the years this system has been improved and remains the state of the art, dramatically increasing shipborne firepower and accuracy against aircraft, cruise missiles, and now ballistic missiles.[38] The Type 052C narrowed the surface-combatant capability gap between the PLA Navy and the United States, Japan, South Korea, and recently Australia, all of which operate Aegis-equipped destroyers in the western Pacific.

What China has devised is not the Aegis combat system per se but, like some NATO navies, a capability that is similar, at least on paper, built around an APAR/AESA. Like the Aegis, these radars eliminate slowly rotating antennas and search for, detect, and track many targets simultaneously while providing command and terminal guidance and target illumination to SAMs. The Chinese APAR is known in Western terminology as the "Dragon Eye."[39] These ships also marked the PLA Navy's first venture into vertical-launch system (VLS) technology, allowing its new DDG to shoot more rapidly.[40]

The six ships of Type 052C started the PLA Navy down the road of state-of-the-art destroyers, but the improved 052D has been favored. For many years the U.S. Navy's *Arleigh Burke*–class DDG has been seen as the "best of breed"; eighty-eight of them are in commission, building, or authorized.[41] On paper the Type 052D is a worthy competitor. Its designers adapted the flat-panel phased-array like that of U.S. and allied Aegis systems but also, more importantly, a sixty-four-cell VLS. These installations, outwardly very similar to the American VLS, are loaded with a mix of surface-to-air missiles, land-attack cruise missiles, antiship cruise missiles, and antisubmarine missile-launched torpedoes.

It has become a commonplace that the key weakness of Chinese multimission destroyers is ASW. Whether that is true or not, the PLA Navy has not shortchanged the Type 052D. It has a full suite of ASW sensors: a hull-mounted sonar, a variable-depth sonar (VDS), a towed

The Luyang III (Type 052D)–class CNS *Hohhot* (DDG 116) was
commissioned in 2019. This class is the PLA Navy's frontline, general-
purpose destroyer. It is often compared to the U.S. Navy's DDG 51 class.
The Type 052D entered service in 2012, whereas the DDG 51 has been in
production since 1991. The most numerous version of the U.S. class, known as
"DDG 51 Flight IIA," is a few feet shorter than the Chinese ship but displaces
about two thousand tons more, because it is beamier than its sleek Chinese
cousin. The U.S. Navy ship loses the beauty contest but makes up for it with
firepower: ninety-six VLS cells as compared to sixty-four in the Type 052D.
http://eng.chinamil.com.cn/

array (commonly called a "tail"), and a helicopter fitted for ASW. Some
experts suggest that these systems are derivative French sonar suites,
manufactured in China under license. For twenty years, from 1972 to
1993, France provided modern sonar technology to China. According to
Jane's, however, the PLA Navy is equipping its new destroyers and frigates
with indigenously developed VDS and towed sonar arrays, although it
is likely that the technology is based on Western systems acquired during the 1970s: "French sonar systems such as the DUBV 23 search sonar
and DUBV 43 low-frequency VDS, which were used to outfit the first
Luda III (Type 051G) conversion in 1990 and the two newly built Luhu
(Type 052A)–class DDGs in 1993. . . . [T]here is strong suspicion that
China has reverse-engineered these devices—along with other Western

products, believed to include a Raytheon DE 1164 VDS—to accelerate development of its own indigenous efforts."[42]

In any event, the Type 052D's medium-frequency, hull-mounted active sonar has a surface-duct range of 10,000 to 18,000 yards.[43] It is the VDS system, however, that provides the 052D's real active-sonar capability: a ship can lower it from an enclosed equipment room in the stern (where it is protected from saltwater corrosion) to the water depth that will yield optimal detection and tracking whatever the ocean environment. Lowering the VDS does impose a speed penalty on the ship, to avoid parting the tow cable, and if one is not careful one can destroy the towed body by dragging it over a shallow spot. Another element of the ASW capability of this ship is its embarked helicopter; the PLA Navy operates both the export version of the Russian Kamov Ka-28 and the Z-8, the Chinese version of the French Frelon. Both aircraft have a dipping-sonar capability, by which, as in VDS, the helicopter lowers the sonar to depths favorable for detection. Both Chinese helicopters perform a vital function in providing ASW protection for the ship and a task group, but both are old, and the PLA Navy is apparently planning a replacement. A Z-18, equipped with a complete suite of ASW sensors and weapons as well as antiship missiles, is being evaluated, along with a lighter Z-20, very similar to the U.S. Navy SH-60 series and suitable for the PLA Navy's destroyers and frigates.[44]

The Keystone of a Carrier Strike Group: The Type 055

The Type 052D has one shortcoming: it does not have enough firepower. Its sixty-four VLS cells have to be divided between four classes of missiles for four types of targets—air, surface, submarine, and land. The loadout of the VLS cells can obviously be tailored to the intended mission, but for argument's sake assume a notional combination of eight ASW torpedoes, six antiship cruise missiles, and six land-attack cruise missiles; that would leave only forty-four cells for SAMs. (VLS cells cannot be reloaded from replenishment ships at sea, although the U.S. Navy is apparently once again trying to solve that problem.)[45] Although the ship is equipped for the full range of destroyer missions, when operating as an escort for an aircraft carrier or amphibious group its primary responsibilities would be air defense and ASW, for which sixty-four cells seems too few. By contrast, the *Arleigh Burke*s have either ninety or ninety-six VLS cells, depending on when a given ship was commissioned.

The PLA Navy has an answer to this apparent shortfall: the new Type 055 Renhai-class DDG. Four of these DDGs were launched in 2017–18. As of this writing one is in commission, others are fitting out, and hulls five and six are under construction. They are big ships. At 590 feet in overall length, they are seventy-five feet longer and ten feet beamier than the Type 052D. The class is estimated to displace ten thousand tons of ocean water at light load, 13,000 at full load. It has a distinctive high-freeboard, flared hull similar to that of China's large Type 071 LPD, which should improve sea keeping in rough seas and at high speed—a very useful attribute when maintaining station on an aircraft carrier. This class abandons the Type 052D's combined diesel and gas-turbine propulsion and mimics the U.S. cruiser/destroyer arrangement of four gas-turbine main engines. The class is fitted with a Chinese-made state-of-the-art phased-array radar and combat-direction system and with greatly increased firepower (112 VLS cells). Its fit also includes a hull-mounted sonar, a towed-array sonar (TAS), and a VDS; a 130-mm main gun; two helicopter hangars and a flight deck; and appropriate short-range self-defense systems.[46] The radar system is especially interesting. According to one source:

> Two sets of active phased array radars, one being the larger S-band arrays on the vessel's super structure and the other being the smaller set of X-band arrays in the ship's enclosed sensor mast, equip the ship. The S-Band system is used for long range search and track, while the much more sensitive X-band system is used for tracking smaller, stealthier and high-speed objects with greater fidelity at lesser ranges. There are cross-overs in capabilities between the two sensor arrays, which also adds to redundancy. No other ship in China's inventory possesses such a high-end radar system.[47]

The ship is designed to operate with China's aircraft carriers as a primary air-defense unit. Various articles have speculated that the Type 055 could be a ten-ship class. Whether the PLA Navy has decided on the size of a notional carrier escort force is not clear, but with two carriers in the water and one building and given the number of Types 052Ds and 055s in commission, fitting out, or known to be building, it will easily be able to assign five or six multimission, high-end destroyers, an impressive

AAW and ASW defensive force, to escort carrier strike groups. The Type 055 is also another signal that China's navy should no longer be viewed as being in a perpetual "catch-up mode" technologically speaking.

These Types 052D and 055 are also formidable warships independently; they can look out for themselves where the aircraft or cruise-missile threat is limited and can launch land-attack cruise missiles to project power ashore. A relevant example would be the cruise-missile strikes that the United States launched against Syrian chemical weapons facilities on April 14, 2018. A cruiser and four DDGs launched the vast majority of the eighty-eight cruise missiles the United States fired in this raid.[48]

These two classes can also take care of themselves if they encounter hostile destroyers. They load what some have called China's deadliest antiship cruise missile (ASCM): the YJ-18, with a 290-nm range and supersonic closing speed.[49] Supported by shipboard helicopters or remote space-based assets, this is a potent over-the-horizon capability.

Finally, it is worth noting that destroyers with Aegis-like combat systems are expensive warships to build; only a few navies in the world can afford them. For example, by 2020 Japan will have twelve; whereas China already has thirty-one in commission or building.[50]

Blue-Water-Capable Frigates

The Type 054A guided-missile frigate has been another success story for China's warship designers. The lead ship of the class, *Xuzhou*, was commissioned in 2008, and since that time this class has been the workhorse for PLA Navy far-seas antipiracy operations and follow-on presence missions as described above. As of July 2019, forty-five of the sixty-four warships dispatched to the Gulf of Aden have been Type 054A frigates.[51] At 4,100 tons and 440 feet, this twin-screw, diesel-powered frigate is almost exactly the size of the now-decommissioned *Oliver Hazard Perry*–class frigate the U.S. Navy built in the 1980s. For its size the Type 054A is well armed, with long-range ASCMs, a thirty-two-cell VLS launcher with medium-range SAMs, and a helicopter with hangar. The ASW suite is being improved with the addition of the towed array and variable-depth sonars that are already being fitted on China's Type 56 corvettes (in effect, small frigates).[52] This is a planned thirty-two ship class; twenty-eight are in commission at this writing, and all thirty-two are expected to be around 2020.

These ships certainly have demonstrated the range and sea-keeping ability to operate with carrier strike groups throughout the Indo-Pacific region; at issue is speed. The Type 054A is judged to be capable of twenty-seven knots at full power. Under most circumstances when operating with a carrier this should be adequate, but when there is not enough true wind, carriers launching or recovering aircraft may steam faster than that to create sufficient relative wind across the flight deck. It is worth noting that the U.S. Navy routinely used both *Knox-* and *Perry*-class frigates, no faster than the Type 054A, as carrier battle group escorts during the Cold War.

Underway Replenishment

It is safe to assert that after more than a decade of antipiracy experience the PLA Navy quite capable of the logistically sustaining small task groups on distant stations. Underway replenishment has become commonplace for it.[53] But even replenishment ships need to restock from shore facilities, and destroyers and frigates need to visit ports to give crews "liberty call" and to obtain supplies not available from the replenishment ships. COSCO, a state-owned enterprise that is in the logistics-services business worldwide, normally can satisfy the latter need; in COSCO, China enjoys preexisting support structure at virtually all major ports on the Pacific and Indian Oceans. The combination of a state-owned enterprise ashore and modern multiproduct replenishment ships at sea has proved an effective approach to sustainment halfway around the world.

When, as described in chapter 2, the PLA Navy scrambled to increase its replenishment ship inventory, it commissioned six more *Fuchi*-class AOEs between June 2013 and July 2016. These six are slightly larger, at 25,000 tons, than the two that were run ragged in the Gulf of Aden, but they too are powered by twin diesel engines; as a result, they are limited to around twenty knots. This is too slow for sustained carrier strike group operations, and as a result the PLA Navy has introduced a 719-foot, 40,000-ton ship of the AOE type. The ship, known as the Type 901, is a gas-turbine-powered ship and has an estimated maximum speed of twenty-five knots. The first of this class of fast combat support ships was commissioned in 2017, with another commissioned a year later. It seems likely that for every aircraft carrier China commissions it will also introduce a Type 901 AOE.

In a very short period of time, China has created a state-of-the-art, blue-water underway-replenishment force second only to that of the United States in size and capability. At this writing, the PLA Navy has eleven modern multi-product replenishment ships in commission, more than enough to support continuous far-seas deployments in addition to the counterpiracy patrols.[54]

The Expeditionary Amphibious Force

For years, the interest of observers in PLA Navy amphibious shipping has been for assessing the PLA's ability to invade Taiwan. While that contingency requires continued attention, the PLA Navy has also, with scant fanfare, been assembling an impressive blue-water amphibious expeditionary capability. It now has six Type 071 amphibious assault ships (LPDs) of the Yuzhao class in commission; hulls seven and eight are fitting out.[55] Each of these 20,000-ton ships can embark a full battalion of PLA Navy marines or PLA soldiers (five to six hundred men). Each is equipped with a well deck that can load four air-cushion landing craft (LCACs) in addition to a mix of up to twenty lightly armored amphibious tanks or infantry fighting vehicles. These diesel-powered ships are relatively fast, twenty-five knots at full power, and have hangars for two medium-lift helicopters.[56] Significantly, four ships of this class have made antipiracy deployments in the place of a destroyer or frigate. While these substitutions may have been occasioned by the nonavailability of surface combatants, it seems more likely that the PLA Navy leadership is assessing the performance of this new class. An extended deployment provides an opportunity to identify areas of maintenance, training, and command/communications that need improvement.

For some years there was speculation that the PLA Navy was going to build a class of amphibious assault ships with long, straight flight decks to enable multiple-helicopter operations. It has done just that. The PLA Navy's first LHD for "landing helicopter dock" was launched in September 2019 and is currently undergoing a lengthy fitting-out process. These will be big ships, optimized for helicopter-borne amphibious assault and capable of embarking substantial numbers of attack and troop-lift helicopters.[57] It is estimated that the Type 075 LHD displaces between 35,000 and 40,000 tons, with an 870-foot flight deck.[58] It will also have a well deck and be able to embark as many as 1,400 assault troops. Although this class of ship can be used in any amphibious operation, including Taiwan or in the South China Sea, its primary value for China in my judgment will be in peacetime as a contingency presence somewhere along the BRI. More of this below.

In terms of blue-water amphibious ships the humble tank landing ship, the LST, should not be overlooked. Since 2003, the PLA Navy has commissioned fifteen of its large (4,800-ton) Yuting III (Type 072A) class. These diesel-powered ships have a reported maximum speed of twenty-one knots and an estimated operating range of three thousand miles; they can accommodate an LCAC, 250 marines, ten tanks, and a medium-sized helicopter (having a flight deck though no hangar).[59]

To match this buildup in amphibious shipping, the PLA Marine Corps, a component of the PLA Navy, is also expanding. In December 2017, PRC media reported that each of China's three fleets (North, West, and South) was assigned two brigades of six thousand men each, for a total PLA Marine Corps strength of around 36,000. Around five hundred Chinese marines already form the garrison at China's base in Djibouti, putting into practice the expanded expeditionary mission assigned to the PLA Marine Corps.[60] The question remains how the PLA Navy will organize and employ its expanded Marine Corps for routine presence and contingency operations.

The types and numbers of amphibious ships the PLA Navy has and is planning to commission provide some clues. Using the U.S. Marine Corps as a reference, the PLA Navy could decide on expeditionary amphibious ready groups (ARGs) composed of two Type 071 LPDs and one Type 075 LHD. On the U.S. Marine Corps model, this three-ship force could embark approximately 2,500 marines, organized as a ground combat element (a battalion), an aviation combat element (attack and troop-carrying helicopters), and a logistics battalion and command element. Whether the PLA Marine Corps would follow this template is a matter of conjecture at this point, but the main point is that the blue-water amphibious force the PLA is building provides the potential for three ARGs that could be rotationally deployed anywhere that Beijing chose. Amalgamating the three ARGs plus ten or so LSTs to form an amphibious task force would permit approximately ten thousand PLA marines to be deployed globally. Such a force could be well protected, with an aircraft carrier for air cover and air support along with ten or so destroyers and frigates for air defense and antisubmarine escort. Such a force would likely include four to five of China's extant replenishment ships. By around 2025 China will have a very impressive, deployable, power-projection task force—the first since Adm. Zheng He's last deployment to the Indian Ocean in 1431–33 (see note 9).

The Submarine Force

Nuclear-powered submarines are ideally suited for far-seas deployments by virtue of their long range, high underwater speed, and ability to stay submerged for very long periods of time. Despite these advantages, however, even SSNs require logistical support and voyage repair when on sustained deployments thousands of miles from traditional support bases. This is why the U.S. Navy deploys forward a submarine tender either in Guam or at Diego Garcia. China is likely to make similar support arrangements for far-seas-deploying SSNs. Djibouti would be a possible location, as would Gwadar, Pakistan, for some sort of submarine support ship.

The PLA Navy has long had a small SSN force, but in the past few years it has created the embryo of a modern SSN force with the commissioning of six Shang-class (Type 093) boats. (Western submariners refer to their ships as "boats"; whether this usage has been adopted by the PLA Navy is not known.) It is expected to introduce a new class that could bring the inventory to seven to eight SSNs in the 2020–22 period, which would exceed the British and French SSN forces and place China third globally in operational nuclear-powered attack submarines, behind the United States and Russia.[61] With this size inventory, it could maintain an SSN on station in either the Indian Ocean or in the eastern Pacific, perhaps off the coast of Hawaii or California. (The Soviet Union routinely operated its nuclear submarines off both the east and west coasts of the United States. The Russians periodically do so today.)[62]

Whether PLA Navy nuclear attack submarines would be included in a notional PLA Navy carrier strike group has been a matter of speculation among bloggers and newspaper columnists. It seems unlikely that they would be at this stage of their development. Using an SSN in direct support of a carrier creates difficult tactical problems. Responsive tactical communications with submerged submarines is likely to be a constant problem, as well as keeping track of them so the strike group's helicopters do not mistake them as intruders. There is also a tactical incompatibility issue. If a direct-support submarine is to be any help, it has to be tethered in some fashion to the carrier's movement. However, a submarine hunting another submarine must remain very quiet, search at a moderate speed, and freely operate at different depths; meanwhile a carrier needs to go fast, move around unpredictably "chasing the wind," and respond quickly to evolving operational circumstances. Finally, according to the U.S. Navy's Office of Naval Intelligence, the PLA Navy's current submarine force, including its SSNs, are optimized not for hunting other submarines but for sinking ships.[63]

The PLA Navy has around fifty-four operational conventionally powered submarines, of three Chinese classes along with twelve of the Russian Kilo class. They are primarily focused on near-seas defense in the Yellow, East, South China, and Philippine Seas, but the newest conventionally powered submarines are capable of operations beyond them.[64] The PLA Navy's most modern of these is the Yuan class (Type 039A/B), equipped with air-independent propulsion.[65] It has been in series production since 2004, and there are as many as twenty now.[66] One of these large (3,500 tons underwater displacement) boats was sent to the Indian Ocean, calling at Karachi, Pakistan, in April 2015. It was the third submarine the PLA Navy had deployed to the Indian Ocean, the earlier ones having been a Type 093 SSN and a Song (Type 039)–class conventional boat.[67]

In July 2018, India's Chief of Naval Staff reported that since 2013 the PLA Navy has been conducting two submarine deployments to the Indian Ocean every year. "They last three months," he said, "and alternate between a conventional boat and an SSN."[68] China's growing undersea presence in the Arabian Sea and the Bay of Bengal, Indian naval commanders say, is meant to display increased naval capability and strategic intent in areas near India's most important sea-lanes.[69] The pattern is clearly intended to familiarize PLA Navy submariners with the Indian Ocean's operating environment and suggests that deployments there are likely to become routine, along the lines of the Soviet Navy's routine submarine presence in the northern Arabian Sea during the final two decades of the Cold War.[70]

Putting China's Blue-Water Capabilities in Perspective

It is difficult to appreciate the magnitude of PLA Navy's development of—pick the term—blue-water, far-seas, or open-ocean protection capabilities without context. The best way to get that context is comparison to the other great navies of the world. Table 3 sets the classes of Chinese blue water–capable ships that were discussed in this chapter alongside similar classes of other naval powers, including the United States. This is *not* a comparison of orders of battle, counting every ship, only those discussed above; it is, rather an illustration how the PLA Navy has leapt ahead of other large navies that have historically operated around the world. Table 3 makes clear that in terms of modern warships and submarines (and, again, speaking here *only* in those terms) China outstrips its erstwhile peers, except the United States.

The main point is that the PLA Navy's far-seas capabilities do not measure up against America's far-seas naval forces, albeit they are very impressive when measured against the rest of the world. Of course, virtually all of America's warships are built to be blue water–capable, to operate "overseas" across the Pacific or Atlantic Oceans, while China is able to include in its total warship numbers many small units suited only for operations in its near seas. The United States has both qualitative and quantitative advantages in aircraft carriers, high-end air-defense cruisers and destroyers, large amphibious ships, and nuclear attack submarines. But in terms of warfare near China's only seacoast, all of China's ships are homeported directly on it, whereas most the U.S. Navy is based thousands of miles away.

This point leads to an inevitable imbalance in favor of China in the western Pacific. Beyond the ships listed above, the PLA Navy also has around 175 other destroyers, frigates, corvettes, older submarines, and missile-attack craft that are capable of operating in the East and South China Seas—in other words, out to the first island chain. Thus, on a day-to-day basis the Seventh Fleet, forward-deployed in the western Pacific, faces as many as 270 PLA Navy ships and submarines that could shoot advanced weapons at them, as could all of the land-based air and missiles forces that will be discussed in chapter 5. In short, in its home waters, China possesses a formidable and still-growing navy that on a day-to-day, routine basis—and this is the most important point—overshadows the United States alone, or even the combined capabilities of the United States and Japan.

Table 3. Blue–Water–Capable Ships of Major Naval Powers (in Commission or Fitting Out, ca. 2021)

	China	U.K.	France	Japan	India	Russia	United States
Carriers	2	2	1	2 (*Izumo* class being adapted for F-35B aircraft)	1	0	11
Aegis-like Destroyer[a]	36	6	4	6 (Aegis) 6 (Aegis-like)	4	0	90 (CGs and DDGs)
Modern Frigate (FFG)	30	13	6 (FREMM)[b]	0	4	10	0 (25 LCSs are not FFGs)
Large Amphibious	9	3	3	3+2 DDH	1	0	34
AOR/AOE	11	3	3	5	5	3 very old	30
SSN	8	6	5	0	1	17+8 SSGN	53+4 SSGN
SS	30			22	16	19	0
SSBN	6	4	4	0	1	13	14
Total	132	37	26	46	33	70	236 (plus 25 LCSs)

a. "Aegis-like" ships are modern destroyers with phased–array, electronically scanned radars and mission suites optimized toward air defense, having surface-to-air missiles with sufficient range for area as opposed to unit defense. For the PLA Navy these are Types 052C/D and Type-055. Japan has both U.S.-supplied Aegis radar and combat system and domestically developed Aegis-like systems. Others are the U.K. Type 045 *Daring* class, the French Horizon class, the Japanese *Kongo* and *Atago* classes, and the Indian *Kolkata* and *Visakhapatnam* classes.

b. FREMM: *Frégate européene multi-mission*, European Multipurpose Frigate. *Sources:* DoD *Annual Report to Congress: Military and Security Developments Involving the People's Republic of China*, 2012, 2018, 2019; *Jane's Defense Weekly* announcements of ship commissionings; International Institute of Strategic Studies, *Strategic Balance*, 2019, for all countries listed in the table; websites for the Indian Navy, Royal Navy, French Navy. Rick Joe's *Diplomat* series on the future of the PLA Navy; Ronald O'Rourke's semiannual update of his Congressional Research Service report *China Naval Modernization*; Office of Naval Intelligence; The Russian Navy 2015: *A Historic Transition*, and ONI's *The PLA Navy: New Capabilities and Missions for the 21st Century.*

On one hand, Chinese land-based airpower and missiles would seem to represent collectively a decisive edge in any campaign in the near seas before U.S. naval and air force reinforcements could arrive. On the other hand, the PLA Navy cannot simply ignore its sea-lanes: an attack on Taiwan (to pick the most familiar scenario) in which the United States becomes involved is likely to become quickly a global war at sea and draw forces away from the East China Sea. The PLA Navy would have to have sent substantial surface and maritime-patrol aircraft forces to its South China Sea bases and Indian Ocean facilities, including Djibouti, before it (say) attacked Taiwan, ready to defend the sea-lanes from the moment the first shot was fired. This would of course reduce its firepower advantage in the East China Sea.

Implications

This chapter has focused on the portion of the PLA Navy capable of far-seas or blue-water operations. As a general rule, Chinese surface combatants are extremely well armed. On paper they are able both to attack and to defend themselves and seemingly are equipped with effective antiship cruise missiles and in some cases with land-attack cruise missiles. China's blue-water amphibious force is modern and with a good deal of training would be capable of state-of-the-art amphibious assaults beyond China's littoral. When its LHDs enter service the PLA Navy will be second only to that of the U.S. Navy in terms of a large, globally capable, expeditionary amphibious force.

Virtually all of the PLA Navy ships discussed in proceeding paragraphs have been commissioned since 2004; the obvious conclusion is that China's open-ocean-protection mission will be executed by a new and modern far-seas force. This force, clearly well balanced across the board, increasingly resembles nothing more than a smaller version of the U.S. Navy. The question is: Will Beijing employ its blue-water forces the way Washington uses its navy? The last fifteen years have seen the PLA Navy, albeit with small numbers of ships, operate as the U.S. Navy does when in distant seas, conducting the whole range of "peacetime presence" activities: naval diplomacy, emergency evacuation, disaster relief, and exercising with friendly navies.[71]

What has not been seen is aircraft carrier–centered presence—yet. Whether that will become routine remains to be seen; the PLA Navy still has to become proficient in blue-water carrier operations and learn how to sustain and maintain both the ship and its air wing a long way from home. *Liaoning*'s deployments have largely been short excursions from its home port in Dalian south to Hong Kong or around Hainan in the South China Sea. However, in May 2018, following the fleet review in the South China Sea, *Liaoning* with five escorts (three DDGs and two FFGs) entered the Philippine Sea and conducted carrier-group training for several days. On May 31 the Chinese Ministry of Defense announced at its monthly press conference that "the carrier group's exercises have been deepened to include combat operations in the open seas. It has initially formed a system combat capability . . . [and] comprehensive system of offense and defense has been effectively tested."[72]

Depending how shakedown and training goes with the PLA Navy's second carrier, it likely will be 2022–23 before a Chinese aircraft carrier–centered task force makes an extended deployment to the western Indian Ocean, perhaps even to the eastern Mediterranean. When that happens, though, and it almost certainly will, China will have truly arrived as a blue-water naval power. China's global prestige will grow. The image of a Chinese "global" expeditionary navy would likely over time attenuate perceptions of American power, especially in maritime regions where only the U.S. Navy or its friends had operated freely since the end of the Cold War. The PLA Navy already sends its small antipiracy task groups to show the flag; when large formations, especially with an aircraft carrier or LHD, start showing up, they will be visible manifestations of China's new stature.

How Big Will China's Blue-Water Navy Become?

To appreciate how far the PLA Navy has come in a short time, it is useful to look back. Writing in 2003, Dr. Bernard Cole, a published expert on the PLA Navy, described the severe limits of the PLA Navy's blue-water capability:

> The Chinese navy currently includes fewer than 20 warships capable of operating in even a limited early 21st-century naval environment. And these ships—2 Sovremenny-class, 1 Luhai-class, and 2 Luhu-class guided-missile destroyers (DDGs), and approximately 12 Jiangwei-class guided-missile frigates—are armed with very

limited antiair warfare weapons systems. Another 40 or so surface combatants are armed with antisurface ship cruise missiles and, in a non-air-threat environment, could perform SLOC defense duties in *Chinese littoral waters*. The PLA Navy' ability to deploy is further limited by the presence of only three replenishment-at-sea ships in the fleet.[73]

As we have seen, this is no longer the case. As we have also seen, China does not reveal how many ships and submarines it intends to build. This lack of transparency gives rise to great uncertainty over how large a blue-water PLA Navy will become. If one takes seriously Xi's 19th Party Congress work report—that the national objective is to have a completely transformed, "world class" navy by 2050—one could expect it to become very large indeed. History provides a hint at what is possible in East Asia. In 1941 the Imperial Japanese Navy was a formidable force: ten battleships, twelve aircraft carriers, eighteen heavy cruisers, twenty light cruisers, 126 destroyers, and sixty-eight submarines.[74]

CHAPTER FOUR

Combat in China's Near Seas

Area Denial

The last chapter focused on the blue-water navy that China is building. It addressed the mission the PLA has elected to call "open seas protection" and the sorts of capabilities it would need to execute it. This and the next chapter focus on the war-fighting mission that China's 2015 DWP *China's Military Strategy* calls "offshore waters defense." Recall how the DWP distinguished between defense of China and defense of overseas interests and SLOCs: "The PLA Navy will gradually shift its *focus* from 'offshore waters defense' *to the combination of 'offshore waters defense' with 'open seas protection*,' and build a combined, multifunctional and efficient marine combat force structure."[1]

The military objective the PLA seeks to accomplish through "offshore waters defense" is command of the sea and air, or at a minimum denial of that command to the United States, on, over, and under the surface of its maritime approaches. This objective was publicly announced well over a decade and a half ago, when it was spelled out in China's 2004 defense white paper: "While continuing to attach importance to the building of the Army, the PLA gives priority to the building of the Navy, Air Force and Second Artillery force to seek balanced development of the combat force structure, *in order to strengthen the capabilities for winning both command of the sea and command of the air, and conducting strategic counter strikes*."[2]

The goal of Chinese command of the sea and air, or as it is often termed, sea and air control, is to dictate who can use these domains, in this case the nation's maritime approaches, whenever the Central Military Commission elects to do so and for as long as it chooses. At a minimum, this implies the PLA's preventing their use by any interloper. Each of the PLA services plays a role. The PLA Navy, the Air Force, the Rocket Force, and the Strategic Support Force (for cyber, space, and electronic warfare) all have important responsibilities associated with gaining sea and air control in the western Pacific and defending the Chinese mainland from air and missile attacks. In practice, the exercise of air and sea control means finding enemy aircraft, ships, and submarines at sea or over the sea and defeating them before they can attack China or interfere with PLA operations against its near neighbors—and then maintain control until the conflict ends.

Offshore-Waters Defense Is the Same as Anti-Access/Area Denial

A word about the term "offshore waters defense" is in order. This is a new Chinese formulation of concepts usually rendered in English as "active defense" or "offshore defense." The U.S. military has coined its own term to characterize the PLA's operational concept; it is called anti-access (A2) and area denial (AD), commonly referred to as A2/AD. Whether one uses Chinese or American terms, in practice it is a PLA joint-service campaign with a dual operational objective: first, keeping approaching hostile forces at bay by attacking them before they gain access to areas where they could do harm—thus *anti-access*; second, if anti-access fails or hostile forces are already in combat theater (e.g., U.S. forces stationed in Japan), defeating them before they can gain freedom of operational and tactical action—*area denial*.[3] To be clear, anti-access and area denial are American-coined terms, introduced into the official Defense Department lexicon by the 2001 Quadrennial Defense Review.[4] Another term often used to describe the PRC's approach to defense is "counterintervention." This too is a Western construct, and the term is not found in authoritative Chinese sources.[5] However, along with A2/AD, it is a useful characterization; both describe the military operational objective (or military effect) the PLA is trying to accomplish if the United States elects to attack China or intervene on behalf of potential antagonists.[6]

The best open source on defending China's sea frontier is the PLA's *Science of Military Strategy*: "Active defense is the essential feature of

China's military strategy and is the keystone of the theory of China's strategic guidance." This textbook argues that "active defense" is actually a "strategic counterattack," because if an enemy "offends our national interests, it means the enemy has already fired the first shot." The PLA "must do all [it] can to dominate the enemy by striking first." It goes on to instruct that "*we should try our best to fight against the enemy as far away as possible*, to lead the war to the enemy's operational base . . . and to actively strike all the effective strength forming the enemy's war system"[7]

For simplicity, this chapter will use "counterintervention" or "A2/AD" for China's "offshore waters defense"; in the context of a conflict in the western Pacific between the United States and China, they imply the same concept of operations. From China's perspective, such a campaign is inherently defensive, designed to react to U.S. forces close to or closing the mainland. While the PLA has created its A2/AD plan with a Taiwan contingency in mind, the concept itself has broader military applicability. The military capabilities that the CCP has assembled amount essentially to a layered defense of the western Pacific Ocean. The concept and its associated capabilities are as important to the defense of the Chinese mainland from attack from the sea—a vulnerability that has plagued China since the Opium Wars era—as to the protection of a Taiwan invasion force. Thus, even if the prospect of conflict over Taiwan evaporates, the PLA capabilities associated with A2/AD will remain essential and almost certainly will not disappear. In his recent book on China's military strategy, Dr. Taylor Fravel argues that the PRC's "main strategic-direction that defines the geographic focus of strategy" remains the same, oriented to Taiwan and China's southeast, but may have expanded to something akin to a Taiwan Strait–western Pacific orientation.[8]

For the foreseeable future, Beijing's primary military competitor—the United States—will maintain a significant naval and air presence on China's doorstep. If Beijing uses force to effect reunification with Taiwan or resolve some maritime claim, the United States is the only country that could thwart Beijing militarily. American air and naval presence in the region also counterbalance (some would argue deter) the potential use of the PLA to settle sovereignty claims by force majeure in peacetime.

A2/AD and the PLA Navy

In geographic terms, a PLA counterintervention campaign would meet the classic American definition of "jointness": it requires unitary command and control of units from all of China's services. It would be fought on the waters, in the airspace, and among the islands of the East and South China Seas and from there eastward across the Philippine Sea some 1,650 nautical miles to the "second island chain": from the Commonwealth of the Northern Marianas, through the U.S. territory of Guam, then southward to just north of the Indonesian province of Papua.

A2/AD (counterintervention) is not limited to combat inside the first island chain. It is a range-dependent concept of operations, not bounded by fixed land features, island chains, or erstwhile lines in the water. The stated PLA objective is to intercept approaching U.S. forces as far away from the PRC as possible, certainly before these forces approach close enough for its aircraft or land-attack cruise missiles to reach the Chinese mainland.

The announced range of the Tomahawk cruise missile is 900 nautical miles; the tactical radius of the carrier-based FA-18E/F Super Hornet jet is between 550 nm (unrefueled) and 900 nm (with one aerial refueling). That means, assuming the Super Hornets would be refueled in the air, Chinese planners need to be able to attack U.S. surface forces, probably organized as aircraft carrier strike groups, and also to locate and track attack submarines some 1,000–1,200 nm from China's coast. It also means that the PLA would be very concerned about U.S. Air Force heavy bombers on Guam, aircraft that could reach China.

PRC strategists considering an attack on Taiwan or Japan have two separate but related problems when it comes to potential U.S. involvement. The first is dealing with U.S. air and naval forces permanently stationed on the territory of Japan: the Seventh Fleet, Fifth Air Force, and III Marine Expeditionary Force (MEF), in the home islands or on Okinawa in the Ryukyu chain. These units would be America's "first responders" to an act of Chinese aggression against Taiwan or Japan— or, potentially, other American allies (say, the Philippines over a South China Sea dispute). This factor is the crux of this chapter.

The United States also has the Seventh Air Force stationed in the Republic of Korea, whose mission is to deter an attack by North Korea. The position of the South Korean government has been that U.S. forces

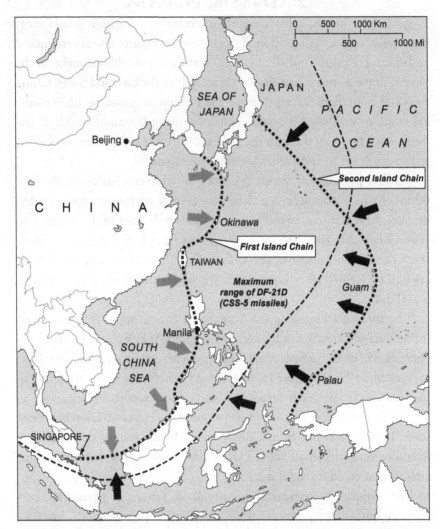

Map 1. First and Second Island Chains. This map displays the first and second island chains, along with the maximum-range arc of China's primary long-range antiship ballistic missile. The large black arrows depict a wartime scenario of U.S. forces seeking to gain access to the Philippine Sea in order to defend either Japan, Taiwan, or the Philippines. The large gray arrows depict the PLA objective of denying the U.S. military access to friends and allies, essentially trying to keep reinforcements from the United States from moving east through the Philippine Sea.

Harry J. Kazianis, "Air–Sea Battle Concept: An Attempt to Weaken China's A2/AD Strategy," October 26, 2014, collapsechina.blogspot.com/2014/10/air -sea-battle-concept-attempt-to.html.

stationed on its territory would not be permitted to attack Chinese forces in a Taiwan contingency. However, the famously unsentimental PLA planners must surely consider it necessary to be prepared to deal with interference from these aircraft.

The second basic problem for the PLA, which will be the focus of the next chapter, is how to slow down or halt American reinforcements leaving Guam, Hawaii, the Middle East, or the continental United States. It is unlikely that American reinforcements (except for SSNs) would be available immediately to respond to a short-notice attack, so this second planning problem might well be separated in time, perhaps by weeks, from the first, which would permit the PLA to deal with the two sequentially.

Area Denial

The best way to explore the area-denial element of counterintervention is to look at it through the lens of the PLA's most stressing near-seas scenario, that of militarily convincing or forcing Taiwan to unify itself with the mainland. Because the geography is nearly identical, a Taiwan scenario is, for this purpose, also relevant to a contest between Japan and China over the Senkakus/Diaoyus. The U.S., Chinese, and Japanese forces involved would be almost the same, and accordingly, that scenario will be left implicit.

I deem Taiwan most stressing because the PLA would have to deal with U.S. naval and air forces already in the neighborhood. For decades, these forward-deployed American forces have enjoyed permanent access in East Asian waters and airspace: the Fifth U.S. Air Force presence in East Asia predates World War II, the Seventh Fleet was established in 1943, and III Marine Expeditionary Force in 1944. In any case, for all practical purposes Taiwan is the center of the Sino-American security universe. Either directly or indirectly, it has been the cause of the vast majority of security issues between the PRC and the United States since the outbreak of the Korean War in 1950.[9] For the PLA it has been and remains, because of potential American involvement, the most important driver of modernization.[10] As noted China expert Dr. David Schambaugh has written:

The dispatch of two aircraft carrier battle groups (CVBGs) during the 1996 crisis signaled to Beijing, Taipei, and the world that U.S. involvement, under certain conditions, is a distinct possibility. The

United States has made clear, and the TRA [Taiwan Relations Act] suggests but does not require that an unprovoked attack or other coercive behavior toward the island (including blockades) would likely trigger a U.S. military response, although the policy of "strategic ambiguity" has long dictated that exactly what that military response might consist of would depend on the circumstances. The U.S. government and president regularly say that PRC military action would be judged with "grave concern."[11]

More specifically, the geographic focus of action in this chapter comprises the East China Sea and the Japanese territory that constitutes a large portion of the first island chain. Of necessity, it also addresses the role the Japan's Self-Defense Forces, because its Maritime and Air services are likely to play important roles.

Why Would Taiwan Be a Cause for War between China and America?

Taiwan is a de facto (not de jure) independent democratic nation known to its citizens and friends around the world as the Republic of China. Given the choice, most of Taiwan's citizens would vote to become independent, but as a practical matter mainland China forecloses that option by threatening war should Taiwan attempt it. Beijing has gradually amassed the military capability to make that warning credible. As a result, Taiwan's citizens prefer to continue being neither a legally independent state nor legally a component part of the PRC. For the people of Taiwan this increasingly uneasy status quo is preferable to either war with or reunification to what used to be called "communist China"—simply put, it is the best deal Taiwan can get under the current circumstances.[12]

For almost a quarter of a century (1954–79) Taiwan was protected by a formal defense treaty with the United States and by its own large, conscript military force and competent air force and navy. In 1979, Washington terminated the treaty, having decided that the PRC, not the ROC, should be recognized as the lawful Chinese state. The ROC was expelled from the United Nations and recognition as the lawful government of China was withdrawn by the vast majority of nations in favor of the People's Republic. Since that time Taiwan has depended, aside from its current volunteer force, on the combination of a security guarantee from Washington implied in the Taiwan Relations Act of 1979; the periodic purchase of defense equipment from the United States (currently the only country that has the courage to sell arms to Taipei); and the geographic gift of what is called the Taiwan Strait but is effectively a hundred-mile-wide, often very rough, moat.[13]

Until the mid-1990s, the mainland could only make hollow threats against Taiwan, since the PLA did not have the ability even to reach out and inflict serious damage on Taiwan, much less invade and seize the island. In those years Taiwan was judged to have the most capable military force on either side of the Taiwan Strait, especially in its air force. Those days are long gone. Since the mid-1990s the PLA has been dedicated

Map 2. Taiwan and Taiwan Strait. Taiwan, the Taiwan Strait, Pescadores (Penghu), and Taiwan's offshore islands.

to a comprehensive military modernization, the results of which have been impressive. PLA has surpassed Taiwan in virtually every aspect of modern warfare. In particular, it has invested in a serious improvement of its navy and air force and in the manufacture of well over a thousand conventionally armed, very accurate, short-range ballistic missiles.

The Current Situation

The primary war-planning focus of the PLA, the "main strategic direction," remains Taiwan.[14] The PLA defines the major strategic direction as "the focal point of the struggle of contradictions between ourselves and the enemy . . . in the overall strategic situation, it is the vital point of *greatest importance*."[15]

On January 2, 2019, General Secretary Xi gave a long speech on unification for Chinese and Taiwanese audiences. He emphasized the long-standing PRC understanding of "one China," saying, "The two sides of the Strait belong to one China and together we will work together to achieve national unification."[16] The way to do this was through the "one country, two systems" (1C2S) formulation that had been used with Hong Kong and Macao.[17] (Given how Hong Kong's political freedoms have been constricted, this course of action likely filled the citizens of Taiwan with dread rather than enthusiasm.)[18] He was not willing, he implied, to wait forever for unification talks to begin but that Beijing's goal of peaceful unification remained his objective.

Beijing remains willing to use force—reluctant, but willing. Xi made clear that keeping force on the table is intended to deter interference from outside forces (i.e., the United States) or from the small minority of hard-core independence advocates. There was nothing very new in the presentation, but it did signal that resolution of the Taiwan issue is now firmly embedded in Xi's overarching goal of "achieving the great rejuvenation of the Chinese nation." This linkage is a veiled warning that Taipei needs to consider seriously how long the status quo can be its *best possible* future.[19]

It is notable that Xi's speech was also a shot across America's bow, a warning to stop reinforcing Taipei's reluctance. He reemphasized that any use of force against Taiwan would be primarily directed against interfering "external forces" (again, the United States). Currently, it is not likely that China would launch an unprovoked attack on Taiwan to settle the unification issue once and for all. If it did, there is a high probability, but not an absolute certainty, that the United States would intervene to attempt to halt it. A commitment to do so is implied (as David Schambaugh notes, above) in the TRA.[20] Despite the "strategic ambiguity" employed (again, as Dr. Schambaugh points out), for planning purposes the Chinese military must assume the worse and count on American intervention.

At this writing, tension has increased across the Taiwan Strait for a number of reasons, primary among them the fact that Beijing simply does not trust Taiwan's ruling party, the Democratic People's Party (DPP), which has long advocated eventual independence. Beijing especially does not trust the current president of Taiwan, Madam Tsai Ing-wen, who helped craft the independence language in the DPP Party Charter and who in January 2020 won a second term in a landslide.[21] This vote has been interpreted, correctly in my view, as a massive rejection by the citizens of Taiwan of Beijing's "1C2S" strategy. Nonetheless, preliminary indications suggest Xi is unlikely to back away from 1C2S, implying Beijing believes that it has time on its side.

This suggests there will be no letup in PLA demonstrations of its military prowess in and around Taiwan. This has been going on since Tsai first took office in 2016. The PLA has, especially its air force and navy, been operating around the island to remind Taipei's military and people of its growing capabilities. PLA activities include increased ground exercises on the opposite coast, flights around Taiwan, and naval exercises in the East China Sea.[22]

As a result, the Trump administration and Congress have taken steps to tangibly support Taiwan's vibrant democracy—gestures that unfortunately could make the situation worse. Washington is systematically rolling back well-established diplomatic protocols and agreements with Beijing that had circumscribed "official" government interaction with Taiwan officials. This greatly irritates and agitates Beijing, which increasingly sees Washington as intending (including with frequent U.S. Navy warship transits of the Taiwan Straits) to encourage independence-oriented politics in Taiwan and implicitly discourage discourse on reunification. Beijing's concerns were voiced by a well-known Chinese scholar at a December 2018 conference organized by the state-sponsored newspaper *Global Times*:

There are several key figures in the Trump administration that support Taiwan. Despite the Democratic Progressive Party's loss in local elections, the United States continues to support Tsai Ing-wen because she refuses to compromise with China. The internal U.S. position is, as long as Tsai Ing-wen does not declare "Taiwan independence," she can do anything else. I am worried that the United States will do something unprecedented since the U.S.-China relations were established and cause serious friction on both sides.[23]

The Role of the PLA Navy in a Cross-Strait Conflict

PLA war planners studying an attack on Taiwan have two problems to overcome if victory is to be achieved before the weight of U.S. military power can be brought to the fight. The first is quickly destroying Taiwan's capable, if much smaller, navy and air force. The other is dealing with the permanently stationed American air and naval forces located in Japan's home islands and Okinawa.

No one other than those planners knows precisely how the PLA would choose to attack were Beijing's patience to be exhausted or Taipei to cross a "red line" (such as declaring independence, building a nuclear weapon, or even simply refusing to discuss the issue).[24] The discussion that follows draws on my own understanding of how the PRC could employ its capabilities to execute an attack, not on any insider knowledge.[25] However, the particulars of the PLA plan need not be known to appreciate that the geography of the East China Sea region around Taiwan makes certain operational factors obvious. It is a long-understood imperative sea and air control must be established over an amphibious objective area before a major assault, especially one that crosses across a hundred miles of water. Clearly there have been hints in doctrinal writings, such as the *Science of Military Strategy*, of PLA thinking on the matter. Ian Easton's recent analysis, *The Chinese Invasion Threat*, makes extensive use of Chinese and Taiwanese sources to outline how a campaign might be fought.[26]

Keep in mind that Beijing does not need to launch an amphibious assault from a standing start. Nor could it conceal preparations to do so. Troop movements, truck convoys to known embarkation ports, "surges" of ships and submarines to sea are all detectable by today's reconnaissance systems and provide early warning. Such movements might be given a pretext, probably an announcement that the PLA was about to conduct a major exercise. The defense authorities in Taipei are perfectly aware of such deceptive covers and over the years have increased readiness whenever the PLA exercises amphibious forces opposite Taiwan.

It is necessary to provide a snapshot of the military capabilities available on a routine basis in the western Pacific to all the likely participants in this conflict and to identify and characterize the sources on which it based. The data given in tables 4, 5, and 6 reflect operational units as of April 2019 and do not include units under construction, outfitting, or conducting sea trials.[27] The PLA and Taiwan force numbers are from the 2019 Department of Defense's *Annual Report to Congress on Military and Security Developments Involving the People's Republic of China*. These annual reports are the most authoritative open-source documents available; helpfully, each year's report includes a "net assessment" of the forces on each side of the strait. The sources for the U.S. forces stationed in Japan are on the internet—unit websites and "fact sheets." Sources for Japanese force numbers are identified in endnotes.

Tables 4, 5, and 6 also identify the portions of China's total capability that would be initially involved—that is, those under the Eastern and Southern Theater Commands. DoD estimates these commands and the forces assigned to them would have the lead in any Taiwan operation, while the other eastward-facing regional command, the Northern Theater Command, would be primarily responsible for China's maritime approaches.[28] Of the 1,020,000 personnel in the PLA ground forces, it is estimated that 915,000 are in combat units, 360,000 of them in the Taiwan Strait area.

The PLA Navy is the largest force of destroyers, frigates, corvettes, and submarines in Asia. These ships are armed with antiship cruise missiles or torpedoes, as well as impressive submarine-detection capabilities. The PLA Navy also has the largest amphibious force in Asia. In a major Taiwan conflict, the Eastern and Southern Theater naval components would participate in direct action against the Taiwan navy, the U.S. Seventh Fleet, and likely the Japan Maritime Self-Defense Force (the latter will be discussed below). The Northern Theater could, in addition to protecting the sea approaches, support other fleets with mission-critical assets. Conversely, the other fleets could, and probably would, provide resources to the Northern Theater depending on the course of the conflict, which is likely to be sequential as opposed to simultaneous.

As described in earlier chapters, Beijing has embarked on an ASW surface-warship building spree. In this scenario the corvette and frigate numbers are important since they would be protecting the South China and East China Seas SLOCs. The PLA has airfield and port facilities in the Paracels and Spratlys that allow its ASW forces to be

Table 4. The Peacetime Western Pacific Naval Balance around Taiwan (July 2019)

	China Total	Eastern and Southern Theater	Taiwan	U.S. Seventh Fleet	Japan Maritime Self-Defense Force
Aircraft Carriers	1	0	0	1	0
Cruisers/ Destroyers	33	23	4	10–14	47 (includes 4 DDHs)
Frigates	54	43	22	0	6
Corvettes	42	33	0	0	0
Missile-Equipped Attack Craft	86	68	44	0	6
Diesel Attack Submarines	50	34	2	0	18
Nuclear Attack Submarines	6	2	0	8–12	0
Subtotal (Ships That Can Shoot with Aircraft, Cruise Missiles, or Torpedoes)	272	203	72	19–27	77
Amphibious Ships (all classes)	59	41	14	3–4	3
Totals	331	244	86	22–31	80

Sources: "China and Taiwan Naval Force," in *DoD Annual Report to Congress 2019*; U.S. Seventh Fleet, "Fact Sheet," n.d. [2018], https://www.c7f.navy.mil/Portals/8/doc uments/7thFleetTwoPagerFactsheet.pdf?ver=2017-09-20-040335-223; Japan Ministry of Defense, *Defense of Japan 2018, Japan Defense White Paper*, March 2018, https://www.mod.go.jp/e/publ/w_paper/2018.html, 21.

deployed along the length of the South China Sea SLOC. The PLA Navy introduced the Type 056 corvette (Jiangdao class) in 2013 and already (mid-2019) has forty-two in commission. Total class strength is not clear, although some sources suggest a total of more than sixty are planned. The 295-foot-long Jiangdaos displace 1,500 tons and are built in two variants: a multipurpose Type 056 with hull-mounted sonar and an ASW-specialized Type 056A that adds a towed array and VDS. For a small ship this is an impressive array of ASW sensors. When the class is at full strength it will represent an important piece of the PLA Navy near-seas submarine-detection network: passive detection arrays on the ocean floor, special-purpose ships (three launched to date) that tow long arrays, land-based maritime patrol aircraft, and island-based ASW helicopters.[29]

Both Type 056 variants are able to defend themselves: their fit includes four YJ-83 antiship missiles, a point-defense, short-range missile system, and a 76-mm main gun. The ASW variant is also equipped with two 324-mm triple ASW torpedo launchers. The ships have no hangar but do have flight decks large enough to accommodate a Harbin Z-9 helicopter with dipping sonar.[30] In the South China Sea, all six of China's man-made bases in the Spratlys have facilities for helicopters, as do many of its facilities in the Paracels. This means ASW helicopters can be island based and flown to Type 056s for short periods, say twenty-four to forty-eight hours. This class is well suited for patrol and SLOC-protection missions, particularly since it would be operating where Chinese land- or island-based air cover and airborne ASW support are readily available.[31]

PLA Air Force and PLAN Naval Aviation

The air balance of power would be particularly important in a Taiwan Strait conflict. Gaining air superiority in and around Taiwan would be crucial if the PLA hoped to conduct any "projection operation" against Taiwan. Conversely, failure would likely end any PRC hope of compelling reunification by occupation. This is not to say that Taiwan would escape unscathed: PLA missile and cyber capabilities do not require air superiority to inflict large-scale damage and destruction. Table 5 displays estimated totals of operational military aircraft in both the PLA Air Force and PLAN Naval Aviation. China will continue to field fourth-generation aircraft (now about six hundred) and probably will become a majority-fourth-generation force within the next several years. "Fourth generation" essentially refers to such contemporary frontline fighters and fighter-attack aircraft as the U.S. F-15, F-16, and F-18 or the Chinese J-10, J-11 and J-15 (along with its Sukhoi derivatives). Taiwan, whose fighter force is largely older fourth generation, is in the process of upgrading its F-16 fleet to what can be characterized as "generation 4.5."[32]

In addition, the PLA Air Force possesses one of the largest inventories of advanced long-range surface-to-air systems in the world, a combination of Russian S-300 (SA-20) battalions and domestically produced CSA-9 battalions. Beijing is in the process of introducing the latest Russian SAM system, the S-400 (SA-21), whose slant range of 215 nm covers, depending on how far inland its batteries are, a substantial portion of the airspace over the East China Sea—a missile-engagement-zone (MEZ) that allows it to engage fighters in and around the Taiwan Strait and Taiwan's medium-altitude airspace.

Beijing's decades-long investment in rocketry has amply paid off for the PLA; the combination of space-based navigation systems and ballistic missiles (discussed in detail in the next chapter) now holds the military capabilities of its near neighbors, and also American forward-stationed forces, at risk. A glance at table 6 reveals how much of the PLA's warfighting capability in the western Pacific is resident in the Rocket Force (SRF). If the high-end estimate of missile inventory is anywhere near correct, the PLA could overwhelm antimissile defenses. In any case, it

Table 5. Peacetime Western Pacific Fighter/Strike Air Balance around Taiwan (July 2019)

	China Total	Eastern and Southern Theaters	Taiwan	U.S. in Japan	Japan
Fighters	1,500	600	350	153 (includes USN/ USMC)	293 (does not include 52 old F-4s)
Bombers/ Attack	450	250	0	N/A	0

Sources: DoD *Annual Report to Congress 2019*; *Defense of Japan* 2018, 460; "China and Taiwan Naval Force."

Table 6. PLA Rocket Force and Taiwan

System	Launchers	Missiles	Estimated Range Band
Short-Range Ballistic Missiles (SRBMs)	250	750–1500	160–530 nm (can cover Taiwan, some can reach Okinawa and Ryukyu chain)
Medium-Range Ballistic Missiles (MRBMs) (includes DF-21D antiship missile, approx. 1,000-nm range)	150	150–450	530–1,600 nm (at max. range can cover virtually all of Philippine Sea and South China Sea)
Intermediate-Range Ballistic Missiles (IRBMs) (includes DF-26 antiship variant, 2,100-nm range)	80	80–160	1,600–2,650 nm (can cover Guam, much of western Pacific, the South China Sea, and northern portions of Indian Ocean)
Ground-Launched Cruise Missiles (GLCMs)	90	270–540	>425 nm

Source: DoD *Annual Report to Congress* 2019, 45, 117.

must be noted these missile inventories are likely to continue to grow and improve.

In its totality the inventory of military force at Beijing's disposal is impressive and daunting. In it can be seen tangible fruit of Beijing's increases in the PLA budget by an average of 10 percent per year from 2000 to 2016.[33] A Department of Defense 2019 annual report on China's military stated:

China's leaders are committed to developing military power commensurate with that of a great power. Chinese military strategy documents highlight the requirement for a People's Liberation Army (PLA) able to fight and win wars, deter potential adversaries, and secure Chinese national interests overseas, including a growing emphasis on the importance of the maritime and information domains, offensive air operations, long-distance mobility operations, and space and cyber operations.[34]

While spending budgetary largesse on impressive new capabilities, the PLA has also focused on realistic training, emphasizing mission-focused exercises, multiservice (joint) operations, mobility, command and control, staff work, and responsive logistic support. The PLA Navy, like all the other PRC military services, has been busy replicating American employment of technologically advanced networked systems—what the PLA calls "informatized" (real-time, data-networked) warfare.

Informatization figures prominently in PLA writings and is roughly analogous to the U.S. military's "net-centric" concept: a force's use of advanced information and communications technology to gain operational advantage. PLA writings highlight the ways in which near-real-time shared awareness of the battlefield enables quick, unified effort to seize tactical opportunities.[35]

A Sequenced Approach against Taiwan: Area Denial in Practice

The analysis of how the area-denial aspect of China's counterintervention operation might unfold will proceed using the premise of a sequenced (phased escalation), three-step operation consisting of a coercion phase, neutralization of Taiwan and regional airpower, and if necessary, invasion. This categorization is an artificiality, since the campaign would probably have many overlapping activities.

The PLA Eastern Theater Command, with its headquarters in Nanjing, along with the Southern Theater Command, would be responsible for executing the operation against Taiwan, although it is likely that the CMC in Beijing would be watching closely.[36] Starting with coercive measures that do not directly kill or maim people or physically destroy property or infrastructure, the PLA could inflict grievous economic harm through large-scale cyber attacks aimed at shutting down the banking system, stock market, selected power grids, and airports. If combined with the declaration of a blockade or maritime exclusion zone of perhaps fifty miles around the island to keep commercial shipping from bringing goods in, this first coercive step might be enough to bring the people of Taiwan to demand that the government agree to discussions leading toward unification.

In this phase the PLA Navy would station surface warships in a picket line to warn away merchant ships bound for Taiwan. The navy might also be assigned to cut the underseas cables that connect Taiwan to the global internet and other high-speed digital data networks associated with financial transactions. Obviously, the PLA Navy would have to be prepared for the possibility of escalation. For example, Taiwan's small navy might be ordered to escort Taiwan-flagged merchant ships to port, and the PLA Navy could be ordered to prevent that. This means that even if the Central Military Commission thinks it is just in the coercion phase, combat at sea could break out against the ROC navy.

It is important at this point to emphasize how formidable a force the PLA Navy is in Chinese home waters. Even discounting the land-based air and missile firepower that can be brought to bear against enemy ships, on any given day the PLA Navy could call on some large proportion of the 270 or so surface units and submarines that, stationed along the PRC's seaboard, can promptly sortie into the East China Sea and the vicinity of Taiwan. As we have seen, all of China's surface combatants are very well armed with antiship cruise missiles.[37]

It is also likely that once China elected to use force against Taiwan and the United States opted to respond, the war at sea would likely spread globally very fast, after which whenever and wherever around the world the U.S. Navy and PLA Navy encountered one another, combat would ensue. Further, Beijing's fears regarding attacks on its SLOCs would almost certainly come true, perhaps (as mentioned briefly in the last chapter) in the form of a U.S. Navy "distant blockade." If the PLA Navy intended to defend trade it has to have adequate forces in such areas as the northern Arabian Sea before the shooting started. That complication might be eased if, as is altogether possible, Xi and the CMC choose in time to expand and regularize PLA peacetime presence in the western Indian Ocean by transforming its antipiracy mission into a standing force—an air-sea-submarine Indian Ocean Squadron based at Djibouti. This prospect is explored further in the chapter that discusses the Indian Ocean.

The Air and Missile Attack

If China's attempt at largely nonviolent coercion failed to convince the government of Taiwan to begin a unification dialogue, Beijing's next hypothetical step would be air, missile, and, as necessary, submarine attacks against early-warning radars, surface-to-air missile sites, and,

most important of all, airfields. The primary goal would be to eliminate Taiwan's air force and defensive antiair and antimissile systems and
thereby gain air superiority over Taiwan and the Taiwan Strait. That
superiority would be necessary to allow the PLA Air Force to pummel
Taiwan very deliberately with ground-attack weapons, and it would also
be a prerequisite to starting an amphibious force toward Taiwan.

The PLA Navy can contribute to the destruction of Taiwan's airpower in this scenario. Its new DDGs equipped with the HQ-9 long-
range SAMs can act as seaward extensions of China's national SAM
belt, covering low-altitude gaps and "shadow zones" in land-based radar
coverage, contributing to the air defense of Chinese forces, or engaging
airborne fighters.[38] All of this would be not dissimilar to what would be
expected of them screening a PLA aircraft carrier or amphibious force.
While these destroyers have their own ASW capabilities, it is likely that
if in relatively fixed sectors they would require ASW screens themselves,
drawn from the large inventory of frigates and corvettes. Meanwhile,
PLA Navy submarines could be expected to attack Taiwan-flagged merchant ships or warships.

Managing the exclusive zone around Taiwan would become very
important at this point. Beijing would not want to initiate unrestricted
submarine warfare—that is, against *any* merchantmen or warships within,
say, fifty miles of Taiwan. Commencing hostilities against Taiwan after its
refusal to negotiate would be signal enough to third-party shipowners and
insurers to keep them clear of what had turned into a de facto war zone.

By this point readers may be wondering why the U.S. military, in
particular the Seventh Fleet and Japan-stationed Fifth Air Force, has not
been mentioned. They routinely operate in and around the East China
Sea and for all practical purposes are America's "first responders" to any
contingency that arises in the western Pacific. In the scenario I have suggested, it is uncertain what the U.S. government would do during the
coercive phase, other than mounting a "full court" diplomatic effort and
involving the UN to calm tensions and forestall shooting. Washington
could, but not necessarily would, encourage Taipei to conduct some manner of exchange with Beijing, to learn what it wanted. Does Beijing want
Taiwan to (figuratively) "come out with its hands up"? Would something
less than complete surrender do, such as discussion of what "one country,
two systems" would mean? Militarily, meanwhile, Washington would

likely place all Pacific forces, especially those in Japan, in a very high readiness condition and get ships under way. For the time being, however, assets would likely be directed to stay out of the exclusion zone around Taiwan and to do nothing that could provoke actual use of weapons.

Whether Japan too elected to improve the readiness condition of its forces would be of great importance to both Beijing and Washington. The United States depends on Japanese air defenses for the protection of its bases on Japanese territory; Washington would be very anxious, and likely diplomatically insistent, that Tokyo increase its readiness posture in step with U.S. forces. Beijing, for its part, would hope Tokyo was more worried about provoking China than eager to get ready to fight.

The Decision to Attack Japan

Beijing has had years to weigh the relative costs and benefits of attacking U.S. facilities on Japanese soil concurrently with striking Taiwan. On the minus side of the ledger, such an attack, especially if any Japanese citizens were killed, would very likely bring Japan's very capable navy, the MSDF, and its forty-odd destroyers and frigates and twenty or so submarines into the fight. In addition, Japan's air force, the Japan Air Self-Defense Force (JASDF), is well trained in air-to-air combat and would be ready to add to the overall air-defense equation in the southern half of the East China Sea, where the contested Senkakus are. What would essentially be a surprise attack on Japan would draw global opprobrium, but the veto power of China's permanent seat on the UN Security Council could frustrate any onerous UN sanctions. Temporarily putting air bases out of commission is clearly possible for Beijing. Its real problem would be political: whether to broaden the war by attacking U.S. facilities on the territory of Japan (or, if it comes to that, South Korea).[39] Would Beijing be willing to add to its enemies by attacking its neighbor's territory?

On the plus side of attacking Japan, the PLA would have a very good opportunity to hamstring regional U.S. airpower before it could involve itself in the fight. Attacks on American air bases and defensive SAM systems with conventionally armed ballistic and land-attack cruise missiles could well ground or destroy Air Force and Marine Corps fighter and support aircraft. A directly related question, should Beijing decide to do this, is whether it should broaden the air-base attack to include JASDF fighter bases to take them out of the fight too. If Beijing assumes

Japan would "be in" once it attacked U.S. bases on Japanese soil, it makes operational sense to attempt to take out a portion of Japan's tactical airpower also.

A related (and also tough) issue for Xi and company, should they decide to attack U.S. facilities in Japan, would be whether the PLA Rocket Force strikes Guam at the same time. Militarily, attacking Guam to destroy long-range bombers and tankers stationed at Anderson Air Force Base makes sense. But as Guam is sovereign American territory, striking it would justify a U.S. response in kind, against mainland China. The complexities of exploring in detail the bundle of issues related to land-based airpower that could interfere with PLA operations are beyond the scope of this book, but it would be another of the many difficult choices the leadership of China would have to confront. For the purposes of scenario development in order to illustrate PLA Navy roles, let us assume that Beijing did approve attacks on U.S. and Japanese airpower in Japan and on Guam. Attacking Taiwan has high political stakes for Xi Jinping, the Standing Committee of the Politburo, and the Central Military Commission; failure would likely cost them their positions and perhaps more.

Destroying Land-Based Airpower

In PLA strategic literature, a "Joint Fire Strike Campaign" is described as an "integrated fire assault offensive campaign undertaken against key enemy targets . . . to destroy, sabotage key enemy targets, paralyze enemy's operations system, undermine the enemy's will to resist, and weaken the enemy's capacity for war."[40] If the objective is forcible reunification, the airpower of Taiwan, that of the United States in the region, and that of Japan all qualify as "key enemy targets."

The PLA Rocket Force and Air Force would play the leading roles attacking air bases, although submarines fitted with land-attack cruise missiles could contribute. The basic operational approach would be straightforward: attack bases with ballistic and cruise missiles to destroy aircraft on the ground and damage the airfields and support structures beyond use. Chinese sources state that conventional ballistic-missile attacks by the PLA Rocket Force would primarily be aimed at "the enemy's surveillance/early warning systems, electronic warfare systems, air defense/antimissile formations, air troop bases and other targets."[41]

Conventionally tipped ballistic missiles have been used to attack fixed land targets since the Germans began launching V-2 rockets at England in 1944. These early rockets were used essentially as terror weapons, having little strategic or operational value because of their small explosive payloads and extremely poor accuracy. Today things are very different. Satellite-enabled navigation has revolutionized positional accuracy for virtually all military activities, and the United States no longer has a monopoly on it. China has been creating its rival to the Global Positioning System (GPS); as of April 2019 the Chinese version, the Beidou Satellite Navigation System, had forty-four satellites in orbit. The Beidou constellation will be completed some time in 2020. According to Chinese marketing material it will yield accuracy of five meters. Just as GPS offers the U.S. military, Beidou almost certainly reserves a more accurate capability for the PLA. Beidou means that the PLA can fire suitably equipped ballistic or cruise missiles at specific latitudes and longitudes and reasonably expect them to hit very close to the aim-points. That in turn means that Washington could no longer frustrate PLA ballistic-missile attacks on fixed land bases by turning off GPS access.

These missiles carry a relatively small conventional payload (a thousand pounds of explosives, in the case of the PLA's CSS-6 and CSS-7 short-range ballistic missiles).[42] Therefore, the keys to putting airfields out of commission are missile accuracy and numbers, for attack and reattack; probability of success is a function also of the adequacy of active missile defenses, the effectiveness of passive defenses, such as hardened aircraft shelters, and the efficacy and rapidity of runway repair. Fortunately, testimony before the U.S.-China Economic and Security Review Commission by a RAND expert provides a useful summation:

RAND has looked at the effects of various TBM [theater ballistic missile] and cruise missile warheads against air-base targets, and numbers on the order of thirty to fifty TBMs per base appear to be sufficient to overload and kill air defenses, cover all of the open parking areas with submunitions to destroy aircraft parked there, and crater runways such that aircraft cannot take off or land. If thirty to fifty cruise missiles were fired along with the TBMs, they would complicate the air-defense problem and could also damage or destroy a squadron's worth of aircraft shelters. There would likely

also be damage to other critical air-base systems such as fuel storage
and handling or maintenance facilities and equipment. Following
such an attack, U.S. forces would have to extinguish burning aircraft, clear the airfield of debris and unexploded ordnance, repair
runway craters and fly in replacement aircraft and support equipment before the base could generate useful combat sorties.[43]

There are only two American air bases in Japan close enough to the
theater of operations to be hit—Kadena Air Force Base on Okinawa and
Iwakuni in southern Honshu. The Japanese air force is more dispersed,
with two fighter squadrons on Okinawa. Two other airfields house three
fighter squadrons each on the southern main island of Kyushu. The
JASDF also bases two squadrons of fighters on the west coast of Honshu.
This is not the entire fighter strength of Japan, only that portion in the
bases close enough to the scene of action to be among the most immediate PLA targets. The Eastern Theater commander would also have to
neutralize all of Taiwan's fighter bases, which adds to the challenges of
missile allocation (and stocks), targeting, and timing. Optimally, all bases
would need to be struck at nearly the same time; a simultaneous PLA
Navy, Air Force, and Rocket Force attack on five American and Japanese
air bases simultaneously, plus Guam, *plus* the ROC's on Taiwan, would
demand a high degree of skill and coordination.

If the Yokosuka-based aircraft carrier, USS *Ronald Reagan* (CVN 76),
were in port at the time (say, for a scheduled stand-down or maintenance
period, all indications and warning of conflict having been missed), the
PLA might be able to catch its air wing ashore at Marine Corps Air
Station Iwakuni.

Removing a good chunk of American airpower, and possibly Japan's
as well, would buy back for China some of time that was sacrificed by its
deliberate, phased escalation.

What about U.S. Carriers?

The optimum date to strike is something that Beijing would have to
decide. Many considerations would be at play, aside from, obviously,
the readiness of the PLA. Weather is a major consideration; the Taiwan Strait is notoriously rough at certain times of the year. Good flying
weather would be required. Another consideration would also be the state

of preparedness of the ROC, and so on. The list would also include the strength and location of U.S. forces already in the region, which would certainly include the location of the *Reagan* carrier strike group, known as Task Force 70 (TF 70). China keeps close global track of all U.S. carrier movements; it seems safe to assume that the PLA updates TF 70's position every few minutes, even nearly continuously if the carrier is not electronically silent. (The next chapter discusses the PLA ocean surveillance system in more detail.)

From a PLA operational perspective, what would be its *best* location—in port in Yokosuka? at sea near Guam (where at least once a year it conducts an exercise)? off Australia? or where? My guess is that for the PLA, the farther the carrier is from the Taiwan Strait, the better. TF 70 could not respond immediately if it were upward of 1,500 nm away except by moving toward the scene of action around Taiwan, during which time it would be vulnerable to the full range of PLA anti-access capabilities. A complete discussion of the PLA's A2 forces is in the following chapter.

The main point is that TF 70's air wing is an important piece of total U.S. airpower routinely stationed in East Asia, and taking American and Japanese airpower out of the regional power equation would make it easier for the PLA to seize air superiority in the vicinity of the Taiwan Strait and to deal with the vastly outnumbered ships of the Seventh Fleet and Japan Maritime Self-Defense Force. The Seventh Fleet has only between ten and fourteen cruise-missile-firing surface warships available on a routine basis.[44] These "first responding" forces will have to confront PLA Navy ships and submarines, PLA Naval Air Force and PLA Air Force regiments, and ASBM ballistic missiles from the PLA Rocket Force.

Coping with American and Japanese Submarines

Meanwhile, PLA Navy air and surface forces optimized for ASW work would be very busy in the East China Sea trying to find and eliminate any American and Japanese submarines, especially near Taiwan and its smaller islands, where they could create havoc with PLA amphibious forces. The PLA Navy has, as we have seen, been working hard to improve its ASW capabilities. All of its newest destroyers, frigates, and eventually its corvettes have or will have hull-mounted sonar, a stern-mounted variable depth sonar, and many have acoustic tails as well; all are capable of embarking an ASW helicopter. The quality of training is unknown, but the hardware appears more than adequate.

The PLA Navy is investing in ASW aircraft as well; it has an improved helicopter apparently in the works and is in the process of introducing a turboprop maritime patrol aircraft, the KQ-200. The PLA Navy sees regional ASW—dealing with the American and Japanese submarines in and around the two island chains—as necessarily an "all hands on deck" matter. The PLA Navy can already count on an established network of fixed ocean-bottom arrays, underwater fiber-optic cables connecting sensors that can passively detect sounds or other emissions from submarines.[45]

The Seventh Fleet website indicates that at any given time it has between eight and twelve SSNs and nuclear-powered cruise-missile submarines (SSGNs).[46] This is a formidable force; four of them are permanently stationed in Guam, the rest rotationally deployed from Hawaii and the West Coast. The U.S. submarine force could put a severe crimp in Beijing's plans, if for no other reason that when at sea they can move fast and are immune to all of the PLA's missilery and to the PLA Air Force's tactical aircraft, which are neither trained nor equipped to locate and attack submarines. In addition, SSNs from Pearl Harbor or San Diego are likely to the first reinforcements to arrive, since they could make high-speed, nonstop submerged transits. (At twenty knots sustained submerged speed it would take approximately nine days to travel from Pearl Harbor to the Taiwan Strait.)

All Japanese submarines are conventionally powered, but the *Soryu* class now being introduced is judged to be the best in the world, with excellent underwater endurance and weapons load of torpedoes and cruise missiles. Like those of the U.S. Navy, Japanese submariners are very well trained.[47]

For the PLA, then, time is important, but realistically the campaign will take weeks not days. Once Beijing decided to start shooting, its goal would have to be to get Taipei to run up the white flag as soon as possible. The military objective would be to accomplish this before American reinforcements could gather in the eastern Pacific, Hawaii, and Guam and move to positions where U.S. military power could have a decisive effect. The PLA wants but will unlikely to be able to present Washington, and the world, with a fait accompli.

Area Denial in Practice for the PLA Navy

The PLA Navy's growing inventory of well-armed blue-water surface warships would make a serious contribution to the counterintervention campaign, mainly in the AD phase. It is not likely that China's surface ships (even its carriers) would deploy deep into the Philippine Sea to engage an approaching task force, because once beyond land-based fighter cover, perhaps seven hundred nautical miles out, their vulnerability to hostile air and submarine attack increases.[48]

These forces, however, would have plenty to do in the East China and South China Seas, dealing with American, Japanese, and ROC first responders and preparing for amphibious operations. The Japanese contribution could be decisive. Once Japan decided to defend itself it would have to be "all in." If the United States lost the battle for Taiwan, how could it hope to help defend Japan? The capabilities that the PLA employed to win that campaign are the ones they could use against Japan over the Senkakus. A failure to help Washington rescue Taiwan would put the American defense commitment to Japan, including the U.S. nuclear umbrella, in serious jeopardy. Why would Washington risk nuclear war with China to defend Japan if the United States had needed help and Tokyo had not responded with its full strength?

Importance of Taiwan's Outer Islands

During the attack (coercion) phase the PLA is expected to capture or neutralize Taiwan's outer islands.[49] Available PLA studies on a Taiwan campaign highlight the importance of those islands. One of them, Jinmen (or Quemoy), is itself an archipelago of fifteen granite islands, honeycombed with tunnels dug during the 1950 and '60s, when the mainland routinely shelled them. One of the outer islands is only a few miles from the mainland commercial port of Xiamen.[50] Another of Taiwan's holdings, 125 miles farther north along the Chinese coast, is the Matsu group of twenty-eight granite features. These are also well fortified and cover the approaches to Fuzhou, which like Xiamen, is an important commercial port. The Kinmen and Mazu archipelagoes sit squarely where the PLA would assemble its amphibious assault forces; also, obviously, once the mainland began to attack Taiwan, their garrisons could attack two important Chinese cities and interfere with key shipping areas.[51] Capturing them makes good military sense.

Ian Easton makes the useful point that PLA planning for an invasion of Taiwan resembles the World War II Central Pacific island-hopping campaign, in miniature. The next "hop" would be from Kinmen to the Penghu (Pescadores) Islands. The Penghu chain consist of sixty-four features of various sizes, the largest being Makung. It has a fine natural harbor that the Japanese used in World War II, is only thirty-five miles from the central coastline of Taiwan proper, and would be on the flank of an invasion force headed to suitable beaches in the either the northern or southern ends of Taiwan. This island fortress too would need to be taken before a landing on Taiwan itself could begin.[52]

Stopping Short of Invasion

If the attack phase in this notional plan did not convince Taipei to yield, Beijing would have two choices. First, it could go ahead and execute the invasion plan. If, however, the military portion of the coercion campaign had gone so poorly that an invasion attempt seemed liable to be a complete disaster, it could simply stop and declare victory. By this point Beijing would presumably have collected Taiwan's offshore East China Sea islands (and maybe while it was at it the two in the South China Sea, Itu Aba and Pratas). Beijing could honestly claim Taiwan had been taught a severe lesson regarding its willingness to use force, and with the seizure of the offshore islands, especially Penghu, it would have significantly enhanced its already sizeable military advantage. Retired lieutenant general Wang Hongguang, a former vice commander of the Nanjing Military Region, recently made the point during a Beijing conference that the "seizure of outlying islands" was one potential scenario, besides a direct landing, or a "siege" of Taiwan proper, of pressuring Taipei into surrendering.[53]

Of course, China would not be able to call it quits were the United States unwilling to do so itself. It would not be hard for Washington to stop even if Taipei wanted to fight on, since Beijing's overture would have indicated it was not going to execute a full-scale invasion. Even if American losses thus far were more severe than the damage it had inflicted on the PLA, Washington could also declare victory, claiming to have halted the attempt by the mainland to capture Taiwan forcibly. If Washington agreed with Beijing on a cease-fire, Japan would likely see no point in continuing, especially if the damage the PLA had absorbed had somewhat leveled the regional military balance. What would be the political point of continuing the fight if Beijing indicated it were willing to stop without invading Taiwan?

At this point, however, a great many people would have died, both military and civilian, and enormous destruction would have been inflicted on Taiwan, so it would be difficult to agree to a cease-fire—which would simply restore the uneasy geopolitical status quo ante. Each party would probably then lick its wounds and prepare for another round—unless the CCP altered its framework for permanent rapprochement with Taiwan, it would go through this all over again.

———

For the PLA success or failure would depend on four big uncertainties. First, would Taipei fight hard, or, deciding that independence is not worth the destruction of much of what it had achieved over the past thirty-five years, agree to negotiate unification? Second, could the PLA deal with the U.S. first responders, or will those responders put up a good enough fight to impede PLA progress significantly? Third, would the Japanese commit their military wholeheartedly to fight in conjunction with U.S. first responders? Fourth and finally, would the PLA's counterintervention operational concept effectively slow down American forces moving to the rescue?

The PLA Navy has a good deal to do regarding each of these uncertainties. The most immediate problem that the PLA Air Force, Naval Aviation, Rocket Force, and Navy would face would be the U.S. Seventh Fleet units active at the time in or around the first island chain. Similarly, if Japan is involved, these PLA assets would be hunting for its warships and submarines as well. Finally, the PLA surface navy has another important role if the conflict involves an invasion of the ROC: it would be its job to get the PLA ground force to Taiwan.

Its frigates and corvettes would together play an important role in antisubmarine protection for PRC sea-lanes in the South China Sea, East China Sea, and Yellow Sea, and should the conflict expand in geographic scope and in time, they might also be needed to protect Chinese shipping in the Indian Ocean. The HQ-9 armed destroyers, as noted earlier, could supplement mainland air defenses.

The purpose of this chapter is to explore the role of the PLA Navy in an area-denial role; let us play the Taiwan scenario through. If China did

elect to invade Taiwan proper, the PLA Navy would need to keep doing
what it had been during the attack (coercion) phase:

1. Contributing to the anti-access phase of the counterintervention
   fight against American reinforcements. This would largely involve
   submarines and land-based PLAN Naval Aviation strike aircraft.
2. Continuing the area-denial phase of the fight in and around the
   East China Sea against U.S. and Japanese first-responding ships
   and submarines.
3. Related to number 2, conducting a dedicated ASW campaign
   against allied submarines in and around the East China Sea.
4. Protecting South China Sea shipping lanes against American
   submarines. This would involve land-based ASW-oriented
   aircraft and helicopters, along with frigates and corvettes as
   merchant-ship escorts. It would be possible to assemble inbound
   convoys in the vast harbors created in the Subi, Mischief, and
   Fiery Cross Reefs in the Spratly Islands, the better to focus
   protection for the final thousand nautical miles of their transit.
5. Escorting high-value merchant ships and tankers through the
   Indian Ocean and dealing with U.S. attempts to interrupt sea-
   lanes there. Indian Ocean forces would need to defend themselves
   from the Fifth Fleet in the Persian Gulf. Djibouti and other
   PLA base facilities in the Indian Ocean region would risk being
   overrun by U.S. forces unless adequate defensive measures were
   undertaken.
6. Supporting any ongoing operations against Taiwan's offshore
   islands.
7. In addition, for the invasion phase of the operation, the most
   important mission of all: getting the PLA landing force to Taiwan.
   This involves keeping assault forces safe in their transit to the
   invasion beaches, conducting a successful assault(s), protecting
   the invasion beaches and lodgments, providing gunfire support
   to the landing force, managing the flow of supplies and men to
   the beachhead(s), and providing seaborne medical support and
   evacuation.

The PLA Navy must certainly have war-gamed the fight over Taiwan many, many times and thereby have a good idea of how many of each class of warship and submarine it needs. I have not done this; the discussion in this chapter is mission-based—working from what a navy would be expected to do and how it might go about it. Either way you look at it, however, to execute all phases of a Taiwan scenario and then fight the global war at sea into which I assume it would horizontally escalate, the PLA Navy of 2020 does not have enough warships.

As one example, assume that 20 percent of the PLA Navy would not be able to get under way for one reason or another; all mission areas would be affected. In particular, there seems to be a shortfall in submarines. The U.S. Defense Department's annual report on the PLA for 2019 indicates that PLA had fifty conventional submarines and six SSNs in its order of battle that year (see table 4). If eleven (20 percent) of the fifty-six are not able to get under way, only forty-five would be available for tasking. I estimate that the Chinese would station between fifteen and eighteen submarines in the Philippine Sea, organized in three "wolf packs" of five or six boats each, for the A2 portion of counterintervention. (These numbers, by the way, are my estimates, not something I have found in Chinese writings.) The PLA Navy would need at least one rotation of boats ready to go as reliefs. Eleven boats unready for sea that only leaves between nine and fifteen available in all. One solution might be to dedicate as many SSNs as possible to the Philippine Sea and leave them on station longer, freeing more conventional boats for the first island chain. The point here is to highlight an aspect of force-level planning that presumably dictates, in this case, how many submarines the PLA Navy needs to maintain in inventory. It also highlights the value of the endurance of SSNs.

When Xi Jinping says the purpose of the PLA is "to fight and win wars," the Taiwan problem is likely what he has in mind. If that is the case, he really will need a world-class navy. He will not have that for another fifteen or twenty years.

CHAPTER 5

Keeping the Americans Away

Anti-Access and the Taiwan Campaign

This chapter concludes the discussion of the PLA Navy's role in counterintervention. The geographic focus shifts away from the East China Sea and first island chain to the PRC's more distant maritime approaches, mainly the Philippine Sea, between the first and second island chains. It is the most likely avenue of approach for a U.S. reinforcing group headed toward China. The canonical scenario is an American response launched in response to an unprovoked PRC attack on Taiwan, but the response could also be to an attack on treaty ally Japan. The scenario also posits that serious combat, as described in the last chapter, has already broken out in the waters near China and that there is a real possibility that Japan will also be involved, if not already.

What this chapter covers, then, are the anti-access elements of a counterintervention campaign, those that involve keeping U.S. forces as far away from the scene of action as possible. They have received the most public commentary from Japanese, Indian, and Western security and military professional and analysts, because of the threat that the PRC's ballistic (or, potentially, and over the longer term, hypersonic) missile forces present to Guam and westbound aircraft carrier–centered strike groups sailing west to roll back Chinese aggression (see map 3).

What follows a detailed discussion of the capabilities that the PLA has or is putting in place to execute the anti-access aspect of counter-intervention.[1] Although in practice the PRC's "offshore-waters defense" campaign would be an integrated effort, I have elected to disaggregate the discussion. One reason for doing so is clarity, another the fact that in practice the campaign could unfold in a phased manner, the first phase being the area-denial operation (previous chapter).

Surveillance:
The Prerequisite for Counterintervention

It goes without saying that if you want to shoot at a specific target you need to know where it is. The same thing applies to attacking ships and submarines at sea and aircraft in the air. For the PRC, then, the first and most important requirement for defense of the seaward approaches is an effective surveillance of the western Pacific Ocean. Finding ships on the high seas is very difficult, because of the vastness of the oceans when compared even to the largest ships. Also, determining the location of a ship just once is not very helpful, because ships move. Ships at sea travel around the clock, night and day, and even at their relatively modest speeds, over a twenty-four-hour period they cover substantial distances. For example, in that time a ship at fourteen knots covers 336 nautical miles (387 statute miles).

The Soviet military pioneered solutions to this problem. The Soviets created something the United States called the Soviet Ocean Surveillance System (SOSS). It was a blend of radio-direction-finding arrays, long-range surveillance radars, and space-based satellites. There were also, often, "tattletales"—individual Soviet ships that simply tagged along with U.S. carrier battle groups in international waters. A tattletale's job was to notify Moscow periodically where a target of interest, mainly the aircraft carrier it was following was. The high point of Soviet maritime defense occurred in the mid-1980s, when the Kremlin had in place about 270 attack submarines, 280 major surface combatants, and over 1,300 land-based naval aircraft distributed among the North Atlantic, eastern Mediterranean, and Pacific approaches to the Soviet Union.[2] The Soviet concept combined open-ocean surveillance, long-range land-based aircraft with antiship cruise missiles, and nuclear-powered submarines with large loads of antiship cruise missiles to form an A2/AD capability that was imposing when the Cold War ended. The PLA has put a remarkably similar concept in place.

The PLA's Approach:
First, Find Enemies at Sea to Shoot At

Compared to the Soviets' era, modern technology has greatly eased the open-ocean surveillance problem for the PLA, although the area it must search is vast—some thirty-two million square miles of the western Pacific Ocean. China hopes its surveillance will find approaching naval forces, so PLA commanders can direct submarines to ambush them, vector land-based aircraft to attack them, and target and launch antiship missiles. Without surveillance, the PLA cannot do any of these tasks effectively. As a result, it has made a serious investment in an overlapping land-, air-, and space-based ocean surveillance system with the goal of reliable coverage out to at least two thousand nautical miles.

The land-based portion of this system consists of a network of very-long-range, over-the-horizon (OTH) radar systems that can detect large ships throughout the Philippine Sea and elsewhere. Because these systems use frequencies too low for resolution precise enough to launch long-range missiles with any hope of hitting the target, their main purpose is early warning. OTH radar detection can also help reduce uncertainty, by suggesting promising areas for other PLA surveillance systems to search. While OTH is imprecise, the overall system in which it is fused has the potential to provide real-time surveillance and targeting-quality data.[3]

The backbone of that overall system is space-based, in particular its remote-sensing, high-resolution earth-observation element. At this writing it operates twenty-eight different types of satellites, for a total of roughly 134 remote-sensing satellites: a blend of electro-optical/infrared (EO/IR) and video imaging of the surface of the ocean, synthetic-aperture-radar (SAR) detection of ships, and electronic-intelligence (ELINT) identification of shipborne radar and other electronic transmissions. Ten of these satellites are the Jilin series of high-resolution optical remote-sensing satellites. China is expanding this constellation with a goal of having sixty Jilin-1 satellites in orbit by 2020 and 138 by 2030. In addition to high-resolution video they will also carry an EO payload. The total constellation, thanks to its numerical size, has very short revisit times (i.e., between successive "looks") over certain high-interest areas (addressed in detail below).[4] It is safe to assume that China keeps track of U.S. carrier movements globally and that when one is headed toward China and gets within approximately two thousand nautical miles, the

Chinese intelligence, surveillance, and reconnaissance (ISR) system can update its position every few minutes, and (as suggested earlier) continuously if the carrier is not electronically silent. According to one technically sophisticated assessment:

> In the task of finding a U.S. carrier at sea, China's satellites would vary in their usefulness according to sensor type and resolution. Of the sensors deployed on China's satellites, synthetic aperture radar (SAR) is the most useful for hunting maritime targets, as it can sweep a relatively wide swath at a resolution good enough to image fairly small targets. SAR can produce imagery regardless of weather or sunlight. Instead of merely looking for a carrier group itself, SAR can capture ship wakes trailing over large stretches of ocean, making it particularly useful for finding moving targets.[5]

Since these low-earth-orbiting (LEO) satellites are looking for moving ships, a very short revisit time is essential for near-real-time location and targeting. A typical LEO will revisit the same area on the earth between every 84 to 127 minutes. The only way to shorten revisit time for a given point on earth is to increase the number of satellites that pass over it, hence, "constellations" of satellites. With enough satellites the revisit time can be shortened nearly to zero. For example, the ideal LEO constellation for a broadband cellular network would have 292 satellites.[6] While coverage of the western Pacific Ocean by space-based-radar or other remote-imaging satellites would not require a constellation this size, the 138-satellite Jilin constellation referred to above can provide information accurate enough to locate and target approaching warships on a near-real-time basis. This means it could maintain near-continuous space-based surveillance of U.S. Navy ships, especially large ones, such as an aircraft carrier. The pace of PRC satellite launches has been impressive; in 2018 it led the world with thirty-nine space launches, compared to the United States (thirty-one) and Russia (twenty).[7] It duplicated this feat in 2019, again leading the world with thirty-two successful launches compared to twenty-two for Russia and twenty-one from the United States.[8]

The air-breathing leg of the PLA's ocean surveillance network will soon involve long-range high-altitude drones (UAVs). According to the National Air and Space Intelligence Center (NASIC), "China has been developing a wide range of UAVs including long-range and low-observable systems that are capable of conducting reconnaissance and strike missions."[9] Its Cai Hong–5 (CH-5) is similar in in appearance to the well-known Reaper drone and when fully added to the ocean surveillance inventory will give added capability in China's near seas.[10] In peacetime, China can send these UAVs beyond the near seas, using satellite relay—the PRC has approximately forty-one communication satellites in orbit—to control them and receive surveillance data from them.[11] In time of conflict, however, drones that venture too far beyond PLA-controlled airspace are susceptible to being shot down. The downing by Iran of an American RQ-4A Global Hawk surveillance drone operating in international airspace on June 2019 highlights this vulnerability.

The Airpower Leg of Counterintervention

The land-based aircraft component of the counterintervention layered defense consists of bombers and strike fighters of both the PLA Air Force and PLAN Naval Aviation. Unlike the Russians, China as yet does not have an equivalent to the Cold War–era Soviet Tu-22M supersonic long-range Backfire bomber, which carried high-speed antiship cruise missiles with which to attack U.S. carrier forces approaching the Soviet Union. What China does have is a version of the old Soviet Tu-16 Badger bomber, newly produced in China as the H-6. China obtained the rights to build these bombers decades ago and has since been improving and modernizing the design. The latest and most comprehensive upgrade entered service in 2009. Known as the H-6K, this bomber has new more powerful engines and modern systems that include infrared and electro-optical sensors and a data link for networking with friendly forces. For counterintervention missions the H-6K can carry an underwing loadout of six YJ-12 supersonic antishipping missiles, which have a range of between 160 and 210 nm (depending on the source).[12] That means that if a single regimental-sized raid of eighteen aircraft could reach firing positions unscathed it could launch 108 ASCMs.[13]

An important caveat is needed at this point. PLA aircraft bent on attacking U.S. naval forces in the Philippine Sea have to overfly or pass between Japan's Ryukyu Islands to reach them. This means they have to be able to penetrate American and Japanese air defenses on the way to the attack and on their return. During peacetime the PLA Air Force and

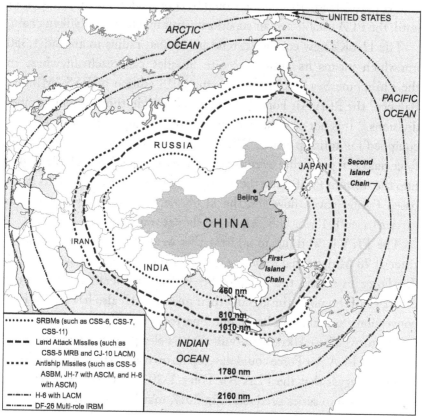

Map 3. Conventional Ballistic and Cruise Missile Coverage of the Indo-Pacific. China's Antiship Ballistic Missile (ASBM) ranges are illustrated by the 1,010-nm dot-dashed line (CSS-5/DF-21D); the latest ASBM (DF-26) has a 2,160-nm range that is depicted by the dashed line. Note that the DF-21D can reach most of the Bay of Bengal and the entrance to the Malacca Straits, while the DF-26 covers the entire second island chain, as well as a large portion of the northern Indian Ocean. Note also that the range of the H-6K bomber is the same as the range of the DF-21D when carrying ASCMs. When armed with a land-attack cruise missile the H-6K could attack Guam. See the 1,760-nm range ring. If given third-party overflight permission by South Asian countries, the H-6K bomber-missile pairing is also a credible Indian Ocean weapon. *2018* Annual Report to Congress, *45.*

Naval Air Force training over the Philippine Sea overfly international airspace above Japan's Miyako Strait (a 130-nm gap between Okinawa and Miyako Island); that option would be contested in wartime, unless, or until, the PLA established air superiority over much of the Ryukyu chain.

The H-6K's new engines extend its combat radius to around 1,350 nm,which means its antiship cruise missiles can reach anywhere in the Philippine Sea.[14] According to the 2018 edition of IISS "Military Balance" the PLA Air Force has ninety H-6Ks, in three or four bomber divisions.[15] It is not clear how many of those are organized, trained, and equipped for antiship strike. What is clear is that since 2016 the H-6K force has been practicing overwater missions, conducting multiple flights into the western Pacific and the South China Sea;[16] once beyond its land-based fighter cover, however, the H-6K becomes highly vulnerable to carrier-based F-18s or U.S. Air Force fighters on Guam.

The PLA is working to address this weakness. The acquisition of three Il-78 Midas aerial refueling tankers from Ukraine allows the PLA Air Force to extend the range of Su-30 fighter aircraft so they could escort H-6K bombers throughout their mission.[17] (It also has several H-6 conversions to tankers in hand, but reportedly these have been less than satisfactory.) These Ukrainian-built tankers also provide a template from which the PLA Air Force could develop its own aerial tanker fleet. Some experts suggest that the PLA Air Force Y-20 heavy transport aircraft, which went into series production in 2017, may be the airframe the Air Force will convert into a tanker;[18] this speculation was echoed in a *Global Times* article in November 2018.[19] It seems inevitable that the PLA Air Force will eventual develop a credible airborne "tanking" capability; when it does, that will be a major contribution to the PRC's ability to fight for sea control throughout the Philippine Sea.

The PLA Navy's aviation force operates two regiments of the older H-6G, which can carry four of the 135-nm-range YJ-83 antiship cruise missiles. Apparently the PLA Navy is also having its older H-6 variants upgraded to the new reengined, longer-range H-6K (or perhaps a J model).[20] On paper, the PLA Air Force and Naval Aviation combined have seven regiments of H-6G/K bombers potentially useful for maritime strike operations.[21]

In 2002, the PRC purchased twenty-four Russian Su-30 MK2s for the navy, making it the service's first fourth-generation fighter aircraft.

These aircraft feature both extended range and maritime radar. With a combat radius of 725 nm, it can reach well into the Philippine Sea from its Eastern Theater Command base.[22] This allows the Su-30 MK2 to strike enemy ships at long distances, defending itself with a good air-to-air capability. They carry the supersonic but very-short-range (fifty-five-nautical-mile) Kh-31A (AS-17A) air-to-surface missile; they would have to enter well into the air-defense range of U.S. destroyers or cruisers screening a carrier before they could launch.[23]

Perhaps the best maritime-attack aircraft in either of China's air forces is the fast (1.75 Mach maximum speed), 1980s-era JH-7 Flying Leopard. With its 590-nm combat range, it needs to be refueled in flight to strike beyond the first island chain. It can carry up four ASCMs; however, not all of the PLA Air Force JH-7 inventory is dedicated to maritime strike, because the JH-7 is also a good ground-attack fighter-bomber. The PLA Air Force has 140 JH-7s in inventory plus two brigades of Russian-built Su-30MKKs that could be used in antiship roles.

PLAN Naval Aviation has about 120 JH-7/7As (six regiments) also capable of carrying up to four subsonic YJ-83K ASCMs (135 nm range).[24] The PLA Navy has publicized that its carrier-capable J-15 fighters can also employ the YJ-83 missile.[25] Given the number of JH-7/7As in the navy and air force, these strike fighters present a difficult challenge to warships operating within the first island chain, but without in-flight refueling their role in the Philippine Sea is quite limited.

The bottom line is that together the PLA Air Force and Naval Aviation could mount multiregiment/brigade-sized strikes against naval targets virtually anywhere inside the second island chain. Against targets closer to the PRC in the East or South China Seas, such as Seventh Fleet units that routinely patrol these waters, all of these aircraft could be involved. This is why the dramatic growth in overwater air force training is so significant. PLA airpower is becoming comfortable with overwater operations and is becoming a very credible, full partner with the PLA Navy and PLA Rocket Force in the counterintervention mission.

The PLA Navy's Contribution to the Counterintervention Fight

The PLA Navy submarine force is the Navy's most important counterintervention capability, because finding a submarine is perhaps the single most difficult operational task that any military faces, for the simple reason that water is neither transparent to nor penetrable by search radars and the effectiveness of acoustic detection systems is often dramatically hindered by water temperature conditions. History suggests that searching for submarines that are trying not to be found requires a large investment of ship and aircraft resources. China understands this; as the U.S. Department of Defense points out, "The PLA Navy places a high priority on the modernization of its submarine force."[26] The reason for this has been explained by the U.S. Navy's Office of Naval Intelligence (ONI), "China has long regarded its submarine force as a critical element of regional deterrence, particularly when conducting 'counter-intervention' against [a] modern adversary. The large, but poorly equipped [submarine] force of the 1980s has given way to a more modern submarine force, optimized primarily for regional anti–surface ship missions near major sea lines of communication."[27]

The size and eventual composition of the PLA submarine force are state secrets, and as a result projecting the overall size and quality of that force is a bit of a guessing game. There seems to be consensus within the U.S. government, however, that there will be over seventy boats of all classes.

- DoD stated in 2018 that "by 2020, [China's submarine] force will likely grow to between 69 and 78 submarines."
- ONI stated in 2015 that "by 2020, the PLA Navy submarine force will likely grow to more than 70 submarines." In an accompanying table, ONI provided a more precise projection of seventy-four, including eleven nuclear-powered boats and sixty-three non-nuclear-powered.[28]

The modern Chinese strategic nuclear-powered ballistic-missile-launching submarine (SSBN) force is included in these totals. Its mission is to remain hidden in the vastness of the ocean as a survivable potential second nuclear strike force; therefore it does not hunt for ships to attack. Subtracting these five or six SSBNs from the total submarine estimates shows that the vast majority of the PLA Navy submarine force (seventy-odd) is potentially available to attack hostile surface ships. Obviously not all submarines are in a perfect state of readiness at all times, nor are all of them likely to be assigned to go after enemy warships. For argument's sake, if 35 percent of the force is assigned other tasks or is not ready to deploy at any given time, that still leaves around forty-five boats available for counterintervention warship hunting.

Another important point is that the PLA Navy submarine force is believed to have only six nuclear-powered attack submarines in commission with perhaps two or three more in various stages of construction. The advantage of an SSN is a virtually unlimited source of fuel. This translates into underwater speed and endurance that permits the submarine to move rapidly from one patrol station to another, escape quickly if detected, cover long distances in a hurry to attack newly discovered targets, or remain on station as long as food holds out—all the while remaining submerged.

The speed, mobility, and covertness of the bulk of the PLA Navy submarine force is much less, since these submarines rely on some combination of diesel engines, which require air when surfaced or snorkeling, and batteries for propulsion and electricity when submerged. The newer Yuan class (discussed in chapter 3) has the benefit of air-independent propulsion (AIP), which allows it to recharge batteries while submerged and increase underwater endurance to between fourteen and eighteen days—if, that is, speed is limited to ten knots or less.[29] Nonetheless, AIP is an important capability, and it makes Type 039A boats formidable weapons. The remainder of China's submarine force, non-AIP and conventionally propelled, has the significant operational drawbacks of limited underwater endurance and speed. This why the PLA ocean surveillance network is so important; early detection of an approaching armada permits operational PLA Navy commanders to position submarines correctly to intercept.

Today, even numbers alone make the PLA Navy submarine force imposing and well armed. ONI estimates that 64 percent of PLA submarines are able launch antiship cruise missiles.[30] Eight of the twelve Kilo class purchased around the turn of the century from Russia are armed with the highly capable, Russian-made SS-N-27 Sizzler ASCM.[31] While ASCMs, especially the long-range (290 nm) YJ-18, are rightly matters of concern as antiship weapons, modern torpedoes remain the most effective ship killers: when they explode, the result is a big hole below the waterline.[32] Many torpedoes are designed to explode under a ship's keel, which is almost certain to sink a ship as large as nine-thousand-ton destroyer, by breaking it in half.[33] PLA Navy submarines are capable of firing both wire-guided and wake-homing torpedoes; the latter can be very difficult for surface ships to counter.[34]

Operationally, the PLA Navy's submarine force plays an important role. Some of its units could be stationed around a thousand nautical miles from their East China Sea bases, between the first and second island chains in the Philippine Sea. It would be primarily oriented toward the A2 phase, attempting to make the U.S. Navy fight for its own survival so it cannot interfere in the battle for Taiwan, either delaying its arrival there or inflicting so much damage that the United States is incapable in any reasonable amount of time of affecting the Taiwan conflict without escalating to all-out war.

One approach, as suggested in chapter 4, "wolf packs," requires a significant investment in submarine presence. But of the prospect of upward of eighteen PLA Navy submarines roaming around the Philippine Sea could cause approaching U.S. Navy forces to hesitate until they were deemed under control. If they do so, the PLA Navy submarine force will have accomplished its mission. If the PLA can, by means of its antiship ballistic missile (ASBM) threat and an aggressive submarine posture in the Philippine Sea, delay American reinforcements for many days, let alone many weeks, its objectives against either Taiwan or Japan could be accomplished without undue interference.

The Antiship Ballistic Missile in Counterintervention

The PRC is adding a new and very threatening element to the layered defense that constitutes counterintervention. It is, in fact, a unique PLA capability—to use ballistic missiles to attack moving surface warships. Traditionally, ballistic missiles have been considered poor weapons against ships at sea: ships move, and once fired on a ballistic trajectory, a missile's aim point cannot, by definition, cannot be altered to account for that motion.

The PLA has developed, and in July 2019 conducted a long-anticipated test of against a target at sea, a weapon system that links conventionally armed ballistic missiles with very accurate location information from the ocean surveillance network. Surveillance provides geolocation and target-tracking data to shore-based missile batteries. It may also generate course corrections even when the warhead is in space. Effectiveness depends upon a technology known as the maneuverable reentry vehicle (MaRV) warhead, which contains sensors to guide it to a target, especially one that is moving. The PLA has successfully developed target seekers in the high-explosive missile warhead that activate as the warhead descends and then steer it to the moving ship. This is a task that depends not only on gaining very accurate surveillance data but also on slowing down the warhead so the seeker is not burned up by the heat of reentry.

The DoD 2009 *Annual Report* cites what it describes as an authoritative 2004 article for readers in the Second Artillery Corps (now Rocket Force) describing how the ASBM could employ "penetrating sub-munitions" to "destroy the enemy's carrier-borne planes, the control tower and other easily damaged and vital positions."[35] The Rocket Force has worked on this problem for some time. The authors of a paper published by the Second Artillery Engineering College, as it was then known, conclude that

> providing terminal guidance to ballistic missiles is critical to the successful launch of a precision attack on a slow-moving large target at sea. Based on the results from simulation, missiles with terminal guidance capability can have a relatively large range of maneuverability, which may be as large as 100 kilometers (53 nm). . . . Large surface targets at sea, such as aircraft carriers, are relatively poor in maneuverability. It cannot effectively escape an attack within a short period of time. Therefore, a ballistic missile with terminal guidance capability . . . is fully capable of effectively attacking this type of target with high precision.[36]

The missile with this capability that has been tested is the Dong-Feng 21D (DF-21D). It is a two-stage, solid-fuel-rocket, single-warhead, medium-range ballistic missile with a maximum estimated range of a thousand nautical miles. A newer, long-range version is the DF-26, which has an estimated range of 2,100 nm.[37] For well over a decade ASBMs have been dubbed "carrier killers." Frankly, though, it is not absolutely certain that this complex system would work against a moving ship over a thousand miles away. Almost ten years ago, Adm. Robert Willard, then commander of U.S. Pacific Command, gave an interview in which he said that the DF-21D had reached IOC, initial operating capability. In the United States, IOC means the missile itself has been tested and implies that the warhead had been tested as well; Admiral Willard did note, however, that the United States had not detected a test at sea against a moving target. In turns out that his assessment of IOC was premature: only now, nearly a decade later, has the DF-21D finally been tested at sea. Willard's successor several times removed, Adm. Philip Davidson, said in a speech that the PLA Rocket Force had fired a six-missile salvo at a target in the South China Sea.[38] He did not say whether or not the test shots hit the target, and as of this writing, neither has the PLA. The missiles did all apparently land in the area that Beijing had designated in notices to airmen and mariners issued ahead of the tests themselves. Over time, I suspect, more information will become available on how well the ASBM system performed in practice. The main point for this discussion is that the PLA is likely to continue to invest effort and money into making the DF-21D and DF-26 ASBMs credible weapons.[39]

Capt. Sam Tangredi, USN (Ret.), an anti-access expert, makes the following important observation regarding the implications of the PLA's ASBM capability: "Whether or not the DF-21 would be effective in combat, its impact on naval strategy debates in the United States has been profound and continuing. Critics of new American aircraft carrier construction cite cost comparisons between a large arsenal of DF-21Ds and a single aircraft carrier. Numerous studies suggest the U.S. Navy cannot operate within the first island chain, which stretches from Japan to Malaysia. Adding to the debate is the development of the follow-on land-attack/antiship DF-26."[40]

To be sure, the technical difficulty associated with production of a reliable missile warhead, the command and control problem of accurately locating an aircraft carrier, the networking issue of getting that information to a missile-firing unit in a timely fashion, and the processing requirements of translating positional information into a guidance solution for the missile, make for a complicated challenge:

A complete ASBM system will require the ability to detect, identify, track, target, and engage a threat and then perform damage assessment upon it—this is the "kill chain." Each of these sensor-to-shooter steps must be executed in a time sensitive manner, since the intended target would be maneuverable—a U.S. aircraft carrier. A complete kill chain entails a wide range of technologies, from penetration aids on board the missile, space-based and other sensors, data processing and exchange networks, and other infrastructure to achieve a high degree of integration of both the weapon platform and its command and control.[41]

An assessment of China's advanced weapons systems by *Jane's* reinforces the assessment that to be effective these weapons require an extensive infrastructure of data networks, communications systems, and sophisticated navigational technologies, all amalgamated into a workable system.[42] It goes without saying that this system must be able to withstand attempts to jam or otherwise interrupt it. Nevertheless, in 2009 a senior intelligence officer assigned to ONI was quoted as saying, "ASBM development has progressed at a remarkable rate. . . . In a little over a decade, China has taken the ASBM program from the conceptual phase to nearing an operational capability. . . . China has elements of an [over-the-horizon] network already in place and is working to expand its horizon, timeliness and accuracy."[43]

Now, ten years later, the DF-21D has been deployed to operational forces. The DF-21D, the numerically large submarine force, land-based air forces, and the growing number of capable surface combatants add up to a serious operational challenge for the U.S. Navy when it penetrates the second island chain into the Philippine Sea.

———

A great deal of the public discourse in the United States concerning how the PRC might execute a counterintervention, or A2/AD, campaign, has revolved around China's rocket and missile forces. This is because of the ASBM weapon and its two unique attributes. First, it can be fired at targets as far away from the PRC as a thousand nautical miles, perhaps two thousand if the DF-26 develops as anticipated. Not only can targets be engaged at a great distance, but the weapons will arrive in minutes. Obviously, the closer targets are to the Chinese mainland the shorter the time of flight. The second attribute is that because the weapon is a ballistic missile traveling at incredible speed, it is very hard to shoot down. This attribute, however, is also a potential weakness, since to hit a moving ship its warhead requires embedded terminal guidance, which in turn must survive reentry into the atmosphere. When, as noted above, the warhead accordingly slows down, shipborne missile systems have a fleeting opportunity for a better shot. Naturally, warhead terminal-guidance systems are also susceptible to a host of countermeasures, such as electronic jamming, false targets, and decoys. The biggest weakness of the ASBM system, however, is its dependence on exquisitely precise locating and target surveillance systems—that is, in the military vernacular, the PLA's intelligence, surveillance, and reconnaissance system.

History has demonstrated that the other two key components of the PLA's counterintervention "troika," land-based aircraft and submarines, can be useful in the absence of *precise* locating information; this is not the case with the ASBM. Not to gainsay the potential decisiveness of a functional ASBM system, for which the PLA continues to strive, but the very complexity of the system, as discussed, and the array of attacks, countermeasures, and deceptions designed to degrade its surveillance and support network, make it less than the ultimate defensive system.

On the other hand, the PLA Navy submarine force, the Chinese navy's major contribution to the anti-access element of counterintervention, does not need such rarefied targeting. Submarines have onboard sensors to fine-tune target location enough to close and attack. In submarine warfare, numbers matter, quite a lot, and the PLA Navy submarine force is growing as it modernizes. If reports regarding a new Chinese SSN construction capability are accurate, the number of new, more capable nuclear attack submarines available for this mission could grow exponentially in the next few years. China scholar Dr. Lyle Goldstein of the U.S. Naval War College reports that China has developed a new nuclear submarine construction facility with a 430,000-square-foot assembly hall containing two parallel production lines, large enough to build four SSNs simultaneously.[44]

Neither is the land-based attack-aircraft portion of anti-access completely dependent on extremely precise targeting to be effective. In addition, all aircraft-launched ASCMs have integral seekers; they are not launched until the radar in the aircraft has detected a target vessel. Naturally, constant target position updates from the PLA's ISR system, even if degraded, are necessary, given the length of time—well over ninety minutes—it takes aircraft to reach firing positions in the Philippine Sea.

Some observers assume that counterintervention is primarily a PLA Navy show. In China's near seas the navy does have a very significant role, as the last chapter indicated, but in the anti-access realm it is not the lead player. To succeed, a counterintervention campaign has to be genuinely joint; the PLA Navy, Air Force, Rocket Force, and Strategic Support Force must work together seamlessly. This is a big problem for the PLA, which is not yet a joint force. Xi and the rest of the PLA leadership recognize this problem and are working hard to resolve it. But as the U.S. military has learned from the aftermath of the 1986 Goldwater-Nichols Act, which mandated a joint force, it takes many years, decades actually, to create a credible joint approach to fighting.

In sum, the PLA objective, once it has decided to launch a military campaign that is likely to trigger U.S. involvement—most probably against Taiwan, with attacks on American air and naval forces stationed in Japan or at sea in the vicinity of the first island chain—is to deal promptly with these U.S. "first responders." This fight would constitute the area-denial portion of A2/AD. The PLA then has to be able to repostion its forces, especially ships and submarines, to begin its sea-denial effort against American reinforcing forces in the Philippine Sea or on Guam before they can interfere with PLA operations. This would be the anti-access portion.

CHAPTER SIX
_____

The PLA Navy and
the South China Sea

B efore addressing China's interests in the South China Sea and how
the Chinese navy contributes to the advancement of those interests, it
is necessary to set the stage with a brief overview of the mix of sovereignty,
international law, and conflicting strategic interests that make the South
China Sea such a complex problem.

The land features in the South China Sea—approximately 180 named
islands, rocks, shoals, sandbanks, reefs, and cays above water at high tide;
plus many others that are only above water at low tide; along with unnamed
shoals and submerged features distributed among four geographically
different areas of that sea—are claimed in whole by China and Taiwan
and in part by Vietnam, the Philippines, Malaysia, and Brunei.[1] Japan
claimed and occupied all of the major features in the South China Sea
from 1939 onward and placed them under the jurisdiction of the governor
general of Taiwan.[2] When World War II ended in 1945 Japan evacuated
its garrisons and formally renounced its claims in the 1951 San Francisco
Peace Treaty; unfortunately however, the renunciation documents did not
also entail "devolution," reversion of territory to any previous owner or
claimant.[3] Many of the Japanese garrisons surrendered to the Republic of
China, which in turn occupied a handful of the largest features.

The People's Republic of China, as the legal successor state to the
Republic of China, claims all the land features in the South China Sea, on
the basis of history and first discovery by Chinese seafarers. The Republic

of China on Taiwan maintains an identical claim to the Paracel Islands, the Spratly Islands, and Scarborough Shoal. Both the PRC and Taiwan also claim the Pratas Islands, which Taiwan occupies; no other country contests the PRC/ROC Pratas claim.[4] Since 1956, Taiwan has continuously occupied the largest feature in the Spratly chain, Itu Aba (or Taiping Island). For reasons of its own, Beijing has permitted Taiwan to maintain itself there, though it could easily seize it. Itu Aba has a natural water supply, facilities for a garrison, and an airfield capable of handling C-130s. During World War II the Imperial Japanese Navy used it as an advanced submarine base.

China also occupies in the Spratlys what formerly were four small rocks and three "low-tide elevations," defined by the UN Convention on the Law of the Sea as features below water at high tide and as not subject to appropriation. Through massive dredging, all seven have been turned into substantial man-made island bases. Before these reclamation efforts none met the UNCLOS definition of an island, nor does any today. Artificially changing the nature of a feature does not change its legal status as far as the law of the sea is concerned. They remain rocks and low-tide elevations under international law.[5]

In the 1970s and 1980s the Philippines and Vietnam joined Taiwan in the Spratlys and began to occupy above-water features. This "land rush" was triggered by rumors of vast petroleum reserves. As a result, all of the fourteen or so largest naturally formed Spratly features were already "taken" when Beijing, finally deciding to act, occupied six Spratly features in 1988 and in 1995 snatched Mischief Reef from the Philippines.

Vietnam claims the Paracel and Spratly archipelagoes in their entireties. Its representative at the 1951 San Francisco Peace Treaty with Japan conference claimed them.[6] Vietnam occupies the most features in the Spratlys—twenty-one, according to the "South China Sea Island Tracker," a website maintained by the Center for Strategic and International Studies (CSIS); it has also constructed small (100 to 250 square meters) platforms on six totally submerged shallow spots.[7] Vietnam's claims in the Spratlys derive from French claims made in 1933, largely to keep them out of Japanese hands. Following World War II full-time garrisoning did not begin until 1974, when the Republic of Vietnam (RVN, i.e., South Vietnam) sent garrisons to six features. In 1975, three weeks before the fall of Saigon, North Vietnam seized these six to ensure they did not fall into Chinese hands.[8] After Vietnam's unification in 1975, its Spratly occupations gradually expanded in scope.

The Philippines claims Scarborough Shoal and a significant section of the Spratlys, which it has named the Kalayaan Island Group (KIG). The Philippines bases the claim to Scarborough Shoal on continuous occupation and administration starting when the Philippines was a U.S. colony. The Philippines only occupies seven features and two submerged reefs, which sit on its continental shelf.[9] The Philippines became involved in Spratly claims in 1956, when the features were suddenly "discovered" and claimed by enterprising Philippine businessman Tomas Cloma, who issued a proclamation naming his discovery "Freedomland." The Philippine government was greeted with a storm of protests from South Vietnam, the ROC, the PRC, and France (which at that point still claimed the Spratlys). However, choosing to do nothing, Manila never totally disowned the Cloma "discovery," and in 1971 President Ferdinand Marcos formally announced a claim to fifty-three of the Spratly group on the basis that the islands were *res nullius* (land without an owner) and six years later formally annexed them all.[10]

Malaysia claims seven islands or rocks in the Spratly group and occupies five. It also claims two low-tide elevations and three totally submerged reefs that are on its continental shelf. The Malaysian claim dates from 1979 and is based on the fact the features it claims are all on its continental shelf.[11] Brunei claims one feature in the Spratlys, Louisa Reef (which may be a low-tide elevation and not an island), because it is on is on its continual shelf.[12]

China's Strategic Interests

As we will see, the PLA Navy has been central to China's efforts to reclaim what it considers lost Chinese territory. China's strategic objective in the South China Sea (SCS) is to achieve complete de jure sovereignty over all the islands, islets, reefs, and shoals scattered through the sea, as well as all the maritime rights to territorial seas and exclusive economic zones (EEZs) that sovereignty yields. Beyond complete sovereignty over all the land features, it also claims "historic rights" to the resources (fish, oil, and gas) in much of the South China Sea. Collectively, the combination of claims to land features, even if submerged, and historic resource rights makes the South China Sea, as the Chinese put it, "a core" national interest.

Historic Rights and the Nine-Dashed Line

One of the most confounding aspects of the SCS disputes is the existence of the so-called nine-dashed line (9DL), a U-shaped line that encompasses about 80 percent of the South China Sea. Beijing inherited the 9DL from Taipei, which first created it in 1947. It has appeared on maps issued by the People's Republic of China since 1949. Neither the ROC nor the PRC has ever defined exactly what the line was originally intended to indicate, although for some years Beijing has by its actions made clear that in its view the line bounded the area of the South China Sea where China possessed "historic rights." As portrayed on Chinese charts, the 9DL clearly infringes on the EEZs of the sea's other claimants, as well as on Indonesia's EEZ around Natuna Island and its associated gas fields. In short, Beijing is using the 9DL as a pretext to claim well over half the resources found in the EEZs of the other coastal states—outright theft, on a grand scale. Largely because of this infringement, the government of the Philippines took China to court in 2013, asking the Permanent Court of Arbitration (PCA) in The Hague to rule on the 9DL and other Chinese transgressions against the Philippines. Much to the surprise of many, the PCA found in the Philippines' favor.[13]

The July 2016 PCA award addressed the historic rights issue head on. It found that there was "no legal basis for China to claim historic rights to resources in the sea areas falling within the 'nine-dash line,'" and that there was "no historic evidence that China had historically exercised exclusive control over the waters or their resources."[14] China dismissed this finding, then days later officially claimed for the first time "historic rights in the South China Sea." China also claimed internal waters and other maritime entitlements "based on" all the islands in the South China Sea (in Chinese, Nanhai Zhudao).[15]

The United States officially delivered a demarche challenging Beijing's official assertion six months later, in December 2016. It says in part, "These statements appear to assert expressly, for the first time, a Chinese maritime claim in the South China Sea that would include 'historic rights.' The United States objects to such a claim as *unlawful*, insofar as it would be inconsistent with international law as reflected in the Law of the Sea Convention."[16] This diplomatic note is important, because it puts the United States on record for the first time regarding China's unlawful behavior over the years (see below) as well as blatant intent to steal resources, including fish, belonging to the coastal states under UNCLOS. It also bears directly on how China pursues its quest for SCS energy resources.

The Energy Issue

The Republic of Vietnam issued its first oil concession in July 1973 and shortly thereafter annexed ten Spratly features and militarily garrisoned the two largest, ostensibly to protect the exploration.[17] Meanwhile, China was becoming anxious that its domestic oil fields could not meet the demand of its growing economy. When, by 1993, it had become a net oil importer, Beijing became convinced that South China Sea could be a solution to the oil shortfall. The prospect of vast energy resources raised the stakes regarding sovereignty over otherwise inconsequential islets and features.[18] Dr. Erica Downs, one of America's leading experts on resource issues, notes that "nobody knows how much oil is in the South China Sea because it has not been fully explored. . . . The key question then becomes whether the Chinese government views the South and East China Seas as potentially having enough oil to substantially reduce China's dependence on imported oil. There is no shortage of Chinese press reports referring to the SCS [South China Sea] as China's 'Persian Gulf.' It is also worth noting that CNOOC (China National Offshore Oil Company) believes that deep-water SCS has enormous potential."[19]

Skeptics include the U.S.-based Energy Information Administration. It issued a report that throws cold water on the possibilities of huge Spratly or Paracel discoveries: "EIA's analysis shows that most fields containing discovered oil and natural gas are clustered in uncontested parts of the South China Sea, close to shorelines of the coastal countries, and not near the contested islands. Industry sources suggest [that] almost no oil and less than 100 billion cubic feet of natural gas in proved and probable reserves exist in fields near the Spratly Islands. The Paracel Island territory has even less natural gas and no oil."[20]

In short, any large quantities of oil and gas in the South China Sea are mostly to be found on the continental shelves of Vietnam, the Philippines, Malaysia, Indonesia, and Brunei, not around the Spratly and Paracel chains. This is why the 9DL has turned out to be so important to Beijing: the line cuts through areas where hydrocarbons *are* most likely to be found. It gives Beijing a (purported) basis on which to insist that it must participate in the exploration and development of any gas or oil discoveries within the 9DL. It also provides a rationale for the China Coast Guard's officially sanctioned harassment of exploration attempts undertaken by coastal states in partnerships with European or American firms. Vietnam and the Philippines are dependent on the expertise and technology developed over decades by Western oil companies, which are now reluctant to become involved in ventures that will lead to face-offs with the China Coast Guard.[21] Take as an example of the result the case of the Philippines and the Reed Bank, a hydrocarbon-rich area on its continental shelf. Manila's only hope of exploiting Reed Bank for its own impending energy crunch is to deal with Beijing on a joint-development basis. This seems like a clear case of extortion.[22]

The Defense of China

The South China Sea has been an avenue of approach by which to attack China since the nineteenth century. The British and then the French came by sea to southern China to trade, then eventually with naval and military force to attack China, invade its coastal ports, and twice march to the capital of the Qing Empire in Beijing and force humiliating treaties on it.

This history alone is enough to make sense of Beijing's long-established ambition to achieve control of the South China Sea and the airspace above it. Chinese control would eliminate the possibility that southern China could once again be attacked from across the South China Sea.

The South China Sea SLOC

Command of the South China Sea in times of conflict is important for China also because its SCS sea-lane is long: some 2,200 nm from Singapore to Shanghai. China wants to nullify any attempt by a littoral state or the United States to disrupt shipping exiting the Singapore Strait en route to China. This sea-lane passes the west of the Spratlys and is China's primary export sea route to the Indian Ocean and on to Europe. It connects China with Persian Gulf oil and African and Australian minerals, and it carries finished goods to Europe. It is also the initial leg of the much-touted Twenty-First-Century Maritime Silk Road. As discussed in earlier chapters, the PLA is very worried about the vulnerability of its sea lines of communication generally. Controlling the SCS islands, which are adjacent to the SLOCs there, is the best way to make certain no one else does.

The fact that Vietnam, a rival claimant and traditional antagonist, now stations six Kilo-class submarines on Cam Ranh Bay and operates Russian-built attack aircraft capable of threatening Chinese shipping suggests that sea-lane anxiety is not an idle concern. Even more troubling for Beijing is that Philippine president Duterte, despite his tilt toward Beijing, has not canceled the 2014 Enhanced Defense Cooperation Agreement (EDCA) with the United States and in fact reaffirmed it in November 2017 in a meeting with President Trump. This agreement gives U.S. forces access for extended-stay rotations to five Philippine Armed Forces bases, four of them airfields.[23] After two years of legal wrangling, the Philippine Supreme Court ruled in 2016 that the agreement is constitutional. While there have been no recent rotations, this agreement represents a latent capability that could be activated for use against Chinese sea-lanes.[24]

Finally, U.S. nuclear-powered attack submarines would be a major threat to South China Sea SLOCs. A little-known aspect of the operations of American submarines in World War II is how much time they spent in the South China Sea, going after Japanese warships and shipping, especially tankers carrying oil from the Dutch East Indies to Japan. For example, between October and December 1944 there were an average of fifteen U.S. Navy submarines on patrol somewhere in the South China Sea.[25] This history is a proof of concept of successful submarine attacks against the very same sea-lane that China worries about today.

Strategic Depth

Commanding the South China Sea also affords defense in depth to the important PLA Navy submarine base at Yulin, not far from the resort area of Sanya on the southern end of Hainan Island. Since 2000, the PLA has transformed Yulin into a heavily fortified and well-defended naval base, complete with tunnels for submarines and facilities for surface combatants.[26] Yulin is where China has decided to homeport its small SSBN fleet, presumably because of its proximity to deep water and its relatively straightforward access to the open ocean. This location also capitalizes on the defensive shield of the PLA bases in the Spratlys and Paracels. Throughout the Paracels are useful helicopter facilities, and on

Woody Island is a major air base that can help "delouse" PLA Navy SSBNs (i.e., detect any U.S. Navy submarines trailing them) when they depart Yulin for deterrence patrols.

To accomplish the three strategic objectives of defending its South China Sea SLOC, providing defense in depth against an attack on southern China, and protecting its SSBN home port at Yulin, Beijing has systematically constructed a network of bases. Starting with Hainan itself and proceeding southward through the Paracels and then on to the Spratlys, China has over the decades constructed a chain of facilities that cover the length of the South China Sea. It has built excellent harbor facilities and airfields capable of accommodating the full range of PLA Navy and China Coast Guard ships and craft, as well as PLA Air Force and Naval Air Force combat and support aircraft. This has not taken place by accident but through a patient plan.

China's Efforts to Achieve Control of the South China Sea

The PRC began this campaign seven decades ago, in 1955. It is important to keep in mind that Beijing "inherited" its South China Sea claims from the Republic of China: the PRC asserts that ROC claims to the South China Sea features became its own when in 1949 Nationalist Party leader and ROC president Chiang Kai-shek decamped to the island of Taiwan with much of what was left of his army. (Chiang's departure ended, for all practical purposes, the Chinese civil war, although it took the PLA another six months to overrun Hainan.)

In 1955, Beijing occupied abandoned Nationalist Chinese holdings in the eastern Paracel Island chain. Since then it has inexorably collected islands, rocks, and other features in the SCS by the occupation of unoccupied features and, when necessary, the application of force (e.g., in 1974 and 1988 by the PLA Navy against Vietnam). It used force majeure in 1994 and 2012 to gain control of features legitimately belonging to the Philippines. In recent years, Beijing has also employed its maritime-law-enforcement vessels and maritime militia to intimidate, arrest, or physically injure or damage coastal-state fishermen and their craft. In short, Beijing has a long record of coercive behavior in the SCS. (See appendix II for a complete discussion of the militia.) The following paragraphs briefly describe how Beijing's SCS plan has unfolded.

Gaining Full Control of the Paracel Islands

Following World War II, the Paracels (Chinese, Xisha) were split between France (eventually devolved to South Vietnam), which held the southwestern (Crescent) group of islands, and the ROC which from 1946 held the northeastern (Amphitrite) group. When in 1950 Mao's People's Liberation Army finally overran Hainan, Chiang ordered its evacuation. With U.S. Navy assistance, some 66,000 Nationalist troops and civilians were moved from Hainan to Taiwan, including the Nationalist garrisons in the Paracel and Spratly Island chains.[27]

Five years later, Beijing began an occupation and gradual buildup of forces in the abandoned eastern Paracel group centered on Woody Island, the largest feature in the archipelago. An opportunity to seize the portion of the archipelago occupied by South Vietnam arose twenty years later, on January 17, 1974. The last U.S. forces had left Vietnam eight months earlier, and there was no political enthusiasm in Washington for any further military involvement in Southeast Asia, and certainly not with China.[28] President Nixon had made his historic visit two years before but was now deeply distracted by the growing threat that the Watergate scandal posed to his presidency. Washington turned down South Vietnam's requests for intervention by the Seventh Fleet. A week later Secretary of State Henry Kissinger met with the director of the PRC's Liaison Office in Washington, DC, and informed him that the United States did not support Saigon's attempts to bring the Paracel issue to the United Nations or to the Southeast Asia Treaty Organization (SEATO).[29] This was the first of a succession of occasions in which Washington chose not to confront China over its behavior in the South China Sea.

The fight itself was over quickly. The PLA Navy won a helter-skelter naval shoot-out with the South Vietnamese navy and followed up with a well-planned and -executed amphibious assault that drove treaty ally South Vietnam from the western portion of the Paracels.[30] This gave Beijing control of the entire Paracel chain. Dr. Toshi Yoshihara, a U.S. Naval War College faculty member, has written an excellent assessment of the battle, using Chinese sources. He writes that "newly available Chinese-language sources reveal a far more complex naval operation than is commonly depicted in Western scholarship. Hitherto-unknown details of the battle illustrate how Chinese strategists tailored their tactics so as to coerce, deter, and defeat a rival claimant."[31] Yoshihara placed emphasis on the importance of this campaign for the PLA Navy:

> For the People's Liberation Army Navy, the campaign is etched into the service's institutional memory; constituting an essential part of the navy's "glorious history." The "counterattack in self-defense" vanquished South Vietnam's navy and secured China's control over the Paracels. It is considered the PLA Navy's first sea battle against an external enemy. (The fighting against the Nationalists along the mainland coast in the 1950s and 1960s is regarded as an extension of the Chinese civil war.) The battle was also the first time that the PLAN [PLA Navy]—then largely a coastal-defense force composed of obsolescent Soviet vessels—operated so far from China's shores. The disparity in naval power that seemingly favored South Vietnam (Republic of Vietnam, or RVN) has helped Chinese commentators mythologize the triumph.[32]

Today Hanoi still refuses to recognize China's occupation, claiming to be the real sovereign of the Paracel chain. China has no intention of leaving, arguing that its claim of sovereignty is superior to that of Hanoi. Meanwhile, as mentioned, Beijing has gradually improved the military usefulness of the Paracels. It has undertaken substantial upgrades to the islands' military infrastructure and developed several features as military outposts. Woody Island's airfield mentioned above is a dual-use civilian and military airfield, with sixteen hangars for combat aircraft and four larger hangars. The harbor can now accommodate ships as large as the Chinese cruise ships that bring tourists to enjoy beaches and water sports.[33]

The PLA also occupies nineteen other outposts throughout the Paracels; three of them now have protected harbors capable of handling large numbers of naval and civilian vessels. Five of the islands contain helipads, Duncan Island a full helicopter base.[34] Helicopters flying from these facilities can cover to the west of the Paracels. ASW-specialized helicopters are likely to be assigned, presumably, as suggested earlier, to operate off the Yulin base complex.

The civilian infrastructure of Sansha City on Woody (Yongxing) Island has not been neglected. Besides cruise ships and ferry service from Hainan,

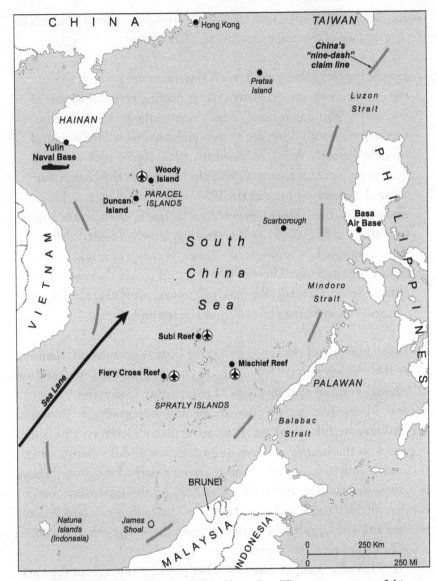

Map 4. Major PLA Bases in the South China Sea. The main purpose of this map is to illustrate the distribution of China's most important island bases in the South China Sea. Specifically, in the Paracels, Woody Island hosts a jet fighter– and bomber-capable runway, hangars, and other support facilities. There is also a major helicopter facility on Duncan Island. Three of China's seven island bases in the Spratlys (Fiery Cross, Subi, and Mischief) also have new airfields and facilities. Scarborough is listed as a potential base because of its location in the northeast portion of the South China Sea. If Scarborough were to be transformed into a facility similar to Mischief Reef, it would complete overlapping island-based air coverage of the entire body of water. These bases provide defense in depth for the PLA Navy's SSBN base at Yulin on Hainan island.

there are now daily Hainan Airlines flights from Haikou, Hainan.[35] Woody was designated the administrative center of China's holdings throughout the SCS in 2012. It was made a prefecture-level city of Hainan Province and given the responsibility for the administration of all of China's claimed island chains in the SCS.[36] In practice, this meant making Sansha City into a hub for the China Coast Guard, the maritime militia, and surveillance and information networks. President Xi Jinping himself, during a visit to Hainan in April 2013, emphasized the importance of Sansha City: "Xi directed the province to develop a well-functioning government in Sansha to fulfill the Party's four aims in the South China Sea: protection of rights, protection of stability, preservation of the maritime environment, and development."[37]

The Spratly Islands

By 1988, despite Beijing's long-standing claim to the Spratly chain (in Chinese, Nansha), Taiwan was the only Chinese national entity actually maintaining a foothold there. The PRC had quietly fumed that all the "best" features (those with a reasonable parcel of land above water) were already occupied by Taiwan, Vietnam, the Philippines, or Malaysia. According to Adm. Liu Huaqing, former commander of the PLA Navy, the PLA was particularly aggrieved by what it considered the illegality of this occupation of important strategic territory that belonged to China:

Soon after I came to the Central Military Commission [1987] I was confronted with a task: To study and deal with the Nansha issue. Throughout my years of service in the Navy, I had been constantly concerned about the Nansha issue. Among the South China Sea Islands, the Nansha Islands are the southernmost archipelago, which occupies the largest area and contains the largest number of islands and reefs. . . . Strategically, the Nansha Islands are of great importance because they are located in the important sea-lane linking the Indian and Pacific oceans and on the route by which China makes contacts with foreign countries through the South China Sea, and they serve as an important southern protective screen for the safety of the motherland. . . .

By the time I started to work with the Central Military Commission, almost all above-water islands and reefs of this beautiful and rich archipelago had been occupied by Vietnam, the Philippines, and Malaysia.[38]

By this time, the CMC had decided to take action in the Spratlys. The pretext was a 1987 United Nations Educational, Scientific and Cultural Organization (UNESCO) request that countries establish monitoring stations to survey the world's oceans. Between April and November of 1987, China dispatched several small PLA Navy ships to Fiery Cross Reef to conduct survey work aimed at construction of an outpost that would also meet the UNESCO request.[39]

The Vietnamese came to understand that the PLA Navy was intent on taking control of unoccupied Spratly features; Fiery Cross had been occupied first, thanks to the UNESCO pretext. Next was Cuarteron Reef (Huayang), only ten miles from a Vietnamese outpost. The Vietnamese navy had been shadowing PLA Navy surveying and building activity and determined to beat the Chinese to an unoccupied feature called Johnson Reef (Chigua).[40] The PLA Navy got there first anyway, landing a survey team. According to Admiral Liu, this is what transpired:

> At 0625 on 14 March [1988], a landing craft, No. 505, and two military transport ships, Nos. 604 and 605, of the Vietnamese navy suddenly came to the waters of Chigua Reef. They dispatched 42 officers and men, armed with light machine guns and assault rifles, to make a forced landing on the reef. A hand-to-hand fight was imminent. The Chinese and Vietnamese officers and men stood in the water, facing each other, weapons in hands.
>
> Our naval officers and men shouted out to the Vietnamese officers and men again and again, saying that this is China's territory and ordering them to leave. The Vietnamese officers and men not only ignored the order, but, on the contrary, made the first strike by using assault guns to shoot our personnel. At the same time, several light machine guns on transport ship No. 604 simultaneously opened fire at our personnel on the reef and aboard our ships. One of our sailors was wounded instantly.
>
> Under such circumstances, our naval officers and men were compelled to fight back in self-defense, killing over two dozen of the Vietnamese who had landed on the reef and captured nine of

them. One Vietnamese transport ship was sunk, while the other two ships were badly damaged. The battle lasted only 28 minutes. Two of our personnel were wounded.

As small a scale clash as it was, the Chigua Reef battle demonstrated the might of the Chinese Navy. I no longer had the feeling that we were controlled and humiliated by others. The grievance that had existed in my heart for years had disappeared. . . . The Chigua Reef battle cheered and inspired every Chinese. Like others, I was excited beyond description. As a serviceman, however, I had to consider how to maintain our permanent presence on the Nansha Islands and safeguard our national interests really effectively.[41]

This is the Chinese view. Vietnam counters that—as a Chinese video of the shootout that surfaced years later on YouTube seems to bear out—many of its men were needlessly shot down.[42] The main point is, however, that China held onto the reef; Vietnam never again attempted to use force to defend its claims in Spratly Islands. For the rest of 1988 the PLA Navy occupied and built facilities on three additional features, ending the year with six footholds in the Spratlys.

The 1995 Seizure of Mischief Reef

China added a seventh Spratly feature to its holdings when it seized Mischief Reef in 1995 despite protests from Manila that it was on its continental shelf. Chinese construction activity was not discovered until it was well under way, when a Philippine fishing boat unsuspectingly arrived on the scene. China has occupied Mischief ever since. The seizure was consequential and clearly unlawful, since the reef, despite its name, is actually a low-tide elevation rising from the Philippine continental shelf; as such it was not subject to appropriation according to the UNCLOS treaty, which Beijing would ratify the next year (1996). This was the first of a long list of violations of the Law of the Sea Treaty perpetrated by Beijing in the pursuit of its strategic objectives in the South China Sea.

The building activity itself was led by the PLA Navy, which supervised the construction of the raised platforms (called "fisherman shelters" by Beijing) equipped with satellite communications dishes. Bill Hayton, whose analysis of the incident is the most comprehensive, correctly calls it another turning point in Chinese behavior in the Spratlys. Before Mischief, Vietnam had been the only SCS rival claimant to suffer from China's "creeping control" strategy. Manila was surprised that China had infringed on its continental shelf; in the ensuing tempest Beijing issued a series of denials and lies. Hayton speculates that China's motivation for selecting Mischief, aside from Manila's military weakness, was because Mischief Reef is near Reed Bank, where the Philippines (see above) intended to survey for gas and oil—something about which Beijing had previously complained to Manila.[43]

Washington issued a statement of concern—in May 1995, several months after the fact, at the daily State Department briefing—but took no further steps. Even so, the statement did publicly define the basic policy framework that Washington follows to this day:

> The United States is concerned that a pattern of unilateral actions and reactions in the South China Sea has increased tensions in the region. The United States strongly opposes the use or threat of force to resolve competing claims and urges all claimants to exercise restraint and to avoid destabilizing actions.
>
> The United States has an abiding interest in the maintenance of peace and stability in the South China Sea. The United States calls upon claimants to intensify diplomatic efforts that address issues related to the competing claims, taking into account the interests of all parties, and which contribute to peace and prosperity in the region. The United States is willing to assist in any way that the claimants deem helpful. The United States reaffirms its welcome of the 1992 ASEAN [Association of Southeast Asian Nations] Declaration on the South China Sea.
>
> Maintaining freedom of navigation is a fundamental interest of the United States. Unhindered navigation by all ships and aircraft in the South China Sea is essential for the peace and prosperity of the entire Asia-Pacific region, including the United States.
>
> The United States takes no position on the legal merits of the competing claims to sovereignty over the various islands, reefs, atolls, and cays in the South China Sea. The United States would, however, *view with serious concern any maritime claim or restriction on maritime activity in the South China Sea* that was not consistent with

international law, including the 1982 United Nations Convention on the Law of the Sea.[44]

Meanwhile, Beijing had assured Manila that it was not to worry, its only aim was to improve the shelters that fishermen used.[45] Beijing (in an implicit self-contradiction) then offered the preposterous excuse that the occupation had been ordered by low-level personnel who had "acted without the knowledge and consent of the government." As one contemporary observer notes, "the possibility that a low-level Chinese bureaucrat had authority to dispatch seven naval vessels to set up an outpost 1000 KM [kilometers] from mainland China" was absurd.[46]

In any case, Beijing did not subsequently withdraw from Mischief to "correct" this low-level error, and Manila did worry. It took the matter to ASEAN, with the result in August 1995 that Beijing, perhaps influenced by the American use of "view with serious concern" (diplomatic code words implying the possibility of a resort to force), agreed to a bilateral code of conduct to prevent future incidents.[47] This triggered a spate of Sino-Philippine high-level visits, some involving the PLA, between 1995 and 1999. In fact, the second meeting in 1995 produced a joint code of conduct, of sorts, in which the two sides pledged to abide by certain general principles of behavior. However, as so often is the case with the PRC in the South China Sea, there was no progress whatsoever on the question of the Mischief Reef. Meanwhile, the PRC worked to turn its "fisherman shelters" into more permanent military facilities.[48] Eventually the notion of a code of conduct was taken up by ASEAN, and in 2002 Beijing agreed to participate in the development of such a code. Now, some eighteen years later, an ASEAN-China code of conduct remains a work in progress.

In 2002 Beijing also agreed to a Declaration on the Conduct of Parties in the South China Sea (DOC). Subsequently it has been judged ineffective, "too vague and had no means to resolve disagreements. As a result, most parties violated the text while insisting that they were still in compliance and pointing their fingers at others."[49] In fairness, however, since 2002 China has not explicitly violated the DOC pledge to "refrain from inhabiting presently *uninhabited* islands, reefs, shoals, cays and other features." It has focused on building on features it had already inhabited. China does not inhabit Scarborough Shoal but surrounds it—on which more below.[50]

Between 1988 and 2013 China expanded its footholds, seven small features, so that small military garrisons could be more comfortably housed and communications equipment, radar, and defensive armament accommodated. Other claimants did the same, and the Spratlys "garrison club" members managed to coexist in a stable, "live and let live" environment.

China Changes the SCS Status Quo

This relative stability came an end when in 2012 China seized control of Scarborough Shoal, legally a "rock," claimed by both Beijing and Manila, not part of either the Paracel or Spratly Islands. The Scarborough episode is addressed separately below, since Scarborough has not been turned into a Chinese base, at least so far. But its takeover marked a turn for the worse in Beijing's SCS behavior, not coincidently coinciding with Xi Jinping's assumption of authority as party secretary of the CCP and head of the Central Military Commission. What China scholar Bonnie Glaser said in 2012 remains the case today:

> China's behavior in the South China Sea is deliberate and systematic: its actions are not the unintentional result of bureaucratic politics and poor coordination. In fact, the spate of actions by China in recent months suggests exemplary interagency coordination, civil-military control and harmonization of its political, economic and military objectives. The clear pattern of bullying and intimidation of the other claimants is evidence of a top leadership decision to escalate China's coercive diplomacy. This has implications not only for the Philippines and Vietnam, the primary targets of China's coercive efforts, but also has broader regional and global implications.[51]

A crucial feature of the Chinese approach is the full-time presence of several PLA Navy warships in the South China Sea. The PLA Navy pays close attention to units of the U.S. and other navies that transit through the South China Sea or exercise in its waters. Inevitably, foreign warships are shadowed during their operations in the SCS.[52] As Adm. Harry Harris, then Commander, U.S. Pacific Command testified, "Across the South China Sea, China's air force, navy, coast guard, and maritime militia all maintain a robust presence. Routine patrols and exercises ensure Chinese forces are in and around all the features, not just the ones they occupy.

China routinely challenges the presence of non-Chinese forces, including other claimant nations, and especially the U.S., often overstating its authority and insisting foreign force either stay away or obtain Chinese permission to operate."[53]

On the other hand, the PLA Navy carefully avoids getting involved with "maritime rights and interests" evolutions, leaving that to the Chinese Coast Guard and China's maritime militia. The PLA Navy is always nearby in case trouble occurs, but it is the coast guard and maritime militia that lead in aggressively asserting claims to territory and fishing grounds. Their most publicized acts include chasing non-Chinese fishing boats from Chinese-claimed fishing grounds, trying to forestall Philippine efforts to resupply its marines on a grounded hulk on Second Thomas Shoal, and keeping Philippine fishermen away from their traditional fishing grounds around Scarborough Shoal.

In May 2014, China positioned its first deep-sea oil exploration rig in Vietnam's EEZ. The Chinese claimed it was within their EEZ/continental shelf that extends from the western portion of the Paracel Islands, which they have occupied since 1974. Since the Vietnamese do not recognize Chinese sovereignty over the Paracels, they argue that this was their EEZ and that by drilling in it the Chinese were clearly violating Vietnamese sovereignty.

Obviously anticipating trouble, Beijing put the PLA Navy in charge of protecting the rig. It was initially escorted by around eighty vessels—a mix of fishing boats, coast guard vessels, and, reportedly, seven PLA Navy ships, all under the command and control of the PLA Navy.[54] Vietnam responded by dispatching about twenty coast guard and fisheries surveillance ships. The ensuing melee ebbed and flowed for over a month, ships routinely ramming one another and inundating one another with high-pressure water cannons. One Vietnamese fishing boat capsized after being rammed; fortunately, the crew was rescued. After two months, the rig was moved from Vietnam's EEZ, probably to avoid an approaching typhoon.[55] As one expert has observed, "It looks to Southeast Asia like China has taken off the gloves."

He was referring to the hard-nosed approach that China has been pursuing in the South China Sea since it effectively seized control of Scarborough Shoal from the Philippines in 2012. In effect, Chinese actions are "scaring the hell out of Southeast Asia."[56]

Gaining Control of Scarborough Shoal

On April 8, 2012, a group of Chinese fishing vessels were discovered anchored in Scarborough Shoal, a feature that Manila claims and had exercised control over since independence (Scarborough is within the Philippine EEZ). Manila dispatched its largest frigate (a decommissioned U.S. Coast Guard cutter acquired from Washington) to disrupt what it viewed as illegal fishing. The Philippine warship reached the shoal thirty-six hours later, entered the large lagoon, inspected the Chinese fishing boats, and made preparations to arrest the fishermen for illegally fishing in Philippine waters. The fishermen apparently radioed Chinese authorities in Hainan for help, and soon thereafter two unarmed China Marine Surveillance (CMS) vessels already in the vicinity took positions outside the narrow mouth of Scarborough Shoal's lagoon and essentially blocked the Philippine warship from leaving except by shooting its way out. The Philippines sensibly chose not to do this. Manila hoped to settle the dispute diplomatically.

What no one had anticipated was a three-month-long stand-off that ended when the American assistant secretary of state for East Asia made a deal with a Chinese counterpart. The Philippine ship was allowed to withdraw and did so with the understanding that the Chinese ships, by this time as many as eight, would also do so. It did not work out this way; the Philippine navy left, the Chinese stayed. They put a boom across the entrance, and the China Coast Guard has ever since guarded the shoal and chased Philippine fishermen away.[57] According to press reports, the Obama administration deeply resented how the Chinese appeared to have double-crossed American diplomats who understood there would be a mutual Philippine-Chinese withdrawal. Nonetheless, it appeared unwilling to reopen the discussion with Beijing and push for a Chinese withdrawal.[58]

In 2016, the newly elected President Duterte also decided not to revive the stand-off diplomatically, it having become clear that China had no intention of loosening its grip on the shoal. He signaled to Beijing that he wanted to improve relations and sharply downgraded the importance of Manila's relations with the United States. He also indicated he would not insist that the Permanent Court of Arbitration award had been an overwhelming legal victory for the Philippines. What he wanted in return was Chinese economic help in developing

Philippine infrastructure and willingness to allow Philippine fishermen to resume fishing around the shoal.[59]

In this, Duterte may have been influenced by PLA posturing. China had not only dismissed the PCA award "as a scrap of paper" but had also decided to show Manila some military muscle. Carl Thayer, an astute Australian observer, recounts the military signals that were sent to Duterte:

> In the aftermath of the arbitral tribunal's ruling, China was not only dismissive of the award, but mounted displays of military force.... On July 18, 2016, China aired a video showing two J-11 fighters and an H-6K bomber flying over Scarborough Shoal. In September, Chinese H6-K bombers, Su-30 jet fighters, and air refueling tankers conducted a combat training exercise over the Bashi Channel to the north of the Philippines. And in December, China deployed a Xian H-6 nuclear bomber to patrol around the nine-dash line, which denotes China's claims to the South China Sea.[60]

Duterte's volte-face provided Beijing an opportunity to demonstrate that, as it had long insisted, solutions to South China Sea disputes could be found only through *bilateral* negotiations. It almost instantly defused the international "blowback" on China's refusal to honor the PCA findings, and it was not a bad outcome from Duterte's perspective. Filipino fisherman are back fishing near Scarborough, Duterte got promises of large loans from Beijing (which have yet to materialize as of this writing), and he still has the U.S.-Philippine Mutual Defense Treaty (MDT) in his back pocket.

Then, in early 2016, Scarborough Shoal suddenly became a serious issue again, this time for American officials. The *Washington Free Beacon* claimed to have obtained information that the PLA was making plans to turn the 150-square-kilometer shoal and lagoon into an artificial island, as they had done in the Spratlys.[61] Whether this was in fact China's intent is unknown, but Washington reacted as though it was. Whatever information the Department of Defense had was credible enough to trigger a "full-court press" to dissuade Beijing from taking this step. Scarborough is ideally located to "control" the northeast exit of the South China Sea through the Luzon Strait, an important choke point. If

Scarborough were a PLA base with a jet-capable airfield, the PLA would be able to establish air control over the northern Philippines and would be able to declare a credible South China Sea Air Defense Identification Zone (ADIZ). This would be one more step in asserting administrative control over the entire body of water and associated airspace.[62] A modern Scarborough airfield with radar and other ISR facilities would put the PLA within 250 nm of several Philippine bases where the United States has been granted "rotational access" (see below).

Scarborough is a little over three hundred nautical miles east of the major PLA air base on Woody Island in the Paracels and three hundred south of Taiwan-controlled Pratas Island. Pratas, in turn, is the last step to Beijing's goal of controlling the airspace over the entire SCS: it is adjacent to the main sea-lane from Singapore to the entrance of the East China Sea and six of China's ten largest ports. PLA planners have probably concluded that eventually Pratas will become under its control, at which point the PLA can expand the existing airfield to accommodate jet fighters, medium bombers, and support aircraft. Woody Island, Scarborough Shoal (if developed by the PLA), and Pratas Island (when it comes under mainland China's control) would form a chain of a mutually supporting network of airfields, similar to what exists in the Spratlys. This network would give Beijing control of the northeast entrance/exit of the South China Sea and flank Taiwan from the southwest. Another strategically important benefit of such a scheme is the possibility of overlapping air support; from these air bases PLA Navy maritime patrol ASW aircraft could fly long-endurance missions over the waters that PLA Navy SSBNs have to cross from Yulin into the Philippine Sea and central and northern Pacific Ocean.

The American response to suspected Scarborough base building included the rotational deployment of a small task force of Air Force tactical aircraft to the Philippines and presence operations of the USS *John Stennis* (CVN 74) strike group in the South China Sea for much of March, April, and May of 2016. According to *New York Times* reports, President Obama mentioned Scarborough Shoal to President Xi Jinping during their meeting on the margins of the Nuclear Security Summit: "The stakes are so high that Mr. Obama warned the Chinese leader, Xi Jinping, during their recent meeting in Washington not to move on the Scarborough Shoal or invoke an air defense zone, said an American official who was briefed on the details of the encounter and spoke anonymously because of the diplomatic sensitivities."[63]

The flurry of activity regarding Scarborough in those three months was intended to signal Beijing that the United States sees Scarborough as being different from the Paracels and Spratlys. Although official U.S. policy of taking no position on the merits of sovereignty claims in the South China Sea applies to Scarborough Shoal, Washington was all but saying that it was strategically important to keep Scarborough out of Chinese hands lest it become yet another important PLA base. The Trump administration probably shares this view, given its attempts to reassure Manila regarding the MDT, but I have found no public statement to confirm this hunch.

Island Building on a Grand Scale

It is necessary to return to 2014 and the Spratlys. An almost quarter-century of stability, more or less, in the Spratlys was sundered in 2014 when publicly available satellite photography revealed that China was using a fleet of dredgers to build artificial islands. What riveted the attention of the world, especially that of the other coastal claimants and the American security bureaucracy, was that China had undertaken a massive and well organized and executed civil-engineering effort to turn the seven tiny specks it occupied into man-made islands, simultaneously. In late 2013 China had quietly begun dredging to reconfigure the four rocks and three low-tide elevations it had occupied for twenty-five years.[64] By the early months of 2016, these PRC holdings had become de facto islands. They had become full-fledged military bases, three of them with very long runways. The strategic balance in the Spratly Island chain had been decisively altered. When fully staffed and equipped, the new island bases will militarily overshadow the garrisons and defenses of the features occupied by Taiwan, Vietnam, the Philippines, and Malaysia. Overshadowed or not, however, it is important to keep in mind that between them these other Spratly claimants occupy forty-odd features in the Spratlys; China is not alone there.

China has created a military-base design that will accommodate a large garrison; more military equipment, including defensive and offensive missile systems, than was possible before; fuel and ordnance storage; and in three cases very large new harbors that can easily accommodate the largest PLA Navy warships.[65] For the first time, Beijing has the ability to bring land-based aircraft in significant numbers to the southern half of the South China Sea. Each of the three new airfields and support structures is capable of supporting a regiment of fighters (twenty-four aircraft) plus support airplanes. Accordingly, the PLA could have as many as seventy-two fighters in the Spratlys on a full-time basis. With the Spratly bases, those in the Paracels, and the many already existing facilities on Hainan, the PLA has nearly completed its objective of a defensive island-base network. Once the Spratly outfitting is complete, this fully militarized network will represent a capability that, the PLA hopes, can defend its SCS sea-lane and command air and sea approaches on that axis to China.[66]

In addition, the three main Spratly bases with large harbors and wharfs—Subi, Fiery Cross, and Mischief Reefs—would be useful as "forward bases," for supporting PLA Navy operations into the Central Pacific or Indian Ocean with water, fuel, and other logistical support. In many respects, the physical layout of these installations reminds one of the U.S. facility on Diego Garcia atoll in the Indian Ocean. The Spratly bases could easily accommodate surface-ship and submarine tenders, along with maintenance facilities to support PLA Navy, Air Force, and China Coast Guard aviation assigned there for patrol and rights protection—again, as the U.S. Navy and Air Force have demonstrated on Diego Garcia.

In peacetime, the Spratly bases make it possible for Beijing to monitor air traffic through the southern half of the SCS and over much of maritime Southeast Asia; enforce fishing regulations dictated by Beijing; otherwise harass the fishermen of all the other littoral states; and intimidate other Spratly occupiers, to persuade them that their military positions are hopeless and that they must leave.

Like all remote island bases, however, Paracel and Spratly outposts are also vulnerable in case of a major war, particularly to precision weapons launched from submarines, aircraft, and surface warships. Also importantly, the entire SCS is ringed by air bases in the hands of Vietnamese, Filipinos, Malaysians, and Indonesians. In practical terms, in fact, all of China's facilities in the South China Sea are "surrounded" by the air bases of the other SCS littoral nations. If (as is often pointed out) unlike aircraft carriers island bases do not sink, they also do not move, and the precise latitude and longitude of each of China's are known. As a result,

This photograph of Subi Reef shows the fighter jet–capable runway plus a massive enclosed deepwater harbor over two miles wide. A visual comparison, at the same scale, of Subi Reef with a satellite photo of the U.S. Naval Station at Pearl Harbor, Hawaii, illustrates how large the harbor of this island base is: large enough to anchor or berth several dozen PLA Navy ships and small craft. *Thomas Shugart, "China's Artificial Islands Are Bigger (and a Bigger Deal) Than You Think," War on the Rocks, September 21, 2016. Modified by author*

naval and potentially ground forces armed with long-range land-attack cruise missiles and aircraft with stand-off weapons flying from airfields in the littoral countries could attack these island bases.

The United States and the South China Sea

This is a book about the Chinese navy and its maritime power ambitions and not about Sino-U.S. competition in China's near seas. However, this chapter would not be complete without a brief discussion of Washington's approach to the South China Sea and of the ongoing maritime interactions there between the U.S. and PLA Navies. "There should be no mistake: the United States will fly, sail and operate wherever international law allows. . . . America, alongside its allies and partners . . . will not be deterred from exercising these rights. . . . [T]urning an underwater rock into an airfield simply does not afford the rights of sovereignty or permit restrictions on international air or maritime transit."[67] The first sentence of this statement (delivered at the high-profile Shangri-La Dialogue in Singapore on May 30, 2015) has become an important policy mantra. Initially coined as a reaction to China's artificially created islands, it has become a formula used by the American officials speaking broadly about naval and air operations in both the South China and East China Seas. It is an important phrase because it conveys future intent: "This is what the United States is going to do, because it is legally permissible." It also implies, ". . . and don't try to stop us."

Disagreements over the Law of the Sea

One source of constant trouble has been U.S. military surveillance in and over China's EEZ. The two countries decidedly differ in their opinions on what military activities are permitted by the law of the sea in the EEZ of China. Washington argues that UNCLOS permits nations to exercise all its "high-seas freedoms" in the EEZs of coastal states and that by definition, coastal states have jurisdiction over the resources but do not possess sovereign rights over the waters. These "high-seas freedoms" include *peaceful* military activities, which in turn include, inter alia, surveillance and military surveys. China disagrees, claiming that the latter are unfriendly or "hostile." This disagreement regarding surveillance has resulted in two serious incidents. The first was the 2001 midair collision over China's EEZ near Hainan between a U.S. Navy surveillance aircraft (an EP-3) and an intercepting Chinese navy fighter. The second was the 2009 episode in which Chinese fishermen and paramilitary ships dangerously harassed USNS *Impeccable* (T-AGOS 23), which was conducting undersea surveillance, again in the EEZ around Hainan.

The United States believes that nothing in UNCLOS or state practice changes the right of any nation to conduct military activities in EEZs without notice to or consent of the coastal state. China disagrees; it claims that any nation that undertakes reconnaissance activities in China's EEZ without having notified China and received its permission is in violation of both international and Chinese domestic law. Capt. Raul "Pete" Pedrozo, a retired U.S. Navy maritime lawyer, succinctly summarizes the U.S. view:

China's views on coastal State authority in the exclusive economic zone (EEZ) are not supported by State practice, the negotiating history of the United Nations Convention on the Law of the Sea

(UNCLOS), or a plain reading of Part V of the Convention. All nations may legitimately engage in military activities in foreign EEZs without prior notice to, or consent of, the coastal State concerned. Efforts were made during the negotiations of UNCLOS to broaden coastal State rights and jurisdiction in the EEZ to include security interests. However, the Conference rejected these efforts and the final text of the Convention (Article 58) ultimately preserved high seas freedoms of navigation and overflight and other internationally lawful uses of the seas related to those freedoms, to include military activities, in the EEZ.[68]

Despite the unambiguous negotiation record, China is attempting to undo this carefully balanced compromise between coastal and user states. Both Beijing and Washington have recognized the obvious danger created when Chinese units trail or shadow U.S. military ships and aircraft operating in its EEZ, and sensible safety rules regarding such encounters are now in place.[69] For its part, however, Washington continues to ignore Beijing's interpretation of UNCLOS. It has *not stopped* conducting these lawful activities and does not ask permission, much to the continued irritation of Beijing.[70]

The Obama Administration Gets Involved in the SCS

Between March and May 2009, Washington was presented with a series of aggressive PRC actions, the one just mentioned against USNS *Impeccable* in the South China Sea and another against USNS *Victorious* (T-AGOS 19) in the Yellow Sea. Both were operating in international waters but within China's EEZ. No one knows why China decided to press its position on the EEZ in such an aggressive fashion—perhaps it was an attempt to create a "new normal" with a new American administration. If that was the case, it backfired; it, combined with other heavy-handed episodes with China's maritime neighbors, caused Washington to pay more attention to the SCS.

The first major indication of pushback took place at the ASEAN Regional Forum in Hanoi in 2010, when then Secretary of State Hillary Clinton publicly and directly involved the United States in South China Sea disputes, apparently surprising and infuriating the Chinese representative. This marked the beginning of direct diplomatic involvement of

Washington, in a way that was probably unforeseen at the time, into the complex web of South China Sea issues.[71] Clinton stated, "The United States has a national interest, as every country does, in the maintenance of peace and stability, respect for international law, freedom of navigation, [and] unimpeded lawful commerce in the South China Sea. The United States does not take a position on competing territorial claims over land features, but we believe the nations of the region should work collaboratively together to resolve disputes without coercion, without intimidation, without threats."[72]

In hindsight, by choosing to be so publicly involved Washington put itself into the position of trying to shape Chinese activity in the South China Sea with absolutely no practical leverage short of the use of force or imposition of trade or economic penalties. (The U.S.-China trade war, ongoing at this writing, is focused on Chinese trade practices and not the situation in the South China Sea.)

Instead, Washington frequently indicated unhappiness with Chinese activities, especially island building. Its policy approach involved all the normal, noncoercive engagement and diplomatic tools available. It specifically included official exhortations, permanent military presence (which expanded or contracted over time), periodic "freedom of navigation" operations (detailed below) to protest excessive Chinese maritime claims, improved security-oriented relations with China's South China Sea neighbors, and diplomatic notes protesting bad Chinese behavior. The Obama administration stopped short, however, of direct economic penalties and wisely elected not to use force to try to halt island building. The administration believed that the United States had more important matters, such as North Korea, Iran, and climate change, in which it needed to work with Beijing and did not want the South China Sea to become the central issue in Sino-U.S. relations.[73]

China understands this. The South China Sea has been and remains much more important to Beijing than to Washington. Beijing's view is that the South China Sea is a core national interest because sovereignty is in play. It is hardly surprising, given this context, that over the years Beijing ignored American exhortations to behave. China's responses to such criticism can be generally characterized as telling everyone, including Washington, to mind their own business—that the Spratly Islands are sovereign Chinese territory and China can do with them what it likes, that the improved facilities permit China to "better safeguard national territorial sovereignty [i.e., the Spratly Islands] and maritime rights and interests."[74]

The 2014 Enhanced Defense Cooperation Agreement (above) with the Philippines has the potential to add credibility to the deterrent implicit in the U.S.-Philippine Mutual Defense Treaty. While the Philippine air force has no capability to put the new Chinese bases at risk or defend its own troops on Manila's Spratly holdings, the U.S. Air Force rotational detachments certainly do. Washington has long resisted Philippine requests that the MDT also cover Philippine claims in the Spratlys, likely because the legal basis for such an extension would be weak, but it does apply if Philippine armed forces are attacked. Secretary of State Mike Pompeo made this perfectly plain in March 2019. The intent of his statement was to reassure Manila about America's fidelity to the MDT obligation—but also to reinforce deterrence. Beijing has never tested the MDT by shedding Filipino blood trying to force garrisons off Spratly holdings, but in case they were considering it, this was a reminder that an attempt could bring the United States into the fray.[75]

The Trump Administration: Island Building and Militarization Are the Culprits

The most comprehensive Trump administration statement on the South China Sea was made by then Secretary of Defense James Mattis at the June 2018 Shangri-La Dialogue. In his keynote speech, he indicated that China's behavior called into question China's assertions that it sought peace and stability and raised questions about China's broader regional goals. Mattis suggested that China's coercive approach in the South China Sea foreshadowed how it would behave toward its neighbors in the future.[76]

Freedom of Navigation Operations

Despite its apparent indifference to criticism, one thing that does get Beijing's attention are operations in the SCS of the U.S. Navy's Freedom of Navigation (FONOPS) Program. These are well-choreographed warship transits through areas where claims or regulations—here, those of Beijing, elsewhere of other capitals—do not comply with the law of the sea. The program is an operational expression of the legal point that the

United States does not recognize and considers excessive the claim in question.

In a meeting of Secretary Mattis with embarked correspondents during his flight to the Shangri-La Dialogue, Chinese complaints about FONOPS came up. Mattis responded unequivocally that "a steady drumbeat" of FONOPS would continue.[77] Whether this is wise is open to question. The notion of a "steady drumbeat," in effect steady nagging, begins to divert the FON Program away from its intended purpose—protesting excessive maritime claims—and toward using its operations as shows of defiance.

They irritate Beijing but have not caused it to modify any offending claim. That irritation has on occasion gone beyond rhetoric, as evidenced by photographs of a dangerous encounter at sea released by the United States. The incident involved the guided-missile destroyer USS *Decatur* (DDG 73) and a PLA Navy destroyer, and it took place on September 30, 2018. The Chinese warship violated the agreements its government made with Washington and also the International Rules of the Road. It is highly unlikely the ship's commanding officer decided on his own to overtake *Decatur* and then abruptly cut in front, nearly causing a collision. This was clearly a signal despite that agreements between Washington and Beijing for safety in encounters at sea, Beijing feels free to ignore them to signal that it is fed up with certain forms of U.S. activity. In the future FON operations may become riskier than in the past, with the possibility of a more serious incident.[78]

So far, the Trump administration seems to be struggling with the same problem the Obama administration faced. Short of actual use of force, it is hard to change the status quo or roll back China in the South China Sea, particularly since at this point it seems clear that the administration shares its predecessor's view that the South China Sea is not the most important Sino-U.S. issue.

A Military Assessment of Where We Are Today
In his confirmation hearing the incoming commander of U.S. Indo-Pacific Command, Adm. Philip Davidson, offered this assessment of Chinese activities in the South China Sea:

China's development of forward military bases in the South China Sea began in December 2013 when the first dredger arrived at

Johnson Reef. . . . Today these forward operating bases appear complete. The only thing lacking are the deployed forces. Once occupied, China will be able to extend its influence thousands of miles to the south and project power deep into Oceania. The PLA will be able to use these bases to challenge U.S. presence in the region, and any forces deployed to the islands would easily overwhelm the military forces of any other South China Sea-claimants. *In short, China is now capable of controlling the South China Sea in all scenarios short of war with the United States.*[79]

His last sentence drew considerable attention, since by definition no one actually controls the high seas in peacetime. What the admiral was conceding is the reality that China's military capabilities are such that if Beijing elected to use force it could overwhelm the other littoral claimants and quickly gain sea and air control over the South China Sea. Were the Unites States to involve itself, China would have to fight in order to achieve or maintain control. He wisely did not comment as to what might be the outcome of such a fight, because he would have had to say that the balance of military power in East Asia is shifting to favor the PRC. In the unlikely event a SCS conflict between America and China began, it could easily escalate horizontally to a regional or even global war at sea, in which case it would have been only the first skirmish in a bigger conflict.

The fact is that China's still-growing, comprehensive, land-based air and missile power and virtually its entire fleet make the SCS what Beijing assuredly considers part of China's home waters—an extremely dangerous place for U.S. first responders should war break out. Conflict is unlikely because neither Washington nor Beijing wants a fight over the South China Sea. Should matters come to that, however, the United States would have to struggle to gain sea and air control there. Access to bases in the Philippines would be essential. This brings us to the key point: the United States may not *want* to contest control of the SCS but simply to inflict as much punishment as possible and leave it at that. U.S. control of the SCS might not be necessary. Also, even if both sides sought to limit the fight to the SCS, that might not be possible. Should the conflict spread to include Taiwan, for example, Washington might choose to limit its attention to the PRC sea-lane.

In this regard World War II provides a useful example: the main line of advance for the U.S. Navy toward East Asia was the Central Pacific, not the South China Sea.

———

But the United States is not at war with China, and no vital American interest has been compromised in the SCS. Freedom of navigation has not been physically interrupted. Commerce has not been impeded. Shipping continues, while the United States ignores (daily, if you believe Chinese complaints) Beijing's requirement for prior approval for military operations in China's EEZ. The Trump administration has embraced the policy that the U.S. Navy and Air Force intends to sail, fly, and operate where international law permits. An uneasy stability exists.

But that stability should not be understood as a signal that Beijing is satisfied with the current situation. The South China Sea is a core Chinese interest since the issue is *sovereignty*. That point was made unmistakable when James Mattis met with Xi Jinping in Beijing in June 2018. According to press reports, when Mattis raised the topic of the South China Sea, Xi responded, "Our stance is steadfast and clear-cut[:] when it comes to China's sovereignty and territorial integrity, any inch of territory passed down from our ancestors cannot be lost."[80]

In short, there is still a great deal of unfinished business as far as Beijing is concerned. It still has to solve the problem of getting the Filipinos, Vietnamese, and Malaysians off the forty or so features they collectively occupy in the Spratlys, without starting a war. It still has to turn Scarborough Shoal into a base, so it can complete an air base network to control all SCS airspace in times of conflict. It still needs to persuade the government of the Philippines to cancel the EDCA access agreement with the United States, in order to diminish the prospect of U.S. airpower returning to the Philippines. Eventually the PLA Navy is likely to play a leading role in getting these items addressed.

Nevertheless, Beijing has demonstrated over the past seven decades a patient, step-by-step approach to regaining what it firmly thinks is its territory in the SCS. Arguably, China knows exactly what it is doing. Its leaders can read a map. The realities of geography are that other claimants are always going to live in the shadow of China. Certainly, it overshadows them militarily, both individually and collectively. China is already the largest trading partner of all its Southeast Asian neighbors, and all their economies are increasingly interlinked.[81] During a meeting I attended in 2018, one ASEAN participant captured this reality perfectly: "We are all afraid of China, but we are also afraid of what China might do to our economy if we cross them."[82]

So far, China's actions in the South China Sea have not harmed its own economy or its neighbors': its neighbors still line up seeking to improve relations and to participate in its Belt and Road projects. Beijing understands that its smaller neighbors do not want to choose between the United States and China. They all want the best possible relationships with both.[83] Since these small countries will always be China's neighbors and they will always need China more than it needs them, China can permit itself great flexibility in how it redresses what it believes to be illegal occupation of Chinese sovereign territory. Today, then, when it comes to the South China Sea, China has asymmetric advantages in terms of geography, history, military capabilities, and interests. It can afford to be patient—whether it will remains to be seen.

CHAPTER SEVEN

The PLA Navy in the Indian Ocean

The Chinese flag has become ubiquitous on the high seas around the world, especially in the Indian Ocean (IO), where annually many hundreds of Chinese-flagged tankers, container ships, and bulk carriers pass engaged in the trade that made China the world's largest trading nation in 2013. The presence of Chinese warships has also become routine, especially in the Arabian Sea, where in late 2008 the PLA Navy began to protect a portion of its sea-lanes from Somali pirates. It is still at it; in the nearly twelve years since that first PLA Navy deployment China has adroitly blended its shipping-protection mission with traditional naval diplomacy (discussed in chapter 3) by having its returning deployers conduct goodwill visits and naval exercises with most of the Indian Ocean littoral countries.

China's interests in the Indian Ocean in general and the Arabian Sea in particular are directly tied to two related imperatives. The first is President Xi Jinping's signature strategic and economic objective, Belt and Road Initiative (detailed in chapter 1), whose aim is to connect Eurasian, Middle Eastern, and East African nations in a vast global trading network. China is to be at the center of this network; with regard to maritime trade, all sea-lanes are to lead to China. The Twenty-First-Century Maritime Silk Road (also chapter 1) is the maritime component of the network.

The second imperative, closely related to the first, is concern about the vulnerability of its sea-lanes to interruption. China's sea-lane anxiety has been explored earlier in this work and will not be belabored here, except to note that tankers cross the Indian Ocean every day either carrying oil from either the Persian Gulf or Angola in West Africa to China or returning empty for another cargo. At the same time, large numbers of container ships travel much the same sea-lane but carrying cargo in the opposite direction, delivering Chinese exports to the Middle East and Europe. To remind, China's 2015 defense white paper lays out Beijing's concerns: "With the growth of China's national interests, its national security is more vulnerable to international and regional turmoil, terrorism, piracy, serious natural disasters and epidemics, and the security of overseas interests concerning energy and resources, strategic sea lines of communication (SLOCs), as well as institutions, personnel and assets abroad, *has become an imminent issue.*"[1]

Having the ability to protect its shipping should the need arise is the most important of China's overseas security interests in the Indian Ocean region, because the nation's most important sea-lanes cross this body of water. For example, in 2017 China imported an average of 8.4 million barrels of crude oil per day, approximately 50 percent by ship from the Persian Gulf.[2] That means that on any given day approximately eighty-four tankers of the "very large crude carrier" (VLCC) type are under way somewhere in Indian Ocean or South China Sea in the China oil trade.[3]

PLA Navy Presence in the Indian Ocean

For the past decade the PLA Navy presence in the Indian Ocean as a whole has averaged four surface warships, two replenishment tankers, and, for six months a year, a submarine. The surface ships are organized into two independent task forces, or as the Chinese prefer, "flotillas." One task force, two warships and a replenishment support ship, is directly involved in the UN-authorized antipiracy mission in the northern Arabian Sea and Gulf of Aden. The other, similarly organized, task force is either under way in the northern Indian Ocean headed to the Arabian Sea to relieve the on-station antipiracy force, or, having been relieved of that responsibility, is conducting bilateral exercises or naval diplomacy missions along the Indian Ocean or Mediterranean Sea littoral before returning to China.

The PLA Navy has since 2014 also deployed submarines to the IO. According to the former commander of U.S. Pacific Command, the PLA Navy sends a submarine to the IO twice a year, each normally for three months.[4] Chinese sources have claimed that these submarines patrols contribute to the antipiracy operation.[5] That submarines might perform covert coastal surveillance for pirate camps on beaches is possible, of course, but seems unlikely. More probably they deploy to gain experience in blue-water operations a long way from home and collect data on water conditions and thermal layers, so important to submarine operations. In sum, the PLA Navy submarine force is amassing experience that will eventually make possible stationing at least one boat in the IO region full-time. This would not be the first time that a Northeast Asian navy dispatched submarines in the western Indian Ocean; during the final two decades of the Cold War the Soviet Union's Pacific Fleet maintained a routine submarine presence in the northern Arabian Sea.[6]

Today, the PLA Navy presence in the IO is small and not especially threatening. Its units are far from home and well away from the protection of land-based air and missile forces. In East Asia, the PLA has the huge operational advantage of being in familiar waters; there it is the "home team." In the Indian Ocean its small task forces are very much "visiting teams," vulnerable to India's vastly superior navy and land-based airpower. Similarly, when the PLA Navy arrives in the northern Arabian Sea, it is operating in waters that are "home" for the U.S. Fifth Fleet, headquartered in Bahrain.

Thus, on a day-to-day basis, in the IO the PLA Navy operates in areas where much of the airspace can be controlled by the United States or India—that is, with zero air cover. On the other hand, submarines as a general rule are difficult to locate, even in the best of conditions, and the Indian navy's ASW capabilities are not strong, so it is possible that PLA Navy submarine deployments may also be deterrent, reminding the Indian navy that two can play the game of threatening vital SLOCs.

This is the situation today, but this chapter is about the future. It is about what the current PLA Navy presence foreshadows for the coming decade. It is about the growth of a significant portion of the PLA Navy that is able, or shortly will be, to operate a militarily credible number of well-designed, large, seagoing warships—with air cover, globally, but especially the Indian Ocean—and sustain them there for months at a time.

As mentioned in chapter 3, over 130 ships capable of occupying Indian Ocean stations for months have joined the PLA Navy over the past fifteen years.[7] Significantly, this figure is not a final building objective, simply a current count on the way to an unknown endpoint. China continues to build these blue-water-capable ships and submarines with no publicly known numerical force-structure objective. In other words, as argued earlier, we simply do not know how large the PLA Navy will become, because Beijing, unlike every other major naval power in the world, refuses to reveal that fact. What we do know is that China already has in hand a powerful, well-balanced mix of warships that are capable of operating anywhere in the world. They will be especially drawn to the Indian Ocean, because of the Maritime Silk Road and SLOC anxiety.

To Look Forward, We Start by Looking Back

This is not the first time that a traditional Eurasian land power has found reason to deploy warships to the IO region. For the last twenty years of the Cold War, the Soviet Union maintained a substantial number of ships there. The intent here is to establish some historical context for projections for the future. As Mark Twain purportedly quipped, "History does not repeat, but it often rhymes."

Soviet Presence in the Indian Ocean (1968–1990)

Washington and Moscow long competed for political influence in the IO region. Each side attempted to gather "Third World" countries (i.e., aligned with neither superpower) into its camp. The Indian Ocean region was not unique in this regard; the competition went on globally. However, the number of newly independent states that had emerged in Africa, the Middle East, South Asia, and Southeast Asia because of the decolonization of the Indian Ocean littoral in the wake of World War II made it a particularly active arena. The Soviet Union's decision to deploy what came to be a substantial naval presence to the Indian Ocean was motivated by the anti-Western, anti-imperialist, anti-Israel attitudes that already roiled the region, in a symbiotic relation with the "in-your-face" nationalism of military strongmen like Egypt's Gamal Abdel Nasser. Soviet arms sales, even outright grants, were successfully sought by new nations that embraced socialism or Marxism to guarantee their security. Soviet armament largesse was also seen as a tangible expression of great-power political/military support. In return, many of these countries were quite willing to grant access to the Soviet Navy.[8]

Moscow hoped to exploit the vacuum occasioned by the British pull-out from "East of Suez." In those days, before the establishment of U.S. Central Command or Africa Command, the Persian Gulf and Red Sea were responsibilities of European Command, while Pacific Command, at the time deeply engaged in Vietnam, covered the entire Indian Ocean. The only full-time U.S. Navy presence was the tiny Middle East Force in and around the Persian Gulf commanded by a rear admiral who flew his flag at the British base in Bahrain. The force itself consisted of a permanently assigned flagship (a 2,700-ton converted seaplane tender) and two (eventually, late in the decade, four) rotationally assigned destroyers. For much of the 1970s, the Persian Gulf and northern Arabian Sea collectively remained a backwater for the U.S. Navy. Its presence was not welcomed by a majority of the Muslim states, because of Washington's support of Israel. By 1974, twenty-eight ports in eleven regional countries were closed to it.[9]

From the spring of 1969 onward, the Soviets too maintained a continuous naval presence, largely focused on the Gulf of Aden. This was a studied decision on Moscow's part, reached despite a difficult logistical situation created after June 5, 1967, when Egypt closed the Suez Canal at the beginning of the Six-Day War. At the end of that conflict Suez stayed closed while Egyptian and Israeli armies faced each other across the canal. In fact, the canal remained closed until the end of a second conflict—the Yom Kippur War—and subsequent peace negotiations eight years later, in 1975.

The Indian Ocean Squadron's ships came from the Soviet Navy's Pacific Fleet in Vladivostok, the Soviet fleet concentration closest to Aden. It was only 6,600 nautical miles away, compared to 12,000 nm for the Northern Fleet and 11,200 nm for the Black Sea Fleet. (With the canal closed, ships from the two Europe-based fleets needed to circumnavigate Africa in order to reach the Indian Ocean.) Six thousand miles was far enough, but the Soviet Pacific Fleet was up to the time/distance challenge. In order to save fuel and also wear and tear on diesel engines, the Soviets often towed their diesel-powered submarines and small frigates to the Gulf of Aden and back.[10]

Soviet Navy presence in the Indian Ocean region jumped from two hundred ship-days in 1967 to just under 4,200 ship-days in 1969.[11] By 1971, the Soviet Indian Ocean Squadron presence had increased to 8,900 ship-days, with a mix of five or six surface combatants and between two and four submarines, plus support ships. By 1980 the Soviet Indian Ocean Squadron had reached the unprecedented strength of between thirty and thirty-two ships: eleven surface combatants, three to five submarines, and sixteen auxiliaries (tenders, barracks ships, oilers, etc.).[12]

The Soviets relentlessly sought privileged access to naval facilities around the western Indian Ocean littoral and largely succeeded. The People's Democratic Republic of Yemen (PDRY), also known as South Yemen, and soon thereafter Somalia were their big success stories. The PDRY made the major port of Aden available, as well as anchorages around Socotra Island in the Gulf of Aden. Besides Socotra, the Soviet Navy anchored semipermanent mooring buoys off the Seychelles west of Diego Garcia, along the Cargados Carajos Shoal, 268 nm northeast of Mauritius and east of Madagascar, near the Comoros Archipelago.[13]

Gaining access to the Somali port of Berbera in 1972 was of significant benefit to the Soviet Navy, since it was sheltered and deep enough to accommodate large ships pierside, greatly facilitating logistics, voyage repairs, and crew rest. (Think of Berbera and Aden as surrogates for Djibouti today; they are both within 220 nm of Djibouti, Berbera only 150.) Thanks to Berbera, on-station time for Soviet Pacific Fleet ships increased from five months to almost a year.[14]

The Soviets reached an agreement with the Somali government to improve and modernize the port in return for access beyond the port itself. The Soviet Union eventually built Berbera into a significant base that included a missile-storage facility for the Soviet Navy, an air base with a 13,500-foot runway and fuel storage that was capable of handling large bombers, and extensive radar and communications facilities. By 1975 the Soviet Navy was flying long-range Il-38 May ASW aircraft from there. Berbera and other Somali airfields gave the Soviets reconnaissance and ASW capability over much of the Arabian Sea.[15]

But the Soviets overplayed their hand and as a result forfeited bases in Somalia. They took advantage of an opportunity to replace Washington's influence in neighboring Ethiopia following a 1974 army coup.[16] But Soviet attempts to keep both Mogadishu and Addis Ababa happy failed dramatically when the Somalis decided to invade the Ogaden region of Ethiopia before Soviet military assistance to Ethiopia could tip the military balance against them. Moscow found itself supplying both sides and attempted to mediate a cease-fire. When that failed, Moscow effectively abandoned Somalia and threw its support behind Ethiopia. Soviet military aid and advisors flooded into Ethiopia, along with 15,000 Cuban combat troops air- and sea-lifted by the Soviets from Angola, in West Africa. The invading Somalis were driven out of Ogaden.[17] Infuriated, Somalia annulled its treaty with the Soviet Union and expelled all Soviet advisors from the country.[18]

The Soviet Submarine Problem

A dramatic increase in full-time U.S. Navy presence began in mid-1978, with the beginning of the Iranian revolution. When the American embassy in Tehran was stormed on November 4, 1979, the Carter administration dispatched a second carrier battle group to the northern Arabian Sea. It was this that triggered the increase in the size of the Soviet Indian Ocean Squadron mentioned above.

The Soviet increase included more submarines. The three to five submarines in the Soviet Indian Ocean Squadron were a major headache for U.S. Navy forces operating in the same body of water. The Soviet Navy began a nearly continuous SSN presence and increased the number of conventional *Foxtrot*-class diesel/electric boats. The SSNs often included two Victor IIIs, the Soviet Navy's most modern.[19] Suddenly, keeping track of Soviet SSNs and an occasional Charlie-class SSGN in these waters became a major operational task for the Americans. Regional U.S. commanders accordingly requested substantial resources: a full range of air, surface, and submarine ASW assets, as well as air bases from where land-based maritime patrol aircraft could operate. Eventually, Soviet submarines could be tracked by dedicated assets from the time they entered the Indian Ocean until they arrived on station.[20] This preoccupation was partly dictated by the unlikely but nagging concern that the Soviets might launch a surprise attack, but more immediately by fear of being embarrassed by a Soviet submarine slipping through the carrier screen undetected and making its presence known within close firing range—a naval "gotcha" moment (and something the PLA Navy did to a U.S. carrier in 2006).[21]

Everything changed when Mikhail Gorbachev became general secretary of the Communist Party of the Soviet Union in 1985. He instituted a new look in Soviet foreign policy, making it less menacing, promoting *glasnost'* (openness) and *perestroika* (restructuring) at home and pledging peace and cooperation abroad. This policy shift had a direct impact on the Soviet naval posture in the Indian Ocean. By 1986, submarines were no longer deployed to the region. Reconnaissance aircraft deployments to Aden ceased, and the Soviets abandoned the facilities at Ethiopia's Dahlak Island and Yemen's Socotra Island. In February 1991 a final withdrawal from the Indian Ocean region occurred: the Soviet Indian Ocean Squadron sailed home.[22] Ten months later the Soviet Union put itself out of business.

The "So What" Question

What is the relevance of this twenty-year slice of Cold War history? The short answer is, "It depends." It depends first on what Beijing's Central Military Commission decides to do in coming years about PLA Navy presence in the Indian Ocean. This brief summary of the last two decades of the Cold War in the Indian Ocean is intended as a cautionary tale, an example of how a modest naval presence—then by the Soviets, today by the Chinese—can dramatically grow and have a decided impact on the balance of power in the western half of the Indian Ocean. It also depends on how one forecasts the future of the Sino-U.S. relationship. Will it continue to be as contentious as today? This seems likely, because on the American side there is widespread bipartisan support in Congress and among Asia security specialists for the Trump administration's decision to shift the strategic context of America's relationship with China from "engagement" to "strategic competition."[23] The rationale for this change was first describing the White House's 2017 *National Security Strategy* (NSS), released over President Trump's signature, which declared, "A geopolitical competition between free and repressive visions of world order is taking place in the Indo-Pacific region."[24]

Before 2017 there was a more or less "live and let live" relationship between the United States and China in the Indian Ocean region. since then strategic competition between the two, playing out largely in the political and economic realms, has arrived, largely because Washington has elected to become more competitive. This competition is relatively new for Washington, but it is not new for the region. New Delhi and Beijing have been engaged for many years in strategic competition with respect to political and economic relationships with India's neighbors—

Sri Lanka, the Maldives, Bangladesh, and of course with India's traditional antagonist Pakistan. The ongoing contestation between India and China for strategic partners and military access now coexists with one between Washington and Beijing.

America's approach to competition has largely been confined to outspokenly critical U.S. government analysis of "Chinese debt-trap diplomacy," a reference to loans associated with building or expanding port and airport facilities along the Twenty-First-Century Maritime Silk Road.[25] More significantly for the security implications of competition, the NSS also expanded the official scope of America's Asian security interests from its traditional East Asian and Pacific Ocean orientations to include the Indian Ocean. It defined the "Indo-Pacific" as stretching from the west coast of India to that of the United States.[26] This definition confused many, since it left out much of the western Indian Ocean and virtually all of the Arabian Sea, where the PLA Navy has been most active. In practice, this does not really matter, because policy has treated the Indian Ocean region seamlessly. The fact that the Trump administration's definition of the Indo-Pacific does not cover the entire Indian Ocean does not change the reality of the expansion of the geographic scope of security interests to include the region. To emphasize this shift, the name of combatant command responsible for it was changed to U.S. Indo-Pacific Command.[27] In short, the American 2017 strategy document should be considered the opening shot in an expansion of Sino-U.S. competition to the Indian Ocean region.

As a follow-on to the NSS, the Pentagon produced two additional strategy documents, first the 2018 *National Military Strategy* and then the 2019 *Department of Defense Indo-Pacific Strategy Report*. They both doubled down on competition, asserting that China "seeks *Indo-Pacific regional hegemony* in the near-term and displacement of the United States to achieve global preeminence in the future."[28] The documents provide no evidence for this claim, nor do they define the nature of the "hegemony" Beijing seeks. Hegemony is commonly understood as some blend of leadership, dominance, and predominant influence or authority. It has been commonplace to suggest that China ultimately seeks to play the leading role in East Asia and wants to supplant the United States as the predominant power in that region. What these two official U.S. government claims imply, however, is that China's hegemonic ambitions are no longer limited to the western Pacific region but now include the Indian Ocean region as well. We should soon know: if China does have hegemonic goals, an early manifestation should be an increase in its military presence in the region.

Comparing the Soviet Experience to China's Current Indian Ocean Posture

Among the obvious differences between today and the Cold War period just discussed is that today's U.S. Navy posture in the Indian Ocean is the direct opposite of that of the 1970s. Then the American footprint was tiny, and the Soviets', from the late 1960s, was substantial. Today it is the PLA that has the small footprint, whereas the U.S. Fifth Fleet, headquartered in Bahrain, is the predominant naval power in the western Indian Ocean. The other obvious difference is that the Soviet motivation for involvement in the Indian Ocean was ideological, the philosophical political-economic struggle between communism and capitalism (the free world); it was a zero-sum, often violent, struggle between the communist bloc led by Soviet Union and (at least originally) "Red" China and the "West," led by the United States, to gather like-minded states to their respective sides.

Geoeconomics Is the Reason the PLA Is in the Indian Ocean

Serious geoeconomic Chinese considerations regarding the security implications of its growing economic footprint along the Indian Ocean predate by a decade Xi Jinping's 2013 kickoff of the Belt and Road Initiative. As a result of its study and analysis, the CMC concluded that the nation's growing overseas economic interests had created political and security issues that needed to be addressed. This judgment was made public in 2004, when the PLA's top mission guidance was changed. The party secretary, then Hu Jintao, announced as head of the CMC a new set of "Strategic Missions and Objectives" for the Chinese armed forces.[29] This document was a major turning point in Chinese thinking about the role of the PLA Navy, in that it assigned to the military a greater role in "safeguarding China's expanding national interests." It called on all the armed forces to broaden their views of security to account for China's evolving national interests, especially its expanding global economic footprint (comprising in part overseas investment and the number of

Chinese civilians abroad, particularly in Africa). It also emphasized the central importance of imported natural resources, especially oil. What it meant was that the entire PLA needed to become more expeditionary and that the navy, in turn, needed to develop blue-water capabilities—to become able eventually to provide security as far away as East Africa.

Experience in Distant-Theater Naval Operations

When the Soviet Navy decided to create the Soviet Indian Ocean Squadron (*Eskadra*, in Russian) in the late 1960s it had already learned how to sustain squadrons or flotillas in the eastern Mediterranean to pursue national political objectives; what was new was logistical support thousands of miles away. The Soviets' solution was permanently mooring support ships—repair ships, berthing barges, oilers, dry cargo carriers, etc.—in politically friendly ports or roadsteads by which its warships could be provisioned and maintained. This was a rough approximation of the U.S. Navy approach during the Pacific campaign of World War II.

Looking to the future, this is a technique the PLA Navy could employ if it decides to create a larger footprint independent of its anti-piracy mission. To be sure, China has so far never created and deployed a naval squadron expressly for broad regional political, economic, or security objectives. But over time PLA Navy leadership has learned to capitalize on the counterpiracy presence in the northern Arabian Sea, as we have seen. This would not be possible if their ships were not operationally reliable. It is doubtful that the PLA Navy would send ships after six or so months of steady operations to remote West African or eastern Mediterranean ports, far from ready maintenance support, if it were worried about them breaking down. Beijing's use of the PLA Navy as a diplomatic tool, flying the flag and showing off its handsome new ships in distant ports, is very much in the tradition of how the United States and other powers employed their navies in the post–World War II period.

Basing Issues

One of the most obvious similarities between the Soviet IO experience and China's current activity is the desire for basing facilities in the Horn of Africa. At first glance the Soviets appear to have been more ambitious, because their political-ideological agenda. Over a twenty-year span in and around the Horn of Africa the Soviets established major naval and air support facilities in Berbera, Somalia; Ethiopia's Dahlak Islands in the Red Sea; and Aden and Socotra Island in the PDRY.

China is as eager as the Soviets were to gain access in as many places as possible along the Indian Ocean littoral, especially the Horn of Africa. But their approach is distinctive, one that can be characterized by the phrase "place and base." That is, China has many places potentially available to it, thanks to friendly political relations with most of the littoral nations. In many of them the ubiquitous COSCO and other state-owned enterprises reliably provide food, fuel, fresh water, and especially shore electrical power (without which ships' generators cannot be shut down for maintenance).[30]

This sort of support was adequate for counterpiracy task forces for nine years, but Beijing eventually found it necessary to abandon its long-standing condemnation of overseas bases as hegemonic. The navy now realized it needed something more substantial and permanent than places to pull into for food, fuel, and liberty ashore. Like the Soviets, the Chinese navy wanted something of its own—a *base*. As a result, we now have the spectacle of Beijing rationalizing Djibouti as a logistics "outpost," as a necessary contribution to regional security and development—which Djibouti might well be.

The attractiveness of politically stable Djibouti as basing facility—for the United States, Japan, France, Italy, and now China—contrasts usefully with the political turmoil in host countries that bedeviled the Soviets, and to a lesser degree the Americans, during the Cold War. China reached agreement with the government of Djibouti in 2015 and by August 1, 2017, had opened its first overseas base. In return, the president of Djibouti was granted a four-day state visit to Beijing, where a number of economic deals were arranged.[31]

When it comes to sea-lanes, the significance of the port of Djibouti and the adjacent port of Doraleh, located as they are at the Bab el Mandeb choke point (leading to the Red Sea and Suez Canel) is obvious. In addition however, it can support PLA Navy missions that are not related to antipiracy. This is not a modest facility: it has the potential, and likely the mission, to support Chinese UN peacekeeping forces in Africa, stage Chinese diplomats, businessmen, or laborers evacuated from troubled African countries, contribute to both PLA Navy presence throughout the western Indian Ocean and, in case of crisis with India or the United States, the protection of sea-lanes.

Crucially, this facility also provides the PLA with a permanent intelligence focal point, one that can provide PLA forces in the region with evaluated, finished regional information. Significantly, it appears large enough to become in the future the headquarters of a PLA regional commander, conceivably with responsibility for PLA Navy activities throughout some portion of the Indian Ocean. Finally, unlike the Soviets, the Chinese have significant and legitimate economic and interests in the Horn of Africa that make the Djibouti facility practical and understandable. These latter are clearly spelled out in an *East Asia Forum* article:

> China's capital exports to Africa are on the rise. . . . China's stock of overseas direct investment in Africa more than doubled between 2011 and 2015 from US$16 billion to $35 billion. China also extended loans totaling US$63 billion to African nations for power, transport and other projects over the same period.
>
> This growth of investment in and lending to Africa has contributed to an increase in Chinese citizens on the continent. Official Chinese statistics show that from 2011–15 the number of Chinese citizens working in Africa increased from 180,000 to 264,000, while unofficial estimates of the overall number of Chinese citizens in Africa range from 1 to 2 million. China also continues to be a large contributor to UN peacekeeping efforts in Africa—particularly in South Sudan, where Beijing has invested billions in the oil sector.[32]

Some 1,500 nm east of Djibouti across the Arabian Sea lies the Pakistani port of Gwadar. It is perfectly placed to become a base for PLA Navy ships patrolling the approaches to the Strait of Hormuz. The Soviets did not have to worry about oil sea-lanes from the Persian Gulf; China does. According to the U.S. Department of Defense, Gwadar is likely to be the next "place" Beijing chooses to make into a base.[33] In 2015, China obtained a forty-year lease to manage the port. Gwadar is the maritime terminus of the China-Pakistan Economic Corridor (CPEC), an ambitious project that includes highways, dams, hydropower, railways, and pipelines.[34]

Making Friends in the Indian Ocean Region

The Soviets capitalized on the popularity of socialist or Marxist political-economic systems among emerging nations and on the ability of their own defense industry to produce military assistance in massive amounts to gain and sustain "friendships" in the region. China too wants regional relationships but is using different tools. Where the Soviets offered Marxist political mentorship and modern weapons at "friendship prices," Beijing eschewed (until the beginning of Xi's second five years in office) any hint of political competition and instead offered "win-win" economic arrangements (infrastructure development, no-questions-asked loans) to gain access. To this package Xi now adds its own model of development and techniques of social control as a ways for fellow authoritarians to maintain political stability.[35]

China's move into Djibouti has a significant and specific economic component. It relates to Ethiopia, which has been among Africa's fastest-growing economies and the leading investment destination in sub-Saharan Africa for China. Between 2006 and 2015 Chinese entities loaned more than $13 billion for infrastructure and industrial parks, although in 2018 investment slackened, on concerns about Ethiopia's political instability.[36] The Addis Ababa–Djibouti Railway was built between 2011 and 2016 by the two Chinese companies that also manage the railway and operate its passenger, freight, and maintenance services. It links Addis Ababa in Ethiopia with the port of Doraleh in Djibouti. It provides landlocked Ethiopia with railroad access to the sea: more than 95 percent of Ethiopia's trade passes through Djibouti, accounting for 70 percent of the activity at the port of Djibouti.[37] China has over four hundred separate investment projects representing four billion U.S. dollars' worth of foreign direct investment (FDI) in Ethiopia.[38] But the June 2019 coup attempt in Ethiopia will have reminded Beijing, just as the Soviets were reminded before them, that with Horn of Africa nations long-term political stability can never be assumed.[39]

The Twenty-First-Century Maritime Silk Road

The Soviet Navy was sent to the Indian Ocean region out of political opportunism, to lend tangible support to the many newly independent colonies Moscow hoped to enlist as card-carrying members of the global socialist camp. China, for its part, comes seeking raw materials, investment opportunities, and export markets. It comes also because the most cost-effective way to transport its exports to the Middle East Africa and Europe is by sea through the Indian Ocean. By 2013, when Xi Jinping inaugurated the BRI, the "the maritime silk road" sea-lane was a long-established fact.

As we saw in the first chapter, the series of interrelated sea-lanes that run from China's major ports through the Indonesian straits, along the Indian Ocean's northern littoral and East Africa (including Djibouti), up the Red Sea, and through the ancient predecessors of the Suez Canal into the eastern Mediterranean have formed a trading route for millennia. This "road" has in modern times been heavily traveled by China's shipping, as well as that of other nations. Notwithstanding the emergence of piracy as a serious concern for a few years, the fact is that since the end of World War II no country has attempted to severe this link. Today it is implicitly guarded by maritime nations along the way—especially Australia and India—and by forward-deployed U.S. naval forces.

The piracy problem had in large measure dissipated by 2017, but the PLA Navy antipiracy patrols continued relentlessly. This suggests a broader interest by Beijing: it wants the presence of Chinese warships in the far reaches of the Indian Ocean to become normal, a fact of life. The downturn in piracy has permitted the implicit broadening of the mission of its counterpiracy task force to encompass the full range of operational responsibilities implicit in the phrase "safeguarding China's expanding national interests." It should also be noted that the PLA Navy is a still a relative newcomer to the blue-water navy club, so training and gaining experience are important to the PLA Navy's professional development even if there are few pirates to shoo away. Just as forward deployments are a way of life in the U.S. Navy in peace or war, for the PLA Navy there is no substitute for actually operating ships for months at a time thousands of miles away from home bases and overcoming the challenges that arise there.

Submarines in the Indian Ocean

From the earliest days of the Soviet naval presence in the Indian Ocean, submarines formed an important part of it. PLA Navy submarines have belatedly begun to do the same, deploying to the Indian Ocean and apparently to the Arabian Sea as part of antipiracy task forces. Because submarines remain the most difficult type of warship to keep track of, the Chinese have in this way triggered anxiety on the part of the Indian navy, which worries about its own sea-lanes to East Africa and the Persian Gulf. Prior experience with the Soviets suggests that, depending on the pace of PLA Navy submarine deployments to the region, it may be necessary for the United States and perhaps its allies to develop a theater-wide approach to submarine monitoring, one that includes Australia and India.[40]

One reason for the Soviets' naval presence in the Indian Ocean was anxiety over suspected American SSBN deployments there. Today, the issue has reemerged, with an entirely different cast of players. In August 2016, India commissioned its first SSBN, INS *Arihant*. This indigenously built submarine is the first of a planned class of five. In November 2018 *Arihant* was declared operationally ready, having completed its first deterrence patrol.[41] New Delhi's goal is an assured nuclear second-strike capability against Pakistan and China. This is a new threat for China, one that raises the question of whether it should respond by mounting an effort to keep track of India's SSBNs or by deploying its own SSBNs to the Indian Ocean and thereby threatening India from a new and different azimuth.[42]

Implications for the Future

Consider that China is making major investments all the way from the MSR's western termini in Italy and Greece, through the Suez Canal and Red Sea to Ethiopia and Djibouti, along the littoral of the subcontinent to Pakistan, Sri Lanka, and the Maldives, through the Indonesian straits, to home. Beijing is unlikely to remain willingly dependent on the forward-stationed naval power of the United States and India for sea-lane security. After all, navies have the ability to interrupt sea-lanes as well as guard them. Starting from the western Indian Ocean, it is the U.S. Fifth Fleet that is the predominant naval force; in the central and eastern Indian Ocean it is the Indian navy that is supreme; while in the eastern Indian Ocean and approaches to the Indonesian straits stand the Australian navy and U.S. Seventh Fleet. Collectively these forces hold the security of China's Maritime Silk Road in their hands.

All this suggests that as China's stake in the Indian Ocean expands Beijing will call upon its navy to introduce more capability into the region, to redress the current imbalance there in maritime power. This means

Chapter Seven

there will eventually be more Chinese bases present and more warships
rotating in and out.

The PLA Navy already has all the necessary pieces in hand—carrier air,
land-attack cruise missiles on multimission destroyers, sophisticated air-
defense-capable destroyers, antisubmarine-warfare frigates, multiproduct
replenishment ships, and large amphibious ships—to assemble into a very
credible multimission naval task force. China now has the second-largest
modern amphibious capability in the world (after the United States), probably able to embark between five and six thousand marines for operations
anywhere in the world. Such a force, escorted by modern destroyers and
frigates and defended by an aircraft carrier, would surely represent true
PLA power projection.

During the Cold War, Washington saw its competition for access
as a zero-sum game. That is not the case today, as the case of Djibouti
illustrates. If there is a game for influence today it is between New Delhi
and Beijing; Washington is not playing. Washington pursues access and
basing agreements with Indian Ocean littoral states based solely on its
military needs and (so far) does not actively seek to counter Chinese
attempts to gain influence.

Beijing's fixation with SLOC defense and the related protection of
the maritime leg of BRI has put the PLA Navy into an unfamiliar situation. The PLA Navy is forced to play an "away game" and operate in
the shadow of the most capable military in the region, that of India. But
India, other than preventing terrorists from landing along its extensive
coastline, apparently has no unifying theory for the defense of maritime
approaches, nothing that resembles China's A2/AD. Until now, India
has not needed one. In the future, though, depending on New Delhi's
perception of the PLA Navy's presence, India may need to capitalize
on its geographic position to put in place a joint area-denial capability
to defend its maritime interests. A useful example would be Australia,
in the eastern Indian Ocean, where very capable armed forces already
pursue a sea-denial-based defense strategy that couples submarines,
land-based airpower, and advanced open-ocean surveillance.

Should the PLA Navy begin to maintain a routine naval presence
in the Indian Ocean in addition to its antipiracy operations, it can be
expected to increase Indian apprehension regarding long-term Chinese objectives. That could increase its incentives for an even closer

Indian-American naval relationship. The pace of that relationship's strengthening will naturally be dictated by the overall state of Sino-Indian relations; however, it is conceivable that an increase in PLA Navy presence, especially submarines, could result in some sort of combined India-U.S. ASW organization. China's growing regional influence generally has spurred Indian engagement with its near neighbors, Sri Lanka and the Maldives, as well as with the islands states of Mauritius and the Seychelles.

It is reasonable to suggest that by mid-decade the PLA Navy could keep a carrier-centered group of from fifteen to twenty ships in the western Indian Ocean. Assuming a generous turnaround ratio (i.e., how many units one must own to keep one on station continuously) of five to one, the PLA Navy could now maintain eighteen warships in the western Indian Ocean full-time. The major shortfall is in carrier-based aircraft: such a group would not now always enjoy carrier-based air. The gap could potentially be filled by fighters flying out of Djibouti or Gwadar. This makeshift would have its own problems, a major one being host-nation approval. Also, China would have to construct the fields—expensive and controversial at best, in the case of Djibouti involving the upgrading of an existing airfield adjacent to China's base that is too short for military jets. (Experts from Djibouti suggest in personal conversation, however, that the runway could be readily extended into the Indian Ocean to be made capable of handling military aircraft.)

In short, it is entirely possible that by 2025 China's blue water force could be around 150, including three carriers. It seems very likely that for the reasons discussed here Beijing will gradually build up its daily presence in the Indian Ocean, beyond the antipiracy deployers.

The strategic impetus would be Sino-U.S. competition. Despite China's formulaic protestations that its intentions are peaceful, Indian Ocean nations will presumably become more concerned as PLA Navy presence grows. This has already happened in East Asia, where China's desire to ensure its own security through military modernization and an assertive posture has made its neighbors feel less secure.

This future is not preordained. The CMC could easily conclude that protecting a sea-lane across the Indian Ocean is simply not feasible and accordingly keep the majority of its blue-water navy active in East Asia. It may well conclude that its naval-presence needs can continue to be met as they have been for the last decade—with a handful of ships. That the

CMC would so choose, however, given the investment already made in Djibouti, the continuing importance of the Maritime Silk Road, and Xi Jinping's "world-class navy," seems unlikely. The U.S. Department of Defense holds that Djibouti is just the first step, that "a more robust overseas logistics and basing infrastructure would allow China to project and sustain military power at greater distances. China's advancement of projects such as the 'One Belt, One Road' Initiative (OBOR) will probably drive military overseas basing through a perceived need to provide security for OBOR projects. China will seek to establish additional military bases in countries with which it has a longstanding friendly relationship and similar strategic interests, such as Pakistan."[43]

The past may indeed be prologue in the Indian Ocean.

CHAPTER EIGHT

Opposite Sides of the Same Coin

Maritime Power and the PLA Navy

This book has briefly explored the operational history of the PLA Navy in the twenty-first century as it matured and expanded beyond the imagination of most foreign observers, perhaps even beyond the hopes and dreams of some within the navy itself. It has explored how the PLA Navy might be employed at home and abroad and has speculated that it may be on a trajectory leading to permanently deployed major naval formations in the western Indian Ocean. The Chinese achieved none of this by accident. The world is witnessing the fruits of careful, long-range strategic planning, mixed with what the Chinese themselves would call "the objective facts" of the PRC's geoeconomic circumstances. These "facts" have resulted in a truly remarkable public acknowledgement from the military of an ancient continental power that "the traditional mentality that land outweighs sea must be abandoned, and great importance has to be attached to managing the seas and oceans and protecting maritime rights and interests."[1] "Managing oceans" starts with control, and "protecting interests" requires a navy. As those interests grew, so too did the necessity for a great one. If there were any doubts about this within China's leadership, especially in senior uniformed ranks, what seems to have tipped the scales toward greatness, to world-class stature, is the ambition—what Xi Jinping has dubbed the "China Dream"—to restore (as Xi sees it) the nation to a position of global preeminence. This is not the vision of Xi alone; his predecessor too linked military power with growing global stature.

The PRC's newfound enthusiasm for things maritime of necessity required development of all the capabilities associated with maritime power, especially shipbuilding, a large merchant marine under the state's control, and first-rate port facilities. The PRC has done all of this and more. Restoring what the Chinese consider China's ancient position of centrality takes more than rhetorical exhortations. It takes the tangible capacity and capability that the PRC's go-out strategy brings. Announced in 1999, "going out" unleashed a torrent of investment around the world, accompanied by characteristic Chinese entrepreneurial skill. The aim was to gather foreign know-how by purchase or other means, secure guaranteed access to raw materials and food, and create business opportunities abroad, many of them dedicated to global, especially maritime, trade.[2] As many observers have noted, "going out" might be better called "going global," with the Belt and Road Initiative as the primary example.

Beijing realizes that its maritime great-power goal encompasses more than just naval strength; Xi Jinping's goal that the PLA Navy became "a world-class navy" is widely seen—correctly, in my judgment—as a prerequisite of great maritime power. For Xi, building China into a maritime power "is of great and far-reaching significance for promoting sustained and healthy economic development, safeguarding national sovereignty, security and development interests, realizing the goal of completing the building of a well-off society, and subsequently realizing the great rejuvenation of the Chinese nation."[3] This linkage—maritime power with the China Dream—makes it a foregone conclusion that maritime power and a navy of world class are not passing fancies but firmly embedded in the grand strategy of the PRC.

That they are is related to the need "to control." Under Xi, strengthening party control has become an obsession, and it is no surprise that he perceives control as one of the great advantages of maritime power. The Chinese Communist Party's theoretical journal has authoritatively made this connection, laying it down that historically a country that was a great maritime power was one that could "exert its great comprehensive power to develop, utilize, protect, manage, and control oceans." China, it declared, would not become a maritime power until it could control its maritime sovereignty, rights, and interests and deal with the threat of containment from the sea.[4]

For the PLA Navy "controlling oceans" includes addressing the "threat of containment from the sea." It is essentially a concrete military "requirement," one that underwrites the "requirement" for a world-class navy, since the only country that could hope to contain China happens to be the only one with a world-class navy. The idea of "containment from the sea" rests on the belief, as the 2005 edition of the PLA's *Science of Military Strategy* puts it, that "the predominant strategic power [read United States] who is unwilling to see the rising and growing of new powers always [tries] to contain them before their rise." In any case, China's "lifeline to communicate with the outside world" is the collectivity of its sea-lanes, the defense of which is a very complex problem.[5]

Being put upon by foreign naval powers is not a new experience for China. The "Century of Humiliation," which did not end until 1949, had to be endured because China's navy and its army-manned maritime defenses were too weak to prevent foreigners from invading, carving up, and imposing their will on China. Today, Beijing is determined not to be weak, especially at sea, but worries that the United States is able to prevent it from achieving the China Dream by virtue of its ability to amass power in China's near seas. Finally, maritime power is associated with so many of the world's historically dominant powers.[6] While it is important not to overstress this element, it is also true that in the nineteenth and twentieth centuries nations with "world-class navies" were also world powers and actors of global consequence.

Even before Xi used the language of "world class," the idea that China required a "powerful" navy was the conceptual center of its maritime ambitions.[7] The Chinese quite logically conclude that the sine qua non of maritime power is the ability to control waters where China's "maritime rights and interests" are involved, to enforce those maritime rights and interests, and to deter or defeat attempts by the United States to derail China's growth by choking off its maritime commerce. In the view of experts in the PRC, until it can do all this China cannot be considered a maritime power.[8]

Addressing SLOC Anxiety

A major theme of this book has been Beijing's worries about the security of its seaborne trade. The 2013 edition of *Science of Military Strategy* notes that more than thirty key sea-lanes of communication link China to over 1,200 ports in 150 countries and that these SLOCs are vital "lifelines" for the nation's economy and social development. The prominence given to SLOC protection and the protection of overseas Chinese citizens and interests in both the 2015 DWP and the *Science of Military Strategy* leaves little doubt that SLOC security will continue to be a major preoccupation for the PLA Navy. Certainly it remains one in China's latest (July 2019) defense white paper, *China's National Defense in the New Era*, which is at pains to highlight the importance of "maintaining the security of strategic SLOCs."[9]

Nevertheless, and despite its impressive growth, the PLA Navy's shortcomings become obvious when one considers it fighting alone, away from the friendly shore-based air and missile forces of the western Pacific. This has not been a worry during the decade of peacetime operations in the Indian Ocean, but these deployments are nonetheless constant reminders that in crisis or conflict in the Indian Ocean or mid-Pacific the PLA Navy would be conducting "protection missions in the far seas" without air cover. Yet it is in those very waters that the PLA Navy would be expected to defend China's SLOCs or overseas interests and citizens, and even possibly in the eastern Mediterranean, where the Maritime Silk Road terminates at Greek and Italian ports. These operations would be "road games," played under the air superiority of the Indian air forces or the carrier-based airpower of the United States.

If I seem to keep referring to air cover for surface ships that do not have it but are in range of hostile air forces, I do so because it is crucially important. Adm. Liu Huaqing recognized the vulnerability of ships operating alone. He did so on the basis of an accurate appreciation of what happened in World War II, notably the sinking by Japanese land-based aircraft (flying from Vietnam) of the battleship HMS *Prince of Wales* and the battle cruiser HMS *Repulse* in the South China Sea three days after Pearl Harbor. These ships had been operating without air support. In his writings—in the days before the airfield on Woody Island in the Paracels was built—Admiral Liu worried about the risk of sending ships to the Spratlys and southern part of the South China Sea. The potential threat (thanks in part to a large air force "inherited" from the former government of South Vietnam) from the newly established Socialist Republic of Vietnam was his major concern. Neither the Chinese navy nor air force had aircraft that could cover ships that far from Hainan. This is why he became an early and persistent advocate of a Chinese aircraft carrier.[10]

The nagging problem of "containment from the sea" is largely one of sea-lane protection, a problem that exists in both the PRC's near and far seas and will not go away as long as the possibility of conflict with the United States remains. If military planners in Beijing hope to ameliorate it, the PLA must develop the kind of air and missile power that can support its navy in distant seas. That means a combination of overseas bases with access rights for land-based fighters (similar to what the United States enjoys), land-based antiship missiles stationed abroad, and anti-access surveillance that covers the Indian Ocean and cues long-range ASBMs like the DF-26. (I assume that the PRC already has the ability to surveil the Indian Ocean; whether it can do so with the accuracy and timeliness required for ASBM employment is another matter.) The evidence suggests that Beijing realizes a larger, more sophisticated carrier-based air force is going to be necessary as well—two carriers are in commission, and a much larger third one is building.

Those capabilities and overseas facilities with airfields and PLA garrisons will not appear overnight, if they do at all. But they could by 2035. There are many diplomatic obstacles to overcome, but that they could be is not out of the question: Beijing is persistent, wealthy, and well armed. The PLA Navy's stature and reputation have gone from insignificance to impressiveness in the past fifteen years, and it is possible that fifteen years hence China might be in a position to contest seriously for control of waters anywhere its sea-lanes and interests are to be found.

When the maritime-power objective was announced in 2012, the Obama administration's "rebalance" or "pivot" to the Pacific was much in the news. Many Chinese analysts were writing that U.S. presence in the western Pacific was now going to be an impediment to Chinese maritime ambitions. The rebalance was widely misinterpreted in Asia as a dramatic buildup of American power in East Asia. It was never intended to be that, and sure enough, it was not.[11] But believing itself faced with that prospect, China charged ahead, strengthening and expanding every conceivable facet of maritime power, especially the navy, coast guard, and maritime militia. It has thrown resources and human talent at the problem so unrestrainedly that it now has the largest navy, coast guard, and maritime militia in the world. Nor, as the U.S. Defense Department clearly sees, are they "junkyard" forces:

The majority of China's missile programs, including its ballistic- and cruise-missile systems, are comparable to other international top-tier producers. China's production of a wide range of ballistic, cruise, air-to-air, and SAMs for the PLA and for export has probably been enhanced by upgrades to primary assembly and solid rocket motor production facilities.

China's aviation industry has advanced to produce a large transport aircraft; modern fourth- to fifth-generation fighters incorporating low-observable technologies; modern reconnaissance and attack UAVs; and attack helicopters. China's commercial aircraft industry has invested in high-precision and technologically advanced machine tooling and production processes, avionics, and other components applicable to the production of military aircraft. However, China's aircraft industry remains reliant on foreign-sourced components for dependable, proven, high-performance aircraft engines.

China is the top ship-producing nation in the world and has increased its shipbuilding capacity and capability for all types of military projects, including submarines, surface combatants, naval aviation, sealift, and amphibious assets. China's two largest state-owned shipbuilders—the China State Shipbuilding Corporation and Shipbuilding Industry Corporation—collaborate in shared ship designs and construction information to increase shipbuilding efficiency. China now produces its naval gas turbine and diesel engines domestically—as well as almost all shipboard weapons and electronic systems—and is almost entirely self-sufficient with little dependence on traditional foreign suppliers for shipbuilding.[12]

Xi Jinping's October 2013 renaming as the "Twenty-First-Century Maritime Silk Road" of a centuries-old, well-traveled, and very long sea-lane raised its strategic importance and removed any doubt that maritime power was for the PRC a global, not regional, ambition. To be sure, many of China's maritime concerns will remain concentrated in regional waters—that is, the near seas—but the 2015 DWP indicated that its maritime strategy was moving from single-minded "offshore waters defense" to broader, global strategic missions. Now, five years later, that objective remains urgent: the 2019 DWP states, "The PLAN *is speeding up* the transition of its tasks from defense in the near seas to protection missions on the far seas."[13]

By Any Objective Measure China Is a Great Maritime Power Today

It is not as if China embarked on a quest for maritime power with a metaphorical blank sheet of paper. When in late 2012 the goal was announced, China was already a world leader in shipbuilding by tonnage; it had the world's largest fishing industry (one that has since continued to grow); and its merchant marine was close to being number one in total ship count (today it is first). Its navy and coast guard are the largest such services in the world, by ship count. In sum, in terms of tangible measures—warships and civilian vessels of all kinds and the infrastructure needed to maintain them and build more—China already is a maritime power.

The excellent contributed appendices are in-depth looks at, respectively, the Chinese Coast Guard and the PLA Maritime Militia. Both play significant roles in asserting the PRC's "maritime rights and interests," frequently with a very heavy hand, in both the South and East China Seas. Their combined activities have become so notorious that the U.S. Department of State was compelled in July 2019 to protest, and (as diplomats say) very "frankly" state:

The United States is concerned by reports of . . . China's repeated provocative actions aimed at the offshore oil and gas development of other claimant states threaten regional energy security and undermine the free and open Indo-Pacific energy market.

As Secretary Pompeo noted earlier this year, "by blocking development in the SCS through coercive means, China prevents ASEAN members from accessing more than $2.5 trillion in recoverable energy reserves."

China's reclamation and militarization of disputed outposts in the SCS, along with other efforts to assert its unlawful SCS maritime claims, including the use of maritime militia to intimidate, coerce, and threaten other nations, undermine the peace and security of the region.

China's growing pressure on ASEAN countries to accept Code of Conduct provisions that seek to restrict their right to partner with third party companies or countries further reveal its intent to assert control over oil and gas resources in the South China Sea.

The United States firmly opposes coercion and intimidation by any claimant to assert its territorial or maritime claims.

China should cease its bullying behavior and refrain from engaging in this type of provocative and destabilizing activity.[14]

When one considers all the categories that collectively add up to comprehensive maritime power—navy, coast guard, militia, merchant marine, port infrastructure, shipbuilding, fishing—one sees that China is already is already the global leader, or is among the top two or three in the world.[15] No other country can match China's maritime capabilities across the board. For example, the United States has the world's leading navy, but in terms of quantity, and some cases quality, its shipbuilding, merchant marine, coast guard, and fisheries pale in comparison with China's. In 2013, China caught 16.3 million tons of fish compared to the American 5.2 million tons. The comparison of coast guard cutters (those of over five hundred tons) is equally stark: Chinese Coast Guard, 225, versus U.S. Coast Guard, 40.

So much of this book having been about SLOCs, let us end with a brief look at the Chinese merchant marine that travels them. China's goal is self-sufficiency in sea trade.[16] During the past ten years, China's state-owned merchant fleet has more than tripled in size. As of January 2018, the nation owned some 5,552 ships, well ahead of Greece (4,371) and Japan (3,841). For comparison, the United States is in sixth place, owning 2,073 ships.[17] In determining the size of merchant fleets, much depends on what you count. For example, while China owns more ships than Greece or Japan, in total deadweight tonnage (DWT) it slips to third, behind these two countries. What this means is that Greece owns more very large ships, a great many more. Its holdings are slightly over 330,000,000 DWT, China's only 183,000,000.

Nonetheless, China does have a very big merchant fleet, and we can expect continued growth. The European Council on Foreign Relations reports that only 25 percent of Chinese trade is carried by its shipping companies; this is not self-sufficiency.[18] Trying to reach that goal accounts for the pace of growth of China's merchant marine, faster than anywhere else in the entire world fleet, in all ship types.[19]

China's merchant marine also has a military role. It is becoming more integrated into routine PLA operations, compensating for shortcomings in the PLA's organic long-distance sealift capacity. Large roll-on/roll-off (Ro-Ro) ships already participate regularly in PLA exercises, and they support troop and unit movements for all services. This is likely to increase as more civilian ships are built to national defense specifications and the military operates farther from China's coasts.[20]

The PLA Navy, moreover, does not have to fight alone in the western Pacific. The combat power of the PLA Air Force and Rocket Force would change the equation in favor of China, at least until the United States could organize and bring to bear the power to gain and maintain sea control in the western Pacific. This situation is going to become worse (from the Western viewpoint) as the PLA Navy adds capability, especially more submarines. Some day the PLA will be able to claim it could keep the United States at bay long enough for China to accomplish its objectives against Taiwan or Japan.

The total PLA Navy warship/submarine/replenishment ship strength today is in the range of three hundred. As of this writing the U.S. Navy is projected to have force structure of around 264 *similar classes* of ships by the end of 2020.[21] While the American number includes many more high-end ships, the number of warships and submarines the PLA Navy will be able to muster for a maritime campaign in China's near seas continues to grow.

Considerations Regarding a "World-Class" PLA

Xi's goal of a "world-class" military should be viewed as a general, high-level concept of force development and not as a strategy for how China plans to use its armed forces—an intention to catapult the PLA into the top tier of military powers. China wants to be able compete effectively against the best. One way to think about this question is to expect China to achieve widely recognized benchmarks associated with top-tier militaries today (e.g., aircraft carriers, nuclear weapons, long-range bombers, and space assets and capabilities).[22] China is also focused on the future; as the 2019 DWP reaffirms, its vision of future warfare is of one that emphasizes information technology, intelligence, surveillance, reconnaissance, and precision strike.[23]

Retrospectively, world-class militaries have been so judged and accorded that professional standing by contemporaries based on success in combat. A world-class PLA would be able to achieve the CCP's political objectives, especially in the face of armed resistance from the United States. Beijing is not looking to fight any foe at any time anywhere. It seeks to have an unsurpassed military advantage in the contingencies it assesses it may face. The primary contingency focus of the PLA is to improve its ability to conduct joint operations in a Taiwan scenario in which it has to fight the United States.

A Taiwan scenario could play out in many ways. In chapter 4 my objective was to explain how the PLA Navy would be employed by China's Central Military Commission and Eastern Theater commander in a conflict with the United States. In the scenario China elects to use force out of impatience with Taiwan's unwillingness to begin a process of becoming a province of the PRC. It would be a blatant act of aggression, despite Beijing's likely assertion that the matter of Taiwan is an internal problem and that everyone else should mind their own business. I have not attempted any judgments about how well the PLA Navy would do in this sort of conflict against two of the best navies in the world—the U.S. Navy and Japan Maritime Self-Defense Force. In short, I have not conducted a dynamic war game of my scenario.

The scenario in chapter 4 does assert, however, that Beijing has initiated a "war of choice" against Taiwan. This also means that the CCP's top leadership is going to be "all in," because they have to be: if the conflict goes badly they are going to lose their jobs and maybe more. This makes a fight over Taiwan all the more dangerous because it would engage two nuclear-armed opponents in all-out conventional war at sea and in the air. The risk of escalation to the use of nuclear weapons would be present from first shots between them. Beijing seems to appreciate this danger and when in the 2019 DWP it restated its long-held commitment to a policy of "no first use" of nuclear weapons, it added the phrase "at any time and under any circumstances." This implies that Beijing would not resort to nuclear weapons in conventional conflict over Taiwan even to forestall defeat.[24]

How Good Is the PLA Navy?

Over the years the approach the PLA Navy has taken in turning a coastal defense force into a world-class navy (at least in peacetime) has been impressively systematic. China's shipbuilding and warship-design processes are also impressive. The result is a formidable force. However, we have no real idea how well the officers and men, their networks, command-and-control systems, and weapons would perform in the stress of combat. Neither does the PLA, but judging by high-level pressure from Xi on down to improve training, it is far from confident.

PLA Navy ships and crews seem to hold up well in counterpiracy operations, which provides a clue regarding the general level of competence and equipment reliability within the navy. That, however, is peacetime: Xi Jinping as commander in chief and his CMC are painfully aware of the lack of experience in actual combat of the PLA as a whole. When Xi assumed power, the first thing that needed correction was the PRC high command: it needed to be brought into the twenty-first century. By 2015 Xi had achieved sufficient political control of the PLA to launch a major reform of the "legacy" military organizational structure. The traditional military regions were disestablished and replaced by five joint theater commands. These commands are assigned planning and war-fighting responsibilities oriented outward from China's frontiers. Theater commanders are responsible for their respective "strategic directions" and command forces from all the appropriate services; these commanders can be likened to America's regional joint-force commanders.[25]

Another major change, again mirroring the U.S. Department of Defense, was the removal of individual service headquarters from the operational chain of command. The CMC was expanded and strengthened, assuming many of the responsibilities of the now disestablished four general departments of the high command. This organizational shakeup is profound and is going to take several years to be completed. Xi set the target of 2020, but many American experts hold that it will take longer to become truly effective. Meanwhile, the command-and-control system of the PLA is in a state of flux.[26]

The most important reason behind the reform at the outset was that Xi and his trusted military advisors shared the opinion that the operational capabilities of the PLA needed to improve. The PLA needed to become a joint war-fighting force in practice, not in name only. More specifically, the objective of this very disruptive organizational initiative is to put in place a command-and-control framework that can train the PLA to prevail in "information intensive joint operations in the maritime-aerospace domain." As Dr. David Finkelstein notes, "The more vexing issues for the PLA seem to reside on the institutional side. There appear to be deep seated concerns [on the parts of Xi and the CMC] . . . that the *capacity* to produce first rate weapons and systems does not automatically translate to operational *capability*."[27]

The missing ingredient is an organizational structure that encourages—when necessary, demands—joint approaches to operational problems. But it is hard for commanders to know what to demand when they themselves have little operational know-how. The PLA is conscious that "it has not been tested in battle for many years." Apparently Xi himself has weighed in on this problem with blunt criticism of operational commanders, accusing them of shortcomings he calls the "Five Cannots." Commanders cannot:

- Analyze a situation
- Understand higher-echelon intent
- Make a decision on a course of action
- Deploy forces
- Handle unexpected situations.[28]

Coming from the boss, this is a very harsh assessment, but it is not the first the PLA has received. Much has been written over the years on the PLA's lack of combat experience, much of it by commentators within the PLA itself. As Dennis Blasko reports, PLA media organs frequently urge forces to overcome "peace disease," "peacetime habits," and "peacetime practices."[29]

I take the PLA's critics at their word, but it is possible that they are focused more on the army and air force than the navy, simply because of the nature of operations at sea. It is, however, also true that the U.S. Navy lacks experience in high-level, multidomain conflict like a Taiwan contingency. In the years since World War II, the U.S. Navy's pilots and aircrew have seen more combat than those of any other navy, and most other air forces—and they continue to do so. But they have not had to face, on a sustained basis, sophisticated air defenses or modern fighter aircraft since the end of the Vietnam War (or fighters *in large numbers* since Korea). During the Cold War American submarines, especially, operated in near-combat conditions when snooping around Soviet submarines, and they probably continue to do so around Russian and Chinese boats in certain situations, but they have not fired a torpedo in anger since

1945. Since Vietnam, the surface navy has fired many hundreds of cruise missiles, mainly at land targets, but only in a small number of cases was anyone shooting back. The last time the U.S. Navy had to fight to maintain sea control was during the Okinawa campaign in 1945—interestingly enough, in the same waters where a cross-strait conflict would take place.

During the Cold War, like all U.S. services, the Navy invested a good deal of effort at the operational and tactical levels, training to fight an enemy with a world-class fleet, many submarines, and a large number of land-based systems that could reach far out to sea. Thankfully, it never had to find out if the 1980s-era offensively oriented "Maritime Strategy" against the Soviet Union would have worked in practice as well as it did in war games. The Navy is now embarking on the same sort of focused training and serious thinking, this time exploring how to fight in a situation like the Taiwan scenario discussed in chapter 4.[30] Arguably, the PLA Navy has had the luxury of a lot more time to prepare for a battle for Taiwan, because that has been the point of its training, planning, and modernization from the outset.

A Big Uncertainty:
How Large Will the PLAN Be in 2035?

We know Xi wants a "world-class force." We know (from chapter 1) that before him Hu Jintao established an ambitious force-building objective in 2012.[31] We also already know that China's navy force-structure objective remains a state secret. A few experts like Rick Joe and James Fanell have published projections of PLA Navy strength in 2030. What follows below is my own estimate of overall PLA Navy warship strength in 2035.[32]

A good starting point is what has been done over the past fifteen years. This book has divided the PLA Navy into two pieces: one contains the units (discussed in chapter 3) that are suitable for blue-water operations, the other those that are not. Over the last fifteen years China commissioned or has launched 131 blue-water-capable ships including the carriers, surface combatants, major amphibious assault ships, submarines, and large fleet replenishment ships. In the second category are the approximately 115 warships destined for operations only in China's near seas. So, over the last decade and a half China has added a total of roughly 240 new warships to its navy. During several of these years what are now China's most modern shipyards were not yet in production, so it is not unreasonable to forecast that over the next fifteen years China could commission or launch 150 more blue-water ships in order to grow far-seas capacity and replace ships commissioned between 2005 and 2010 (around thirteen ships). In sum, my forecast of, specifically, the PLA Navy's blue-water capability in 2035 is around 265 warships.

I think the 2035 mix would include many more submarines than now, perhaps double the number. Submarines will be increasingly valued since they cannot, yet, be tracked from space. Nuclear-powered attack submarines may constitute a larger proportion of the overall submarine force. If the anticipated new nuclear-submarine construction hall at Huludao actually has the capacity that enthusiasts have suggested, it would not be unreasonable to estimate that over the next fifteen years the PLA Navy could commission an average 1.5 SSNs annually.[33]

The need for air cover for surface ships operating away from China's near seas has been addressed throughout this work, which leads to the question of how large the PLA Navy carrier force will become. It seems that three will be operation by 2025; the issue is how many more carriers the PLA Navy thinks it may need and how many it will have in the water by 2035. The PLA Navy's carrier and air-wing development has been careful and unhurried. In this the navy has demonstrated admirable caution, and I see no reason for that to change.

The third, larger, catapult-equipped carrier under construction (see chapter 3) is an entirely new, and unproven, design. For a ship of this complexity, construction and fitting out could take some time. As the United States has learned to its dismay with its own new-design carrier, the urge to stuff in as much new technology as possible can result in expensive delays.[34] The need for the PLA Navy to invest also in new airframes for its carriers, addressed earlier, is urgent. In fact, it could easily turn out that having enough suitable, combat-capable aircraft for the carrier force will become the "long pole in the tent" for China's sea-based aviation. If one assumes a six-year building and outfitting period for each hull and the design remains fairly stable, the PLA Navy could have five or six carriers by 2035. By that time *Liaoning*, if still in commission, will probably be a full-time aviator-training ship.

PRC shipyards have demonstrated the ability to turn out destroyers, frigates, and corvettes in quantity, so for these types building capacity is not an issue. The PLA Navy will have an important voice in determining the precise mix of surface combatants, but it may be forced to make suboptimal choices if economic or leadership developments cause its budget share to drop. I would guess that over the next fifteen years the number of units of these types will grow, with an emphasis on improved ASW and long-range SAM systems.[35]

Turning to the near-seas category of warships, I estimate that its numbers will remain constant, in the range of 160 ships (115 of them commissioned since 2005). The biggest change will be the replacement of the eighty-odd single-mission *Houbei*-class fast attack craft with frigates or corvettes with the same ASCM punch but ASW capability as well.

Finally, my guess is that the PLA Navy in 2035 will consist of approximately 265 blue-water ships of the classes discussed in chapter 3, plus another 160 smaller ships or special-mission units not well suited for distant waters. The result will be a 425-ship PLA Navy that will be the world's largest, by far. (This number does not include minesweepers, small amphibious ships, and sundry auxiliary ships.) By any measure this navy will have to be judged "world class."

Concluding Thoughts

Throughout this book I have made assumptions that as China's blue-water capability matures one can expect to see the PLA Navy operating in numbers wherever the CMC decides to show the flag or display force. I have also speculated that the PLA Navy, like the Soviets before them, would want to maintain, on a more or less permanent basis, a substantial naval presence in the western Indian Ocean. Finally, I have also speculated that China's SLOC anxiety is so great that it is considering a force large enough to defend its most important SLOCs, even in wartime, from either India or the United States. This all could be very wrong.

Estimating on the basis of circumstantial evidence, however extensive, does not equate to predicting the future. It is certainly possible that Xi's envisioned "world-class" navy is not to be permanently abroad, *comme les Américains*. Xi will be eighty-two in 2035 and is not likely to see his vision of China's navy realized, and his successor's (or successors') idea of how the navy should be employed is unknown. It is also possible that the CMC has concluded, or will that Maritime Silk Road SLOC defense in wartime is simply too hard. Xi's concept of "world class" could easily turn out to mean a very large navy more or less strictly limited to East

Asia, so as to be clearly superior, supported by land-based missile and air forces, to whatever the United States could throw against it. This force would clearly overshadow the Indian navy and be a credible deterrent to any Indian interference with PRC trade, obviating the need for a large squadron in the western Indian Ocean.

It is also useful to think of the U.S. Navy in 2035. As it turns out, current American shipbuilding plans have it arriving at its 355-ship goal in same year as the PLA reaches Xi's objective of "modernization being nearly complete," 2035. (At this writing in early 2020, the prospects for having the resources to accomplish this objective appear problematic at best.) It is also necessary to keep in mind that only 60 percent or so of the U.S. fleet is stationed in the Pacific Ocean region—along the West Coast of the mainland United States, in Hawaii, in Guam, and in Japan. Most of the other 40 percent is homeported along the Atlantic coast, along with a small number permanently assigned in the Mediterranean Sea and Persian Gulf regions. In a crisis that could lead to conflict it is likely the *entire* U.S. military, not just 60 percent, would be involved, including, in the case of the U.S. Navy, the bulk of the Atlantic Fleet.

It is certain that in 2035 the PLA Navy will outnumber the U.S. Navy, especially in Chinese home waters, as it does today. There is no indication that Beijing's warship-building spree is likely to end anytime soon. Of course, an economic slowdown in China could slow military moderniza- tion. For its part, the U.S. Navy, while smaller, does hold several aces that the PRC will take many decades to duplicate or counter, if it ever can. The first is America's all-nuclear-powered submarine force; second is the decided advantage the U.S. Navy holds in sea-based airpower embarked on nuclear-powered carriers; third is its very large, all-Aegis cruiser/destroyer force; fourth, perhaps, comprises the added capabilities now being explored: unmanned ships and undersea units, directed-energy weapons, carrier-based unmanned aircraft, and so forth. While these future systems look terrific on paper, the reality is that for both China and United States the bulk of their naval power that is in the water today will still be in the force fifteen years hence. The other final, and probably decisive, advantage the U.S. Navy has is the tradition, skill and opera- tional experience of its officers and sailors.

What seems indisputable, however, is that American presidents from this time forward face a challenge last faced by Franklin Roosevelt in

1941 after Pearl Harbor. If a conflict with China erupts, the president will be the commander in chief of a navy that will have to fight to gain, and then to maintain, sea control almost anywhere in the western Pacific. Since World War II ended in 1945, the United States has had the luxury of being able to employ its maritime expeditionary capabilities in the pursuit of its interests wherever it thought best, for as long as it thought best, with little or no concern regarding whether those forces could arrive there and stay.

Of course, this was not true during the last two decades of the Cold War in the eastern Mediterranean and North Atlantic, but in East Asia and in the Arabian Sea no American administration has had to worry about the Navy's ability to go where needed. This profound advantage is melting away, mainly because of China's growing naval, air, and missile power but also because the Russians and others (such as the Iranians) have recognized that keeping conventional American power at arm's length severely limits Washington's range of strategic options. This new strategic environment is just around the corner, and China is leading the way.

APPENDIX I

The China Coast Guard

A Uniformed Armed Service
Ryan D. Martinson

This appendix chronicles Beijing's efforts to create a unified, capable maritime law enforcement agency.[1] In his 18th Party Congress Work Report, Hu Jintao, then general secretary of the Chinese Communist Party (CCP), identified four lines of effort that the country would pursue to transform China into a maritime power: raise the country's capacity to exploit marine resources, develop its maritime economy, protect its marine environment, and safeguard maritime rights and interests. China's maritime law enforcement (MLE) forces play an important role in each, and the most important of them is safeguarding China's maritime rights and interests.[2] The key point to keep in mind is that a world-class maritime rights protection force is an inextricable element in the march toward great maritime power.

Xi Jinping became general secretary of the CCP on November 15, 2012, and quickly turned his attention to the semichaotic state of the maritime law enforcement institutions of the People's Republic of China (PRC). The organization now known as the China Coast Guard did not exist at the time. Instead, five different agencies, each with a narrow mission set, performed "coast guard–like" missions. These organizations, which scarcely communicated with each other, competed for funding, missions, and acclaim. This situation—described as "five dragons stirring up the sea"—led to waste, inefficiency, and disarray.[3] None knew this better than Xi himself, who had witnessed it while serving as vice chair of China's Central Military Commission (CMC) and as leader of the CCP's Maritime Rights Protection Leading Small Group, an entity that establishes policy.[4] During 2012 he had observed the inauguration of a regular PRC constabulary presence established near the Senkaku Islands on the pretext that Tokyo had nationalized these disputed, barren rocks. In the South China Sea, China's constabulary forces were also busy as the lead agencies in a several-month-long stand-off with Manila over Scarborough Shoal, a large, mostly submerged feature that both countries claim 140 nautical miles west of Subic Bay. Today, thanks to what took place in 2012, Beijing effectively controls Scarborough, by virtue of a continuous MLE presence. Both the Senkaku and Scarborough operations were successful assertions of Chinese sovereignty claims, but conducting simultaneous sovereignty campaigns in the East and South China Seas placed huge stresses on China's maritime law enforcement forces. These stresses did not end when the campaigns ended; the agencies were subsequently tasked with maintaining permanent presences in the vicinity of these widely separated features.

Two weaknesses stood out. One was an organizational problem, the other that China's maritime law enforcement forces lacked the ships they needed—especially large-displacement cutters—to maintain constabulary presence where and when necessary. The solution to the latter problem was straightforward: by the end of 2012 Chinese leaders had instructed the People's Liberation Army (PLA) Navy to transfer eleven auxiliary vessels to what would become the Chinese coast guard. They were painted white and sent to the "front lines." At the same time, Beijing hastened production of several new classes of oceangoing patrol ships, the first step in what has turned out to be a sustained coast guard building program. As of this writing China has the world's largest coast guard fleet, some 252 cutters and patrol craft, including the two largest cutters in the world, displacing some 12,000 tons. Approximately 115 of China's cutters are large enough to conduct sustained patrols throughout China's claimed waters. The addition of large harbors and docks on three of China's man-made bases in the Spratlys (Subi, Mischief, and Fiery Cross Reefs) also increases Beijing's ability to patrol routinely the farthest reaches of its South China Sea claims.[5]

Once he had assumed control of the civil side of the Chinese party-state by becoming president of the PRC, Xi took prompt action to remedy the organizational chaos as well. At that time maritime law enforcement and maritime rights protection were state, not party, functions. Coast guard reform was one of Xi's first substantive actions, and in March 2013 the National People's Congress (NPC) passed legislation to reconstitute the State Oceanic Administration (SOA), empowering it to oversee an amalgamation of four of the old "dragons." The China Coast Guard was born four months later, on July 22, 2013.[6] This marked the beginning of what turned out to be a long and difficult process to create a coast guard befitting a maritime power. If, however, China's maritime law enforcement reform has encountered many difficulties, it has also achieved major improvements.[7]

Background:
Law Enforcement and Maritime Rights Protection

The term "maritime rights and interests" refers to the rights to be enjoyed, and the interests they engender, within the maritime zones of jurisdiction and sovereignty extending from Chinese territory—all, that is, as defined by China![8] China claims maritime rights to three million square kilometers (1,158,306 square miles) of maritime space, commonly known by the Chinese as the country's "blue national territory" or "ocean territory." This space encompasses the Bohai Gulf; a large section of the Yellow Sea; the East China Sea out to the Okinawa Trough;[9] and all the waters within the "nine-dash line" in the South China Sea.[10] Nearly half of China's ocean territory is—and many of the land features encompassed within it are—contested by other states. Key claimants include South Korea in the Yellow Sea, Japan in the East China Sea, and the Philippines, Malaysia, Vietnam, and Indonesia in the South China Sea. In short, save for Russia, Beijing has disputes with all of its maritime neighbors.

Beijing also asserts the right to regulate peaceful naval operations and surveys in its exclusive economic zone (EEZ).[11] This interpretation of international law is contested by many other states. Some, like the United States, disregard China's position and routinely deploy "special mission" ships to waters off Hainan Island and other strategically important areas. Chinese policy makers believe that these actions violate the country's maritime rights and interests.

China relies on all its sea services—navy, coast guard, and militia (for which, see appendix II)—to defend and advance its positions in these disputes. Their operations are often called "maritime rights protection."[12]

Because of their administrative functions, Chinese maritime law enforcement forces serve as China's "primary instrument of rights protection in peacetime."[13] They perform four primary rights protection missions:

- They sail through and linger in disputed waters to bolster a Chinese claim of ownership, demonstrate China's commitment to its claim, and pressure other states to comply with China's demands.
- They track, monitor, and sometimes obstruct foreign naval vessels operating in China's EEZ.
- They ensure the security of Chinese state and private vessels operating in disputed waters.
- They deny foreign commercial exploitation in Chinese-claimed waters, even those that overlap and infringe on the EEZs of coastal states.

Inherent in all these missions are the important tasks of maritime domain awareness and intelligence collection, which indirectly support China's rights protection efforts.[14]

Official and quasi-official Chinese texts identify "administrative control" *(guankong)* as the desired end state of China's rights protection activities. By this they mean imposing the Chinese legal order over Chinese-claimed maritime space. The "12th Five Year Plan for Maritime Development" calls for China to improve its capacity to achieve administrative control over jurisdictional waters.[15] At the 2013 National Maritime Work Meeting, Xu Shaoshi, head of the Ministry of Land and Resources, declared that China needs to work hard to become a maritime power— meaning, inter alia, "China's rights protection struggle needs to be forceful and effective, and China must do more to strengthen its capacity to exercise administrative control over the sea."[16]

This pursuit of administrative control fits into a larger stated goal of "strategic management of the sea," which means a comprehensive state effort to achieve maritime predominance in peacetime.[17] In the words of then vice commandant of the China Coast Guard, Sun Shuxian, "The ocean of our dreams is a secure and harmonious ocean. [In this vision], our maritime disputes are properly resolved, and our maritime rights/ interests are effectively protected. These represent the strategic vision for strategic management of the sea and administrative control of the sea."[18]

Before Unification: The Five-Dragon Era

Background context is important. What follows is a long narrative digression meant to explain the role of the maritime organizations on the eve of Xi's decision to create a coast guard.[19]

China Marine Surveillance

During the five-dragon era, China Marine Surveillance (CMS) was by far the most important actor in maritime rights protection. It was the maritime law enforcement arm of the SOA.[20] CMS traces its roots to the early 1980s, when it was charged with maritime rights protection responsibilities. Early rights protection missions included compelling foreign oil rigs operating with domestic Chinese partners in Chinese jurisdictional waters to curtail polluting discharge; monitoring undersea cables that passed through Chinese jurisdictional waters; and, in May 1985, harassing a Japanese surveying ship operating in China's claimed jurisdictional waters in the East China Sea.[21]

CMS operated on the basis of a small set of domestic laws, most of which reflected Chinese interpretations of the United Nations Convention on the Law of the Sea (UNCLOS).[22] By enforcing Chinese law, these activities made CMS the most prominent player in China's approach to maritime sovereignty issues and ultimately, because of the experience gained, it became the core of the new China Coast Guard.

At the national level, CMS units operated beyond China's twelve-nautical-mile territorial sea. Their primary responsibility came to be called "rights protection law enforcement."[23] This brought them into contact with foreign mariners. Before 2006, these encounters mostly took place in undisputed Chinese waters. Moreover, presence at sea was "irregular" (i.e., periodic—*bu dingqi*). The units would be dispatched singly, as opposed to being rotated to and from a permanent station at sea. For example, a national-level CMS surface ship, moored at a pier, would receive orders to intercept, track, monitor, and sometimes harass foreign survey and surveillance ships operating in China's EEZ. An early example of this approach to rights protection took place in May 2001, when the CMS tracked USNS *Bowditch* (T-AGS 62), conducting military survey operations in the Yellow Sea.[24]

Eventually, national-level cutters began patrolling on a regular basis. By the middle of 2012 CMS had nine ships at sea at any given time, six of them in the South China Sea.[25] This meant that CMS ships were now regularly active in disputed waters in the East China Sea and the South China Sea. Their primary mission was very basic, that of presence—largely passive presence to demonstrate Chinese sovereignty, presence to collect intelligence (or, to use the Chinese euphemism, "collect evidence," *quzheng*).[26] CMS personnel were civil servants with no police powers, and their ships were unarmed state vessels *(gongwu chuan)*.

That they were unarmed is not to say that national-level CMS forces did not act aggressively on occasion. They had water cannons, sirens, and floodlights with which to intimidate noncompliant foreign seamen, mainly fishermen. In some cases, the CMS skippers used their ships as instruments of coercion, by threatening to bump, ram, or shoulder foreign vessels. For example, in March 2011 *CMS 71* and *CMS 75* tracked and impeded the surveying operations of MV *Veritas Voyager* near the Philippines-claimed Reed Bank (a large seafloor feature in the Philippine EEZ).[27] A year later, at Scarborough Shoal, two CMS captains used their ships to block the Philippine navy frigate BRP *Gregorio del Pilar* (a former U.S. Coast Guard cutter) from detaining Chinese fishermen found poaching giant clams in the lagoon.[28]

CMS ships also supported Chinese state-owned enterprises seeking to exploit resources in disputed waters. For example, in June 2007 a flotilla of CMS ships defended at least one Sinopec surveying vessel under assault from Vietnamese paramilitary vessels.[29] Expanded CMS presence at sea was made possible by the entry into the CMS inventory of thirteen new ships by 2011.[30] All were unarmed. The national-level CMS units also received a material boost in late 2012, the transfer from the PLA Navy mentioned above of eleven large-displacement, if overage, naval vessels, mostly fleet auxiliaries, to the CMS. Some of these ships needed major overhauls before they could be put into service, but several were immediately painted in CMS livery and sent to trouble spots.[31] At the end of 2012, national-level units operated twenty-eight cutters displacing at least a thousand tons, forming China's largest oceangoing MLE force.[32]

Authoritative Chinese sources claim that the Scarborough Reef and Senkaku Island conflicts "sounded the [warning] bell" for building up the fleet.[33] In 2012, the CMS signed the first of a series of contracts for very-large-displacement (three thousand metric tons or more) ships, a type the service had long wanted.[34] By the end of 2012, work was under way on twenty-nine new piers capable of accommodating the coming big ships, as well as on additional infrastructure they would require.[35]

At this time regional contingents commanded aviation units, one detachment each. As part of the regularization of rights protection operations, each region consistently employed aircraft to monitor the maritime domain and establish administrative presence. On the eve of the reform, each detachment operated no more than two fixed-wing aircraft (variants of the Y-12 twin-engine turboprop) and one or two helicopters.[36]

Ultimate command over CMS ships and aircraft resided in Beijing, at the CMS Command Center.[37] This provided a degree of central control over actions at sea, essential given that CMS cutters were often performing enforcement operations with possible repercussions for Chinese diplomacy. The center helped coordinate routine rights protection deployments, balancing resources and requirements, and approved deployment plans submitted by commanders at regional contingents. This centralization allowed for better regional coordination of national policy, especially since deployments often crossed regions. Many CMS ships had satellite communications systems, enabling Chinese leaders particularly close control. During the Scarborough Reef standoff, for instance, SOA director Liu Cigui communicated directly with local commanders via video teleconferencing equipment.[38]

Chinese sources indicate that militiamen with previous military experience are among the very best of the CMS civil servants. In its final years CMS received an infusion of young, college-educated personnel, recruited for fluency in foreign languages, knowledge of engineering and the physical sciences, and awareness of international law. However, CMS also claimed to be a paramilitary organization: it was a uniformed service, and its personnel received some military training. Moreover, national-level cutters, although without deck guns, kept a number of assault rifles on board.[39]

At the local level, CMS units gradually acquired larger, oceangoing cutters. SOA leaders, almost certainly with the permission of national decision makers, eventually decided to expend the mission of local-level cutters to include rights protection law enforcement operations beyond China's territorial waters. For example, in May 2011 Hainan set up a CMS detachment on Woody Island in the Paracels, a "forward" location

for rights protection.[40] Central government support of local participation
in maritime rights protection is best illustrated by the decision to purchase for local contingents thirty-six large-displacement cutters (ranging
from 600 to 1,500 metric tons), identified as "rights protection" cutters.[41]

China Fisheries Law Enforcement

China's national and local fisheries law enforcement organizations—collectively called China Fisheries Law Enforcement (*zhongguo yuzheng*)—
constituted the second entity that was integrated into the China Coast
Guard. The Ministry of Agriculture operated the Fisheries Law Enforcement Command (FLEC—*yuzheng zhihui zhongxin*), located in Beijing.[42]
It was established in May 2000 to coordinate blue-water operations,
which had become increasingly important when UNCLOS went into
effect and China assumed responsibility for managing vast new areas of
maritime space.[43] Since many of these waters were disputed, safeguarding maritime rights and interests was clearly an important consideration
in creating FLEC.[44]

Blue-water fisheries operations for rights protection purposes were
known as *huyu weiquan* (literally, "protecting fisheries rights protection")
and involved both protecting Chinese fishermen and harassing foreign
fishermen operating in Chinese-claimed waters. FLEC units also conducted symbolic patrols in disputed areas. At least one FLEC cutter was
involved in the harassment of USNS *Impeccable* in 2009, an operation
purportedly directed by the then-head of the South China Sea Bureau of
Fisheries Law Enforcement, Wu Zheng.[45]

Over time, blue-water fisheries law enforcement patrols became more
systematic. FLEC planned annual fisheries deployments in China's
EEZ.[46] The annual EEZ patrols, however, failed to curb one of the most
nettlesome problems faced by the service: foreign harassment of Chinese
fishermen in remote sections of China's claims. To improve its capacity
to protect fishermen and their property, China adopted a two-pronged
approach. First, the Ministry of Agriculture began to equip Chinese fishing vessels with satellite navigation and communications hardware. These
systems allowed FLEC units to respond to distress calls more quickly
and to collect information on the disposition of foreign vessels.[47] As this
program unfolded, China Fisheries Law Enforcement also began implementing a convoy system for fishing fleets in what at the time (2010) was

considered one of the more perilous sections of the South China Sea, the Spratly Islands.[48]

Whether national or local, FLEC personnel were uniformed civil servants empowered to impose civil penalties—fines and confiscation. They were not policemen, with the power to arrest or charge with crimes. However, unlike CMS forces, many FLEC ships carried deck-mounted weapons (large-caliber machine guns); also, like some CMS forces, the FLEC vessels themselves were sturdy enough to physically force away foreign fishermen operating in Chinese-claimed waters, especially in the Paracels.[49]

Despite their many pressing missions, the national-level Fisheries Law Enforcement units procured very few new ships in the years leading up to the reform. One noteworthy exception was a very advanced, large-displacement (2,500 metric tons) ship delivered in 2010. Although based in Guangzhou, this ship has performed rights protection operations as far north as the Senkaku Islands and as far south as James Shoal in the South China Sea. It appeared at Scarborough Reef in April 2012, during the stand-off with the Philippines.[50] It was also involved in two separate, tense confrontations with Indonesian coast guard vessels.[51] Fisheries Law Enforcement also received several transfers from the PLA Navy, one of which was involved in the June 2011 molestation of *Viking II*, a Norwegian surveying vessel operating on behalf of the Viet Nam National Oil and Gas Group.[52]

While the national and local units of the Fisheries Law Enforcement possessed far fewer oceangoing ships than did CMS, FLEC was a much larger agency. An April 2012 *Legal Daily* article puts the total force at 33,000 officers, of which 17,000 were involved in maritime fisheries management.[53]

China Maritime Police

The third dragon comprised the maritime units of China's Border Defense Force (*bianfang budui*), a specialized branch of the People's Armed Police (PAP—*renmin wuzhuang jingcha*) under the Ministry of Public Security.[54] Called the *bianfang haijing*, or China Maritime Police (CMP), this service is now frequently referred to as the "old Coast Guard," to distinguish it from the new service set up in 2013.[55] The CMP was a military organization, albeit separate from the People's Liberation Army; its personnel had military ranks, were called soldiers (*guanbing*) or active-duty military (*xianyi*), and wore uniforms. However, they also had functions and attributes like those of policemen. In fact, and unlike CMS and FLEC, they had true police powers to investigate, detain, and arrest suspected criminals. The primary mission of the old Coast Guard was public security (*zhi'an*): drug smuggling, terrorism, theft, illegal border crossing, and civil disputes that turned violent. In theory, the CMP had a mandate to enforce criminal law in all of China's jurisdictional waters, including, of course, large expanses disputed by other states.[56] In practice, however, CMP units seldom patrolled the outer seas.[57] This meant that the CMP played only a small role in supporting China's position in its maritime disputes.

The CMP operated many small craft in and around harbors and along the coast. However, in the years leading up to the integration, the service experienced a quiet buildup, over twenty Type 618B patrol ships. At six hundred metric tons, these ships were capable of operating in blue water, but because of limited fuel and storage capacity and small crews they lacked the endurance for the type of extended presence needed in China's more distant maritime frontiers. These ships were armed, mounting 30-mm deck guns. The "old Coast Guard" also operated three larger-displacement ships, two of them decommissioned PLA Navy destroyers.

Maritime Anti-Smuggling Police and the Maritime Safety Agency

The Maritime Anti-Smuggling Police (MASP), as the fourth dragon was known, was chiefly tasked with enforcing customs regulations. Like the CMP, the Maritime Anti-Smuggling Police had legitimate police powers. Officers were empowered to investigate (*zhencha*), detain (*juliu*), and arrest *(daibu)* those accused of violating the criminal code. They also enforced administrative law.[58] Given the scope of their work, the Maritime Anti-Smuggling Police operated mostly on or near the shore, concentrating in major trading hubs. For these purposes they operated over two hundred small craft, motorboats, and small ships, some of which were equipped with deck guns.[59] While they served very important sovereign functions, they did not operate beyond the inner seas and thus do not figure prominently in this study.

These four dragons, CMS, FLEC, CMP, and MASP, were swept up in the formation of the Chinese Coast Guard in 2013. The fifth dragon, the Maritime Safety Agency, was not included and remained independent. Overseen by the Ministry of Transport, MSA primarily performs missions involving safety of life at sea, including search and rescue and environmental protection (ship discharges, in particular). MSA ships, among China's biggest and most advanced, played a prominent role in Chinese operations to locate the wreckage of Malaysian Airlines flight MH370 in early 2014.[60]

MSA represents the cooperative side of Chinese maritime law enforcement, frequently serving as an instrument of friendly maritime diplomacy with other states. However, it does play a small but noteworthy role in protecting China's maritime rights and interests. Two of its large cutters (which displace 3,000 and 5,400 metric tons) respectively, regularly patrol out to the Chunxiao Oil Fields in the East China Sea. With its several large-displacement ships, MSA is in a position to contribute much more to the rights protection mission and, if advocates have their way, may do so in the future.[61]

The fact that the Chinese government elected not to integrate MSA into the China Coast Guard could reflect a desire not to taint this more cosmopolitan agency by associating it with a new organization centered on maritime rights protection. Chinese policy makers may also have judged that adding a fifth agency to the original four might have made insuperable an already difficult organizational reform.

Fixing Maritime Rights Protection

In the five-dragon era, Chinese maritime law enforcement faced systemic problems. Five agencies housed in five different ministries managed the sea, enforcing different sets of laws. Some law enforcement personnel were civil servants, some were policemen, and some were active-duty military. All agencies vigorously pursued material and personnel expansion without taking into consideration the big picture, causing "duplicative construction" (*chongfu jianshe*).

Responsibilities overlapped. Both the CMP and the MASP were charged with combating smuggling. Both CMS and MSA were responsible for environmental protection. Yet there was little communication between agencies. The fragmentation of the service sometimes led law enforcement officers to turn a blind eye to violations outside of their respective jurisdictions. These issues were especially acute in China's territorial seas, where all five dragons operated, but even in the outer seas, where rights protection took place, CMS and the Fisheries Law Enforcement did not coordinate their operations. On top of all this, individual agencies suffered from a divide between national- and local-level organizations, a perennial challenge in Chinese governance.

In seeking a solution to this mess, PRC analysts often sought inspiration from other coast guards. These usually included the U.S. Coast Guard, the Japan Coast Guard, and the Korea Coast Guard. The U.S. Coast Guard drew considerable Chinese interest, because over the years it had accomplished what China's had wanted to do—gradually absorbed a number of independent maritime-related entities, such as the Lighthouse Service, to form the bureaucratically coherent service that exists today.[62]

Despite the general recognition that China needed to rectify what Dr. Lyle Goldstein has called the "balkanized" state of its MLE agencies, everybody knew that reform would be tremendously difficult.[63] It would require bringing together soldiers, policemen, and civil servants. It would involve powerful national bureaucracies.

Cutting the Gordian Knot

Soon after the 18th Party Congress, SOA director Liu Cigui outlined in public print his understanding of what was already being called China's "maritime power" strategy. To become a maritime power, Liu believed, China would need to "establish maritime administration and maritime law enforcement systems that are authoritative and highly efficient, have fairly concentrated functions, and have uniform responsibilities; that can perform overall planning for both internally oriented administrative law enforcement and externally oriented rights protection law enforcement; and that can provide organizational support for efforts to build China into a maritime power."[64] Simply put, the five-dragon model would have to change. Of course, that is what happened; one suspects that Liu already knew that Xi intended to form a Chinese coast guard and that his article was intended to help set the stage.[65]

On March 10, 2013, the NPC passed the "Plan for State Council Organizational Reform and Transferal of Functions." Provision 5, in the "Reform" section, stated the following:[66]

> In order to promote unified maritime law enforcement and raise law enforcement effectiveness, [we hereby] integrate the forces and responsibilities of the State Oceanic Administration and its China

Marine Surveillance, the Ministry of Public Security's China Maritime Police, the Ministry of Agriculture's China Fisheries Law Enforcement, and the General Administration of Customs' Maritime Anti-Smuggling Police, and reconstitute the State Oceanic Administration, to be managed by the Ministry of Land and Resources. SOA's chief responsibility will be to draft maritime development plans, implement maritime law enforcement for [the purposes of] rights protection, oversee and manage use of the sea, and protect the environment. SOA will perform law enforcement for [the purposes of] rights protection under the name China Coast Guard. It will accept operational guidance from the Ministry of Public Security.[67]

This brief statement did not reveal much, but it did allow for some insights.[68] The document used the word "integrate" (*zhenghe*) rather than "unify" (*tongyi*). This, then, was not to be an organizational unification of the different government agencies but something less: the integration of just those "forces" (*duiwu*) that performed maritime law enforcement functions.[69]

SOA would retain custody over CMS and gain it over three other dragons. On March 18 the government named Meng Hongwei, vice minister of the Ministry of Public Security, as director of the China Coast Guard.[70] Meng had long overseen the Border Defense Force. He had a higher administrative rank than Liu Cigui, who became party secretary of the China Coast Guard. With Meng Hongwei in charge and its guidance authority, the Ministry of Public Security would have a major say in future developments.

In July 2013, the State Council released a redacted version of the plan outlining the structure, functions, and size of the reconstituted SOA.[71] This document, commonly referred to as the "Three Decisions Plan" (*sanding fangan*), made clear that the China Coast Guard and the State Oceanic Administration were to be tightly intertwined. The China Coast Guard would comprise eleven departments (*si*) within SOA, as well as a headquarters (*silingbu*) and a command center (*zhihui zhongxin*). SOA, working through the coast guard, would oversee "unified planning, unified construction, and unified command over the China Coast Guard forces; regularize law enforcement behavior, streamline law enforcement processes, raise the capacity to perform maritime rights protection law enforcement, and safeguard the maritime order and maritime rights and interests." The coast guard would perform maritime rights protection missions on behalf of SOA.

Integration under SOA (2013–2018)

The new China Coast Guard was officially established on July 22, 2013. Within weeks, many Chinese maritime law enforcement units had repainted their ships with China Coast Guard livery and new pennant numbers, and new standardized life jackets had been issued. These superficial signs of uniformity concealed, however, the slow and contentious nature of the reform. What was achieved during the five years in which the CCG was managed by SOA?

On paper, the China Coast Guard established many of the institutional arrangements outlined in the Three Decisions Plan. Within the first two years it created a headquarters in Beijing, three regional branches, and subordinate contingents and detachments in each coastal province.[72] However, only the headquarters was fully functional and integrated.[73] In contrast, regional bureaus and subordinate contingents were led by "preparatory groups" (*choubeizu*), an acknowledgment of their unreadiness. At all levels, staff members continued to wear the uniforms of the services to which they had belonged prior to the reform.

After five years of reform, aside from snazzy new paint jobs, not much had not changed operationally. CMP detachments, for instance, were never dismantled. Still containing only PAP soldiers, they continued to operate from their old bases and facilities, which were identified in the Chinese press by their old names. The China Coast Guard, then, existed as an amalgam of separate agencies, with increasing separation the closer one got to the front lines. Beneath the headquarters level, organizational integration was widely regarded as "not being where it should be."[74]

Frontline forces from different agencies seldom trained together.[75] They employed different doctrines and maintained different cultures and standards of excellence. In many cases, where engagements with foreign mariners were few and small, this may not have mattered, but overall, interoperability suffered. Not surprisingly, since they did not train together, frontline forces from different agencies rarely operated together. There were some exceptions. Former CMS and FLE forces, for example, sometimes conducted joint sovereignty patrols. In the months immediately after the creation of the China Coast Guard, former CMS and Fisheries Law Enforcement ships began sailing together on certain high-profile missions, notably to the Senkaku Islands.[76]

During the five years it was managed by SOA, the reform did yield some benefits. The most important of them was the creation of the China Coast Guard headquarters and its command center, which together improved overall coordination of national coast guard assets.[77] Some provincial-level CMS cutters were also integrated into the national command-and-control architecture.[78] By the end of 2014, the China Coast Guard headquarters alone was tasking frontline forces, issuing orders directly to individual cutters at sea and circumventing unit commanders. This, a former Fisheries Law Enforcement officer explained, was a huge improvement over the past.[79] On January 1, 2018, for instance, the command center received notification from Chinese-occupied Mischief Reef in the Spratlys that a Brazil-registered sailboat (*Pangaea*) had grounded at Livock Reef. It immediately ordered *CCG 3303*, then on patrol, to rescue crew members.[80]

The new command and control arrangements also made possible large-scale mobilization in times of crisis, such as happened south of the Paracels in May 2014. Chinese leaders authorized operations by the China National Offshore Oil Company's drilling rig *HYSY 981* in Vietnam's EEZ. Hanoi reacted forcefully, deploying coast guard and paramilitary vessels to obstruct drilling operations. The PLA Navy, placed in charge of the dozens of maritime law enforcement cutters, arranged them in a perimeter around the rig and physically prevented the Vietnamese from reaching it. This operation, which required a massive effort involving all the former dragons, was successful, but it highlighted the lack of interoperability between the different forces involved.[81] Still, it simply would not have been possible prior to the China Coast Guard reform, when China lacked the means to organize for joint action. The 2015 U.S. Department of Defense *Annual Report to Congress* provides a broader context:

Employment of Chinese Coast Guard (CCG), PLA Navy ships, and the Chinese commercial fishing fleet is one tool China uses in conducting "low-intensity coercion" to advance its position with respect to its territorial and maritime disputes. CCG ships remain at the forefront of responding to perceived challenges to China's territorial and maritime claims as China seeks to avoid a military confrontation. China maintains a near-continuous presence of CCG ships in all disputed areas in an effort to demonstrate its ability to operate when and where it wants. During periods of tension in the South China Sea, China uses the quantity and advanced capabilities of its CCG assets to overwhelm and deter South China Sea claimant nations with the goal of eventually compelling regional acceptance of China's sovereignty claims.[82]

The same can be said about a more recent coast guard operation. In August 2016, Chinese leaders ordered, or at least authorized, over two hundred Chinese fishing vessels to sail near Japan's Senkaku Islands. There is no definitive explanation for Beijing's choice of this moment for a political act of this scale. Nothing like it had occurred since 1978.[83] Beijing assigned twenty coast guard cutters as escorts for the fishing fleet, part of which strayed into Japan's territorial sea. The escort force comprised vessels of several frontline units: CMS, CMP, and FLE, as well as provincial-level maritime law enforcement forces.[84] Again, this operation could not have succeeded without the centralized command of maritime law enforcement assets made possible by the creation of the China Coast Guard.

Unification under the People's Armed Police (2018)

During the SOA period all four dragons continued to exist in some form, but their respective roles changed over time, none more so than those of CMP. The CMP's outstanding performance during the defense of *HYSY 981* seems to have convinced Chinese leaders that PAP "combat power" could make the difference.[85] The CMP, which had once seldom left China's territorial sea, now took on a more prominent role in frontline rights protection, and was duly reequipped. It received new oceangoing cutters, such as the four-thousand-ton Type 818, which is armed with a 76-mm deck gun and two 30-mm cannons and resembles a Type 054 frigate. It also gained vessels formerly owned by civilian law enforcement detachments; for instance, Fisheries Law Enforcement was directed to transfer its three-thousand-ton cutter to a Jiangsu-based CMP unit.[86]

The migration of CMP units to the front lines resulted in a marked militarization of China's maritime frontier. CMP forces began deploying to the Senkaku Islands, Scarborough Shoal, and the Spratlys—once the exclusive domains of CMS and FLEC cutters. In mid-August 2017, for instance, a Hainan-based CMP cutter appeared at Sandy Cay, a tiny feature just west of Philippines-occupied Thitu Island in the Spratlys, as part of a larger force that included militia and naval vessels that pressured Philippine leaders to halt plans to build fishing shelters there.[87]

Xi Jinping's 2013 decision to create the China Coast Guard had been decisive, but it had been made without a definitive vision of what it was to be: a uniformed service like the CMP and the U.S. Coast Guard or a civilian organization like CMS and FLE. Indeed, by all accounts, the reform appears to have been a sudden, top-down decision.[88] In early 2014, Sun Shuxian told Chinese reporters that he favored a civilian orientation. A debate, apparently, was under way, and he was to lose it:[89] the CMP members of the China Coast Guard's senior leadership felt differently. Their view ultimately prevailed, and it was decided to recast the CCG into a uniformed service on the model of the CMP.

To that end they might have simply transferred the entire service to the Ministry of Public Security, which had overseen the CMP and whose vice minister also its commandant. Instead, the party took another approach. China's maritime law enforcement reform was entwined with a decision by Xi Jinping to assert direct party control over all of China's armed forces.[90] In January 2018, the party placed the PAP under the Central Military Commission.[91] With this move, they ensured complete party monopoly over all of China's internal and external armed forces.[92] In the same month, and without any further elaboration, China's Ministry of Defense revealed that "maritime rights protection law enforcement" had become one of the PAP's three primary missions.[93]

This interesting revelation was explained two months later, in two documents. First, on March 14 the National People's Congress issued the "Explanation of the State Council Organizational Reform Plan." It stated that SOA would be eliminated, its responsibilities transferred to the newly created Ministry of Natural Resources.[94] Second, on March 21, 2018, Xinhua released the text of the "Plan for Deepening Party and State Organizational Reform." It outlined the CCP's decision to place the China Coast Guard under the PAP. Details were few: the plan stated only that China Coast Guard forces, hitherto "led and managed" by the SOA, and their "related functions" would be transferred to the PAP. This transfer would occur first, "reorganization" (*zhengbian*) later.[95] The PAP formally took control of the China Coast Guard on July 1, 2018.[96] Of the implications of that one U.S. expert wrote:

> Whereas the 2013 China Coast Guard mixed civilian and para-military personnel, now all coast guard officers will become uniformed active duty People's Armed Police officers. New recruits will enlist as People's Armed Police officers and follow basic training procedures similar to those of the People's Liberation Army. People's Armed Police officers will be given full authority to board, inspect, seize, and investigate domestic and foreign vessels based on domestic Chinese law. Ships will most likely stay the same color and officers will continue to introduce their all-black uniforms seen on recent China Coast Guard patrols.
>
> The China Coast Guard should now officially be regarded as one of China's armed forces, capable of executing a variety of law enforcement duties at sea during peacetime with possible wartime functions. The reform will likely enable the China Coast Guard to train and equip itself to conduct combat operations alongside the navy during conflict. This is an important change from the 2013 iteration of the China Coast Guard.[97]

In key ways, the China Coast Guard reform has improved China's ability to exercise administrative control over its three million square kilometers of claimed maritime space. The new system even in its early days much enhanced command and control over frontline rights protection forces. The reform was supposed to synergize Chinese maritime law enforcement—to form a fist out of formerly ineffectual fingers. This it has done. Deployments are far better coordinated than they were in the past—an outcome of the creation of the China Coast Guard headquarters and command center. Whereas in the past, CMS and Fisheries Law Enforcement forces operated through their respective command bureaucracies, now they reported through a single chain of command to senior decision makers in Beijing.[98] These improvements no doubt strengthened presence at sea and made possible at least two major rights protection operations: the 2014 defense of *HYSY 981* and the August 2016 fisheries escort mission to the Senkakus.

However, much work was not completed. During its five years under SOA, the China Coast Guard did not fully erect the structure outlined in the Three Decisions Plan. Moreover, it took no significant steps toward melding the old agencies into an integrated force with a single identity. To paraphrase one SOA official, China made progress toward achieving a "physical integration" but had failed to achieve a "chemical integration."[99]

The decision to place the China Coast Guard under the PAP is likely to resolve many of the issues faced during the first phase of the reform. Gone are the days of joint oversight by different government ministries. The China Coast Guard now operates with a clear chain of command extending from frontline forces to the Central Military Commission and completely circumventing the state bureaucracy. Debilitating internal debates and political maneuvering can finally end, and the new service can focus on the task at hand.

Placing the China Coast Guard under the PAP will complete the militarization of frontline maritime law enforcement. A CCG under the PAP gives Chinese leaders more options in a crisis. PAP personnel, for instance, can frame a forcible landing on a disputed island as a law enforcement action. Indeed, former CMP units are already training for such scenarios.[100] Nonetheless, the PAP will still face many challenges before it can create a single, homogenous China Coast Guard. CMS, Fisheries Law Enforcement—as well as the General Administration of Customs, not discussed here—personnel will need to be integrated into the PAP, which is a military organization. Some individuals will choose to leave instead; some will fail to meet the age, fitness, or other requirements. The new arrangement could harm recruitment of talented men and women who want to go to sea as civil servants, not soldiers.

To be sure, the transfer of the China Coast Guard to the PAP does not mean the end of civilian maritime law enforcement in China, in that, so far, provincial maritime agencies remain intact. In fact, a new operational concept is being explored in which PLA Navy, China Coast Guard, and local law enforcement forces sail together to disputed areas. If foreign naval forces appear, the PLA Navy moves forward to usher them away. If foreign civilian mariners are found infringing PRC "rights," the China

Coast Guard expels them. If the problem is illegal behavior by Chinese citizens, local law enforcement handles the problem. This new model has already been employed in the Paracels and could expand to other areas.[101] If it does, it will be the next chapter in Beijing's efforts to ensure it can prevail in any peacetime confrontation with neighbors over maritime claims and attendant access to fish and hydrocarbons, including a substantial portion of the EEZ resources that Korea, Japan, Vietnam, the Philippines, and Indonesia are legally entitled to exploit. The fact is that every improvement in the effectiveness of China's coast guard is bad news for its maritime neighbors.

China's Maritime Militia

An Important Force Multiplier
Andrew S. Erickson and Conor M. Kennedy

The People's Armed Forces Maritime Militia (PAFMM) is a state-organized, -developed, and -controlled force operating under a direct military chain of command to conduct Chinese state–sponsored activities.[1] The PAFMM is locally organized and resourced but answers to the very top of China's military bureaucracy: the commander in chief, Xi Jinping. While the PAFMM has been part of China's militia system for decades, it is receiving greater emphasis today, because of its value in furthering China's near-seas "rights and interests."

Traditionally, the PAFMM has been a military force raised from civilian marine industry workers (e.g., fishermen). Personnel keep their "day jobs" but are organized and trained in exchange for benefits and can be called up as needed. Recently, the People's Liberation Army (PLA—in this context, the military generally) has been adding a more professionalized, militarized vanguard to the PAFMM, recruiting former servicemen (by offering them high salaries) and launching formidable purpose-built vessels. This vanguard has no apparent interest in fishing.

This chapter focuses on the current organization and employment of Chinese maritime-militia organizations. It first puts this force into historical context by surveying the PAFMM's background and its changing role in China's armed forces. Next, it examines the PAFMM's current contributions toward China's goal of becoming a great maritime power, in both old and new mission areas. The remaining sections will address specific maritime-militia modes of command and control, intelligence gathering, organization and training and will suggest possible scenarios and implications.

Decades-Long History

China's militia system originated before the Chinese Communist Party (CCP) came to power, but the system of recruiting numerous state-supported maritime militias from coastal populations was not fully implemented until the communists began to exercise greater control of the coastline in the 1950s. This segment of China's population had been relatively isolated from the turmoil of the Civil War; these regions had been under either Japanese or Republic of China (ROC) control in the decades before CCP rule was established. The CCP targeted the fishing communities by creating fishing collectives and work units, enacting strict organizational and social controls, and conducting political education. Factors motivating and shaping this transformation included:

- The PLA's early use of civilian vessels after Chiang Kai-shek's Nationalist Party decamped to Taiwan.
- The fact that fishermen constituted the bulk of China's experienced mariners.
- The requirement during the 1950s and 1960s to defend against Nationalist incursions along the coast.
- Increasingly frequent confrontations with other states' fishing and naval vessels as China's fishermen gradually began to fish farther offshore.
- The transformation of many shore-based coastal-defense militias to the at-sea maritime militia.

The PAFMM has played significant roles in manifold military campaigns and coercive incidents over the years:

- In the 1950s, support of the PLA's island seizure campaigns off the mainland coast
- In the 1960s, securing of China's coast against Nationalist infiltrations

- In 1974, seizure of the western portion of the Paracel Islands in the South China Sea from South Vietnam
- In 1976, harassment of "foreign" naval ships east of the Zhoushan Archipelago (south of Shanghai)
- In 1978, presence mission in the territorial sea of the Senkaku Islands
- In 1995, Mischief Reef encounter with the Philippines stemming from the occupation and development of that reef
- In 2009, harassment of USNS *Impeccable*
- In 2012, Scarborough Shoal stand-off with the Philippines
- In 2014, blockade of Philippine-occupied Second Thomas Shoal
- In 2014, repulse of Vietnamese vessels from disputed waters surrounding the China National Offshore Oil Corporation's (CNOOC's) oil rig *HYSY 981*
- In 2014, harassment of USNS *Howard O. Lorenzen*
- In 2016, large surge of fishing craft near the Senkaku Islands
- In 2017, envelopment of Philippine-claimed Sandy Cay in the northern Spratly Islands.[2]

The important point to note is that many of these actions were not merely reactive. In some cases PAFMM participation was preplanned and guided by PLA organs: the 1974 seizure of the western Paracels from Vietnam, reconnaissance and sovereignty patrols during the February 2014 blockade of Second Thomas Shoal, and the 2014 defense of the CNOOC oil rig against Vietnamese vessels.[3]

The 2012 Scarborough Shoal stand-off is an example of how militia forces already at sea can rally to an emerging confrontation It was the PAFMM that first arrived to aid Chinese fishermen in danger of being arrested by Philippine officials in an incident that sparked the April 2012 Scarborough Shoal episode. Reports by members of the PAFMM unit present at Scarborough Shoal and their actions there suggest that the PLA exercised command and control over PAFMM forces in subsequent operations to seize the feature from the Philippines.[4]

The PAFMM: A Decentralized, Local Institution

The PAFMM is an important component of China's local armed forces. Its part-time units are part of an armed mass organization of mobilizable personnel who retain their normal economic responsibilities in daily civilian life—a reserve force of immense scale. The militia is organized at the grassroots level: its units are formed by towns, villages, urban subdistricts, and enterprises. It supports China's armed forces in a variety of ways and is seeing the list expand as the PLA continues to modernize. Militia units differ widely from one location to another, as their respective compositions stem from local conditions (*yindi zhiyi*). A good example is the establishment of emergency naval ship-repair units in areas with strong shipbuilding industries.

The PAFMM is found, logically, in port areas with large fishing, shipbuilding, or shipping industries where experienced mariners or craftsmen provide a ready pool of recruits. Citizens can join land-based primary militia organizations between the ages of eighteen and thirty-five. The PAFMM's age requirements are flexible, extending to forty-five for those with special skills, even older in some localities (e.g., Yancheng City of eastern China's Jiangsu Province extended the maximum age for its maritime militiamen to fifty-five).[5] Veterans of the armed forces are prized. For example, Zhejiang Province has established as a recruiting target a 65 percent ratio of veterans to nonveterans for its maritime-militia units.[6]

Local military and civilian leaders appear to have a degree of autonomy in how they build their militias. Most PLA publications state up front that militia building should be suited to the local missions and localities' resources for mobilization. In other words, forces are not built in cookie-cutter fashion imposed by national-level leadership. Rather, they are organized with two things in mind: the local populace and its industrial or institutional capacity and the specific requirements they are intended to satisfy.

Unlike the active-duty forces of the People's Republic of China (PRC), its reserves, among them the militia, are not recruited from a variety of locations. It is the civilian government's job to incorporate militia building into its maritime economic development and to take the lead in militia construction. Government marine agencies such as the China Coast Guard (CCG) are tasked with assisting in organizing PAFMM units and in their training. Local propaganda, finance, and civil affairs departments each become involved, in their respective areas. The navy, in cooperation with other military agencies, provides special technical training and conducts joint exercises with the PAFMM.[7] Finally, county- and grassroots-level People's Armed Forces Departments (PAFDs), directly involved in the normal management and organization of the units, are central to PAFMM organization.

Unit composition is determined by the capabilities of the vessels involved. In principle, PAFMM personnel numbers are determined based on the vessels (*yichuan dingbing*). Vessels and their crews are recruited into tactical-level units—"detachments" (*fendui*)—typically composed of companies, platoons, and squads. Some provinces have developed battalion-sized units. Most counties establish at least one company-sized unit; however, their size and capabilities vary greatly depending on local conditions. Some units comprise oceangoing fishing vessels capable of reaching distant waters, such as the Spratlys, while support units may not possess vessels at all.[8] The PLA's political work is not overlooked; the guideline is for two or more party members on each "mission fishing vessel." Essentially, wherever the maritime militia goes, the party is on board.[9]

The geographical distribution of units is largely driven by the operational needs of a given region. For example, in 2015, the Guangdong Military Region (MR) Mobilization Department proposed a PAFMM force organization based on geographically oriented missions:

- Reconnaissance forces are deployed to distant islands, reefs, and areas around important waterways.
- Maritime militia assisting Maritime Law Enforcement (MLE) forces are primarily deployed around disputed islands, reefs, and sea areas.
- Maritime-militia support forces are deployed to naval stations, ports, piers, and predetermined operational sea areas.
- Emergency response forces make mobile deployments to sea areas around "traditional fishing grounds."

That department opined that units could be organized according to their operational destinations: forces assigned to law enforcement and reconnaissance missions would be organized where its vessels normally fish. Conversely, PAFMM forces responsible for security or loading operations would be organized in the coastal areas in which they are needed. Whether followed exactly or not, this approach suggests how

PLA leaders reconcile the need to deploy these forces with the economic realities of individual militia organizations and their personnel. The PLA is continually experimenting with organizational arrangements to serve the needs of the military and state without imposing unrealistic expectations on a given PAFMM unit. This pragmatic policy means there is no universal model for maritime militia organization.[10]

On the national scale, however, Beijing is creating a leaner militia force generally (not only maritime), reducing the overall number of militiamen and strengthening the training and capabilities of more elite units. Obsolete infantry units have disbanded in favor of technically sophisticated militia that can support modern PLA operations. For the PAFMM this has resulted in the building of "elite" maritime militia units that would be used year-round.[11]

Most descriptions of PAFMM vessel requirements focus on the fishing industry. They prioritize large-tonnage, steel-hulled ships that are fast (by fishing-vessel standards) and capable of withstanding collisions. In many ways, since the PAFMM conducts most rights-protection missions without arms, the vessel itself is the weapon.[12] PAFMM forces also incorporate the logistical benefits of the mother ships that routinely support fishing fleets. Hainan's Sanya Fugang Fisheries Company used a three-thousand-ton supply ship to support its rights-protection operations in the Spratlys from 2012 to 2014, significantly extending the range and endurance of the PAFMM vessels involved.[13]

The PAFMM in the South China Sea

In 2015 Beijing created a special PAFMM unit for the South China Sea, headquartered in Sansha City on Woody Island, the largest of the Paracel Islands. This special-purpose unit appears to be a full-time, militarized organization. It provides the crews for eighty-four purpose-built vessels equipped with high-pressure water cannons and with rugged, reinforced hulls able to withstand physical shouldering of third-party fishing boats and coast guard vessels. Lacking fishing responsibilities, its personnel train for peacetime and wartime contingencies, sometimes with light arms, and deploy regularly to disputed South China Sea features, even during fishing moratoriums.[14] This new full-time Sansha City force has been involved in a recent PAFMM "operation" to keep Philippine and other fishermen away from Sandy Cay, an above-water feature very close to Philippine-occupied Thitu Island. It does this by maintaining a blockading force of at least two PAFMM vessels.[15]

Sansha City, being the municipality that Beijing charges with "administering" the vast majority of the South China Sea, plays a leading role in PAFMM procedural innovation. Starting in 2013, its higher headquarters called for Sansha's maritime militiamen to be deployed to "all areas within the nine-dashed line."[16] In 2015, the municipality was further directed to ensure that maritime militia "achieve[s] regular presence and regular demonstration of rights" in Chinese waters in the South China Sea.[17] To this end, the PLA garrison in Sansha City established the state-owned Sansha City Fisheries Development Company as a PAFMM organization dedicated to maritime rights operations. The Sansha City Fisheries Development Company militia unit was set up first and foremost as a professional paramilitary force, with fishing a secondary mission at best. Military veterans were and continue to be sought for all positions. These militiamen receive hefty salaries atop an array of generous benefits: a crewman can earn over $13,000 annually, a captain over $25,000; all members receive insurance, retirement, and medical benefits.[18] These are princely sums and perquisites by Chinese standards and go far in a coastal fishing village. The money apparently does not depend on meeting actual fishing responsibilities; "trawling for territorial claims" would seem to be what these payments are for.

Sansha maritime militia members have been photographed loading crates labeled "light weapons" onto one of their deployed (they are physically homeported on Hainan) large vessels—the ones with water cannons and sturdy hulls.[19] The largest Sansha maritime militia vessels are 60 meters long and 9 meters in beam, and they likely displace 600 to 750 tons. They are a good deal larger than the 320-ton, 44-meter *Parola*-class patrol vessels Japan is constructing for the Philippines.[20] Some of these new militia ships reportedly have a "weapons equipment room" and "ammunition stores" on board.[21]

The Sansha militia boats, which are painted blue, and are collectively an integral part of the "blue-hull, white-hull, grey-hull" (PAFMM, CCG, PLA Navy), three-tiered defense of China's maritime rights and interests in the South China Sea. To coordinate these multiagency efforts, a six-million-dollar command center has been established on Woody Island.[22] The Sansha garrison operates on at least two Paracel

Islands "informatized" outposts that monitor proximate seas and has begun construction on three other Paracel features. PLA leaders have indicated that these initial outposts will be replicated in the Spratlys and have commenced construction on three features there. Already, the Sansha garrison has established a People's Armed Forces Department (PAFD) on Fiery Cross Reef and a PAFMM element on Mischief Reef, the beginnings of a growing and full-time rotational PAFMM presence in the Spratlys.[23]

The Sansha fleet maintains a continual rotational presence vis-à-vis disputed features in the South China Sea. Sansha's vessels are divided into six companies, stationed at three dedicated and closed-off bases in the Hainan Island harbors of Baimajing, Yazhou, and Qinglan. (There is not enough room on Woody Island, and the locally recruited crews have no desire to be stuck on underdeveloped Woody, or the Spratlys at all, for that matter.) The authors' review of publicly available Automatic Identification System data confirms that a systematic rotation is in effect, apparently a straightforward one-in-three scheme: two of the six companies deployed at any given time, four in port or undergoing maintenance.

Contributions to China's Maritime Power

PLA reforms introduced by Xi Jinping in 2015 made significant changes across all of China's armed forces, including modernization of China's reserve forces, particularly the PAFMM. In the 13th Five Year Plan released in March 2016 the maritime militia was made one of the priorities in optimizing the overall militia system.[24] PAFMM units in China's coastal provinces have since grown visibly and increased in their operational capabilities.

The fishing industry and the maritime militia are valued by Beijing as useful contributors to the consolidation of China's maritime claims, particularly in the South China Sea. Xi Jinping has personally highlighted the importance of the maritime militia. In 2013, he visited the Tanmen fishing harbor in Hainan Province, meeting its maritime militia company and telling them that "Maritime Militia members should not only lead fishing activities, but also collect oceanic information and support the construction of islands and reefs." He praised the militiamen for protecting China's maritime interests in the disputed waters in the South China Sea.[25]

The PAFMM is also important politically as an organic arm of the military and state in the fishing industry. The hope is that militiamen will shape public opinion, setting an example for both enterprises and the masses as "model" mariners, inspiring them to get involved in maritime development and to travel to disputed sea areas, islands, and reefs.[26] This role was highlighted in October 2016 by the PLA Navy's own news service, which described various ways in which the PAFMM can utilize the "Three Warfares" (psychological, public opinion, and legal) in support of maritime rights protection. It cited the militiamen's numerical and geographical advantages and their ability to act as agents of the military and state without inciting suspicion and how such advantages can be leveraged to influence domestic and foreign public opinion. Furthermore, the news service noted, militiamen are granted significant leeway as to how they fulfill their manifold functions, unlike active-duty troops subject to numerous military and international regulations.[27] For example, as numerous sources describe, the PAFMM can use deceptive measures regarding uniforms: "putting on camouflage, they qualify as soldiers; taking off the camouflage, they become law-abiding fishermen."[28] This "plausible deniability" makes maritime militia forces ideal instruments for supporting Chinese maritime claims while insulating Beijing from escalation at sea or criticism abroad.

These advantages underpin China's operational use of the PAFMM. Militiamen are called to "serve in peacetime, respond to emergencies, and fight during war" (*pingshi fuwu, jishi yingji, zhanshi yingzhan*). The maritime militia's dual roles are often referred to as an "ability to fish and fight" (*nengyu, nengzhan*). They are assigned a variety of missions, from traditional logistics for ground forces to more advanced missions in support of the navy. As discussed, during peacetime the maritime militia focuses on protecting China's maritime rights and interests. The PAFMM missions and roles discussed in the following sections are based on PLA doctrine and are not exhaustive.[29]

Support the Front

In "support the front" (*zhiqian*) missions, the PAFMM assists the PLA and PLA Navy. Militiamen augment transport capacity by loading and delivering troops, vehicles, equipment, and materials; they conduct medical rescues and retrieve casualties; provide navigational assistance;

conduct emergency repairs or refits of vessels, docks, and other infra-structure; provide fuel and material replenishment at sea; and conduct various other logistical functions. All along China's coast, militiamen regularly train to support PLA operations.

The PAFMM also trains in minelaying and basic mine clearance. The PLA Navy assists the PAFMM in this area, usually in joint exercises. There appear to be PAFMM mine-warfare detachments that lack the necessary equipment. In some instances, naval reserve craft are integrated with PAFMM vessels to form a "naval reserve minesweeper *dadui*" (bat-talion).[30] Militiamen train on board PLA Navy minesweepers to be ready to execute that mission on their fishing vessels.[31] The Dalian district clearly outlined its PAFMM's mine-warfare and blockade/sea control missions in a catalogue of military actions to ensure maritime border security during a foreign invasion or major internal unrest in a neighbor-ing (unnamed) coastal state. Given Dalian's location on the Yellow Sea the reference is obviously to collapse of North Korean central authority; in such a scenario maritime militia units assist the PLA Navy and CCG in various ways, processing refugees and disarming former armed forces.[32]

Some maritime militia units have a deception mission (often referred to as *weizhuang fendui*), to use corner reflectors to increase their ves-sels' radar cross sections and thereby seem to be major ships on enemy sensors. Training events feature PAFMM vessels steaming in formation with mounted corner reflectors, attempting to resemble, on "enemy" radar, naval groups. The Jiaojiang Maritime Militia Deception Detach-ment conducted such a training event in October 2010; it involved multiple efforts to disrupt enemy surveillance and targeting, including corner reflectors and floated chaff canisters.[33] Another instance, in 2012, involved a naval militia resupply detachment that used smoke screens and corner reflectors against an "enemy" unmanned aerial vehicle (UAV) during a training assignment to rendezvous with a PLA Navy forma-tion.[34] To be sure, it is unclear exactly what is achieved by these relatively crude passive deception measures, but the fact that they are practiced at all indicates that the PLA plans to use every possible resource in any campaign to defend China. It seems likely that the PAFMM's members have realized that making one's fishing boat look like a warship on radar is a good way to get shot at during a conflict. How enthusiastic these units are about such a wartime mission is unknown.

One maritime militia unit under the Wenzhou Military Subdistrict (MSD) that once trained regularly with corner reflectors now employs instead technology capable of "electromagnetic attenuation and absorption."[35] For example, the Ninghai County PAFD in Zhejiang Province has assembled a special-warfare militia detachment of fifty-eight technical experts who conduct electronic warfare using specialized equipment installed on requisitioned civilian vessels. Serving as a "blue force" (i.e., the adversary) for training exercises simulating "blue" electronic signatures, they employ electronic jamming and electronic baiting against Chinese "red forces."[36] While this deception unit may not be the most sophisticated "opposition force" to train against, it offers a capability that the PLA Navy almost certainly appreciates.

Maritime Rights Protection

Over the past few years PAFMM responsibilities to conduct "rights protection" *(weiquan)* have become widely known in Western discourse and in many ways appear to have become the maritime militia's most important mission. This is because of the prominence that China's maritime disputes in the East and South China Seas have gained in Western policy interactions with Beijing, as well as in press and scholarly exchanges.

In 2015, Hainan Military District (MD) leaders outlined the PAFMM's specific missions in rights protection, including "Use of civilians against civilians for regular demonstration of rights" and "Special cases of rights protection by using civilians in cooperation with law enforcement."

In the first instance, the maritime militia will execute presence missions by fishing in disputed (but Chinese-claimed) waters. This mission seeks to normalize a Chinese "civilian" presence and justify the activities of the China Coast Guard to assert administrative control over disputed waters. Militia vessels can also be mobilized to harass or expel foreign civilian vessels found encroaching on fishing rights or disrupting Chinese development of islands and reefs or resource extraction. They can also provide regular escorts for Chinese civilian survey ships.

When operating in direct support of the coast guard, militiamen will "receive orders" from its command to conduct special rights-protection missions. For example, the maritime militia conduct perimeter patrols *(waiwei xunluo)*, enforce sea-area control *(haiqu fengkong)*, alert higher authority to and expel foreign vessels *(jingjie quli)*, confront those ships (*duizhi*), and push them back, with the coast guard (*heli bitui*).[37] In short, the PAFMM is increasingly assigned a core role within the "Maritime Rights Protection Force System" (*weiquan liliang tixi*).[38]

A prime example of the PAFMM's performance in maritime rights protection occurred when the CNOOC placed the drilling platform *HYSY 981* in disputed waters (within Vietnam's EEZ) southwest of Triton Island in the Paracels. The resulting confrontation saw a large-scale mobilization of militiamen from Guangdong, Guangxi, and Hainan Provinces to form a defensive perimeter around the drilling platform when Vietnamese maritime forces attempted to force the oil rig to leave.[39] Militiamen worked closely with the CCG to repulse numerous attempts by Vietnamese fishing vessels to penetrate the screen.

Emergency Response

Many units have been formed for emergency response (*yingji*)—that is, to handle "*tufa shijian*," a broad term that includes such fast-erupting contingencies as natural disasters, accidents, public-health incidents, and societal security incidents that develop rapidly, harm the public, and require unconventional responses.[40] In 2007, the National People's Congress passed the "Emergency Response Law of the People's Republic of China," which requires the militia to participate in relief efforts. Maritime-militia emergency response units are tasked with handling sudden incidents at sea, such as rescue and relief. They make good "first responders," as they may already be near the scene—as expressed by the phrase *jiudi jiujin*, referring to responses made by nearby local forces. All this tends to be a peacetime matter but would also certainly be involved in wartime as well.

One example of recent innovation in maritime-militia emergency response is a "partnership" with privately owned civil-aviation (tourist, advertising, training, and so forth) firms. In January 2016, the Qinhuangdao MSD in Hebei Province established a "maritime militia helicopter rescue detachment" with the resources of a private general-aviation company. The militia detachment has earmarked for its use two helicopters for rescue, patrol, and resupply missions.[41]

Intelligence, Surveillance, and Reconnaissance

The gathering and reporting of intelligence at sea has been a core mission of the maritime militia in both peace and war. Historically, China has used the PAFMM extensively in this role. Hiding in plain sight, maritime militia forces supplement the PLA's surveillance coverage of the near seas, by loitering around targets of interest or reporting sightings during their regular operations at sea. The development and introduction of new navigational and communications technology into China's fishing industry has significantly augmented the PAFMM's ability to provide valuable, timely intelligence to the PLA. PLA commanders are also currently developing maritime militia intelligence, surveillance, and reconnaissance (ISR) capabilities in the "far seas"; this important development will be discussed in detail below.[42] While the ISR mission is also sometimes termed a "support the front" role, its overall contribution to Chinese maritime domain awareness and its fundamental importance merit a more thorough examination in a separate section of this chapter.

Militia building and mobilization, collectively, is a civil-military venture that helps bind together civilian and military leaders—which is increasingly important as the proportion of party leaders with military experience decreases. As local leaders of coastal provinces look to the ocean for new areas of development and China's military strategy focuses more on maritime power, Beijing's national strategy of civil-military fusion will necessarily be at the forefront. The mobilization of China's mariner population into the PAFMM is one way of extending this civilian-military fusion out to sea.

Command and Control

PAFMM leadership follows the same dual military-civilian structure as that under which most militia organizations in China operate, with responsibilities for militia building falling on both local military organs and their government/party counterparts (*shuangchong lingdao*). In general, the responsibilities of both civilian and military entities are outlined as follows: "The Party Committee provides guidance, the military submits requirements, the National Defense Mobilization Committee (NDMC) coordinates, the government implements, and industries are the backbone."[43] This arrangement essentially integrates the civilian and military leadership in a division of labor for the common and required goal.

Many local governments along China's coast are constructing integrated coastal defense systems meant to implement better administrative control over nearby waters. Places such as Weihai City in Shandong

Province and China's newest prefecture, Sansha City, are organizing "military-police-civilian joint/integrated defense systems" (*junjingmin lianfang tixi*), which include maritime militia units. Sansha City's committee has been a focal point for such projects, with "three lines of defense" (militia, coast guard, and navy, in that order). The city has also established a joint defense coordination center, an integrated monitoring command center, and a "Hainan Province Paracels Islands Dynamic Monitoring System."[44]

As described in many Chinese-language sources on the PAFMM, mobilization orders are received from a variety of entities: the theater, sundry provincial and local authorities, or the China Coast Guard. There is significant overlap, because they all share responsibilities for the militia.[45] The main point is that while local governments are required to fund, supply, and support the militia, only the military holds the authority to use it.[46] In practice, this has created problems. Local authorities who have funded the militia have bridled at being told how to use it, especially if the local military commander has decided to employ it on a different task. In short, PAFMM's complex command-and-control structure routinely challenges local active-duty PLA authorities.

What is certainly clear is that militiamen are handed over to the CCG or PLA Navy for temporary use in both rights protection and combat support. The former chief of staff of the Guangdong MD describes the procedure for maritime rights protection as, "Mobilize the maritime militia in accordance with the requirements of the situation and orders given by superiors to go to mission sea areas where they will be transferred over to the command of the rights protection headquarters."[47]

The PLA does pay attention to the quality of the crews of each militia vessel. Promising grassroots-level cadres (*zhuanwu ganbu*) are recruited directly into PAFMM detachments in order to strengthen fishing-vessel command and control. Second, militiamen with "strong character" receive focused training to enhance the PAFMM's political reliability. Third, individuals with backgrounds as specialized "active-duty boat cadres" (*xianyi chuanting ganbu*) and signalmen (*tongxinbing*) are recruited to strengthen fishing-vessel piloting and communication controls.[48] The ambiguous term "boat cadre" connotes experienced people, including fishing-vessel captains, owners, and exceptional crew members.[49] Sources refer to the cadres as "boat bosses/skippers" (*chuan laoda*, 船老大) or simply "captains" (*chuanzhang*). Former active-duty personnel are given priority for entrance into the maritime militia, and they likely assume unit leadership roles, becoming cadres. Cadres make up an important group that helps maintain unit discipline and ensure that militia building is conducted at the grassroots level.[50]

C4ISR Network

As discussed above, intelligence, surveillance, and reconnaissance missions constitute one of the PAFMM's earliest and most consistent missions. They date back decades, replicating the use by imperial Japan of fishing boats as picket ships in its eastern maritime approaches during World War II.[51] As early as 2007, the PLA Navy recognized the need for a modernized civilian vessel and militia maritime-surveillance network and information-support system that capitalized on the country's vast fishing fleet. It wanted satellite services combining the Beidou positioning, navigation, and timing satellite system and automated shortwave radio transmission, fused so as to create near-real-time data connectivity. With it, China's large fishing fleet could supplement the PLA Navy's maritime domain awareness efforts. That same year, the Yuhuan County maritime militia "battalion" reported completion of a PAFMM surveillance and early-warning network covering the "far seas, near seas, and shoreline." Xiangshan County of Zhejiang Province operates a large PAFMM reconnaissance detachment that follows a pattern laid out by the PLA Navy, with thirty-two "mother ships" acting as nodes for 150 vessels forming a network of surveillance.[52]

MLE forces already use a number of communications systems—such as Beidou, very-high-frequency radio, the Automatic Identification System (AIS), cellular coverage when available, and satellite phones—to ensure reliable command and control when at sea. The equipment is provided to the PAFMM by MSDs, which purchase and distribute satellite navigation terminals, navigational radar, radios, and other electronic equipment.

The Ministry of Agriculture has constructed fisheries command and dispatch centers and regional command-dispatch platforms. According to the Fisheries Law Enforcement Command Center's director, a blend of capabilities forms an important part of the nation's emergency-response and early-warning system: fourteen shortwave shore stations, seventy-eight ultra-high-frequency shore stations, fifteen provincial fishing-vessel position-monitoring centers, thirty fisheries AIS base stations, and fifty-nine fishing port video surveillance branches, established nation-wide.[53] This is a redundant communications and monitoring network built and made available to allow the PLA to maintain reliable communications with militia fishing vessels when they are under way.

In addition to this traditional communication network, Beidou satellite navigation and the vessel-monitoring systems in many provinces have yielded an all-weather, continuous monitoring capability that MLE agencies can use to manage fishing fleets. Beidou terminals have been widely installed on China's fishing vessels, allowing the agencies to track their positions and exchange two-way transmissions of up to 120 Chinese characters—enough to dispatch orders to fishing boats as far away as the Spratlys. The growth of the Beidou constellation into global coverage will also expand the range of communications support to China's maritime militia.

In some areas, Beidou has become an important supplement to AIS, which uses shore-based stations to receive ship positioning and identification information. When fishing boats are beyond the range of shore AIS stations, Beidou's AIS transceiver automatically turns on (it turns itself off when within range of the shore station, to avoid duplicate tracks). The widespread implementation of Beidou's vessel-monitoring system, which includes a marine fisheries integrated information service, facilitates control of PAFMM vessels at sea. The head of Zhejiang MD's Mobilization Division has written that military organs use these systems for monitoring fishing-vessel safety and rescue, as part of building a PAFMM–Fisheries Law Enforcement–MSD–PLA Navy information-sharing channel.[54]

Supporting this surveillance network are various local reporting mechanisms. PAFMM reporting channels are typically between vessels and departments of the MD system on shore. For example, Rizhao City's Lanshan District has established a real-time reporting mechanism for its militiamen to use when monitoring the sea and air; it connects vessels at sea with the militia command center, the fisheries bureau command center, and the PAFD's war readiness office.[55] PLA writings indicate that maritime militia reports are increasingly integrated into the theater command's larger intelligence infrastructure.[56]

For example, the PLA garrison in Zhoushan City, an archipelagic municipality in the East China Sea, has made significant progress in developing its maritime militia ISR network. The garrison has tapped into the city's marine-data collection effort to set up a networked center for maritime national defense mobilization, utilizing big-data collection at sea. Fisheries data and vessel monitoring systems give this PLA garrison mobilization office the information it needs to command and control its PAFMM forces in real time. Militia reports flow in constantly, according to the mobilization office's chief of staff, who oversees the twenty-four-hour operations of the garrison's watch-duty room. PAFMM reconnaissance units send video and audio feeds and photography directly to the garrison, giving the PLA "eyes" on board militia vessels. The Zhoushan garrison reported that during 2014–15, militiamen generated over three hundred reports involving military sea and air intelligence, of which more than 130 were of value to the MD and higher-level units.[57] PAFMM reporting deemed "effective maritime intelligence" is processed and disseminated up the chain of command, reaching the theater-command level.[58]

Militiamen are often termed "mobile sentries" at sea. PAFMM-provided data reportedly directly supports PLA targeting and tracking. The PLA garrison in Jiangsu's Lianyungang held an exercise in late 2015 wherein PAFMM forces provided targeting support to a PLA Navy coastal artillery unit (*anfang budui danpao*). In the scenario, a PAFMM vessel reported a "suspicious vessel" forty nautical miles offshore by calling the garrison's watch-duty room directly via satellite phone. The commander then ordered a shore-based signals unit to transfer the PAFMM vessel's video feed to a radar station. After the garrison command had determined the that vessel was an enemy and verified its location, sensor and targeting data were sent to the coastal artillery unit.[59] This account suggests that any foreign warship within China's claimed EEZ and in range of its coastal defenses may be positively identified and targeted, thanks to the maritime militia.

Means to report surveillance information are obviously important, but so is the quality of information reported. Selected militia members are trained as reporting specialists—that is, information personnel (*xinxi-yuan*)—within units. These personnel collect intelligence at sea and use the Beidou and other reporting systems to ensure that the information is sent up the chain. For instance, Fu'an, a city in Fujian Province opposite Taiwan, held a week-long collective training session for its maritime militia information personnel, covering target identification, essentials of collection methods, and operation of the maritime militia vessel-management platform and the Beidou notification terminal. Also, the PLA is implementing secure communications with the maritime militia. A unit in China's southern Guangdong Province reportedly uses prede-signed "secret code tables," "secure walkie talkies," and "secure radios" to maintain PLA Navy–PAFMM ship-to-ship communications.[60] In short, the PAFMM has created a cadre of personnel specifically trained to ensure expertise and professionalism in reconnaissance.

In May 2017 the PRC minister of defense, Chang Wanquan, com-mended the captain of a militia boat assigned to a reconnaissance detach-ment based in China's eastern Jiangsu Province. The militiaman was praised for spotting the missile instrumentation ship USNS *Howard O. Lorenzen* (T-AGM 25). He had led other vessels of his unit in surround-ing, surveilling, and filming the American ship. The minister "pointed out that the maritime militia is very important and has played a key role in filling in maritime reconnaissance blind spots, as 'small boats' transform into a 'maritime defense with eyes that can see for thousands of miles.'"[61] The availability of technology to the militia is increasingly enhancing its ability to provide ISR support to the PLA. In 2018, the PLA garrison in Shanghai conducted a training exercise with a militia UAV reconnaissance detachment. This detachment contains a "maritime unit" for UAV opera-tions at sea.[62]

The PLA is also developing the PAFMM's ability to support under-sea surveillance. A report of the Xiashan PAFD commander in 2014 included "undersea detection radar" (水下探测雷达) among the equip-ment to be allocated to maritime militia.[63] This commander forwarded in March 2016 a photo of a PAFMM vessel deploying an unmanned underwater vehicle. The photo's caption read, "Going to sea on vessels to collect intelligence."[64] Another report mentions a maritime militia rescue company in Hebei Province with towed side-scan sonars.[65]

One province has outlined specific "doctrine" for PAFMM ISR, laying out the following guidelines for training:

- Dispersal to predetermined sea areas for reconnaissance as "fixed sentries."
- Close-in reconnaissance to verify the identities of suspicious targets as required by the PLA Navy.

- Covert tracking and following of enemy ships and aircraft, to be conducted in concert with other dispersed PAFMM vessels, trading off and coordinating to track target movements.
- Special reconnaissance tasking will involve distributing and installing specialized equipment on militia vessels, such as electronic detection instruments and fish-finding instruments.
- Units listen in on enemy maritime radio signals and detect submarines.[66]

Maritime militia ISR operations fluctuate during the year, since most militia reporting ceases during the PRC-declared annual fishing moratorium that begins in May of each year. In those periods of nominally three months, most fishing vessels are in port, but commanders ensure that militiamen maintain readiness to mobilize.[67] PLA leaders in Zhejiang Province MD suggest that some additional types of fishing vessels should be recruited to supplement the larger trawler fleet during the moratorium. Fishing vessels not designed for trawling are subject to a shorter moratorium, as established by the Ministry of Agriculture, and could fill ISR gaps left by the stand-down of the large trawler fleets.[68]

China possesses the world's largest distant-water fishing and merchant marine fleets. The PLA sees great potential in ISR contributions from these fleets, as they operate around the globe in numerous countries' exclusive economic zones and in key shipping lanes. PLA writings increasingly describe PAFMM ISR functions in terms of geographic distance from China's shoreline. For example, the Shanghai PLA garrison's "comprehensive training unit" describes PAFMM ISR in "distant waters" (*yuanyang*) and differentiates between "militia near-seas reconnaissance and early-warning detachments" and "militia far-seas reconnaissance and early-warning detachments." Additional PLA writings describe the need for more PAFMM units that can move from the near seas into the far seas. Some state outright that vessels in oceanic shipping, marine exploration, and even overseas trade should have "distant waters information personnel" (*yuanyang xinxiyuan*) assigned.[69] Presumably, the information from far-seas reconnaissance would be funneled to a centralized command center, not to provincial MD commands.

Two authors from the PLA's Equipment Academy published an article in 2017 about the need to development a "sea and space common operational picture" (*haitian yiti zhanchang tongyong taishitu*) to support the PLA Navy's far-seas operations. They listed PAFMM "armed reconnaissance fishing vessels" and merchant ships among the sources of surface ISR that would build this common operational picture.[70] Such a development, if fully realized, would also involve the command, control, and management of militia organizations on board Chinese ships in distant waters. To date, there has been virtually no Chinese open-source reporting on actual PAFMM operations outside of the near seas. The discussions (see the preceding paragraphs) of extending ISR networks from the near seas to the far seas suggest that the PLA is considering the development of far-seas ISR generated by a global maritime footprint composed of multiple forces. Whether the PAFMM would play any leading role in such a network—covertly or overtly—remains unknown.

In sum, command of the maritime militia depends on the conditions requiring mobilization, in both peace and war. The PLA utilizes the PAFMM in both peacetime and wartime, as and when needed. The coast guard can also call on PAFMM forces for rights-protection or law-enforcement missions but may be required to provide them material support. In all cases, the MD military and civilian leadership would be involved, either directly or in an oversight role. New institutions and technologies are being incorporated into the mobilization system in order to increase the speed with which local commands can transfer war-fighting potential into war-fighting force. From theater command–led joint exercises to MD-level mobilization orders, and from Beidou messages received by captains operating fishing vessels at sea down to individual militiamen receiving local PAFD notifications on their mobile phones, the means of reliably commanding the maritime militia are growing in sophistication and effectiveness. Here is a powerful example of the PLA's concept of "informatization" at the micro level.

Training

Training of militia is not so intense that it harms the militia members' normal work. To compensate, the PAFD active-duty personnel, cadres, battalion/company and militia unit commanders, and the militia information personnel receive focused training. This is essentially a matter of "training the trainers"; these individuals are expected to train individual militia members in turn. Well-trained supervisors are necessary, since rarely can a region make its entire PAFMM force available for a single training event. For example, a PRC district near the Taiwanese-controlled Matsu Islands was able to train only one-fourth of its emergency-response militia personnel during any given exercise.[71] Limited availability for training is one reason why demobilized active-duty soldiers and party members are priority recruiting targets: they tend to have substantially more experience with training, which in itself involves substantial effort. For example, Zhejiang Province in 2015 reportedly mobilized over a thousand maritime militia vessels for training exercises.[72] Given the independence of nature that characterizes fishermen worldwide, keeping a militia force manned by such people sufficiently disciplined and trained to do that requires continuous effort.

Strong political indoctrination is applied to militia organizations generally, but especially to PAFMM units, since they can disproportionately affect events and diplomacy at sea. It is important that militiamen be familiar with national and provincial objectives and policies. They often receive education in the laws of the sea and rules governing what they can and cannot do.

Previously there existed a degree of separation between the PLA services and the militia units built to support them, particularly in management of training. Joint training was conducted, but evaluations and improvements were largely the work of the PLA MDs. The PLA reforms of 2015 stipulated deeper integration between militia units assigned to support the military. Many maritime-militia units assigned to support the navy are now being trained and evaluated directly by naval personnel. In China's northern province of Liaoning, on the Bohai Sea, the Huludao MSD conducted training for five maritime militia detachments at a navy test base in January 2018. Experts from the Naval Aviation Academy, Ministry of Security, and the Maritime Safety Agency were brought in to teach the militia about oceanography, hydrometeorology, shipboard communications equipment, and reconnaissance of land and sea targets. Joint training between maritime militia vessels and actual PLA Navy ships is also increasing.[73]

Incentives

Vessel owners complain about the opportunity cost of being detained dockside by militia obligations. Local governments and regulations concerning vessel mobilization and requisition allow for monetary compensation to vessel owners and personnel for lost income in such cases. In other circumstances, to offset PAFMM expenses and make its units willing to venture farther from home port (e.g., to the Spratlys), many local governments subsidize their fuel.[74] Hainan's Tanmen Village provides fuel subsidies to its PAFMM units for the expense of travel to the Spratlys.[75]

A system of rewards and publicity for militiamen is in place, its events usually held during provincial military affairs meetings. A series of awards recognizes advanced militia units, advanced captains and cadres, and other outstanding individuals; such accolades are meant to instill pride and a sense of national duty. Other efforts are aimed at preventing abuse or neglect of militia obligations; these include requiring each fishing vessel and its crew to have the appropriate National Defense Obligation Certificates for national defense and mobilization. These are reviewed annually to ensure that all are current. If crews violate their obligations, their fuel subsidies are reduced or eliminated, and their fishing permits could be canceled.

Specific missions will require tailored incentives and rewards. For instance, the Shanghai PLA garrison is reportedly trying to implement rewards to PAFMM reconnaissance units for each intelligence report they generate. Dispatches deemed important will generate greater rewards.[76] Such a system could conceivably motivate militiamen to seek out the "big fish" and provide higher-quality intelligence reports for the PLA.

An Important Element of Chinese Seapower

The PAFMM helps China pursue its near-seas claims and operationalize a decisive shift in strategy: from a three-sea-force focus on regional seas to an evolving division of labor in which the PLA Navy is enabled to increase its overseas missions and focus significantly, in part by the assumption of increasing responsibilities in China's near seas by the coast guard and PAFMM. For this the PAFMM has been able to draw on the world's largest fishing fleet.

Continued tensions in the South and East China Seas bring increased attention to the important role the PAFMM plays. Some Chinese scholars and security experts advocate making militiamen China's first line of defense in confrontations over maritime disputes. In many cases they are already deployed to the front lines, such as around Scarborough Shoal.

Since Xi's April 2013 visit to Hainan, numerous *PLA Daily* and *National Defense* articles have recommended increasing support for PAFMM development. Increasing financial resources are allocated to train fishermen and subsidize new vessels. This desire likely drove the rapid construction of Sansha City's new purpose-built, professionalized PAFMM fleet, which in turn has introduced a new model in force development, one which could conceivably be replicated elsewhere as reduced stocks undermine China's fishing industry.

The PAFMM supports China's overall maritime surveillance system. Since the key to China's anti-access/area-denial system is the close monitoring of China's seaward approaches, it is hardly surprising that the PLA has elected to capitalize on the capabilities that its fishing fleet offers. In addition to surveillance, other low-intensity peacetime missions include supporting rights protection (presence missions, obstruction, reef/island development, envelopment, etc.) and dealing with fishing-fleet skirmishes over maritime claims. Should conflicts between China and its smaller regional neighbors break out, the maritime militia might be charged with such wartime tasks as mine warfare, ambush, or island landings. Chinese planners envision employing the PAFMM in unexpected, unconventional ways in addition to its surveillance, rights-protection, and support roles. New reforms introduced to China's armed forces are comprehensively strengthening the nation's PAFMM forces to support future maritime operations in peace and war.

NOTES

Preface

1. Andrew Lambert, *Seapower States: Maritime Culture, Continental Empires and the Conflict That Made the Modern World* (New Haven, CT: Yale University Press, 2018), 313.
2. Xi Jinping, "Secure a Decisive Victory in Building a Moderately Prosperous Society in All Respects and Strive for the Great Success of Socialism with Chinese Characteristics for a New Era," delivered at the 19th National Congress of the Communist Party of China, October 18, 2017, 48, available at http://www.xinhuanet.com/english/ download/Xi_Jinping%27s_report_at_19th_CPC_National_Congress.pdf.

Chapter One. China's Maritime Power Ambition

1. This chapter owes much to the research and written work of Dr. Thomas Bickford, a colleague in the Center for Naval Analyses' China and Indo-Pacific Security Affairs division, especially his (coauthored with Fred Vellucci Jr. and Heidi Holz) *China as a Maritime Challenge: The Strategic Dimension*, CNA Research Memorandum D0023549. A3/1 (Alexandria, VA, rev. October 2010) and his paper "Haiyang Qiangguo: China as a Maritime Power," for the "China as a Maritime Power Conference" held at the Center for Naval Analyses in July 2015, https://apps.dtic.mil/dtic/tr/fulltext/u2/1014584.pdf.
2. Liza Tobin, "Underway: Beijing's Strategy to Build China into a Maritime Great Power," *Naval War College Review* 71, no. 2 (Spring 2018). She writes in endnote 3 that Hu's phrase 建设海洋强国 is to be translated as "build [a] maritime great power" or "build [China] into a maritime great power." "Maritime great power" (海洋强国) also could be translated "strong maritime nation" or simply "maritime power." However translated, the intent is clear to this author, who will use "maritime great power" and "great maritime power" interchangeably.
3. "Full Text of Hu Jintao's Report to the 18th Party Congress," *Embassy of the People's Republic of China in the United States of America*, November 11, 2012, http://www.china -embassy.org/eng/zt/18th_CPC_National_Congress_Eng/t992917.htm.
4. Alice Miller, "How to Read Xi Jinping's 19th Party Congress Political Report," Hoover Institution, *China Leadership Monitor*, issue 53 (Spring 2017).
5. The source—an article from *People's Navy* in December 2006—for the Hu quotes is found in endnote 30 of Andrew Erickson and Lyle Goldstein, "Gunboats for China's New 'Grand Canals'? Probing the Intersection of Beijing's Naval and Oil Security Policies," *Naval War College Review* 62, no. 2 (Spring 2009). Erickson and Goldstein's article is an invaluable early effort by American scholars to understand Chinese thinking about oil security and sea-lane vulnerability. It offers useful insights into China's anxieties regarding its growing dependence on imported oil carried to China on ships.
6. Xi Jinping, "Secure a Decisive Victory," 48 [emphasis added].
7. David M. Finkelstein, "Breaking the Paradigm: Drivers behind the PLA's Current Period of Reform," in *Chairman Xi Remakes the PLA: Assessing Chinese Military Reforms*, ed. Phillip Saunders et al. (Washington, DC: National Defense University Press, 2019).

8. Daniel Hartnett and Fredric Vellucci, "Toward a Maritime Security Strategy: An Analysis of Chinese Views since the Early 1990s," in *The Chinese Navy: Expanding Capabilities, Evolving Roles,* ed. Philipp C. Saunders et al. (Washington, DC: National Defense University Press, 2011).

9. Beyond issues associated with building China into a maritime power, the 2012 white paper is important also because it defines specific "far seas"–related operations for the PLA Navy: humanitarian missions, escort operations, evacuation of Chinese citizens abroad in periods of crisis or natural disaster, and joint exercises with foreign partners. Finally, the 2012 white paper justifies the PLA's deploying for "diversified missions" that support China's international standing and its security and developmental interests. See Daniel Hartnett, *China's 2012 Defense White Paper: Panel Discussion Report,* CNA China Studies, CCP-2013-U-005876 Final (Alexandria, VA: Center for Naval Analyses, September 2013).

10. See State Council Information Office, *The Diversified Employment of China's Armed Forces* (Beijing, April 2013) [emphasis added]. The official English translation is available at http://news.xinhuanet.com/english/china/2013–04/16/c_132312681.htm. Hereafter, this and other defense white papers from China will be referred to and cited as "[YEAR] DWP."

11. Geoffrey Till, *Seapower: A Guide for the Twenty-First Century,* 3rd ed. (New York: Routledge, 2013).

12. Even Mahan, who coined the term "sea power," did not define it, but it is clear that in his seminal work he equated sea power with success in major naval battles. See Alfred Thayer Mahan, *The Influence of Sea Power upon History, 1660–1783* (Boston: Little, Brown, 1890; repr. London: Methuen, 1965).

13. The definition is drawn from a first-rate work by Dr. Ian Speller, *Understanding Naval Warfare* (New York: Routledge, 2014), 6.

14. Adm. Thomas Collins, Commandant, U.S. Coast Guard, address before the International Sea Power Symposium, October 27, 2003, in John B. Hattendorf, ed., *Sixteenth International Sea Power Symposium: Report of Proceedings* (Newport, RI: Naval War College, 2012), 43.

15. Bickford, Vellucci, and Holtz, *China as a Maritime Challenge.* The legal analysis of China's maritime rights and interests is drawn from Isaac Kardon, "China's Maritime Rights and Interests: Organizing to Become a Maritime Power," paper for the "China as a 'Maritime Power'" Conference, July 2015, Center for Naval Analyses, Alexandria, VA. The policy implications are my own.

16. Chris C. P. Chung, "Drawing the U-Shaped Line: China's Claim in the South China Sea, 1946–1974," *Modern China,* August 11, 2015, and Bill Hayton, "The Modern Origins of China's Claims in in the South China Sea," *Modern China,* May 4, 2018.

17. Xi is cited in Dean Cheng, "China's 'Core' Maritime Interests: Security and Economic Factors," testimony before the Subcommittee on Asia of the Committee on Foreign Affairs, U.S. House of Representatives, Washington, DC, February 28, 2017.

18. Kardon, "Maritime Rights and Interests," 45–48.

19. Liu Kefu, "Push Forward the Construction of Maritime Power with Threefold Efforts," *Zhongguo Haiyangbao,* September 17, 2013, cited in Kardon, "Maritime Rights and Interests," 7 [emphasis added].

20. "Xi Jinping Stresses the Need to Show Greater Care about the Ocean, Understand More about the Ocean and Make Strategic Plans for the Use of the Ocean, Push Forward the Building of a Maritime Power and Continuously Make New Achievements at the Eighth Collective Study Session of the CPC Central Committee Political Bureau," Xinhua, July 31, 2013.

21. "Xi Jinping Stresses the Need to Show Greater Care about the Ocean."

22. Military Strategy Research Department of the Academy of Military Science, *The Science of Military Strategy* (Beijing: Academy of Military Science Press, 2013), 100, 210 [emphasis added].

23. Military Strategy Research Department, 99.
24. Good works on China's Century of Humiliation include: Julia Lovell, *The Opium War: Drugs, Dreams, and the Making of China* (London: Picador, 2011); Robert Bickers, *The Scramble for China: Foreign Devils in the Qing Empire, 1832–1914* (London: Penguin Books, 2011); S. C. M. Paine, *The Sino-Japanese War of 1894–1895: Perceptions, Power, and Primacy* (New York: Cambridge University Press, 2003); and Rana Mitter, *Forgotten Ally: China's World War II, 1937–1945* (Boston: Houghton Mifflin Harcourt, 2013).
25. Xi Jinping, 19th Party Congress work report, 11.
26. Military Strategy Research Department, *Science of Military Strategy*, 209.
27. Angela Monaghan, "China Surpasses US as World's Largest Trading Nation," *Guardian*, January 10, 2014.
28. Jiang Zemin, "Report to the 14th Party Congress," *Beijing Review*, March 29, 2011 (full text, unpaginated), www.bjreview.com.cn/document/txt/2011-03/29 /content_363504.htm.
29. Wayne M. Morrison, *China's Economic Rise: History, Trends, Challenges and Implications for the United States* (Washington, DC: Congressional Research Service, February 5, 2018).
30. U.S. Energy Information Administration, "China Surpassed the United States as World's Largest Crude Oil Importer in 2017," *Today in Energy*, February 5, 2018.
31. "China's Top Commodity Imports and Exports," Commodity.com, https://commodity .com/country-profiles/china/#chinas-top-5-commodity-imports.
32. Erickson and Goldstein, "Gunboats for China's New 'Grand Canals'?"
33. United Nations Security Council, Resolution 1838 (2008), S/RES/1838 (2008), October 7, 2008.
34. "ICC Commercial Crime Services," *International Chamber of Commerce*, https://www .icc-ccs.org/.
35. State Council Information Office, *China's Military Strategy*, May 2015, 3, http://eng .mod.gov.cn/Database/WhitePapers/index.htm.
36. Riu Zhao, Stephen Hynes, and Guang Shaun He, "Defining and Quantifying China's Ocean Economy," *Marine Policy* 43 (2014).
37. Quotation in Tabitha Grace Mallory, "Preparing for the Ocean Century: China's Changing Political Institutions for Governance and Maritime Development," *Issues & Studies* 51, no. 2 (June 2015): 111–38. This article also helped me understand Beijing's expansive vision of ocean development.
38. Zhang Hongzhou, "China's Fishing Industry," in *Securing the "Rice Bowl": China and Global Food Security* (Basingstoke, U.K.: Palgrave Macmillan, 2018), 125–53; Zhang Hongzhou, "Security Implications of China's Rising Appetite for Seafood," June 28, 2018; Stop Illegal Fishing, "Cracking Down on China's Distant Water Fishing Fleet" (blog), September 21, 2018, https://stopillegalfishing.com/press-links/cracking-down -on-chinas-distant-water-fishing-fleet-what-impacts-closer-to-home/.
39. Qing Hong, "Research Summary on the Construction of Marine Food System," *Marine Sciences* 39, no. 1 (2015).
40. Richard C. Bush, "8 Key Things to Notice from Xi Jinping's New Year Speech on Taiwan," *Order from Chaos* (Brookings Institution blog), January 7, 2019, https://www .brookings.edu/blog/order-from-chaos/2019/01/07/8-key-things-to-notice-from-xi -jinpings-new-year-speech-on-taiwan/.
41. Stacy Hsu, "Over 80% Reject 'Two Systems,' Poll Finds," *Taipei Times*, January 10, 2019, http://www.taipeitimes.com/News/front/archives/2019/01/10/2003707656.
42. David M. Finkelstein, "China's National Military Strategy: An Overview of the 'Military Strategic Guidelines,'" in *Rightsizing the People's Liberation Army: Exploring the Contours of China's Military*, ed. Roy Kamphausen and Andrew Scobell (Carlisle, PA: U.S. Army War College, 2007).

43. Bruce A. Elleman, *High Seas Buffer: The Taiwan Patrol Force, 1950–1979*, Newport Paper 38 (Newport, RI: Naval War College Press, 2013).

44. Jiang Zemin, *Jiang Zemin's Selected Works* (Beijing, 2006), 289, cited in M. Taylor Fravel, "Shifts in Warfare and Party Unity: Explaining China's Changes in Military Strategy," *International Security* 42, no. 3 (Winter 2017): 37–83.

45. For an authoritative discussion of the crisis, see Robert L. Suettinger, *Beyond Tiananmen: The Politics of U.S.-China Relations, 1989–2000* (Washington, DC: Brookings Institution Press, 2003, 247–63. As to whether U.S. aircraft carriers sailed through the Taiwan Strait: they did not until some months later (see 260).

46. Cited in Richard Bush, "What Xi Jinping Said about Taiwan at the 19th Party Congress," *Order from Chaos* (Brookings Institution blog), October 19, 2017, https://www.brookings.edu/blog/order-from-chaos/2017/10/19/what-xi-jinping-said-about-taiwan-at-the-19th-party-congress/.

47. Peng Guangqian and Yang Youzhi, eds., *The Science of Military Strategy* (Beijing: Military Science Publishing House, Academy of Military Science of the People's Liberation Army, 2005), 442–43.

48. U.S.-China Economic and Security Review Commission, *2018 Annual Report, Chapter 3, Section One*, November 14, 2018, 272–75, https://www.uscc.gov/.

49. Xi Jinping, "Work Together to Build a 21st Century Maritime Silk Road," and Xi Jinping, "Promote the Silk Road Spirit, Strengthen China-Arab Cooperation," in *The Governance of China* (Beijing: Foreign Languages Press, 2014). See also the website of the Asian Infrastructure Investment Bank, www.aiib.org; and Yun Pumin, "A Second Wind for an Ancient Route," *Beijing Review*, February 5, 2015, http://beijingreview.sinoperi.com/en20156/885487.jhtml.

50. Jeffery Becker and Erica Downs, "China's Djibouti Military Base the First of Many," *East Asia Forum*, June 27, 2018.

51. Jonas Parello-Plesner and Mathieu Duchatel, *China's Strong Arm: Protecting Citizens and Assets Abroad*, Adelphi Series (London: Routledge for the International Institute for Strategic Studies, May 2015), 9. The Chinese themselves understood that this event reflected a significant growth of China's comprehensive national power; "Chinese Naval Vessels Evacuate Hundreds from War Torn Yemen," Xinhua, April 8, 2015, *China Development Gateway*, en.chinagate.cn/2015–04/08/content_35270564.htm.

52. *China's Military Strategy*, 2015, 3.

53. James Mulvenon, "The Cult of Xi and the Rise of the CMC Chairman Responsibility System," Hoover Institution, *China Leadership Monitor*, issue 55 (Winter 2018).

54. Michael Swaine, "Chinese Views of Foreign Policy in the 19th Party Congress," Hoover Institution, *China Leadership Monitor*, issue 55 (Winter 2018).

55. A literal rendering of the Chinese characters would be a "comprehensive, first rate, world-class military." Thanks for this information to Dr. Thomas Bickford, who tells me that this phrase is now considered part of "Xi Jinping thought."

56. Xi Jinping, 19th Party Congress work report, 29, 48.

57. Xi is quoted in "China Has Put Missiles on Islands in the South China Sea," *Economist*, May 10, 2018.

58. Dennis Blasko, "PLA Weaknesses and Xi's Concerns about PLA Capabilities," Testimony before the U.S.-China Economic and Security Review Commission, Washington, DC, February 7, 2019.

Chapter Two. Getting Started

1. This chapter includes a distillation of my "PLA Naval Exercises with International Partners," which first appeared in *Learning by Doing: The PLA Trains at Home and Abroad*, ed. Roy Kamphausen, David Lai, and Travis Tanner (Carlisle, PA: Strategic Studies Institute, U.S. Army War College, November 30, 2012).

2. David G. Muller Jr.'s 1983 *China's Emergence as a Maritime Power* was reissued as *China as a Maritime Power* (Lexington, VA: Rockbridge Books, 2016), 200, 220–31.

3. Muller, 211. Another excellent discussion is in Christopher D. Yung et al., *China's Out of Area Naval Operations: Case Studies, Trajectories, Obstacles and Potential Solutions*, INSS China Strategic Perspectives (Washington, DC: National Defense University Press, December 2010), 9.

4. Yung, 10–11.

5. See Michael McDevitt, "The Modern PLA Navy Destroyer Force: Impressive Progress in Achieving a Far Seas Capability," in *China's Evolving Surface Fleet*, ed. Peter A. Dutton and Ryan D. Martinson, China Maritime Study 14 (Newport, RI: Naval War College Press for the China Maritime Studies Institute, 2017), 55–65.

6. Huang Li, *Sword Pointed at the Gulf of Aden: The PLAN's Far Seas Shining Sword* (Guangzhou, PRC: Zhongshan University Press 2009), 217.

7. I have personal experience with underway replenishments in bad western Pacific weather in small destroyer-type ships. As a junior officer in the late 1960s I served in one of the renowned World War II–era 2,500-ton (full load) *Fletcher*-class destroyers that still was in commission.

8. Interestingly, they were powered by General Electric LM 2500 gas-turbine engines, the type that power U.S. Navy destroyers today. These engines had been sold to China in the 1980s, before post–Tiananmen Square sanctions were applied. Because the sanction regime cut off spare parts, they may have been replaced during a major refit in 2011 with the Ukrainian gas-turbine engines in widespread use in the PLA Navy today.

9. See McDevitt, "Modern PLA Navy Destroyer Force," 59–62.

10. Shahryar Pasandideh, "Less Visible Aspects of Chinese Military Modernization," *Diplomat*, September 21, 2018.

11. Edward J. M. Rhoads, *Manchus and Han: Ethnic Relations and Political Power in Late Qing and Early Republican China, 1861–1928* (Seattle: University of Washington Press, 2000), 150.

12. "Chinese Cruiser Welcomed to Port: First Ship Flying the Yellow Dragon Flag to American Waters," September 12, 1911, https://timesmachine.nytimes.com/.

13. Gabriel Collins and Michael C. Grubb, *A Comprehensive Survey of China's Dynamic Shipbuilding Industry*, China Maritime Study 1 (Newport, RI: Naval War College Press for the China Maritime Studies Institute, August 2008), 32.

14. Li Jianguo, "Keeping the Seas Safe," *Beijing Review*, March 22, 2007, http://www .bjreview.com/print/txt/2007–03/19/content_59601_2.htm.

15. See McDevitt, "PLA Naval Exercises with International Partners," 99.

16. Lu Desheng and Li Gencheng, "'Xiangfan' Returns in Triumph after Joining Maritime Exercise of WPNS," *PLA Daily (Jiefangjun Bao)*, May 24, 2007, OSE Product ID: CPP20070525715007.

17. Andrew Forbes, "Western Pacific Naval Symposium," in *Australian Maritime Issues 2006: SPC-A Annual*, Papers in Australian Maritime Affairs 19, 2006, ed. Andrew Forbes and Michelle Lovi (Canberra: Australian Department of Defense, 2007), 183–87.

18. "PRC, Spanish Navies Conduct 'First Ever' Joint Military Exercise in Atlantic Ocean," Xinhua, September 18, 2007, OSE Product ID: CPP20070918968182; "China, France Conduct Joint Naval Exercise in Mediterranean," Xinhua, September 25, 2007, OSE Product ID: CPP20070925968163; "Two Chinese Warships Arrive in Portsmouth for Good-Will Visit," Xinhua, September 6, 2007, OSE Product ID: CPP20070906968242.

19. Xia Hongping and Hou Yaming, "Chinese Navy Task Force Back from Visits to Australia, New Zealand," November 4, 2007, www.china.org.cn/english?China /223960.htm.

20. United Nations Resolution 1816 (2008), adopted by the UN Security Council on June 2, 2008, https://www.securitycouncilreport.org/. In the review of the draft resolution before passage, China's UN ambassador said, in part, "The rise of piracy off the coast of that country constituted a great threat to its peace process and international efforts

for humanitarian relief. Somalia had asked for assistance in combating piracy, and the international community was widely supportive of that request. The Council had authorized Member States to assist the Government in combating piracy, and China supported prompt adoption of the text"; UN Security Council press release, "Security Council Condemns Acts of Piracy, Armed Robbery off Somalia's Coast, Authorizes for Six Months 'All Necessary Means' to Repress Such Acts," June 2, 2008, https://www.un.org/.

21. Alison Kaufman, *China's Participation in Anti-Piracy Operations off the Horn of Africa: A Conference Report*, CNA China Study D0020835.A1 Final (Alexandria, VA: Center for Naval Analyses, July 2009).

22. The Shared Awareness and Deconfliction initiative began in 2008 as an organized process for coordinating and deconflicting activities of the countries and coalitions involved in military counterpiracy operations in the Gulf of Aden and the western Indian Ocean. The meetings are held in Bahrain at regular intervals and are cochaired on a rotational basis by the Combined Maritime Forces, NATO, and the European Union Naval Force. Since the beginning in 2008, military and civilian representatives from thirty-three countries, fourteen international organizations, maritime industry, and several governments have joined the meetings. See P. K. Ghosh, "Shared Awareness and Deconfliction: Can the Success Story Be Applied to Southeast Asia?," *Indo-Pacific Defense Forum*, February 13, 2016, https://ipdefenseforum.com/.

23. For more detail on China's role, see Andrew Erickson and Austin Strange, "China and the International Anti-Piracy Effort," *Diplomat*, November 1, 2013.

24. Li Jie, "China's Navy Still Has Far to Go," *China Daily*, August 8, 2009, www.chinadaily.com.cn/opinion/2009–08/14/content_8568918.htm.

25. "JFJB Marks 2nd Anniversary of Start of PRC Navy Escorts off Somalia," *Jiefangjun Bao Online*, December 24, 2010, CPP20110105088005.

26. "Qiandaohu (Fuchi)–Class Auxiliary Oiler Replenishment Ship," Globalmil.com, www.globalmil.com/. This class comprises the first PRC-built AOEs—that is, capable of resupplying fuel, water, stores, and ammunition, whereas previous indigenous replenishment ships were actually fleet oilers. The ships can support general-purpose task groups, amphibious task groups, or even aircraft carrier battle groups.

27. Jiao Bofeng, Hou Rui, and Yu Qizheng, "Crisscrossing the Four Seas and Making Its Might Known Everywhere: The 'Qiandaohu' Open-Sea Fleet Replenishment Ship," *People's Navy (Renmin Haijun)*, September 16, 2010, 1, OSE Product ID: CPP20100915478014 [emphasis added].

28. Jonathan Weng, "Chief Designer Talks about PLA Navy Replenishment Ship," *China Defense Mashup Report*, Beijing, February 12, 2009.

29. Bernard D. Cole, "China's Navy Expands Its Replenishment-at-Sea Capability," *Interpreter*, August 26, 2015.

30. Salalah was used as liberty port as well: "The officers and men on board ship who have been at sea for a long period of time will take rest in turns and go ashore for exercise"; "PLAN Navy Berths in Port Salalah for First Replenishment," *Chinese Military News*, cited in chinamil.com, 27 April 2010, www.china-defense-mashup.com/?p=3704.

31. Li Jie, "China's Navy Still Has Far to Go."

32. "PLAN Navy Berths in Port Salalah for First Replenishment."

33. "China to Establish a Naval Base around Somalia," *Newstime Africa*, January 2, 2010, http://www.newstimeafrica.com/archives/9895.

34. For example, "Navy Has No Plan for Overseas Bases," *China Daily*, http://www.chinadaily.com.cn/china/2010–03/11/content_9570126.htm.

35. "China Opens First Overseas Base in Djibouti," *News Djibouti*, http://www.aljazeera.com/news/2017/08/china-opens-overseas-base-djibouti-170801104040586.html.

36. Ben Blanchard, "China Launches Charm Offensive for Overseas Naval Base," Reuters, March 23, 2016; Blanchard, "China Hints More Bases on Way after Djibouti," *CANMUA Net*, March 8, 2016, http://canmua.net/world/china-hints-more-bases

-on-way-514571.html [emphasis added]; John Lee, "China Comes to Djibouti: Why Washington Should Be Worried," *Foreign Affairs Snapshot*, April 23, 2015.

37. "East Seas Fleet Flotilla Explores New Open Ocean Logistic Support Methods," (Beijing) *Renmin Haijun*, September 30, 2010, 2.

38. "The PLA Navy of China Contributions to Counter Piracy," *Contact Group on Piracy off the Coast of Somalia, Capturing Lessons Learned*, January 2, 2016, http://www.lessons frompiracy.net/files/2016/01/PLA-Navys-Escort-Mission.pdf.

39. "PLA Navy of China Contributions to Counter Piracy."

40. "PLA Navy of China Contributions to Counter Piracy."

41. "PLA Navy of China Contributions to Counter Piracy."

42. "East Seas Fleet Flotilla Explores New Open Ocean Logistic Support Methods," 3.

43. "JFJB Marks 2nd Anniversary of Start of PRC Navy Escorts off Somalia."

44. "Italy, China Conduct Joint Naval Exercise off Taranto," (Turin) *La Stampa*, August 3, 2010, EUP20100803058002; "Feature: Chinese Naval Flotilla Visits Greece after Anti-Piracy Mission," Xinhua, August 9, 2010, CPP20100809968.

45. This section is based reviewing the English-language chinamil.com.cn website and reading the press releases under the MOOTW tab. For example, Huang Panyue, "28th Chinese Naval Escort Task Force Ends Friendly Visit to Cameroon," *China Military Online*, June 14, 2018, http://eng.chinamil.com.cn/view/2018-06/14/content_8062519.htm.

46. "Chinese Navy Rescues Tuvaluan Ship from Pirates," *CCTVComEnglish*, CCTV.com text, April 12, 2017, http://english.cctv.com/2017/04/12/VIDEdtd7ofJQ0uDfEUyVEetZ170412.shtml. The PLAN FFG *Yulin* received the distress call at some distance away. It took ten hours to get to the scene. When it arrived, sixteen naval special forces personnel boarded the ship and freed the crew members, who were locked in a safe room. Helicopters provided air cover during the operation. An Indian navy destroyer was also at the scene, and its "helo" helped with air cover, but Chinese accounts failed even to mention Indian cooperation and assistance, which caused irritation in Delhi. See Sutirtho Patranobis, "China Takes Credit Rescuing Ship in Gulf of Aden, Silent of India's Role," *Hindustan Times*, April 10, 2017, https://www.hindustantimes.com/world-news/china-takes-credit-for-rescuing-ship-in-gulf-of-aden-silent-on-indian-navy-s-role/story-SeiSNf4d3JGRhMVv7R9QVM.html.

47. "Chinese Navy Forces Carry Out Anti-Pirate Exercise," China.org.cn, December 27, 2012, http://www.china.org.cn/video/2011–12/27/content_24257074.htm.

48. Dong Zhaohui, "China's Logistic Hub in Djibouti to Stabilize Region, Protect Interests," *Global Times*, March 15, 2016, http://english.chinamil.com.cn/news-channels/china-military-news/2016–03/15/content_6961515.htm; Zhao Yinan, "Li Vows to Protect Rights of Chinese Working Abroad," *China Daily*, May 5, 2014, http://www.chinadaily.com.cn/world/2014livisitafrica/2014–05/10/content_17497900.htm.

49. Yoon Jung Park, "One Million Chinese in Africa," *SAIS Perspectives*, May 12, 2016, http://www.saisperspectives.com/.

50. Kevin Wang, "Yemen Evacuation a Strategic Step Forward for China," *Diplomat*, April 10, 2015.

51. "Symposium on Third Anniversary of Chinese Naval Escort Held," *PLA Daily*, January 13, 2012, http://eng.chinamil.com.cn/news-channels/china-military-news/2012–01/13/content_4768273.htm.

52. "PLA Navy Awards Commemorative Badge for Major Mission Performance," *PLA Daily*, December 29, 2011, http://eng.mod.gov.cn/DefenseNews?2011–12/29/content_4332515.htm.

53. Lu Desheng and Li Gencheng, "'Xiangfan' Returns in Triumph after Joining Maritime Exercise of WPNS."

54. Lu Desheng and Li Gencheng.

55. Xinhuanet, "China to Mark 70 Year Anniversary with Multinational Naval Events," April 20, 2019, http://eng.mod.gov.cn/news/2019–04/20/content_4839897.htm.

56. "The PLA Navy of China Contributions to Counter Piracy," *Contact Group on Piracy off the Coast of Somalia, Capturing Lessons Learned*, January 2, 2016, http://www.lessonsfrompiracy.net/files/2016/01/PLA-Navys-Escort-Mission.pdf. Here is an excerpt illustrating the use of helicopters in antipiracy operations: "On August 6th, 2009, the MV 'Zhenhua 25' was attacked by pirate boats in Bab El-Mandeb Strait. Because that area was beyond the cover range of the ship-borne helicopter, the Commander of the task group immediately ordered that the supply ship be the relay for the helicopter in order to drive off the eight pirate skiffs where the pirates were attempting to embark onboard the MV."

Chapter Three. The PLA Navy Becomes a "Blue-Water" Navy

1. The epigraph can be found at http://news.xinhuanet.com/world/2015-05/12/c_127791919.htm.
2. See Michael McDevitt, ed., *Becoming a Great "Maritime Power": A Chinese Dream* (Alexandria, VA: Center for Naval Analyses, June 2016), passim, available only at https://www.cna.org/CNA_files/PDF/IRM-2016-U-013646.pdf.
3. M. Taylor Fravel, Testimony before the U.S.-China Economic and Security Review Commission Hearing on "A World Class Military: Assessing China's Global Military Ambitions," Washington, DC, June 20, 2019, https://www.uscc.gov/sites/default/files/Fravel_USCC%20Testimony_FINAL.pdf. See also Fravel, *Active Defense: China's Military Strategy since 1949* (Princeton, NJ: Princeton University Press, 2019), 230–35, 272–77.
4. *China's Military Strategy* [emphasis added], 9.
5. Deputy Chief of Naval Operations for Warfare Systems (N-9), *Report to Congress on the Annual Long Range Plan for the Construction of Naval Vessels for Fiscal Year 2019* (Washington, DC: Office of the Chief of Naval Operations, February 2018), 3, http://www.secnav.navy.mil/fmc/fmb/Documents/19pres/longrange_ship_plan.pdf.
6. Li Xuanliang and Mei Shixiong, "At a CMC Meeting on the Reform of Policies and Institutions, Xi Jinping Stresses That It Is Necessary to Have a Clear Understanding of the Importance and Urgency of Pushing Forward Reform on Military Policies and Institutions and Build a Socialist System of Military Policies and Institutions with Chinese Characteristics," Xinhua Domestic Service in Chinese, November 14, 2018 [emphasis added].
7. *China's Military Strategy*, 8 [emphasis added].
8. State Council of the People's Republic of China, *China's National Defense in the New Era* (Beijing, July 2019), 28.
9. Contrary to the portrayal of Zheng He by the Communist Party (and some Western popular historians) as a benign explorer, Ed Dreyer's account makes clear that his expeditions were sent because the emperor "wanted to display his soldier in strange lands in order to make manifest the wealth and power of the Middle Kingdom. . . . [T]hose who did not submit were pacified by force." Edward L. Dreyer, *Zheng He: China and the Oceans in the Early Ming Dynasty, 1405–1433*, Library of World Biography (New York: Pearson Longman, 2007), 180.
10. Ship count: two aircraft carriers, six very large Aegis-like Type 055 DDGs, thirty Aegis-like type DDGs (Types 052C, 052D), eleven replenishment ships (Types 901, 903), thirty large FFGs (Types 054, 054A), eight large Type 071 amphibious ships, one Type 075 LHD, six nuclear attack submarines (Type 093 SSNs), twenty-eight conventional submarines with AIP (Types 039, 039A SSs), and six nuclear-powered ballistic-missile submarines (Type 094 SSBNs). *Jane's Defense Weekly* (various), International Institute for Strategic Studies *Strategic Balance 2019*, Rick Joe's *Diplomat* series, and Director of Naval Intelligence, *The PLA Navy: New Capabilities and Missions for the 21st Century* (Washington, DC: Office of the Chief of Naval Operations, 2015).
11. These include almost sixty well-armed corvettes, or light frigates, for near-seas ASW work and eighty-three missile-attack craft. Small ships lack sea-keeping ability

(performance in rough seas primarily a function of a ship's length), range, endurance, and sustainability.

12. Christina L. Garafola and Timothy L. Heath, *The Chinese Air Force's First Steps toward Becoming an Expeditionary Air Force* (Santa Monica, CA: RAND Project Air Force, 2017): "In recent years . . . [t]he PLA Air Force (PLAAF) has made incremental progress in its ability to carry out overseas operations, including organizing and deploying a long-distance strategic airlift unit capable of carrying out various non-war missions around Asia and as far as Africa. The PLAAF has focused heavily on developing a small number of elite units to carry out these high-profile overseas missions. Fighter and other aircraft have built on the experience gained from domestic long-distance deployments to take part in multilateral exercises, competitions, and demonstrations in other countries. . . . While the PLAAF's expeditionary deployments to date remain small and limited by Western standards, an increasing need to safeguard Chinese interests abroad suggests that the development of expeditionary capabilities will remain a priority for the PLAAF for years to come" (page vi).

13. The term "MOOTW" is yet another PLA "borrowing" from the U.S. military. See *Joint Doctrine for Military Operations Other than War*, Joint Publication 3-07 (Washington, DC: Joint Staff, June 16, 1995).

14. Ian Storey, "China's Malacca Dilemma," *Jamestown Foundation China Brief* 6, issue 8 (April 12, 2006). For an official U.S. statement regarding China's concern about its SLOCs, see U.S. Department of Defense, *Annual Report to Congress: Military and Security Developments Involving the People's Republic of China 2017* (Washington, DC, May 15, 2017) [hereafter 2015 *Annual Report to Congress*], passim, but page 5 as an example.

15. *China's Military Strategy*, 3.

16. There have been hundreds of books on all aspects of this struggle. My favorites are Marc Milner, *The Battle of the Atlantic* (Stroud, U.K.: Tempus, 2003), and the more recent Jonathan Dimbleby, *The Battle of the Atlantic: How the Allies Won the War* (Oxford, U.K.: Oxford University Press, 2016).

17. Director of Naval Intelligence, *Understanding Soviet Naval Developments*, 5th ed. (Washington, DC: Office of the Chief of Naval Operations, April 1985), 88–103.

18. All the surface ships classified as DE, DD, FF, FFG, and CVS, along with VP, VS, HS, and HSL aviation squadrons, plus the entire SSN force, had the primary mission of antisubmarine warfare. Naturally, these forces could and did perform many other missions, but their procurement was justified by the Soviet submarine threat.

19. For a short but authoritative account see Tony Judt, *Postwar: A History of Europe since 1945* (London: Penguin Books, 2005), 590–604, 652–57.

20. Yoji Koda, "A New Carrier Race?," *Naval War College Review* 64, no. 3 (Summer 2011). This article traces the evolution of the JMSDF thinking on how best to defend Japan's sea-lanes, with a focus on the importance of a combined force of destroyers, helicopters, and land-based maritime-patrol aircraft.

21. *China's Military Strategy*, 3 [emphasis added].

22. See for example, T. X. Hammes, *Offshore Control: A Proposed Strategy for an Unlikely Conflict*, Strategic Forum 278 (Washington, DC: National Defense University Press, June 2012); Geoff Dyer, *The Contest of the Century: The New Era of Competition with China and How America Can Win* (New York: Knopf, 2014), chap. 2; and Sean Mirski, "Stranglehold: Context, Conduct and Consequences of an American Blockade of China," *Journal of Strategic Studies* 36, no. 3 (2013).

23. For an Indian perspective see P. K. Ghosh, "Game Changers? Chinese Submarines in the Indian Ocean," *Diplomat*, July 6, 2015.

24. Nan Li and Christopher Weuve, "China's Aircraft Carrier Ambitions: An Update," *Naval War College Review* 63, no. 1 (Winter 2010).

25. Duncan Hewitt, "China Sees New Aircraft Carrier as Symbol of Its Growing Power," *Daily Beast*, August 26, 2016.

26. Huang Panyue, "Role of Aircraft Carrier *Liaoning* Shifts from Training to Combat: Executive Officer," *China Military*, April 25, 2019, eng.chinamil.com.cn/view/2019 -04/25/content_9488581.htm.
27. China Power Team, "How Does China's First Aircraft Carrier Stack Up?," *China Power*, updated June 28, 2018, https://chinapower.csis.org/aircraft-carrier; Franz-Stefan Gady, "China's 1st Carrier Strike Group Reaches Initial Operational Capability," *Diplomat*, June 5, 2018, https://thediplomat.com/2018/06/chinas-1st-carrier-strike -group-reaches-initial-operational-capability/. Gady's title is misleading. The Ministry of Defense press conference statement indicated that the carrier strike group had been "effectively tested," not that it had reached initial operational capability. The quotation regarding the night landing more accurately portrays the current state of combat readiness: the PLA Navy "is still working on it."
28. For an excellent discussion of carrier pilot training, especially night landings, see Huang Panyue (ed.), "Navy's Carrier-Borne Jet Force Takes Off to a Higher Level," *China Military*, September 17, 2018, http://eng.chinamil.com.cn/view/2018-09/17 /content_9284305.htm.
29. Huang Panyue, "Role of Aircraft Carrier *Liaoning* Shifts from Training to Combat."
30. China Power Team, "What Do We Know (So Far) about China's Second Aircraft Carrier?," *China Power*, updated June 29, 2018, https://chinapower.csis.org/china -aircraft-carrier-type-001a.
31. Rick Joe, "PLA Navy Projects to Watch in Next 5 Years," *Diplomat*, August 7, 2018; Franz-Stefan Gady, "China Kicks-Off Construction of New Supercarrier," *Diplomat*, January 5, 2018, https://thediplomat.com/2018/01/china-kicks-off-construction-of -new-supercarrier.
32. "Air wing" refers to the total aircraft complement of a carrier. In the U.S. Navy the air wing is a mix of two or three squadrons of fighter/attack jets, a squadron of electronic warfare jets, an AEW squadron, an ASW helicopter squadron, and a variety of logistics aircraft. In the future it will include unmanned aircraft as in-flight refuelers. Because the existing Chinese carriers are much smaller than U.S. CVNs, their airwings are necessarily smaller, but the overall wing concept is the same: a mix of various different types of mission-specialized aircraft that collectively form an integrated aviation combat team.
33. China Power Team, "How Does China's First Aircraft Carrier Stack Up?" For an earlier assessment see Thomas Newdick, "China's Got an Aircraft carrier: What about the Air Wing?" *War Is Boring*, March 3, 2014, https://medium.com/war-is-boring /chinas-got-an-aircraft-carrier-what-about-the-air-wing-c95283bc0279.
34. Andreas Rupprecht, *Modern Chinese Warplanes: Chinese Naval Aviation—Aircraft and Units* (Houston, TX: Harpia, 2018), 20.
35. Minnie Chan, "China Is Working on a New Fighter Jet for Aircraft Carriers to Replace Its J-15s," *South China Morning Post*, updated July 5, 2018, https://www.scmp .com/news/china/diplomacy-defence/article/2153803/china-working-new-fighter- jet-aircraft-carriers-replace; Jaime Seidel, "Fatal Crashes Compel China to Speed-Up Carrier Stealth Fighter Project," *News Corp Australia Network*, July 6, 2018.
36. Admiral Liu's quote from his memoirs is cited in Andrew Scobel, Michael McMahon, and Cortez Cooper III, "China's Aircraft Carrier Program: Drivers, Developments, Implications," *Naval War College Review* 68, no 4. (Autumn 2015), 68.
37. James C. Bussert, "China Debuts Aegis Destroyers," *Signal*, July 2005.
38. U.S. Navy, "Fact File: Aegis Weapons System," Washington, DC, January 10, 2019, https://www.navy.mil/navydata/fact_display.asp?cid=2100&tid=200&ct=2.
39. Sarah Hirschberger, *Assessing China's Naval Power: Technological Innovation, Economic Constraints, and Strategic Implications* (Heidelberg: Springer-Verlag, 2015), 196–97.
40. Franz-Stefan Gady, "China Launches New Guided Missile Destroyer," *Diplomat*, June 30, 2017, https://thediplomat.com/2017/06/china-launches-new-guided-missile -destroyer.

41. Brian Kalman, "Military Analysis: The Type-052D Class Guided Missile Destroyer," *South Front*, May 1, 2016, https://southfront.org/military-analysis-type-052d-class-guided-missile-destroyer.

42. Jane's by IHS Markit, Content preview: "Undersea Dragon: Chinese ASW Capabilities Advance," 2017, 4–5, https://www.janes.com/images/assets/911/72911/Undersea_dragon_Chinese_ASW_capabilities_advance.pdf.

43. James C. Bussert and Bruce Elleman, *People's Liberation Army Navy: Combat System Technology, 1949–2010* (Annapolis, MD: Naval Institute Press, 2011), 132–33.

44. Rupprecht, *Chinese Naval Aviation*, 32–33; Director of Naval Intelligence, *PLA Navy*, 20–21.

45. Hunter Stires, "Exclusive: CNO Announces the Return of Vertical Launch System At-Sea Reloading," *National Interest*, July 5, 2017.

46. "The Type 055 Class Destroyer," *Naval Technology* (June 2017), https://www.naval-technology.com/.

47. Tyler Rogoway, "China's Type 055 Super Destroyer Is a Reality Check for the US and Its Allies," *The Drive: The War Zone*, June 28, 2017.

48. Wesley Morgan, "Pentagon: US Strike on Syria Achieved Its Limited Objectives," *Politico*, April 14, 2018.

49. Lyle J. Goldstein, "China's YJ-18 Supersonic Anti-Ship Cruise Missile: America's Nightmare," *National Interest*, June 1, 2015.

50. China's Aegis-like DDGs: six Type 052Cs, nineteen Type 052Ds, and six Type 055s.

51. Data provided privately to author from PLA expert Dennis Blasko. The count is current through the thirty-second escort group.

52. Andrew Tate, "China Commissions Fourth ASW-Capable Type 056 Corvette," *IHS Jane's Navy International*, http://www.janes.com/.

53. Huang Panyue, "PLA Navy Ends Era of Supply Ship Troika in Its Escort Missions," *China Military Online*, August 9, 2018, http://eng.chinamil.com.cn/view/2018-08/09/content_9247256.htm.

54. Bernard D. Cole, "China's Navy Expands Its Replenishment-At-Sea Capability," *Interpreter*, August 26, 2015.

55. Andrew Tate, "China Increases Construction Rate of Amphibious Assault Ships," *Jane's 360 Sea Platforms*, June 10, 2019, https://www.janes.com/article/89152/china-increases-construction-rate-of-amphibious-assault-ships.

56. Director of Naval Intelligence, *PLA Navy*, 18.

57. Dave Majumdar, "China's New Amphibious Assault Ship: A Big Waste of Time?," *National Interest*, March 31, 2017, http://nationalinterest.org/blog/the-buzz/chinas-new-amphibious-assault-ship-big-waste-time-19961.

58. Director of Naval Intelligence, *PLA Navy*, 18.

59. "Yuting Class Type 072II/072III," *Global Security*, n.d. [ca. 2005], https://www.globalsecurity.org/military/world/china/yuting.htm.

60. U.S. Department of Defense, *Annual Report to Congress: Military and Security Developments Involving the People's Republic of China 2018* (Washington, DC, May 16, 2018).

61. Director of Naval Intelligence, *PLA Navy*, 19.

62. Mark Mazzetti and Thom Shanker, "Russian Subs Patrolling off East Coast of US," *New York Times*, August 5, 2009.

63. Director of Naval Intelligence, *PLA Navy*, 13.

64. U.S. Department of Defense, *Annual Report to Congress: Military and Security Developments Involving the People's Republic of China 2019* (Washington, DC, May 2, 2019), 36.

65. Christopher P. Carlson, "Essay: Inside the Design of China's Yuan-Class submarine," *USNI News*, August 31, 2015, http://news.usni.org/.

66. Director of Naval Intelligence, *PLA Navy*, 19.

67. 2015 *Annual Report to Congress*, 19; Rajat Pandit, "Chinese Submarine in Karachi, India Alarmed," *Times of India*, June 27, 2015, http://timesofindia.indiatimes.com/india /Chinese-submarine-in-Karachi-India-alarmed/articleshow/47845930.cms.

68. Shaurya Karanbir Gurung, "14 Chinese Navy Ships Spotted in Indian Ocean: Indian Navy Monitoring," *Economic Times*, July 12, 2018, https://economictimes.indiatimes .com/news/defence/14-chinese-navy-ships-spotted-in-indian-ocean-indian-navy- monitoring-locations/printarticle/61882634.cms.

69. Abhijit Singh, "Countering China's Submarine Presence in the Indian Ocean," *Lowy Interpreter*, May 24, 2017; author's personal discussions with retired Indian flag officers and analysts in 2018.

70. An authoritative discussion of Soviet naval presence (thirty-two ships in early 1978) in the northern Arabian Sea / Gulf of Aden region of the Indian Ocean is Mark A. Carolla, "The Indian Ocean Squadron," in *The Soviet Navy: Strengths and Liabilities*, ed. Bruce Watson and Susan Watson (Boulder, CO: Westview, 1986), 241–46.

71. Carolla.

72. Chinese spokesman, cited in Gady, "China's 1st Carrier Strike Group Reaches Initial Operational Capability."

73. Bernard D. Cole, *Oil for the Lamps of China: Beijing's 21st Century Search for Energy*, McNair Paper 57 (Washington, DC: National Defense University Press, 2002), 63 [emphasis added].

74. David C. Evans and Mark R. Peattie, *Kaigun: Strategy, Tactics, and Technology in the Imperial Japanese Navy, 1887–1941* (Annapolis, MD: Naval Institute Press, 1997), xix.

Chapter Four. Combat in China's Near Seas

1. *China's Military Strategy* 2015, 8 [emphasis added].

2. *China's National Defense in 2004*.

3. From the perspective of the approaching "Blue" naval force, this means in practical terms that it will have to fight to gain the sea control that is essential to operations and to sustain that control if the naval campaign is envisioned as more than a hit-and-run raid.

4. U.S. Department of Defense, *The Report of the 2001 Quadrennial Defense Review* (Washington, DC: September 30, 2001), 25. The report (no longer available on the DoD website, copy in author's possession) speaks about anti-access and area denial as they relate to one of America's fundamental strategic concepts—*deterring forward*. Specifically, it goes on to say, "Deterrence in the future will continue to depend heavily upon the capability resident in forward stationed and forward deployed combat and expeditionary forces."

5. M. Taylor Fravel and Christopher P. Twomey, "Projecting Strategy: The Myth of Counter Intervention," *Washington Quarterly* 37, no. 4 (Winter 2015), 171–87, correctly points out that it is impossible to find the term "counterintervention" in Chinese strategic discourse. A number of American experts have suggested that Fravel's and Twomey's arguments go too far, that they risk "throwing the baby out with the bathwater." As it happens, the PLA itself has helped to dampen this debate among American scholars, with the introduction of the term "offshore waters defense" to characterize its approach to defending China from attack from the sea.

6. Timothy Heath and Andrew Erickson, "Is China Pursuing Counter-Intervention?," *Washington Quarterly* 38, no. 3 (Spring 2015), 143–56, is a well-crafted rejoinder to Fravel and Twomey, as is Ryan D. Martinson, "Reality Check: China's Military Power Threatens America—The U.S. Can't Just Wish Away China's A2/AD Capabilities," *National Interest*, March 4, 2015.

7. Peng Guangqian and Yang Youzhi, *Science of Military Strategy*, 459–61 [emphasis added].

8. M. Taylor Fravel, *Active Defense: China's Military Strategy since 1949* (Princeton, NJ: Princeton University Press, 2019), 222.

9. When Chiang Kai-shek and his Nationalist Party were driven off the Chinese mainland in 1949 the Chinese Civil War was effectively over on the mainland, and the communists under Mao Tse-tung had won. In Washington, the Truman administration was prepared to concede Chiang's Republic of China to the mainland. Then in June 1950 North Korea invaded South Korea, and everything changed. Perceiving a global communist plot to overrun newly independent states, Washington reversed course and decided to defend Taiwan, sending the Seventh Fleet to the Taiwan Strait. Although there have been many twists and turns since then, Truman's 1950 decision to defend Taiwan from the mainland remains in place some seventy years later. There are many fine books and articles on this topic. An excellent short analysis is Warren I. Cohen, *America's Response to China: A History of Sino-American Relations*, 5th ed. (New York: Columbia University Press, 2000), 166–76.

10. Before determining that what I had written about PLA deployments for one scenario was equally applicable to the other, I had intended to add to the Taiwan scenario one that involved the Chinese in a conflict over the Japanese-administered, and Chinese-claimed, Senkaku/Diaoyu Islands, northeast of Taiwan. Taiwan, which also claims these five uninhabited rocks of scant intrinsic economic or strategic value, would not be involved. It would be a showdown between China and Japan, with Washington in the role of a good ally "warming up in the bullpen" waiting for a call for assistance. It would be difficult for Washington to go to war with China over these rocks, since it does not even recognize Japanese sovereignty over the Senkakus, only its administrative control. Nonetheless, because the Mutual Defense Treaty between Japan and the United States explicitly covers the Senkakus, the United States could find itself involved in a fight with China if Beijing decided to seize them. In truth, it is hard to imagine that either Washington or Beijing, or probably Japan, would have any interest in engaging in a costly naval and air campaign over tiny, uninhabited features in the East China Sea. Because the human and material costs of a fight would be so disproportionately high, American or even Russian mediation could bring a resolution, one that at a minimum involved a mutual pledge to renounce the use of force. For more background on this dispute see Michael McDevitt, "Whither Sino-U.S. Relations: Maritime Disputes in the East China and South China Seas," in *U.S.-China Relations: Manageable Differences or Major Crisis?*, ed. Rorry Daniels and Juliet Lee (New York: National Committee on American Foreign Policy, 2018).

11. David Shambaugh, "A Matter of Time: Taiwan's Eroding Military Advantage," *Washington Quarterly* (Spring 2000), 131–32.

12. "Over 83 Percent of the People in Taiwan Want to Keep the Status-Quo," *Focus Taiwan: News Channel*, November 2018, http://focustaiwan.tw./news/acs /201811020027.aspx. See also Joseph Wu, "The World Must Not Ignore China's Threats to Taiwan," *Sunday Times*, June 11, 2019. Wu is Taiwan's foreign minister.

13. Richard C. Bush, "Thoughts on the Taiwan Relations Act," *Brookings Op-Ed*, April 21, 2009.

14. For more on strategic directions, see David M. Finkelstein, "China's National Military Strategy: An Overview of the 'Military Strategic Guidelines,'" in *Rightsizing the People's Liberation Army: Exploring the Contours of China's Military*, ed. Roy Kamphausen and Andrew Scobell (Carlisle, PA: U.S. Army War College, 2007), 69–140.

15. Peng Guangqian and Yang Youzhi, *Science of Military Strategy*, 230–34 [emphasis added].

16. Tommy Chai, "The Problem with Xi's 40th Anniversary Message to Taiwan," *Foreign Brief: Geopolitical Risk Analysis*, January 12, 2019, https://www.foreignbrief.com/asia -pacific/china/the-problem-with-xis-40th-anniversary-message-to-taiwan/.

17. For a complete discussion of the "one country, two systems" concept, see Richard C. Bush, *Untying the Knot: Making Peace in the Taiwan Strait* (Washington, DC: Brookings Institution, 2005), esp. 36–39.

18. Since the 19th Party Congress in October 2017, during which Beijing emphasized the party's control over Hong Kong. China has further curbed the territory's autonomy and

freedoms guaranteed under the "one country, two systems" policy and the Basic Law, Hong Kong's mini-constitution. Beijing's promise to allow Hong Kong a "high degree of autonomy" is due to end in 2047, and Hong Kong democratic activists are urgently demanding that China keep its commitments. However, the CCP sees these demands as coming from "separatist forces" bent on derailing the peaceful integration of Hong Kong with the mainland. Since Xi's offer to Taiwan is also cast as a "one country, two systems" situation, the people of Taiwan naturally assume what is happening to Hong Kong would happen to them as well. See *2018 Report to Congress of the U.S.-China Economic and Security Review Commission* (Washington, DC, November 2018), 382–411.

19. This paragraph has been informed by Richard C. Bush, "Beijing's Goal with Taiwan Is Unification—Why Can't It Get There?," *Order from Chaos* (Brookings Institution blog), January 7, 2019.

20. Text of the Taiwan Relations Act (Public Law 96–8, 22 U.S.C. 3301 et seq.) of January 1, 1979. https://www.ait.org.tw/our-relationship/policy-history/key-u-s-foreign -policy-documents-region/taiwan-relations-act/. For the best short analysis see Bush, "Thoughts on the Taiwan Relations Act."

21. Anna Fifield, "Taiwan's President Wins Second Term with Landslide Victory over Pro-Beijing Rival," *Washington Post*, January 20, 2020.

22. 2019 *Annual Report to Congress*, 116.

23. "Will Signal Fires Rise Again in the South China Sea and across the Taiwan Strait in 2019?," Global Times Annual Conference, December 8, 2018, CHW2019010971842058 Beijing *Huanqiu Shibao Online* in Chinese, December 3, 2018.

24. The circumstances under which the mainland has historically warned that it would use force have evolved over time. These circumstances have included formal declaration of Taiwanese independence, undefined moves toward Taiwanese independence, internal unrest on Taiwan, Taiwanese acquisition of nuclear weapons, indefinite delays in cross-strait dialogue on unification, foreign intervention in Taiwan's internal affairs, and the stationing of foreign forces on Taiwan. Article 8 of China's March 2005 Anti-Secession Law states that China may use "non-peaceful means" if "secessionist forces . . . cause the fact of Taiwan's secession from China," if "major incidents entailing Taiwan's secession" occur, or if "possibilities for peaceful reunification" are exhausted. 2018 *Annual Report to Congress*, 93.

25. 2019 *Annual Report to Congress*, 84–89.

26. Ian Easton, *The Chinese Invasion Threat: Taiwan's Defense and American Strategy in Asia* (Arlington, VA: Project 20149 Institute, 2017).

27. 2019 *Annual Report to Congress*, 116.

28. 2019 *Annual Report to Congress*, 70–71.

29. Rick Joe, "The Chinese Navy's Growing Anti-Submarine Warfare Capabilities," *Diplomat*, September 12, 2018.

30. Franz-Stefan Gady, "China's Navy Commissions 41st Type-056/056A Stealth Warship," *Diplomat*, June 13, 2018.

31. Rick Joe, "Chinese Anti-Submarine Warfare: Aviation Platforms, Strategy and Doctrine," *Diplomat*, October 16, 2018.

32. Charlie Gao, "Why the F-15, F-16, Su-27 and other 'Old' Fighter Jets Simply Won't Go Away," *National Interest* (blog), August 22, 2018, https://nationalinterest.org/blog /buzz/why-f-15-f-16-su-27-and-other-old-fighter-jets-simply-wont-go-away-29522; and Mike Yeo, "Taiwan Takes Delivery of First Locally Upgraded F-16," *Defense News*, October 22, 2018.

33. Defense Intelligence Agency, *China Military Power: Modernizing a Force to Fight and Win*, January 2019, 3, www.dia.mil/Military-Power-Publications.

34. 2019 *Annual Report to Congress*, ii.

35. 2019 *Annual Report to Congress*, 14.

36. Peter Wood, "Snapshot: China's Eastern Theater Command," *Jamestown Foundation China Brief,* March 14, 2017, https://jamestown.org/program/snapshot-chinas-eastern-theater-command.

37. Units that are counted: two carriers, six SSNs, fifty conventional SSs, thirty-three destroyers, fifty-four frigates, forty-two corvettes, and eighty-six fast attack craft, for a total of 273.

38. 2019 *Annual Report to Congress.* The diagram is on 87.

39. David A Shlapak, David T. Orletsky, and Barry Wilson, *Dire Strait? Military Aspects of China-Taiwan Confrontation and Options for U.S. Policy* (Santa Monica, CA: RAND, 2000), 7–30.

40. U.S. Air University, *PLA Aerospace Power: A Primer on Trends in China's Military Air, Space, and Missile Forces* (Maxwell Air Force Base, AL: China Aerospace Studies Institute, 2017), 7, http://www.airuniversity.af.mil/Portals/10/CASI/documents/Research/PLAAF/CASI_Primer%202017.pdf.

41. Academy of Military Science, *Science of Military Strategy,* 236, cited in U.S. Air University, *PLA Aerospace Power.*

42. Sean O'Connor, *PLA Ballistic Missiles,* Technical Report APA-TR-2010–0802 (N.p.: Air Power Institute Australia, updated January 27, 2014), http://www.ausairpower.net/APA-PLA-Ballistic-Missiles.html.

43. Jeff Hagen, "Potential Effects of Chinese Aerospace Capabilities on U.S. Air Force Operations," testimony before the U.S.-China Economic and Security Review Commission, Washington, DC, May 20, 2010, 2–3.

44. U.S. Seventh Fleet, "Fact Sheet," n.d. [2018], https://www.c7f.navy.mil/Portals/8/documents/7thFleetTwoPagerFactsheet.pdf?ver=2017–09–20–040335–223.

45. Joe, "Chinese Navy's Growing Anti-submarine Warfare Capabilities"; Joe, "Chinese Anti-Submarine Warfare"; Stephen Chen, "China's Underwater Surveillance Network Puts Targets in Focus along the Maritime Silk Road," *South China Morning Post,* January 1, 2018; Pengying, "China's Real Time Global Ocean Network Established," Xinhua, February 6, 2018, http://xinhuanet.com/2018–02/06/c_136953672.htm.

46. Seventh Fleet, "Fact Sheet."

47. The *Soryu* class is the only conventionally powered submarine routinely listed among the ten best attack submarines in the world—in, for example, Christopher McFadden, "Ten of the Deadliest Attack Submarines in the World," *Interesting Engineering,* March 2, 2017.

48. Rupprecht, *Chinese Naval Aviation,* 71. Rupprecht estimates the combat radius of PLAN Naval Aviation's best land-based fighter (the Su-30MK2, or J-11BH) at 724 nm, which would allow fighters launched at Huangyan/Luqiao Naval Aviation Base on the PRC's East China Sea coast to reach well into the Philippine Sea. However, that assessment is based on a straight-line flight profile over the Miyako Strait and assumes the PLA has managed to achieve air superiority over that portion of the first island chain.

49. "With few overt military preparations beyond routine training, China could launch an invasion of small Taiwan-held islands in the South China Sea such as Pratas or Itu Aba. A PLA invasion of a medium-sized, better-defended island such as Matsu or Jinmen is within China's capabilities. Such an invasion would demonstrate military capability and political resolve while achieving tangible territorial gain and simultaneously showing some measure of restraint." 2018 *Annual Report to Congress,* 95.

50. Easton, *Chinese Invasion Threat,* 114.

51. Easton, 115–16.

52. Easton, 119–21.

53. Liu Zhen, "Taiwan Running Out of Time to Discuss Peaceful Reunification, Says Former Chinese General," *South China Morning Post,* December 22, 2019, https://www.scmp.com/news/china/politics/article/3043108/taiwan-running-out-time-discuss-peaceful-reunification-says.

Chapter Five. Keeping the Americans Away

1. The first serious open-source look at A2/AD was a 2003 study by Andrew Krepinevich, Barry Watts, and Robert Work, *Meeting the Anti-Access and Area Denial Challenge* (Washington, DC: Center for Strategic and Budgetary assessments, 2003). A historical treatment of anti-access strategies along with sage commentary on contemporary A2/AD issues is found in Sam Tangredi, *Anti-Access Warfare: Countering A2/AD Strategies* (Annapolis, MD: Naval Institute Press, 2013). Other important analytical work on the topic includes Stephen Biddle and Ivan Oelrich, "Future Warfare in the Western Pacific: Chinese Anti-Access/Area Denial, U.S. Air Sea Battle, and Command of the Commons in East Asia," *International Security* 41 (Summer 2016); Eric Heginbotham et al., *The U.S. China Scorecard: Forces, Geography, and the Evolving Balance of Power, 1996–2017* (Santa Monica, CA: RAND, 2015); and Terrence K. Kelly, David Gompert, and Duncan Long, *Smarter Power, Strategic Partners*, vol. 1 (Santa Monica, CA: RAND, 2016), among many others.
2. This entire section is based upon a now-declassified National Intelligence Estimate, *Soviet Naval Strategy and Programs through the 1990s*, NIE 11-15-82D (Washington, DC, March 1983), which is found in John B. Hattendorf Jr., *The Evolution of the U.S. Navy's Maritime Strategy, 1977–1986*, Newport Paper 19 (Newport, RI: Naval War College Press, 2004).
3. 2018 *Annual Report to Congress*, 63.
4. Kevin Pollpeter, Testimony before the U.S.-China Economic and Security Review Commission Hearing on "China in Space: Strategic Competition," Washington, DC, April 25, 2019.
5. Eric Hagt and Matthew Durwin, "China's Antiship Ballistic Missile: Developments and Missing Links," *Naval War College Review* 62, no. 4 (Autumn 2009), 89.
6. Caleb Henry, "TeleSAT Says Ideal LEO Constellation Is 292 Satellites, but Could Be 512," *Spacenews*, September 11, 2018, https://spacenews.com/.
7. Ivan Couronne, "In Space, the U.S. Sees a Rival in China," Phys.org, January 6, 2019, https://phys.org/.
8. Stephen Clark, "Long March, Soyuz and Falcon Topped 2019's Launch Leaderboard," *Spaceflight Now*, January 2, 2020.
9. NASIC quoted in Michael Chase, Kristen A. Gunness, et al., *Emerging Trends in China's Development of Unmanned Systems* (Santa Monica, CA: RAND, 2015), 4.
10. By near seas I mean here the Yellow Sea, East China Sea, and South China Sea. Franz-Stefan Gady, "New Variant of China's Ch-5 Combat Drone Boasts Extended Range and Endurance," *Diplomat*, April 5, 2018.
11. Pollpeter, Testimony before the U.S.-China Economic and Security Review Commission.
12. Rupprecht, *Modern Chinese Warplanes*, 40, estimates maximum YJ-12 range as 300 km or 159 nm, whereas the 2018 and 2019 DoD *Annual Reports* are silent on the matter. The Missile Defense Advocacy Alliance places the YJ-12's maximum range at 400 km, or 212 nm; YJ-12, Missile Defense Advocacy Alliance, *Fact Sheet*, http://missiledefenseadvocacy.org/. There is unanimity that this supersonic, maneuverable ASCM is a very difficult weapon to defend against, especially since it has the range to be launched before the attacking aircraft must enter the SAM envelopes of U.S. cruisers or destroyers.
13. Sebastian Roblin, "China's H-6 Bomber: Everything You Wanted to Know about Beijing's 'B-52' Circling Taiwan," *National Interest*, December 18, 2016.
14. Rupprecht, *Modern Chinese Warplanes*, 160; Derek Grossman et al., *China's Long-Range Bomber Flights* (Santa Monica, CA: RAND, 2018), 1.
15. "The Military Balance 2018" (on-line), International Institute for Strategic Studies, https://www.iiss.org/publications/the-military-balance/the-military-balance-2018.
16. Grossman et al., *China's Long-Range Bomber Flights*, 1–5.
17. 2017 *Annual Report to Congress*.

18. David Barr, "This Piece of Chinese Military Hardware Could Change the Military Balance of Power in Asia," *National Interest,* November 6, 2017. At the time of his writing, Lieutenant Commander Barr, a career intelligence officer, was assigned to the Intelligence Directorate of the U.S. Navy's Pacific Fleet staff.

19. Liu Xuanzun, "China Develops Y-20 Variants to Perform Aerial refueling Mission: Military Insider," *Global Times,* November 26, 2018, https://thaimilitaryandasianregion .blogspot.com/2018/12/y-20-aerial-refueling-variant-is-now.html.

20. Jeremy Chin, "China's PLANAF Acquires New H-6J Bomber," *CSIS Missile Defense Project,* October 13, 2018.

21. In discussing this section with Mr. Ken Allen, the research director of National Defense University's China Aerospace Studies Institute (CASI), the author learned that both the PLA Air Force and Naval Aviation are in the process of reorganizing into brigades rather than regiments. At this writing fighters and strike aircraft have been so organized, but bombers have not.

22. Rupprecht, *Modern Chinese Warplanes,* 71.

23. Director of Naval Intelligence, *PLA Navy,* 21.

24. Roger Cliff, "The Development of China's Air Force Capabilities," RAND document delivered in testimony before the U.S.-China Economic and Security Review Commission, Washington, DC, May 20, 2010.

25. Martin Andrew and Carlo Kopp, "Advances in PLAN Carrier Aviation," *Air Power Australia,* April 10, 2010 (updated January 2014), www.ausairpower.net/APA -PLAN-CV.html#mozTocId658924.

26. 2017 *Annual Report to Congress,* 24.

27. Jesse L. Karotkin, testimony before hearing on "Trends in China's Naval Modernization," U.S. China Economic and Security Review Commission, Washington, DC, January 30, 2014, 7. Mr. Karotkin was Senior Intelligence Officer for China, Office of Naval Intelligence.

28. Cited in Ronald O'Rourke, *China Naval Modernization: Implications for U.S. Navy Capabilities—Background and Issues for Congress,* CRS Report for Congress, Order Code RL 33153 (Washington, DC: Congressional Research Service, updated May 12, 2018), 17.

29. H.R.P., "Explained: How Air Independent Propulsion (AIP) Works," *Defencyclopedia: The Ultimate Defense Encyclopedia,* July 6, 2016, https://defencyclopedia.com/2016 /07/06/explained-how-air-independent-propulsion-aip-works.

30. Director of Naval Intelligence, *PLA Navy,* 19.

31. Range 150–170 nm, sea skimmer as it approaches target at supersonic speed. CSIS Missile Defense Project, *Missile Threat* (Washington, DC: Center for Strategic and International Studies, modified June 15, 2018), s.v "SS-N-27 Sizzler."

32. One cannot see very far through a submarine periscope. To use a long-range cruise missile at over-the-horizon range a submarine must receive real-time target location data from a remote source, such as an aircraft or a satellite. It would take this 600-mph missile approximately 33 minutes to fly 290 nm; if the target is moving at twenty knots it will have traveled eleven nautical miles during this time. There is no indication that China's ocean surveillance and control network has the ability to update the missile continuously or that the missile could receive and process this sort of data if it were available. In practice, this means that when the missile is close to preset target range and its radar seeker turns on, the seeker has to have a wide enough scan range to "find" its target—or some other hapless ship that happens to be in the area.

33. A still photo of a *Spruance*-class destroyer being sunk by a torpedo is at http://www .navsource.org/archives/05/pix1/0597321.jpg.

34. Charlie Gao, "China's Torpedoes Are Built to Kill (But Just How Good Are They?)," *National Interest,* March 10, 2018.

35. 2009 *Annual Report to Congress,* 21. The literature on ASBMs is extensive. For an excellent single source see Gabriel Collins and Andrew Erickson, "China Deploys

World's First Long-Range, Land-Based 'Carrier Killer': DF-21D Anti-Ship Ballistic Missile (ASBM) Reaches 'Initial Operational Capability' (IOC)," *China Sign Post*, December 26, 2010.

36. Tan Shoulin and Zhang Daqiao, "Determination and Evaluation of Effective Homing Range for Ballistic Missile Attacking Aircraft Carrier," *Information Command and Control System and Simulation Technology* 28, no. 4 (August 2006), 6–9. The authors are associated with the Second Artillery Engineering College, Xian, China.

37. David Axe, "China Just Deployed Its Deadly 'Carrier Killer' Missiles in a Very Slick Way," *The National Interest*, January 14, 2019.

38. Bill Gertz, "PACOM: China Anti-Ship Ballistic Missile Tests a Signal to US, World," *Washington Free Beacon*, July 19, 2019.

39. Brad Lendon, "Ballistic Missiles Can Hit Moving Ships, China Says, but Experts Remain Skeptical," *CNN*, January 29, 2019.

40. Sam Tangredi, "Fight Fire with Fire," U.S. Naval Institute *Proceedings*, vol. 143/8/1347 (August 2017).

41. Hagt and Durwin, "China's Antiship Ballistic Missile," 89. This assessment is based not on any specific knowledge of how the PLA would attempt to accomplish this task but on the normal steps in employing most long-range weapons systems. In a subsequent article in the same journal the "time late" from detection to missile arrival at the aim point was estimated as thirty-five minutes; see Marshall Hoyler, "China's 'Antiaccess' Ballistic Missiles and U.S. Active Defense," *Naval War College Review* 63, no. 4 (Autumn 2010).

42. "China's Advanced Weapons Systems," *Jane's by IHS Markit*, May 12, 2018, 179, https://www.uscc.gov/.

43. Tony Capaccio, "China's New Missiles May Create a 'No-Go Zone' for U.S. Fleet," *Bloomberg*, November 17, 2009. For a more expansive discussion see Director of Naval Intelligence, *The People's Liberation Army Navy: A Modern Navy with Chinese Characteristics* (Washington, DC: Office of the Chief of Naval Operations, August 2009), 26–27.

44. Jeffrey Lin and P. W. Singer, "China Is Building the World's Largest Nuclear Submarine Facility," *Popular Science*, May 1, 2017. See also Lyle J. Goldstein, "China Prepares to Ramp Up Its Shipbuilding Process," *National Interest*, April 2, 2017.

Chapter Six. The PLA Navy and the South China Sea

1. The breakdown of the features above water at high tide is Pratas Islands (two), Scarborough Shoal (one), Paracel Islands (thirty-five), and Spratly Islands (140). Robert Beckman, "The UN Convention on the Law of the Sea and the Maritime Disputes in the South China Sea," *American Journal of International Law* 107, no. 1 (January 2013), 143–45.

2. Merwyn S. Samuels, *Contest for the South China Sea* (New York: Methuen, 1982), 64.

3. Samuels, 77. See also Kimie Hara, "The San Francisco Peace Treaty and Frontier Problems in the Regional Order in East Asia: A Sixty-Year Perspective," *Asia-Pacific Journal* 10, issue 17, no. 1 (April 23, 2012).

4. During World War II, the Japanese military had a weather station and other facilities on Pratas Island. In May 1945 a combined Australian-U.S. raiding party embarked in the submarine USS *Bluegill* (SS 242) stormed the island. They found that the Japanese had already evacuated. They destroyed Japanese facilities, raised the U.S. flag, claimed the island for the United States, and named it "Bluegill Island." The United States never officially pursued the claim. "USS *Bluegill* (SS-242), (SSK-242), (AGSS-242)," *Navsource Online*, http://www.navsource.org/archives/08/08242.htm (a Navy-veteran-maintained website).

5. The international-law distinction as to whether a feature that is permanently above water is a "rock" or an "island" has a major impact on the maritime entitlements the occupying state may claim. A "rock" is entitled to only a twelve-nautical-mile territorial sea (TTS),

whereas an "island" is entitled to both a TTS and a two-hundred-nautical-mile exclusive economic zone (EEZ). The EEZ confers legal jurisdiction over the disposition of the natural resources of the sea and below the seabed. It is not full sovereignty, however. The difference between rocks and islands is legally vague. The UNCLOS treaty merely states an island must be able to sustain human habitation or have an economic life of its own. In July 2016, in the case between the Philippines and China, the Hague Arbitral Panel Award provided important legal clarity: that to be an island, a *feature in its natural condition* must be able to sustain either a stable community of people or economic activity that either is not dependent on outside resources or is purely extractive in nature. Based on this new definition, the panel found that *none of the features* in in the Spratlys met this definition, that therefore there are no "islands" in the Spratlys, only "rocks." In short, none of the features in the Spratlys rates an EEZ. Importantly, this finding applies only to this specific arbitration and is not yet considered customary international law. Permanent Court of Arbitration, press release, *The Republic of the Philippines v. The People's Republic of China,* The Hague, July 12, 2016, https://pca-cpa.org/wp-content /uploads/sites/175/2016/07/PH-CN-20160712-Press-Release-No-11-English.pdf. See also *Law of the Sea: A Policy Primer,* chap. 10, "The South China Sea Tribunal," *The Fletcher School: Tufts University,* https://sites.tufts.edu/lawofthesea/chapter-ten/.

6. On July 30, 1971, the Republic of Vietnam issued a "Declaration on the Sovereignty of the Republic of Vietnam over the Archipelagos of Paracels and Spratly," indicating five points in favor of its claim of sovereignty. First, in 1802, Emperor Gia Long created a "Dio Hoang Sa" (Company of the Paracels) to supervise the exploitation of these islands. Second, in 1830, under Emperor Minh Mang, the Thruong Sa (Spratly) Islands were included as part of the Vietnamese territory on the first maps published by the kingdom. Third, in 1930 and 1933, the French government, acting on behalf of the Vietnamese empire, officially took possession of the Spratly Islands and notified foreign powers of its possession by a letter dated September 29, 1933. Fourth, *during the 1951 San Francisco Peace Conference, . . . [t]he Vietnamese delegate to the conference made a public statement of Vietnamese sovereignty over the Paracels and Spratly Islands. The statement aroused no objections from any of the fifty-one powers represented at the peace conference.* Fifth, on October 22, 1956, the president of the Republic of Vietnam placed the Spratly Islands under the administration of the province of Ba Ria. The declaration concluded, "The Republic of Vietnam remains the only power to possess the most legitimate rights of sovereignty over the Archipelagos of Spratly and Paracels because it has fulfilled the conditions required by the convention of 1885 concerning the establishment of territorial competency." Teh-Kuang Chang, "China's Claim of Sovereignty over Spratly and Paracel Islands: A Historical and Legal Perspective," *Case Western Reserve Journal of International Law* 23, issue 3 (1991).

7. Alexander L. Vuving, "South China Sea: Who Occupies What in the Spratlys?," *Diplomat,* May 6, 2016. This is the most complete and detailed analysis of Spratly outposts. See also CSIS Asia Maritime Transparency Initiative, "Spratly Islands Island Tracker," *Center for Strategic and International Studies,* https://amti.csis.org/island -tracker/spratlysvn.

8. Bill Hayton, *South China Sea: The Struggle for Power in Asia* (New Haven, CT: Yale University Press, 2014), 79. The features seized by North Vietnam from the Saigon government were Amboyna Cay, Namyet Island, Sand Cay, Sin Cowe Island, Southwest Cay, and Spratly Island.

9. Mark E. Rosen, *Philippine Claims in the South China Sea: A Legal Analysis,* CNA Occasional Paper (Alexandria, VA: Center for Naval Analyses, August 2014), https:// www.cna.org/sites/default/files/research/IOP-2014-U-008435.pdf.

10. Hayton, *South China Sea,* 68–70.

11. J. Ashley Roach, *Malaysia and Brunei: An Analysis of Their Claims in the South China Sea,* CNA Occasional Paper (Alexandria, VA: Center for Naval Analyses, August 2014), 10–14, https://www.cna.org/sites/default/files/research/IOP-2014-U-008434.pdf.

12. Roach, *Malaysia and Brunei*, 39.
13. An excellent short synopsis of the finding is Permanent Court of Arbitration, press release, *The South China Arbitration* (The Republic of the Philippines v. The People's Republic of China), The Hague, July 12, 2016, https://pca-cpa.org/en/news/pca-press-release-the-south-china-sea-arbitration-the-republic-of-the-philippines-v-the-peoples-republic-of-china.
14. Permanent Court of Arbitration, *South China Arbitration*, 2.
15. Statement of the Government of the People's Republic of China on China's Territorial Sovereignty and Maritime Rights and Interests in the South China Sea, July 12, 2016, https://fmprc.gov.cn/nanhi/eng/snhwtlcwj_1/t1379493.htm.
16. U.S. diplomatic note of December 2016 regarding SCS arbitration; *2016 Digest of US Practice in International Law*, 519–520 state.gov/s/1, https://www.state.gov/wp-content/uploads/2019/05/2016-Digest-United-States.pdf.
17. Hayton, *South China Sea*, 70–71.
18. Hayton, *South China Sea*, 121–22.
19. Erica S. Downs, Fellow, Foreign Policy, John L. Thornton China Center, Brookings Institution, personal e-mail to the author.
20. U.S. Energy Information Agency, "Contested Areas of South China Sea Likely Have Few Conventional Oil and Gas Resources," *Today in Energy*, April 3, 2013, https://www.eia.gov/todayinenergy/detail.php?id=10651#.
21. Hayton, *South China Sea*, 144–50.
22. Patricia Lourdes Viray, "China's Continued Blocking of Reed Bank Drilling Could Cost Philippine Development—Expert," *Philippine Star*, July 16, 2018, https://www.philstar.com/headlines/2018/07/16/1834042/chinas-continued-blocking-reed-bank-drilling-could-cost-philippine-development-expert.
23. Carmela Forbuena, "Duterte Reaffirms EDCA, U.S. Ties in Meeting with Trump," *Rappler*, November 14, 2017, https://www.rappler.com/nation/188459-duterte-trump-edca-military-ties-asean-summit-2017-philippines.
24. See Gregory B. Poling and Conor Cronin, "The Dangers of Allowing U.S.-Philippine Defense Cooperation to Languish," *War on the Rocks*, May 17, 2018.
25. Theodore Roscoe, *United States Submarine Operations in World War II*, 6th printing (Annapolis, MD: Naval Institute Press, 1958), 303–410.
26. Damon Cook, "China's Most Important South China Sea Military Base," *Diplomat*, March 9, 2017.
27. Edward J. Marolda, "Asian Warm-Up to the Cold War," *Naval History* 25, no. 5 (October 2011).
28. "Both the United States and the Soviet Union adopted a strictly neutral attitude towards the dispute. A State Department spokesman said on Jan. 20: 'The United States is not involved. We have no claims and we support nobody else's claims.' Dr. Kissinger, the Secretary of State, deplored the use of force in the dispute on Jan. 22, but said that he did not regard the Chinese claims to the Paracels and Spratlys as evidence that Peking wished to dominate the region." *Keesing's Record of World Events* (formerly *Keesing's Contemporary Archives*), vol. 20, March 1974, China, South Vietnam, Chinese, 26388, http://web.stanford.edu/group/tomzgroup/pmwiki/uploads/3217-1974-03-KS-a-EYJ.pdf.
29. Memorandum of Conversation (memcon) between Secretary of State Henry Kissinger and China's Ambassador Han Hsu, Acting Director, PRC Liaison Office, Washington, DC, January 23, 1974. The memcon quotes Kissinger as saying, "There are only two points I wanted to make with respect to the Paracel Islands issue. Chinese forces captured Gerald Emil Kosh, an employee of the Department of Defense, during a battle between South Vietnam and China over competing claims to the Paracel Islands. The South Vietnamese government is making a number of representations to international organizations, to SEATO as well as to the United Nations. *We wanted to let you know we do not associate ourselves with those representations* [emphasis added]," https://history.state.gov/historicaldocuments/frus1969–78v18/d66#fn1.

30. See Hayton, *South China Sea*, 70–78, for a detailed account of the 1974 seizure of the Crescent Group from South Vietnam by China. The United States ignored RVN requests for assistance from the Seventh Fleet. For the Chinese perspective see the excellent article by Toshi Yoshihara, "The 1974 Paracels Sea Battle: A Campaign Appraisal," *Naval War College Review* 16, no. 2 (Spring 2016).
31. Yoshihara, "1974 Paracels Sea Battle," 41.
32. Yoshihara, "1974 Paracels Sea Battle," 61.
33. Asia Maritime Transparency Initiative, "Update: China's Continuing Reclamation in the Paracels," *CSIS AMTI Island Tracker,* August 9, 2017, https://amti.csis.org/paracels-beijings-other-buildup/.
34. "Update: China's Continuing Reclamation in the Paracels."
35. For information on the Hainan Airlines flight see www.flightradar24.com/data/flights/hu7417.
36. Zhibo Qiu, "The Civilianization of China's Military Presence in the South China Sea," *Diplomat,* January 21, 2017.
37. Shinsi Yamaguchi, *Creating Facts on the Seas: China's Plan to Establish Sansha City* (Washington, DC: CSIS Asia Maritime Power Initiative, April 17, 2017), https://amti.csis.org/chinas-plan-establish-sansha-city.
38. Liu Huaqing, *Memoir of Liu Huaqing* (Beijing: People's Liberation Army Navy Press, 2004), 534–35.
39. M. Taylor Fravel, *Strong Borders, Secure Nation: Cooperation and Conflict in China's Territorial Disputes* (Princeton, NJ: Princeton University Press, 2008), 292. See pp. 288–96 for a good overview of the interaction between China and Vietnam in the Spratlys, particularly the potential of oil beneath the seabed that created an economic incentive for China to become more proactive in establishing a physical presence.
40. Fravel, *Strong Borders*, 295; Hayton, *South China Sea*, 81–83.
41. Liu Huaqing, *Memoir*, 541–42.
42. Actual combat footage taken from a PLA Navy warship can be seen at https://www.youtube.com/watch?v=Uy2ZrFphSmc. See also Joshua Lipes, "Vietnam Marks Anniversary of Naval Clash with China Over Spratly Island Reefs," *Radio Free Asia*, March 13, 2018, https://www.rfa.org/english/news/vietnam/anniversary-031320 18160914.html.
43. Hayton, *South China Sea*, 84–88.
44. U.S. Department of State, statement read by Acting State Department press spokesman Christine Shelly [emphasis added], http://dosfan.lib.uic.edu/ERC/briefing/daily_briefings/1995/9505/950510db.html.
45. For a prescient and insightful article on how the Philippines, and to a lesser degree the United States, reacted with nonchalance to the continued building on Mischief in 1999, years after the fisherman shelters were first discovered, see Kerry McCarthy, "Reef Wars," *Time*, March 8, 1999.
46. Daniel J. Dzurek, "China Occupies Mischief Reef in Latest Spratly Gambit" (Durham University, U.K.), *International Boundary Unit Research Unit (IRBU) Boundary and Security Bulletin* (April 1995), 67.
47. Hayton, *South China Sea*, 88.
48. Aileen S. P. Baveria, *Bilateral Confidence Building with China in Relation to the South China Seas Dispute: A Philippine Perspective* (Ottawa, ON: Government of Canada, Department of Foreign Affairs and International Trade, February 2001), https://www.researchgate.net/publication/265157899_Bilateral_Confidence_Building_with_China_in_Relation_to_the_South_China_Seas_Dispute_A_Philippine_Perspective.
49. Gregory Poling, "South China Sea Code of Conduct Still a Speck on the Horizon," *East Asia Forum*, September 6, 2018.
50. Association of Southeast Asian Nations, "Declaration on the Code of Conduct of Parties in the South China Sea," November 4, 2002, https://asean.org/?static_post=declaration-on-the-conduct-of-parties-in-the-south-china-sea-2.

51. Bonnie Glaser, "Statement before the House Foreign Affairs Committee, 'Beijing as an Emerging Power in the South China Sea,'" Washington, DC, September 12, 2012.
52. Private discussions between the author and retired naval officers.
53. Harris statement found in U.S.-China Economic and Security Review Commission, *Report to Congress* (Washington, DC: U.S. Government Publishing Office, 2018), 223.
54. Carlyle A. Thayer, "China and Vietnam Square Off in War of Attrition Over Disputed Waters," Asian Studies Institute of Australia, *Asian Currents*, June 2014, https://www .scribd.com/doc/.231875269/Thayer-China-and-Vietnam-Squre-Off-in-War-of -Attrition-Over-Disputed-Waters.
55. Gregory Poling, *Recent Trends in the South China Sea and U.S. Policy*, A Report of the Sumitro Chair in Southeast Asian Studies (Washington, DC: Center for Strategic and International Studies, July 2014).
56. Ernest Bower, director of CSIS East Asia Program, podcast, June 11, 2014, cited in David Tweed, "China Seeks Great Power Status After Sea Retreat," *Bloomberg News*, July 3, 2014.
57. This narrative of the 2012 incident is drawn from Michael J. Green et al., *Countering Coercion in Maritime Asia: The Theory and Practice of Grey Zone Deterrence* (Lanham, MD: Rowman & Littlefield for the Center for Strategic and International Studies, May 2017), e-book.
58. Geoff Dyer and Demetri Sevastopulo, "US Strategists Face Dilemma over Chinese Claim in South China Sea," *Financial Times*, July 9, 2014.
59. Richard Javad Heydarian, "China Rolls Out Red Carpet for Rodrigo Duterte," *Al Jazeera*, October 27, 2016; Heydarian, "Deciphering Rodrigo Duterte's China Triangulation," *National Interest*, October 31, 2016.
60. Carl A. Thayer, "Dead in the Water: The South China Sea Award, One Year Later," *Diplomat*, July 2017.
61. Bill Gertz, "Pentagon Warns of Conflict over Chinese Buildup on Disputed Island," *Washington Free Beacon*, April 29, 2016.
62. An ADIZ is administratively defined airspace, over land or water, asserted in the interest of national security. It normally extends well beyond a country's territorial airspace, to give the country more time to respond to possibly hostile aircraft. It is *not* a claim of any sort of sovereignty over the airspace. Should China establish such a zone in the South China Sea it would be yet another indirect step toward a claim of administrative jurisdiction over large areas of what is today international airspace.
63. Jane Perlez, "U.S. Admiral's Bluntness Rattles China, and Washington," *New York Times*, May 6, 2016.
64. China has occupied the "rocks" Fiery Cross Reef, Cuarteron Reef, Gaven Reef, and Johnson Reef South, along with "low-tide elevations" (submerged at high tide) Subi Reef and Hughes Reef, since 1988. China seized Mischief Reef, another low-tide elevation, in 1994. J. Ashley Roach, "China's Shifting Sands in the Spratlys," American Society of International Law, *Insights* 19, issue 54 (July 15, 2015). The July 12, 2016, Arbitral Tribunal found that Gaven Reef (north) was a rock, not a low-tide elevation.
65. For an assessment of the implications of the new ten-thousand-foot runway on Fiery Cross Reef, see Andrew Erickson, "Lengthening Chinese Airstrips May Pave Way for South China Sea ADIZ," *National Interest*, June 29, 2015.
66. "Build It and They Will Come," *AMTI CSIS*, August 1, 2016, https://amti.csis.org /build-it-and-they-will-come.
67. Ashton Carter, "A Regional Security Architecture Where Everyone Rises," Institute for Strategic Studies, Shangri-La Dialogue, Singapore, May 30, 2015, http://www.defense .gov/Speeches/Speech.aspx?SpeechID=1945.
68. Raul Pedrozo, "Preserving Navigational Rights and Freedoms: The Right to Conduct Military Activities in China's Exclusive Economic Zone," *Chinese Journal of International Law* 9 (2010), 9–29.

69. Memorandum of Understanding between the Department of Defense of the United States of America and the Ministry of National Defense of the People's Republic of China Regarding the Rules of Behavior for Safety of Air and Maritime Encounters, signed November 9, 2014, archive.defense.gov/pubs/141112 _MemorandumOfUnderstandingRegardingRules.pdf.

70. For Chinese views on military activities in their EEZ, see four papers in Peter Dutton, ed., *Military Activities in the EEZ: A U.S.-China Dialogue on Security and International Law*, China Maritime Study 7 (Newport, RI: Naval War College Press for the China Maritime Studies Institute, December 2010).

71. This was intended by the administration to represent the beginning of pushback for what the National Security Council's director for China termed "China's overreach in the SCS." See Jeffery A. Bader, *Obama and China's Rise: An Insider's Account of America's Asia Strategy* (Washington, DC: Brookings Institution Press, 2012), 81–82, 119; and Mark Landler, "Offering to Aid Talks, U.S. Challenges China on Disputed Islands," *New York Times,* July 23, 2010.

72. Hillary R. Clinton, remarks at press availability, July 23, 2010, Hanoi, Vietnam, http://www.state.gov/secretary/rm/2010/07/145095.htm.

73. Jeffery Bader, Kenneth Lieberthal, and Michael McDevitt, "Keeping the South China Sea in Perspective," *Brookings Foreign Policy Brief,* September 2, 2014.

74. "Since 2014, China has reclaimed 2,000 acres—more land than all other claimants combined over the history of their claims. When combined with a range of activities, including: assertion of its expansive Nine-Dash Line claim, relocation of oil rigs in disputed maritime zones, efforts to restrict access to disputed fishing zones, and efforts to interfere with resupply of the Philippine outpost at Second Thomas Shoal, we see a pattern of behavior that raises concerns that China is trying to assert de facto control over disputed territories, and strengthen its military presence in the South China Sea." China's Foreign Ministry spokesman is cited in this statement by David Shear, assistant secretary of Defense for Asian and Pacific Security Affairs, "Statement before the Senate Committee on Foreign Relations," Washington, DC, May 13, 2015.

75. Karen Lena, "Pompeo Assures Philippines of US Protection in Event of Sea Conflict," Reuters, March 1, 2019. For a more in-depth assessment of the state of the alliance, including Manila's concerns caused by the Scarborough Shoal debacle of 2012, see Jay L. Batongbacal, "How to Reinvigorate the U.S.-Philippine Alliance," *Diplomat,* May 2019.

76. James Mattis, "US Leadership and the Challenges of Indo-Pacific Security," *Shangri-La Dialogue,* https://www.iiss.org/events/shangri-la-dialogue/shangri-la -dialogue-2018.

77. Asia Times Staff, "After Beijing's Criticism, Mattis Says, 'Steady Drumbeat' of FONOPS to Continue," *Asia Times,* May 31, 2018, http://www.atimes.com/article /after-beijings-criticism-mattis-says-steady-drumbeat-of-fonops-to-continue.

78. Steven Stashwick, "Unsafe Incident between US and Chinese Warships during FONOP," *Diplomat,* October 2, 2018.

79. U.S. Senate Armed Services Committee, "Advance Questions for Admiral Philip Davidson, USN, Expected Nominee for Commander, U.S. Pacific Command," Washington, DC, April 17, 2018, 18.

80. Steven Jiang, "China Will Not Give Up 'Any Inch of Territory' in the Pacific Xi Tells Mattis," *CNN,* June 28, 2018.

81. Bilihari Kausikan, "ASEAN-China Relations: Building a Common Destiny," *American Interest,* September 23, 2014. In an excellent speech on the topic of China and ASEAN, Kausikan, the former Singapore permanent secretary of foreign affairs, noted, "Chinese investments in infrastructure are binding Southwestern China and Southeast Asia into one economic and hence one strategic and political space."

82. Not-for-attribution conference in Southeast Asia, September 14, 2018.

83. Kausikan, "ASEAN-China Relations."

Chapter Seven. The PLA Navy in the Indian Ocean

1. *China's Military Strategy* 2015, 3 [emphasis added].
2. Chinese customs data in "Table of China December Data on Oil, Oil Product, LNG Imports," *Dow Jones Institutional News*, January 25, 2018.
3. Back-of-the-envelope calculation: It is 6,560 nm from Hormuz to Shanghai via Malacca. An average tanker speed of thirteen knots equates to a twenty-one-day transit. Fifty percent of 8.4 million barrels of daily imports is an average of 4.2 million barrels that has to arrive every day from the Persian Gulf. Each VLCC carries an average of 2 million barrels. Hence two VLCCs need to arrive in Shanghai every day. The result is that on any given day forty-two (21 days × 2) tankers are somewhere along the sea lane to China and a similar number outbound from China to the Persian Gulf.
4. Harry Harris, "Statement of Admiral Harry B. Harris Jr., U.S. Navy Commander, U.S. Pacific Command before the House Armed Services Committee on U.S. Pacific Command Posture," Washington, DC, February 14, 2018, 10, https://docs.house.gov/.
5. PTI [Press Trust of India], "PLA Submarines in the Indian Ocean Legitimate: China," *Economic Times*, July 12, 2018, https://m.economictimes.com/news/defence/pla-submarines-in-indian-ocean-legitimate-china/articleshow/53100318.cms.
6. On the basis of personal experience during the 1980s I can attest to the difficulty of keeping track of Soviet submarines in the northern Arabian Sea. An authoritative discussion of Soviet naval presence (thirty-two ships, including submarines, in early 1978) in the northern Arabian Sea / Gulf of Aden region of the Indian Ocean is given by Carolla, "Indian Ocean Squadron," 241–46.
7. As of December 2019, specifically: two carriers, six Type 055 DDGs, two Type 051 DDGs, six Type 052C DDGs, twenty-four Type 052D DDGs, thirty Type 054/54A FFGs, ten Type 903/901 AORs, eight Type 071 LPDs, eight Type 093/095 SSNs, and thirty SSs (SSBNs not included). See table 3.
8. Richard B. Remnek, "Soviet Access to Overseas Naval Support Facilities: A Military and Political Analysis," in *The Sources of Soviet Naval Conduct*, ed. Philip S. Gillette and Willard C. Frank (Lexington, MA: Lexington Books, D. C. Heath, 1990), 251–67.
9. At the time, only Manama (Bahrain), Port Louis (Mauritius), Karachi (Pakistan), Colombo (Sri Lanka), and Bandar Abbas and Bandar Shapur (Iran) made fuel and other supplies available to transiting U.S. Navy ships.
10. Director of Naval Intelligence, *Understanding Soviet Naval Developments*, 24.
11. Michael Palmer, *Guardians of the Gulf: A History of America's Expanding Role in the Persian Gulf, 1883–1992* (New York: Simon & Schuster, 1992), 87.
12. Director of Naval Intelligence, *Understanding Soviet Naval Developments*, 6th ed. (Washington, DC: Office of the Chief of Naval Operations, July 1991), chart on 40.
13. Geoffrey Jukes, "Soviet Naval Policy in the Indian Ocean," in *Soviet Naval Policy: Objectives and Constraints*, ed. Michael MccGwire et al. (Halifax, NS: Center for Foreign Policy Studies, Dalhousie University, 1975), 479–85.
14. It is worth noting that Berbera still plays an important geostrategic role. The Emirati firm DP World just arranged a deal to run Berbera from the de facto–independent province now known as Somaliland; this arrangement provides the military of the United Arab Emirates a more permanent facility in its fight across the gulf against Houthi rebels in Yemen. Asa Fitch, "DP World to Manage Somaliland Port of Berbera," *Wall Street Journal*, September 5, 2016.
15. Newton Dismukes and James McConnell, eds., *Soviet Naval Diplomacy* (New York: Pergamon Books, 1979), 59.
16. In the late 1960s, Ethiopia was the recipient of the largest U.S. economic and military assistance program and site of the largest American embassy in sub-Saharan Africa.
17. Remnek, "Soviet Access to Overseas Naval Support Facilities," 259–60.
18. Don Oberdorfer, "The Superpowers and the Ogaden War," *Washington Post*, March 5, 1978.

19. James F. Kelly, "Naval Deployments in the Indian Ocean," U.S. Naval Institute *Proceedings* 109/5/963 (May 1983).

20. Director of Naval Intelligence, *Understanding Soviet Naval Developments*, 5th ed., 24.

21. Bill Gertz, "Chinese Sub Stalked U.S. Fleet," *Washington Times*, November 13, 2006. I recall that the destroyer I commanded escorting the carrier USS *Constellation* (CV 64) during operations in the northern Arabian Sea was constantly involved in ASW detection operations when a Soviet submarine got under way from its Socotra Island anchorage.

22. "Statement of Rear Adm. Thomas A, Brooks, USN, DNI, before the Sea Power, Strategic and Critical Materials Sub-Committee of the House Armed Services Committee on Intelligence," Washington, DC, March 7, 1991.

23. The article that made it acceptable for Democrats to agree with the Trump administration's abandonment of "engagement" came from two fairly senior officials from the Obama administration, both with substantial experience of dealing with China: Kurt M. Campbell and Ely Ratner, "The China Reckoning: How Beijing Defied American Expectations," *Foreign Affairs* 97, no. 2 (March/April 2018). The best analysis from the administration's perspective is in a speech by Vice President Mike Pence at the Hudson Institute: "Remarks by Vice President Pence on the Administration's Policy toward China, October 4, 2018," https://www.whitehouse .gov/. Another "engagement failed" article by an experienced China hand is John Pomfret, "Engagement with China Is Failing: Time for 'Constructive Vigilance,'" *Washington Post*, November 28, 2018. Finally, an excellent analysis from a well-regarded China scholar of the debate is Alastair Iain Johnston, "The Failure of the 'Failure of Engagement' with China," *Washington Quarterly* (Summer 2019), 99–114.

24. Donald J. Trump, *National Security Strategy of the United States of America* (Washington, DC: White House, December 2017), 3, 45–46, available at https://www.whitehouse. gov/wp-content/uploads/2017/12/NSS-Final-12-18-2017-0905.pdf.

25. This perspective is reflected well in *2018 Annual Report to Congress of the U.S-China Economic and Security Review Commission: Executive Summary and Recommendations* (Washington, DC: November 16, 2018), available at https://www.uscc.gov/. For example: "Beijing wants to use BRI to revise the global political and economic order to align with Chinese interests. Official Chinese communiques focus on the initiative's economic objectives—building hard and digital infrastructure, fueling domestic development, and expanding markets and exporting standards. But China also seeks strategic benefits from BRI, despite its insistence to the contrary. Beijing's geopolitical objectives for the project include securing energy supplies, broadening the reach of the PLA, and increasing China's influence over global politics and governance. Countries around the world are starting to compare their experiences with BRI projects to China's lofty rhetoric and early promises of easy, no-strings-attached infrastructure financing. As a consequence, some participating countries have begun to voice concerns about BRI projects creating unsustainable debt levels, fueling corruption, and undermining sovereignty" (10–11).

26. *National Security Strategy*, 45–46.

27. Scott Neuman, "In Military Name Change, U.S. Pacific Command Becomes U.S. Indo-Pacific Command," *The Two-Way: Breaking News from NPR*, May 31, 2018, https://www.npr.org/sections/thetwo-way/2018/05/31/615722120/in-military-name -change-u-s-pacific-command-becomes-u-s-indo-pacific-command.

28. James Mattis, *Summary of the 2018 National Defense Strategy of the United States of America*, n.d., 2, file:///E:/2018-National-Defense-Strategy-Summary.pdf; U.S. Department of Defense, *Indo-Pacific Strategy Report: Preparedness, Partnership and Promoting a Networked Region* (Washington, DC: June 1, 2019), 8 [emphasis added].

29. Hu Jintao, "Understand the New Historic Missions of Our Military in the New Period of the New Century," speech to an expanded meeting of the Central Military Commission, Jiangxi Province, December 24, 2004, http://gfjy.jiangxi.gov.cn /yl.asp?idid=11349.htm (no longer posted).

30. For information on regional COSCO offices, see www.cosco.com/en/global_offices
    /staff.jsp?catId=299.
31. Bai Tiantian, "Djibouti President Kicks Off Beijing Visit as China Expands Interest in
    Africa," *Global Times*, November 11, 2017, http://www.globaltimes.cn
    /content/1076682.shtml.
32. Becker and Downs, "China's Djibouti Military Base the First of Many."
33. For an official U.S. government discussion of Chinese overseas access, see 2017 *Annual
    Report to Congress*, 5.
34. "Belt and Road Initiative: China's Super Link to Gwadar Port—A Visual Explainer,"
    South China Morning Post, https://multimedia.scmp.com/news/china/article/One-Belt
    -One-Road/pakistan.html.
35. Bonnie Glaser, "Is China Proselytizing Its Path to Success?," *East Asia Forum*, January
    11, 2018; Jessica Chen Weiss, "A World Safe for Autocrats: China's Rise and the Future
    of Global Politics," *Foreign Affairs* (July/August 2019).
36. "China Scales Back Investment in Ethiopia," *Financial Times*, June 13, 2018.
37. Aaron Maasho, "Ethiopia to Take Stake in Port of Djibouti, Its Trade Gateway: State
    Media," Reuters, May 1, 2018.
38. "Chinese FDI in Ethiopia Reaches USD Four Bln," *Reporter*, September 1, 2018, https://
    www.thereporterethiopia.com/article/chinese-fdi-ethiopia-reached-usd-four-bln.
39. "Killings and Claims of an Attempted Putsch Rock Ethiopia," *Economist*, June 27, 2019.
40. "US helping India Track Chinese Subs," *Indian Defense News*, January 21, 2017, http://
    www.indiandefensenews.in/2017/01/us-helping-india-track-chinese-subs.html.
41. "INS *Arihant*: A Warship Which Can Dive to 300 Metres, Remain under Water for
    Months," *Economic Times*, November 5, 2018, https://economictimes.indiatimes.com
    /news/defence/ins-arihant-a-warship-which-can-dive-to-300-metres-remain-under
    -water-for-months/articleshow/66516888.cms.
42. Kyle Mizokami, "Why China and Pakistan Should Fear India's *Arihant* Class of
    Submarine," *National Interest*, January 22, 2017.
43. 2019 *Annual Report to Congress*, 16.

Chapter Eight. Opposite Sides of the Same Coin
1. 2015 DWP, 9.
2. Hongying Wang, *A Deeper Look at China's "Going Out" Policy* (Waterloo, ON: Centre
   for International Governance Innovation, March 8, 2016), https://www.cigionline.org
   /publications/deeper-look-chinas-going-out-policy.
3. "Xi Jinping Stresses the Need to Show Greater Care about the Ocean"; Liu Cigui,
   "Striving to Realize the Historical Leap from Being a Great Maritime Country to
   Being a Great Maritime Power," *Jingji Ribao Online*, November 2012.
4. Xu Sheng, "Follow the Path of Maritime Power with Chinese Characteristics," *Qiushi
   Online: Organ of Central Committee of the Communist Party of China*, November 2013,
   http://www.qstheory.cn/. (Thanks to Dr Tom Bickford for this quote and citation.)
5. Academy of Military Science, *Science of Military Strategy*, 438.
6. Andrew S. Erickson and Lyle J. Goldstein, "Studying History to Guide China's Rise as
   a Maritime Great Power," *Harvard Asia Quarterly* 12, nos. 3–4 (Winter 2010), 31–38.
7. Chen Mingyi, "China Must Be Built into a Maritime Power by 2050," *Zhongguo
   Haiyang Bao*, January 13, 2014.
8. Liu Cigui, "Striving to Realize the Historical leap." At the time Liu was the director
   of the State Oceanic Administration; he is now (in early 2020) the Communist Party
   secretary of Hainan Province and a member of the Central Committee of the Chinese
   People's Congress.
9. 2019 DWP, 8.
10. Andrew Scobell and Cortez Cooper, "What Is Driving Asian Aircraft Carrier
    Programmes? The Case of China," in *Emerging Strategic Trends in Asia*, ed. Uttam
    Kumar (New Delhi: Institute for Defense Studies and Analyses, 2015), 53–67.

11. See Michael A. McDevitt, "America's New Security Strategy and Its Military Dimension," *Global Asia* 7 (Winter 2012), 14–17.

12. 2018 *Annual Report to Congress*, 85.

13. 2019 DWP, 28 [emphasis added].

14. Morgan Ortagus (spokesperson), "Chinese Coercion on Oil and Gas Activity in the South China Sea," U.S. Department of State press statement, Washington, DC, July 20, 2019.

15. According to the UN, China has seven of the world's largest and most efficient container ports in the world. In 2017 these seven ports, of which Shanghai is number one, handled the amazing total of 164,640,000 twenty-foot equivalent (TEU) containers. United Nations, "Structure, Ownership, and Registration of the World Fleet," in *Review of Maritime Transport* (New York, 2018), 73, available at https://unctad.org/en/PublicationChapters/rmt2018ch2_en.pdf.

16. Richard Scott, "China-Owned Ships: A Rapid Rise to Become One of the World's Largest Fleets," *International Shipping News*, repr. *Hellenic Shipping News*, March 17, 2015, https://www.hellenicshippingnews.com/china-owned-ships-a-rapid-rise-to -become-one-of-the-worlds-largest-fleets.

17. "Merchant Fleet," *2019 e-Handbook of Statistics*, UNCTAD [UN Conference on Trade and Development], https://stats.unctad.org/handbook/MaritimeTransport /MerchantFleet.html.

18. Mathieu Duchatel and Alexandre Sheldon Duplaix, *Blue China: Navigating the Maritime Silk Road to Europe*, Policy Brief (London: European Council on Foreign Relations, April 23, 2018).

19. Scott, "China-Owned Ships," 3.

20. Zhao Lei, "New Rules Mean Ships Can Be Used by Military," *PLA Daily*, June 18, 2015, http://www.chinadaily.com.cn/china/2015-06/18/content_21036944.htm. In 2015 legislation was enacted that required all civilian shipbuilding companies, as well as state-ownedenterprises, to ensure that newly built container ship, Ro-Ro, multipurpose, bulk-carrier, and break-bulk classes of ships are suitable for use by the military in emergency situations. The legislation specifically establishes specifications and design requirements (so-called technical standards) for military use. See also, in Chinese, *Implement National Defense Requirements Standards Ships: Maritime Projection "Second Force,"* Beijing, China Ministry of National Defense, September 1, 2014, http://www.mod.gov.cn/mobilize/2014-09/01/content_4534216.htm.

21. The U.S. Navy total is reached by adding eleven carriers, ninety Aegis cruisers and destroyers, thirty-four major amphibious ships, thirty replenishment ships, fifty-seven SSNs and SSGNs, fourteen SSBNs, three *Zumwalt*-class destroyers, and twenty-five littoral combat ships.

22. Fravel, Testimony, June 20, 2019.

23. 2019 DWP, 4.

24. David Axe, "China: We Won't Use Nuclear Weapons First in a War," *National Interest*, July 24, 2019.

25. Saunders, *Chairman Xi Remakes the PLA*, 3–11.

26. Finkelstein, "Breaking the Paradigm," 54–70.

27. Finkelstein, "Breaking the Paradigm," 59.

28. Finkelstein, "Breaking the Paradigm," 60.

29. Blasko, "PLA Weaknesses and Xi's Concerns about PLA Capabilities."

30. Scott Swift, "A Fleet Must Be Able to Fight," U.S. Naval Institute *Proceedings* (May 2018).

31. "Full Text of Hu Jintao's Report to the 18th Party Congress."

32. See Seth Cropsey, "Transcript: The Rise of China's Navy: A Discussion with Captain James Fanell," Hudson Institute, Washington, DC, May 21, 2019. Fanell projects 450 surface ships and 110 submarines in 2030. See also Rick Joe, "Predicting the Chinese Navy of 2030," *Diplomat*, February 13, 2019, which predicts a total of 110 surface combatants

(not including corvettes or fast attack craft), eighty-four submarines, four carriers, and eleven major amphibious assault ships for a total of 209 ships of these classes in 2030.

33. Rick Joe, "Pondering China's Future Nuclear Submarine Production," *Diplomat*, January 23, 2019.

34. For instance, this paragraph summarizes the problem of introducing many new systems simultaneously: "The delays in the ship development and initial trials pushed both phases of initial operational testing until FY21 [fiscal year 2021] and FY22. The delay in the ship's delivery and development added approximately 2 years to the timeline. As noted in previous annual reports, the CVN 78 test schedule has been aggressive, and the development of EMALS [Electromagnetic Aircraft Launch System], AAG [Advanced Arresting gear], AWE [Advanced Weapons Elevator], DBR [Dual Band Radar], and the Integrated Warfare System delayed the ship's first deployment to FY22." Ronald O'Rourke, *Navy Ford (CVN-78) Class Aircraft Carrier Program*, RS 20643 (Washington, DC: Congressional Research Service July 24, 2019), 21, https://fas.org/sgp/crs/weapons/RS20643.pdf.

35. Phillip Saunders, Testimony before the U.S.-China Economic and Security Review Commission, Hearing on a "World Class Military: Assessing China's Global Ambitions," June 20, 2019, https://www.uscc.gov/. Dr. Saunders provides an excellent overview of the economic aspect of Chinese military modernization and addresses the implications for the PLA if China's economy continues to slow, suggesting that the proportion of defense spending is likely to decline along with the overall annual gross domestic product. Among other ramifications, this portends a slowdown of many expensive new developments and more intense competition for resources among all six of China's military services.

Appendix I. The China Coast Guard

1. Assistant Professor Ryan D. Martinson is a core member of the U.S. Naval War College's China Maritime Studies Institute. A Mandarin Chinese linguist, he researches and writes about China's maritime strategy, especially its coercive use of sea power. He holds degrees from the Fletcher School of Law and Diplomacy at Tufts University and Union College.

2. In the words of the head of the SOA East China Sea Bureau, Liu Kefu, rights protection is a "precondition" for becoming a maritime power. That is, China cannot do all the things it wants to do in its waters until it has full control over them. Liu Kefu, "Using Three Types of Protective Power to Promote Construction of Maritime Power" (*Yi Sanzhong Baohu Lidu Tuijin Haiyang Qiangguo Jianshe*), *China Ocean News*, 17 September 2013, 1, http://epaper.oceanol.com/shtml/zghyb/20130917/35090.shtml.

3. Lyle J. Goldstein, *Five Dragons Stirring Up the Sea: Challenge and Opportunity in China's Improving Maritime Enforcement Capabilities*, China Maritime Study 5 (Newport, RI: Naval War College Press for the China Maritime Studies Institute, 2010).

4. Sources are not clear as to when the Maritime Rights LSG was established. According to Bonnie Glaser it was in mid-2012, before Xi actually assumed the top position in the PRC. A more recent analysis by Glaser's CSIS colleague Christopher Johnson indicates the Maritime Rights LSG was not established until after the 18th Party Congress, when Xi was officially in the positions of party general secretary and chair of the Central Military Commission. The main point is that in either case he was in a position to do something about the organizational mess he had observed during activities in the East and South China Seas. See Bonnie Glaser, *China's Maritime Rights Protection Leading Small Group: Shrouded in Secrecy* (Washington, DC: CSIS Asia Maritime Transparency Initiative, September 11, 2015); and Christopher Johnson, Scott Kennedy, and Mingdu Qiu, "Xi's Signature Governance Innovation: The Rise of Leading Small Groups," *CSIS Commentary*, October 17, 2017.

5. James Hackett, ed., *The Military Balance 2019* (London: Arundel House for the International Institute for Strategic Studies, February 2019), 264. For earlier

information on the size of the Chinese Coast Guard, see U.S. Navy Department, *China's People's Liberation Army Navy (PLAN), Coast Guard, and Government Maritime Forces 2018 Recognition and Identification Guide* (Suitland, MD: Office of Naval Intelligence, July 2018); and Ryan D. Martinson, "China's Second Navy," U.S. Naval Institute *Proceedings* (April 2015).

6. "The Reconstituted SOA and the China Coast Guard Have Been Set Up" *(Zhongzu Hou De Guojia Haiyangju Guapai Zhongguo Haijingju Tongshi Guapai)*, [Government of the PRC website], July 22, 2013, http://www.gov.cn/jrzg/2013-07/22/content_2452257 .htm.

7. Ren Qinqin, "Liu Cigui: Mentioning 'Maritime Power' in the 18th Party Congress Report Has Both Real and Strategic Significance" *(Liu Cigui: Shibada Baogao Shouti "Haiyang Qiangguo" Juyou Zhongyao Xianshi He Zhanlue Yiyi)*, State Oceanic Administration, November 10, 2012, www.soa.gov.cn/xw/ztbd/2012/kxfzcjhh_ xyddsbd/sbddbfc/201211/t20121129_11573.htm.

8. State Oceanic Administration, *China's Oceans Development Report 2013* (*Zhongguo Haiyang Fazhan Baogao*) (Beijing: Ocean Press, 2013), 46.

9. China and Japan have overlapping maritime-boundary claims in the East China Sea. China claims a continental shelf extension up to the Okinawa trough, whereas Japan argues the ECS midpoint is where the two EEZs must be delimited. China's EEZ claim encompasses most of the East China Sea. Japan disputes this claim.

10. For an official analysis of China's nine-dash line see U.S. Department of State, *China: Maritime Claims in the South China Sea*, Limits in the Sea No. 143, December 5, 2014, https://2009-2017.state.gov/documents/organization/234936.pdf.

11. Peter Dutton, "Three Disputes and Three Objectives: China in the South China Sea," *Naval War College Review* 64, no. 4 (Autumn 2011), 42–67.

12. When performed by coast guard forces, they are collectively called "maritime rights protection law enforcement."

13. Duan Zhaoxian, "On the Strategic Objectives of Turning China into a Maritime Power" *(Lun Jianshe Haiyang Qiangguo de Zhanlue Mubiao)*, *China Military Science* *(Zhongguo Junshi Kexue)* (N.p., 2013), 3.

14. For a brief but excellent description of the functions of Chinese maritime law enforcement in disputes, see James Holmes and Toshi Yoshihara, "Small Stick Diplomacy in the South China Sea," *National Interest*, April 23, 2012.

15. "12th Five Year Plan for Maritime Development" *(Guojia Haiyang Shiye Fazhan Shi'er Wu Guihua)*, April 11, 2013, http://www.soa.gov.cn/zwgk/fwjgwywj/shxzfg/201304 /t20130411_24765.html.

16. Huang Ran, "Central Leadership Make Important Instructions Regarding the Opening of the Meeting and Maritime Work" *(Zhongyang Lingdao Dui Dahui Zhaokai Ji Haiyang Gongzuo Zuo Zhongyao Pishi)*, *China Ocean News*, January 11, 2013, 1, http:// epaper.oceanol.com/shtml/zghyb/20130111/30660.shtml.

17. Ryan D. Martinson, *"Jinglue Haiyang:* The Naval Implications of Xi Jinping's New Strategic Concept," *Jamestown Foundation China Brief* 15, issue 1 (January 9, 2015).

18. Sun Shuxian, "Provide Powerful Law Enforcement Support in Order to Realize the 'Maritime Dream'" *(Wei Shixian "Haiyang Meng" Tigong Qiangli Zhifa Baozhang)*, *China Ocean News*, June 28, 2013, 1.

19. For the sake of readability, this study will generally omit "rights protection" in this term.

20. During the "five dragon" era, SOA was overseen by the Department of Land and Resources.

21. Li Mingfeng, *"Yi 'zhongguo haijian,'"* *Ocean Development and Management* (*Haiyang Kaifa Yu Guanli*), June 2011, 26–31.

22. Specifically, the Law of the People's Republic of China on Territorial Sea and Contiguous Zone (1992), Provisions of the People's Republic of China on Administration of Foreign-Related Marine Scientific Research (1996), and the Law of

the People's Republic of China on the Exclusive Economic Zone and the Continental Shelf (1998). State Oceanic Administration, *China's Ocean Development Report (2012)* (*Zhongguo Haiyang Fazhan Baogao [2012]*) (Beijing: Ocean Press, 2012), 349–50.

23. Fan Xiaoting, "Analysis of the Legal Basis of Maritime Rights Protection Law Enforcement" *(Haiyang Weiquan Zhifa De Falv Yiju Zhibian)*, *Xingzheng Yu Fa* (2009), 12. National-level CMS units also performed "administrative law enforcement" *(xingzheng zhifa)*—that is, enforcing laws and regulations governing use of the sea, primarily on and near the coast. For instance, much effort has been expended in recent years to curtail environmentally destructive land reclamation activities and illegal mining of sea sand.

24. Yu Zhirong, Dong Xiji, and Zhang Ying, "Creating Blue Glory in the East China Sea: A Recollection of CMS East China Sea Rights Protection Law Enforcement" (*Hunxi Donghai Zai Zhu Lanse Huihuang—Ji Zhongguo Haijian Donghai Zongdui Haiyang Weiquan Zhifa*), *Ocean Development and Management* (2005), 4. Authoritative U.S. accounts are clear that *Bowditch* was confronted by a PLA Navy frigate, not a CMS unit, which probably had been shadowing from nearby but was unarmed. See Raul Pedrozo, "Close Encounters at Sea: The USNS *Impeccable* Incident," *Naval War College Review* 62, no. 3 (Summer 2009), 101.

25. Zhao Lingfei, "CMS on the Waves: A History of the Development of CMS Regular Rights Protection Patrols" *(Liangjian Shang De Zhongguo Haijian: Zhongguo Haijian Dingqi Weiquan Xunhang Zhifa Gongzuo Fazhan Jishi)*, *Ocean Development and Management* (2012), 6.

26. This appears to have been the motive behind China's first administrative patrol to the Senkakus, in December 2008. For a fascinating account of that mission, see Xu Hui, "Three Year Retrospective of CMS Inaugural Patrol of the Senkaku Islands" (*Zhongguo Haijian Xunhang Diaoyudao Sanzhou Nianji*), *East West South North* (*Dong Xi Nan Bei*), no. 24 (2012), 10–12. Chinese texts frequently describe the purposes of such missions with the twelve-character phrase "show presence, manifest jurisdiction, and declare sovereignty": *xianshi cunzai, tixian guanxia, xuanshi zhuquan.*

27. Carl Thayer, "China's New Wave of Aggressive Assertiveness in the South China Sea," *International Journal of China Studies* (December 2011).

28. Zhao Lingfei, "CMS on the Waves."

29. This episode was covered in a CCTV 4 television program aired on December 31, 2013. See *Travelling around China (Zoubian Zhongguo)*, *South China Sea Travel Notes* (*Nanhai Jixing*), Episode Eight: "Blue Border Guards" (*Lanjiang Weishi*) [hereafter *Travelling around China*], http://news.cntv.cn/2013/12/31/VIDE1388496485764597.shtml.

30. Xi Zhigang, "The Mainland Builds a Quasi 'Coast Guard'" (*Dalu Haijian Dazao Zhun "Haiyang Jingwei Dui"*), *Phoenix Weekly (Fenghuang Zhoukan)*, July 24, 2012.

31. In fact, many of the ships were delivered complete with their PLA Navy crews. Sun Ding, "This Is How CMS Officers Are Trained" (*Haijian Duiyuan Shi Zenyang Liancheng De*), *China Ocean News*, December 27, 2013, 3.

32. See Ryan D. Martinson, *Echelon Defense: The Role of Sea Power in Chinese Maritime Dispute Strategy*, China Maritime Study 15 (Newport, RI: Naval War College Press for the China Maritime Studies Institute, February 2018), 13.

33. "Our Recollections of 2012" (*Pandian 2012 Women De Jiyi*), *China Ocean News*, January 4, 2013, 3.

34. Li Xiaochuan, "The Main Force for Building State Vessels" (*Gongwuchuan Jianli De Zhulijun*), *China Ship Survey* (*Zhongguo Chuanjian*), February 2013.

35. "2012 CMS in Numbers" *(2012 Shuzi Haijian)*, *China Ocean News*, January 2013, 3.

36. See Ryan D. Martinson and Takuya Shimodaira, "Curing China's Elephantiasis of the Fleet," *Jamestown Foundation China Brief* 15, issue 10 (May 15, 2015).

37. When the CMS South China Sea Bureau learned that Chinese fishermen at Scarborough were being threatened with detention by the Philippine navy, it immediately directed *CMS 75* and *CMS 84* to aid them. At the same time it alerted

Beijing, which then took command of the two ships. Long Quan, "Rationally Examining the Sino-Philippines Scarborough Reef Confrontation" (*Lixing Kandai Zhongfei Huangyandao Shijian*), *China Ocean News*, April 20, 2012, 4.

38. "SOA Director Liu Cigui Greets Front Line Forces at Scarborough Shoal via VTC" (*Guojia Haiyangju Liu Cigui Juzhang Shipin Lianxian Weiwen Huangyandao Weiquan Zhifa Yixian Haijian Biandui*), *Ocean Development and Management (Haiyang Kaifa Yu Guanli)*, June 2012.

39. See *Travelling around China*.

40. See "Ten Big Things for CMS in 2011" (*2011 Niandu Zhongguo Haijian Shijian Dashi*), *China Ocean News*, April 6, 2012, 5, http://epaper.oceanol.com/shtml /zghyb/20120406/70195.shtml.

41. Local-level CMS rights protection ships were, in theory at least, subject to orders from the CMS Command Center (*tongyi bushu*). See Yang Chang, "CMS Tianjin Rights Protection Law Enforcement Fleet Is Set Up" (*Zhongguo Haijian Tianjin Shi Weiquan Zhifa Chuandui Guapai*), *China Ocean News*, April 19, 2013, 4.

42. This administrative entity in Beijing approves and coordinates blue-water operations of the three regional contingents. More than just a room with consoles and screens (though it does have those), FLEC is overseen by a director who also serves as the deputy director of the Bureau of Fisheries Administration. A direct translation of the Chinese is "Fisheries Law Enforcement Command Center." The Chinese themselves translate it as "Fisheries Law Enforcement Command."

43. For a useful discussion of China Fisheries Law Enforcement, see Lyle J. Goldstein, "Chinese Fisheries Enforcement: Environmental and Strategic Implications," *Marine Policy* 40 (July 2013), 187–93.

44. *Ocean Development and Management (2012)*, 344. See also Ministry of Agriculture Fisheries Administration, *2009 China Fisheries Yearbook* (*Zhongguo Yuye Nianjian 2009*) (Beijing: China Agricultural, 2009), 335.

45. This is according to retired Rear Adm. Zheng Ming; "Perhaps the Scarborough Shoal and Diaoyu Island Incidents Can Serve as an Entry Point for Formulating and Implementing a Maritime Development Strategy" (*Diaoyudao, Huangyandao Shijian Huo Ke Chengwei Wo Guo Zhiding He Shishi Haiyang Fazhan Zhanlue De Yige Qierudian*), *Modern Ships (Xiandai Jianchuan)* (September 2012). This is confirmed by Liu Bin, "One Year Retrospective after the Creation of the China Coast Guard Bureau: Forces No Longer Operate on their Own" (*Zhongguo Haijingju Zujian Yi Nian Guancha: Zhixing Renwu Bu Zai Danda Dudou Le*), *Southern Weekend (Nanfang Zhoumo)*, October 9, 2014, http://www.infzm.com/content/104611.

46. For a copy of instructions for Fisheries Law Enforcement EEZ patrols in 2010, see http://www.lawyee.org/Act/Act_Display.asp?ChannelID=1010100&RID=660366&K eyWord=.

47. Ju Li, "The Use of Beidou Satellite Navigation System in Oceanic Fisheries" (*Beidou Weixing Daohang Xitong Zai Haiyang Yuye De Yunyong*), *Satellite and Network (Weixing Yu Wangluo)* (March 2013). These systems, already operational by 2007, also played important roles in the *Impeccable* and Scarborough Shoal incidents.

48. Su Taoxiang, "China's First Pair of Fisheries Law Enforcement Ships to Convoy Fishing Vessels Set Sail Yesterday" (*Woguo Shou Dui Nansha Yuzhengchuan Bansuishi Huyu Biandui Zuori Qihang*), *Southern Daily (Nanfang Ribao)*, April 2, 2010, http:// news.163.com/10/0402/10/638P6SBD000146BB.html; Li Mingshuang, "The Ministry of Agriculture Commends Advanced Collectives and Advanced Individuals" (*Nongyebu Biaozhang Huyu Weiquan Xianjin Jiti He Xianjin Geren*), *China Fisheries (Zhongguo Shuichan)* (December 2011), 13–14.

49. M. Taylor Fravel, "China's Strategy in the South China Sea," *Contemporary Southeast Asia* 33, no. 3 (2011), 305.

50. See "The Full Story of the Scarborough Shoal Incident" (*Huangyan Shijian Lailong Qumai*), *People's Navy (Renmin Haijun)*, May 11, 2012, 23.

51. Scott Bentley, "Indonesia's 'Global Maritime Nexus': Looming Challenges at Sea for Jokowi's Administration," *Strategist* (Australian Strategic Policy Institute), September 24, 2014, http://www.aspistrategist.org.au/; Robert Beckhausen, "She Doesn't Look It, but This Chinese Coast Guard Vessel Is One Mean Ship," *War Is Boring*, June 1, 2016.

52. Ramses Amer, "China, Vietnam, and the South China Sea Dispute: Disputes and Dispute Management," *Ocean Development and International Law* 45, no. 1 (2014), 23. See also Fravel, "China's Strategy in the South China Sea," 306–7.

53. See "Pulling Back the Mysterious Veil of CMS and China Fisheries Law Enforcement" (*Jiekai Zhongguo Haijian Yu Zhongguo Yuzheng De Shenmi Miansha*), *Legal Daily (Fazhi Bao)*, April 22, 2012, http://www.legaldaily.com.cn/index/content/2012-04/22/content_3520667.htm.

54. The Border Defense Force operated under a dual command structure that included the Ministry of Public Security and the Central Military Commission. Dennis Blasko, *The Chinese Army Today: Tradition and Transformation for the 21st Century* (London: Routledge, 2012), 27.

55. Its full name is *gongan bianfang budui haiyang jingcha*.

56. This is clearly stated in the Rules on Maritime Law Enforcement Work by Public Security Organs (*gongan jiguan haishang zhifa gongzuo guiding*). An English version of this law is available at http://www.lawinfochina.com/display.aspx?lib=law&id=6429&CGid=.

57. Yang Lin, Huang Jihui, and Zhu Geqi, "Put to Sea, on a Long Patrol!" (*Chuhai, Yuanhang Qu!*), *Frontier Defense Police China (Zhongguo Bianfang Jingcha)*, July 2010.

58. Other relevant documents include the "List of Items Prohibited from Entering or Leaving China," the "List of Items Limited from Entering or Leaving China," and the "PRC Customs Regulations for Protecting Intellectual Property." See *Ocean Development and Management (2012)*, 348.

59. Chen Pengpeng, Gao Qing, Ma Jiang, and Shao Zhijun, "Focus on China's Maritime Law Enforcement Forces" (*Jujiao Woguo Haishang Zhifa Liliang*), *People's Navy (Renmin Haijun)*, 4.

60. The December 2013 issue of *China Maritime Safety* (*zhongguo haishi*) is devoted to a retrospective on the fifteen-year history of MSA.

61. Aside from large oceangoing ships, MSA also operates unmanned patrol craft. One of these vessels operated in the Spratly chain in 2013. Lv Ning, "The Advent of China's First Domestically Developed Unmanned Surveillance Surface" (*Woguo Zixing Yanzhi Kaifa De Shousou Wurenji Celiangting Dansheng*), *China Ocean News*, June 6, 2013, 2. For calls for MSA to play a larger rights protection role, see Tao Jian, "Give Play to MSA's Function of Safeguarding National Sovereignty and Maritime Rights and Interests" (*Fahui Haishi Jigou Weihu Guojia Zhuquan He Haiyang Quanyi Zhineng*), *China Maritime Safety (Zhongguo Haishi)*, May 2013.

62. Zhang Baochen, "What I Have Learned from Other Countries' Organizational Systems for Oceanic and Coastal Law Enforcement" (*Haiyang Daguo Haishang Zhifa Jigou Tizhi De Jiben Guilv Yu Qishi*), *China Maritime Safety (Zhongguo Haishi)* (2008/04), 23–27; Yan Tieyi, "Research on Maritime Police Power" (*Lun Haiyang Jingcha Quan*), *Chinese Journal of Maritime Law (Zhongguo Haishangfa Yanjiu)* 23, no. 2 (July 2012), 78–89; Lin Quanling and Gao Zhongyi, "An Analysis and Consideration of CMS Conduct of Rights Protection Law Enforcement" (*Zhongguo Haijian Weiquan Zhifa De Xingshi Fenxi Yu Celue Sikao*), *Pacific Journal (Taipingyang Xuebao)*; Yan Tieyi and Sun Kun, "On China's Maritime Administrative Law Enforcement Collective" (*Lun Zhongguo Haiyang Xingzheng zhifa Zhuti*), *Journal of Dalian Maritime University, Social Science Education (Dalian Haishi Daxue Xuebao)* (February 2011).

63. Goldstein, *Five Dragons Stirring Up the Sea*, 2.

64. Liu Cigui, "Some Considerations on Building China into a Maritime Power" (*Guanyu Jianshe Haiyang Qiangguo De Ruogan Sikao*), *State Oceanic Administration*, November 26, 2012, http://www.soa.gov.cn/xw/ldhd/lyx/201212/t20121204_19016.html.

65. Cui Taojing, "Looking Back on 2013: The Dream Sets Sail (Part I)" (*Huishou 2013: Mengxiang Cong Haishang Qihang [Shang]*), *China Ocean News*, December 30, 2013, 1; "Commentary: The Reform Will Promote the Maritime Power Strategy" (*Shiping: Dabuzhi Gaigei Jiang Youli Tuijin Haiyang Qiangguo Jianshe*), *National People's Congress*, March 12, 2013, http://www.npc.gov.cn/npc/dbdhhy/12_1/2013-03/12/content_1780160.htm; Yan Hongmo, "Looking Back on a Few Important Decisions Made By the Party Center to Develop Maritime Affairs" (*Huigu Dang Zhongyang Fazhan Haiyang Shiye Jici Zhongda Jueding*), *China Ocean News*, October 8, 2014, 4.

66. Plan for State Council Organizational Reform and Transferal of Functions (*Guowuyuan Jigou Gaige He Zhineng Zhuanbian Fang'an*), [Government of the PRC website], March 15, 2013, http://www.gov.cn/2013lh/content_2354443.htm.

67. Article 5 also establishes a State Oceanic Commission: "In order to strengthen overall maritime planning and comprehensive coordination, [we hereby] establish a high level procedural coordinating body called the State Oceanic Commission. It will be responsible for researching a national maritime development strategy and overall coordination of important maritime-related matters. SOA will undertake the specific work of the State Oceanic Commission."

68. The Q&A session was run by Wang Feng, vice minister of the State Commission Office for public sector reform; http://news.xinhuanet.com/2013lh/2013-03/11/c_124442355.htm.

69. One expert interpreted it to mean that the new China Coast Guard would coordinate the different agencies, which would remain intact. Xing Dan, "The China Coast Guard Bureau Draws Its Sword" (*Zhongguo Haijingju Liangjian*), *China Ship Survey (Zhongguo Chuanjian)* (April 2013).

70. Huang Ran, "CCP Center Appoints the Leadership of the Reconstituted SOA" (*Zhonggong Zhongyang Renming Chongxin Zujian De Guojia Haiyang Ju Lingdao Banzi*), *China Ocean News*, March 19, 2013, 1.

71. Available at http://www.gov.cn/zwgk/2013-07/09/content_2443023.htm.

72. Sometime in the early fall of 2014, probably September, "preparatory groups" for contingents based in China's eleven coastal provinces and directly administered cities were also established. Former CMP forces form their cores. But China Coast Guard recruitment materials released in November 2014 suggest that these *zongdui* also include units from other agencies, including former Maritime Anti-Smuggling Police and Fisheries Law Enforcement units. Wang Pan, "China Begins South China Sea Region Maritime Special Law Enforcement Operation" (*Zhongguo Qidong Nanhaiqu Haiyang Zhuanxiang Zhifa Xingdong*), Xinhua, October 3, 2014, http://news.xinhuanet.com/politics/2014-10/03/c_1112709090.htm. A 2014 recruitment notice for the Guangdong contingent is available at http://gd.offcn.com/html/2014/11/38449.html. The 2014 Zhejiang recruitment notice is available at http://www.gaoxiaojob.com/zhaopin/wenzhirenyuanzhaopin/20141111/134640.html.

73. The preparatory groups as of mid-2017 had not achieved full functionality; Liu Bin, "One Year Retrospective." See Dong Jiawe, "On the Motives and Aims for the Reconstruction of China's Maritime Law Enforcement System," *Journal of China Maritime Police Academy* 16, no. 4 (August 2017), 12. The slow pace of integration at the bureau and contingent levels likely caused the Chinese government to issue "Notice from the State Council Office on Doing More to Promote the Work of Integrating Coast Guard Forces." Mention of this document is found in the public domain, but the author has been unable to track down the text or even a date of issue.

74. See Suo Youwei, Chen Qiren, and Zhou Donghua, "Coast Guardsman Wu Shengbo Has Done Rights Protection Law Enforcement in the South China Sea for 36 Years, Guarding Mischief Reef Forty Times" (*Haijing Wu Shengbo Jianshou Nanhai WEiquan Zhifa 36 Nian, Shou Meijijiao 40 Duo Hangci*), *China News*, May 6, 2015, www.chinanews.com/mil/2015/05-06/7257254.shtml.

75. There were some exceptions: CMS and FLE forces sometimes trained together. See, for instance, Gao Yue, "China Coast Guard 'Flashes Its Sword' in the East China Sea" (*Zhongguo Haijing "Liang Jian" Donghai*), *China Ocean News*, August 23, 2013, 4.
76. Yu Zhirong, "We Need to Attach Lots of Importance to Regular Law Enforcement Patrols to Diaoyu Island" (*Diaoyudao Changtai Xunhang Zhifa Xu Gaodu Zhongshi*), *Military Digest (Junshi Wenzhai)* (March 2014).
77. In May 2014, the Command Center coordinated service efforts to locate the wreckage of Malaysian Airlines flight 370 in March of that year. Chinese journalists covering the story interviewed a PAP senior colonel, Zhang Chunru, who was the center's duty officer; Cui Jingtao, "China Coast Guard Ship Begins Search and Rescue Work in Area Where Malaysian Passenger Jet Lost" (*Zhongguo Haijingchuan Zai Mahang Keji Shilian Haiyu Kaizhan Soujiu Gongzuo*), *China Ocean News*, March 10, 2014, 1. The command center dispatched *CCG 3411*, a former China Fisheries Law Enforcement ship, to the southern Indian Ocean to search for wreckage. See CCTV 13, "China Coast Guard Ship Discovers Two Oil Slicks and Can Inspect as Soon as within One Day" (*Zhongguo Haijingchuan Faxian Liangtiao Jiaoda Youwudai Zuikuai Yi Tian Neng Jianchu*), http://news.ifeng.com/world/special/malaixiyakejishilian/content-4/detail_2014_03/10/34620064_0.shtml.
78. For instance, *CMS 8002*, a Fujian ship, had a direct connection with the CCG Command Center. Zhao Ning, "Demystifying *'CMS 8002'*" (*Jiemi "Haijian 8002" Chuan*), *China Ocean News*, March 15, 2013, 3.
79. See Liu Bin, "One Year Retrospective."
80. Li Jinhong, "A China Coast Guard Vessel Successfully Rescues Three Crew Members Aboard a Foreign-Registered Sailboat Stranded in the Spratlys" (*Zhongguo Haijingchuan Zai Nansha Qundao Haiyu Chenggong Jiuzhu 3 Ming Waiji Geqian Fanchuan Chuanyuan*), Xinhua, January 5, 2018, www.xinhuanet.com/legal/2018-01/05/c_1122217564.htm.
81. Ryan D. Martinson, *The Arming of China's Maritime Frontier*, China Maritime Study 2 (Newport, RI: Naval War College Press for the China Maritime Studies Institute, 2017), 21.
82. U.S. Department of Defense. *Annual Report to Congress: Military and Security Developments Involving the People's Republic of China 2015* (Washington, DC, April 17, 2015), 3.
83. Reinhard Drifte, "The Japan-China Confrontation over the Senkaku/Diaoyu Islands: Between 'Shelving' and 'Dispute Escalation,'" *Asia-Pacific Journal* 12, issue 30, no. 3 (July 27, 2014), 17.
84. "Status of Activities by Chinese Government Vessels and Chinese Fishing Vessels in Waters surrounding the Senkaku Islands," *Japan Ministry of Foreign Affairs*, August 26, 2016, www.mofa.go.jp/files/000180283.pdf.
85. See Martinson, *Arming of China's Maritime Frontier*, 22. One CMP vessel—the Shandong-based cutter *CCG 37102*—was recognized by the State Council and the Central Military Commission for its outstanding performance defending the rig. See "Vessel 3702 of the First Detachment of the Shandong Coast Guard Earns National Award for Excellent Grass Roots Public Security Unit" (*Shandong Haijing Yi Zhidui 37102 Jian Huo Quanguo Youxiu Gongan Jiceng Danwei*), *Weihai Media Web*, May 25, 2017, http://whjyjt.cn/news/whnews/2017/0525/295165.html.
86. "Jiangsu Coast Guard Holds Its First Ship Visit Event in Nanjing" (*Jiangsu Haijing Shouge Jianting Kaifangri Zai Nanjing Juxing*), *Renmin Wang*, February 11, 2018, http://legal.people.com.cn/n1/2018/0211/c42510-29818807.html.
87. Erwin Colcol, "Chinese Vessels Spotted Near Pag-asa Island," *GMA News Online*, August 16, 2017, www.gmanetwork.com/news/news/nation/622062/chinese-vessels-spotted-near-pag-asa-island/story. See also Carmela Fonbuena, "PH Aborts Construction on Pag-asa Sandbar after China Protest," *Rappler*, November 8, 2017, www.rappler.com/nation/187690-ph-china-pagasa-standoff-lorenzana. See also CSIS

Asia Maritime Transparency Initiative, "Confirming the Chinese Flotilla near Thitu Island," August 17, 2017, *Center for Strategic and International Studies,* https://amti.csis .org/confirming-chinese-flotilla-near-thitu-island.

88. One PAP Academy professor wrote that the reform was "strongly put forward by the country's highest level of policymakers"; Li Peizhi, "Thoughts on China Coast Guard Organizational Reform in the Context of the Strategy to Build China into a Maritime Power," *Journal of Chinese People's Armed Police Force Academy* 32, no. 3 (March 2016), 49.

89. Sun soon left the China Coast Guard and became the deputy director of the State Oceanic Administration.

90. With this decision, party leaders may have sought to remove any local control over China's armed forces. See Viola Zhou, "Why China's Armed Police Will Now Only Take Orders from Xi and His Generals," *South China Morning Post,* December 28, 2017, www.scmp.com/news/china/policies-politics/article/2126039/reason-why-chinas -armed-police-will-now-only-take.

91. Kristin Huang, "China Brings People's Armed Police under Control of Top Military Chiefs," *South China Morning Post,* December 27, 2017, www.scmp.com/news/china /diplomacy-defence/article/2125880/china-brings-peoples-armed-police-under-control -top.

92. "The Important Political Decision to Ensure that the Party Has Absolute Leadership Over the PAP" *(Quebao Dang Dui Wujing Budui Jueding Lingdao De Zhongda Zhengzhi Jueding), People's Daily,* February 28, 2017, http://opinion.people.com.cn/n1/2017/1228/ c1003-29732631.html.

93. The other two missions are "safeguard national political security and social stability" and "defensive operations" *(fangwei zuozhan).* See "Ministry of Defense Spokesperson Wu Qian Answers a Question about the Significance of the New PAP Service Flag" *(Guofangbu Xinwen Fayanren Wu Qian Jiu Wujing Buduiqi Yuyi Dawen),* [PRC Ministry of Defense website], January 10, 2018, www.mod.gov.cn/info/2018-01/10 /content_4802153.htm.

94. See "Explanation of State Council Organizational Reform Plan" *(Guanyu Guowuyuan Jigou Gaige Fang'an De Shuoming),* Xinhua, March 14, 2018, www.xinhuanet.com /politics/2018lh/2018-03/14/c_1122533011.htm.

95. The decision to place the China Coast Guard under the PAP was contained in the "Plan for Deepening Party and State Organizational Reform," issued on March 21, 2018. See "Plan for Deepening Party and State Organizational Reform," Xinhua, March 21, 2018, www.xinhuanet.com/2018-03/21/c_1122570517.htm.

96. "Defense Ministry's Regular Press Conference on June 28," [PRC Ministry of Defense website], June 29, 2018, http://eng.mod.gov.cn/news/2018-06/29/content_4818080.htm.

97. Lyle Morris, "China Welcomes Its Newest Armed Force: The Coast Guard," *War on the Rocks,* April 4, 2018.

98. Coordination of China Coast Guard units for inner seas (i.e., internally oriented) missions has not achieved anything close to the same success. The operations organized by the regional preparatory groups in fall 2014 were intended to develop a system to coordinate operations of different coast guard units—meaning, of course, that no such system exists. This system needs to integrate both the national-level units of the four "dragons" and the provincial, municipal, and county units of CMS and Fisheries Law Enforcement—a very formidable task.

99. Zhao Qian, "Make Maritime Law Enforcement More Exacting and Safeguard Maritime Rights and Interests" *(Yange Haishang Zhifa Weihu Haiyang Quanyi), China Ocean News,* December 25, 2014, 3.

100. See Martinson, *Arming of China's Maritime Frontier,* 25.

101. "Joint Navy, Coast Guard, and Civilian Task Force Patrols Paracels for the First Time, Lasting Five Days and Four Nights" *(Junjingmin Lianhe Biandui Shouci Xunluo Xisha Daojiao),* Xinhua, May 20, 2018, www.xinhuanet.com/politics/2018 -05/20/c_1122858765.htm.

Appendix II. China's Maritime Militia

1. The ideas expressed here are those of the authors alone. A compendium of their previous publications on this subject is available at http://www.andrewerickson.com/2018/11/secdef-mattis-calls-for-prc-maritime-militia-to-operate-in-a-safe-and-professional-manner-in-accordance-with-international-law/.

2. China has had an active Maritime Militia presence in the Spratlys since 1985. It was involved in the tensions over Mischief Reef in 1995, when China built structures on the disputed feature. The Philippine navy arrested Tanmen Militia personnel at Half Moon Shoal, much closer to the Philippine coast and over eighty miles southeast of Mischief Reef. Conor M. Kennedy and Andrew S. Erickson, *Model Maritime Militia: Tanmen's Leading Role in the April 2012 Scarborough Shoal Incident* (Washington, DC: Center for International Maritime Security, April 21, 2016), http://cimsec.org/.

3. See Conor M. Kennedy and Andrew S. Erickson, *China's Third Sea Force, the People's Armed Forces Maritime Militia: Tethered to the PLA*, China Maritime Report 1 (Newport, RI: Naval War College, China Maritime Studies Institute, March 2017), 2–3, https://dnnlgwick.blob.core.windows.net/.

4. See Kennedy and Erickson, *China's Third Sea Force.*

5. 民兵工作条例 [Regulations on Militia Work], "关于认真做好2015年民兵整租工作的通知" [Notice on Seriously Completing 2015 Militia Reorganization Work], Sheyang County Huangsha Port Township Government, March 24, 2015.

6. "关于认真做好2015年度民兵整租工作的通知" [Notice on Thoroughly Completing the 2015 Militia Reorganization Work], Qingjiang Township Party Committee, March 23, 2015, http://xxgk.yueqing.gov.cn/YQ119/zcwj/0203/201503/t20150326_1800276.html.

7. Xu Haifeng, "Adapting to New Circumstances: Comprehensively Standardize Maritime Militia Construction," 浙江省加强海上民兵建设 [Zhejiang Province Strengthens Maritime Militia Construction], Xinhuanet, December 4, 2013, http://news.xinhuanet.com/mil/2013-12/04/c_125806747.htm.

8. See Kennedy and Erickson, *China's Third Sea Force.*

9. 李健南 [Li Jian'nan], "抓实建强基层民兵党组织" [Grasp and Strengthen Grassroots Militia Party Organizations], 中国民兵 [China's Militia] 7 (2017), 34–37.

10. [He Zhixiang], "谈海上民兵建设'四纳入'" [Discussion on the "Four Integrations" in Maritime Militia Construction], *National Defense* 4 (2013); He Zhixiang, "适应海防安全形势—建强海上民兵组织" [Adjusting to the Security Situation in Sea Defense: Strengthen Maritime Militia Organization], *National Defense* 1 (2015).

11. 王文清 [Wang Wenqing], "破解海上民兵建设难题" [Cracking the Code on Issues in Maritime Militia Construction], 中国国防报 [China Defense News], July 28, 2016, 3.

12. 张践 [Zhang Jian], "围绕'六化'抓建推动海上民兵转型" [Advance the Transformation of Maritime Militia Centered on "Six Changes"], 国防 [*National Defense*] 10 (2015), 21–23.

13. Andrew S. Erickson and Conor M. Kennedy, *China's Daring Vanguard: Introducing Sanya City's Maritime Militia* (Washington, DC: Center for International Maritime Security, November 5, 2015), http://cimsec.org/.

14. For a detailed examination of the Sansha Maritime Militia and its creation, see Conor M. Kennedy and Andrew S. Erickson, *Riding a New Wave of Professionalization and Militarization: Sansha City's Maritime Militia* (Washington, DC: Center for International Maritime Security, September 1, 2016), http://cimsec.org/. Assessments of deployment patterns are based on the authors' observation of the fleet via the Marine Traffic service, https://www.marinetraffic.com/.

15. The involvement of the PAFMM was confirmed in the Pentagon's 2018 China Military Report; U.S. Department of Defense, *Annual Report to Congress: Military and Security Developments Involving the People's Republic of China 2018* (Washington, DC, August 16, 2018). The presence of at least two PAFMM vessels was determined from

the authors' observation of commercially available satellite imagery; *Digital Globe*, https://www.digitalglobe.com/.

16. He Zhixiang, "Adjusting to the Security Situation in Sea Defense," 48–50. The author uses "militiamen" to cover both male and female PAFMM personnel.

17. Zhang Jian, "Advance the Transformation of Maritime Militia," 21–23.

18. Kennedy and Erickson, *Riding a New Wave of Professionalization and Militarization*.

19. Kennedy and Erickson, *Riding a New Wave of Professionalization and Militarization*.

20. Tonnage estimates were made by: (1) searching for names of known Sansha Maritime Militia at marinetraffic.com, which lists their respective displacements, lengths, and beams; (2) using these data and estimating draft at no more than three meters for vessels in this size category; and (3) employing a block coefficient to calculate displacement; Pia Lee-Brago, "Philippines to Get Nine More Patrol Vessels from Japan," *Philippine Star*, October 14, 2016, http://www.philstar.com /headlines/2016/10/14/1633448/philippines-get-9-more-patrol-vessels-japan.

21. Kennedy and Erickson, *Riding a New Wave of Professionalization and Militarization*.

22. 杨曦 [Yang Wei], "三沙: 军警民联防指挥中心永兴岛奠基开工" [Sansha: Military Police Civilian Joint Defense Command Center Breaks Ground], 南海网 [Hainan Hinews], July 25, 2015, http://sansha.hinews.cn/system/2015/07/25/017715316.shtml.

23. Kennedy and Erickson, *Riding a New Wave of Professionalization and Militarization*; "南海三沙民兵处置侵入领海外籍渔船 部署美济礁" [Sansha Militia Handle Foreign Fishing Vessel Incursions in the South China Sea and Are Deployed to Mischief Reef], 中国国防报 [China Defense News], January 27, 2016, http://www.chinanews.com /mil/2016/01-27/7735164.shtml; "三沙市推动军警民联防机制 构建三线海上维权格局" [Sansha City Promotes a Military Police Civilian Joint Defense Mechanism and Constructs a Three-Tiered Maritime Rights Protection System], 中国新闻网 [China News Network], November 21, 2014, http://politics.people.com.cn/n/2014/1121 /c70731-26071496.html.

24. "军委国防动员部部长: 省军区划归动员部管理 有五职能" [Head of the Central Military Commission National Defense Mobilization Department: Provincial Military Districts to Be Managed under the Mobilization Department with Five Functions], 中国国防报 [China Defense News], March 10, 2016, http://www.guancha.cn/military -affairs/2016_03_10_353475.shtml.

25. "President Pays Visit to Hainan Fishermen," *China Daily*, April 11, 2012, http://usa .chinadaily.com.cn/2013-04/11/content_16394643.htm.

26. He Zhixiang, "Discussion on the 'Four Integrations,'" 36–37.

27. 郑凌晨 [Zheng Lingchen], "发挥好海上民兵优势 打好军民融合攻坚战" [Give Full Play to the Advantages of the Maritime Militia and Fight for Civil-Military Fusion], 中国海军网 [China Navy Online], October 31, 2016, http://navy.81.cn /content/2016-10/31/content_7334774.htm.

28. "海上后备劲旅: 广西北海军分区加强海上民兵建设纪实" [Maritime Reserve Forces: A Record of Guangxi Beihai Military Subdistrict Strengthening Maritime Militia Construction], 解放军报 [PLA Daily], January 6, 2014, http://www.81.cn/lj/2014 -01/06/content_5721123_2.htm.

29. 陈长寿 [Chen Changshou], "关于海上维权与作战动员的研究" [Research on Maritime Rights Protection and Combat Mobilization], 国防 [National Defense] 4 (2017), 21.

30. Terminology used to describe PAFMM units obscures their exact size and composition.

31. 陈青松 [Chen Qingsong], "海防地区支援保障海上作战准备存在的问题与对策" [Issues and Measures in the Preparation for Supporting Naval Warfare in the Maritime Defense Zone], 国防 [National Defense] 10 (2016), 50–51. The Ningbo MSD minesweeper *dadui* is composed of two hundred PLA Navy reservists and sixteen fishing vessels, with an unknown number of fishing vessel captains and crews; "东海大批渔船编入海军预备役" [A Large Number of Fishing Boats in the East China Sea Have Been Incorporated into the Naval Reserve], 中国军网 [China Military Online], March 11, 2015, http://mil.news.sina.com.cn/2015-03-11/1530824043.html.

32. 张国臣 [Zhang Guochen], "海上民兵参加海上封控行动研究" [Research on Maritime Militia Participation in Sea Control Operations], 国防 [National Defense] 11 (2016), 41–43.

33. "真假变幻无踪影—目击浙江省台州市椒江区海上民兵伪装分队演练" [Shifting between Real and False with No Trace: Witnessing the Training Exercise of Zhejiang Province Taizhou City Jiaojiang District's Maritime Militia Deception Detachment], 中国民兵 [China's Militia], 10 (2010), http://kns55.en.eastview.com/kcms/detail/detail.aspx?recid=&FileName=MMZG201010057&DbName=CJFD2010&DbCode=CJFD.

34. "海军民兵补给分队: 民兵'粮草官'驰骋海疆" [Naval Militia Resupply Detachment: Militia "Food Officers" Ride Out to the Sea Frontier], *People's Daily Online*, January 18, 2012, http://military.people.com.cn/GB/172467/16908831.html.

35. 徐守洋, 孟晓飞 [Xu Shouyang and Meng Xiaofei], "海上支援作战能力升浪攀升" [Maritime Combat Support Capabilities Rise with the Waves], *China Defense News*, April 2015, http://news.mod.gov.cn/militia/2015-04/07/content_4578670.htm.

36. "浙江省宁海县人武部58名科技专家编组进民兵'蓝军'" [58 Science and Technology Experts of Zhejiang Province's Ninghai County PAFD Enter the Militia's "Blue Force"], Xinhuanet, November 19, 2014, http://news.xinhuanet.com/mil/2014-11/19/c_127227368.htm.

37. Zhang Jian, "Advance the Transformation of the Maritime Militia," 22.

38. 张荣胜, 陈明辉 [Zhang Rongsheng and Chen Minghui], "关于组织动员海上民兵参与维权行动的几点思考" [Some Thoughts on Organizing and Mobilizing Maritime Militia to Participate in Maritime Rights Protection Actions], *National Defense* 8 (2014).

39. Andrew S. Erickson and Conor M. Kennedy, *From Frontier to Frontline: Tanmen Maritime Militia's Leading Role Part 2* (Washington, DC: Center for International Maritime Security), May 17, 2016, http://cimsec.org/.

40. "中华人民共和国突发事件应对法" [Emergency Response Law of the People's Republic of China], chap. 3, arts. 3 and 17, Baike.com, November 1, 2007, http://www.baike.com/.

41. 王赫 [Wang He], "海上民兵直升机救援分队亮相渤海湾" [Maritime Militia Helicopter Rescue Detachment Debuts in the Bohai Bay], 中国国防报 [China Defense News], May 25, 2016, http://www.mod.gov.cn/mobilization/2016-05/25/content_4664211.htm.

42. 冯文平 [Feng Wenping], "以新时代党的强军思想为引领构建主要战略方向海上民兵侦察情报体系" [Building a Maritime Militia Reconnaissance and Intelligence System for the Main Strategic Directions under the Guidance of the CPC's Thinking on Building a Strong Military in the New Era], 国防 [National Defense] 1 (2018), 44.

43. Feng Wenping, 43–45.

44. 丛黎明, 马绍惠 [Cong Liming and Ma Shaohui], "威海军民推进海防建设融合发展" [Weihai Advances in Civil-Military Integrated Development in Sea Defense], *National Defense News*, January 28, 2015, http://www.mod.gov.cn/mobilize/2015-01/28/content_4567330.htm; "三沙市推动军警民联防机制—构建三线海上维权格局" [Sansha City Promotes Its Military-Police-Civilian Joint Defense Mechanism: Constructs a Three-Line Maritime Rights Protection Structure], 中国新闻网 [China News], November 2014, http://www.chinanews.com/gn/2014/11-21/6803776.shtml.

45. Information Office of the State Council of the PRC, *China's National Defense in 2004*, http://www.china.org.cn/e-white/20041227/.

46. "加速推进后备力量 建设转型发展" [Accelerate and Advance the Construction, Transformation, and Development of Reserve Forces], 中国军网 [China Military Online], March 18, 2016, http://military.people.com.cn/n1/2016/0318/c1011-28209150.html; 贝骁 [Bei Xiao], "状态之变 带来的连锁反应—海南陵水县人武部后进变先闻思录" [A Chain Reaction Brought about by the Changing Situation: The Experience of the People's Armed Forces Department in Lingshui County, Hainan Province], 中国军网 [China Military Online], August 22, 2016, http://www.81.cn/gfbmap/content/2016-08/22/content_154265.htm.

47. Chen Changshou, "Research on Maritime Rights Protection," 21.

48. Zeng Pengxiang, "Scientifically Build a Management System for the Maritime Militia," *National Defense Magazine* 12 (2014).

49. 邓伟余, 赵赵继承 [Deng Weiyu and Zhao Jicheng], "'海上民兵'崛起在蓝色国土" [The Rise of "Maritime Militia" on Blue Territory], *National Defense* 2 (September 2007); 廖刚斌, 王牌, 熊睿 [Liao Gangbin, Wang Pai, and Xiong Rui], "海上民兵分队建设存在的问题与对策" [Issues and Measures in Maritime Militia Unit Construction], *National Defense* 8 (2014), 14–15.

50. "大冶市2012年度民兵军事训练计划" [Daye City 2012 Annual Militia Military Training Plan], http://m.ishare.iask.sina.com.cn/f/32QO2B1WEz5.html.

51. During World War II, Japan commandeered many fishing boats as picket boats, primarily to observe the sea to the east of the mainland and provide early warning of any approaching U.S. task force. One of them, a steel-hulled, ninety-foot fishing boat, spotted the carrier USS *Hornet* carrying Jimmy Doolittle's B-24 bombers to bomb Tokyo in April 1942; the picket radioed Tokyo, causing the planes to launch early at 700 rather 450 miles from Tokyo. See Ian W. Toll, *Pacific Crucible: War at Sea in the Pacific, 1941–1942* (New York: W. W. Norton, 2012), 285–89.

52. Zuo Guidong, Li Huazhen, and Yu Chuanchun, "Heroic Primary Militia Battalion, Strengthening Construction of Maritime Specialized Detachments," Taizhou Net.

53. 居礼 [Ju Li], "北斗卫星导航系统在海洋渔业的应用" [Applications of the Beidou Satellite Navigation System in Marine Fisheries], *Chengdu Guowei Communications Technology Co., Ltd.*, February 4, 2014, http://gwsatcom.com/Trends /inform/2015-06-23/79.html.

54. Xu Haifeng, "Adapting to New Circumstances."

55. 曹树建, 刘健 [Cao Shujian and Liu Jian], "大海成为民兵练兵战备主战场" [The Sea Has Become the Main Battlefield for Militia Training and War Readiness], *National Defense News*, November 3, 2014, http://www.81.cn/gfbmap/content/2014–11/03 /content_91820.htm; 何军毅, 赵继承, 奏景号 [He Junyi, Zhao Jicheng, and Tai Jinghao], "千船齐发, 向着蓝色国土" [A Thousand Vessels Go Out to the Blue Territory Together], *National Defense News*, May 25, 2015, http://www.mod.gov.cn /mobilize/2015-05/25/content_4586486.htm.

56. Feng Wenping, "Building a Maritime Militia Reconnaissance and Intelligence System," 43–45.

57. "动员参谋从后台回归" [Mobilization Chief of Staff Comes Out from behind the Desk], 中国军网 [China Military Online], February 14, 2017, http://www.81.cn /gfbmap/content/2017-02/14/content_169350.htm; "海上织网: 浙江省舟山警备区探索智慧动员纪事" [Maritime Network: A Record of Zhejiang Province Zhoushan Garrison's Exploration of Intelligent Mobilization], 中国军网 [China Military Online], November 17, 2016, http://www.81.cn/gfbmap/content/2016-11/17/content_161792 .htm; "国防建设巡礼: 浙江省舟山市" [National Defense Tour: Zhejiang Province, Zhoushan City], 国防 [National Defense] 11 (2015), 86.

58. 管伟同 [Guan Weitong], "连云港: 对基层民兵党组织建设的积极探索" [Lianyungang: An Active Exploration into Grassroots Militia Party Organization Construction], 中国民兵 [China's Militia] 4 (2017), 24–26.

59. "民兵出海, 渔船成为流动岗哨" [Militia Go Out to Sea, Fishing Vessels Become Mobile Sentries], 中国渔业报 [China Fisheries News], December 14, 2015, http://szb .farmer.com.cn/yyb/html/2015-12/14/nw.D110000yyb_20151214_3-04.htm?div=-1.

60. 陈青松 [Chen Qingsong], "海上作战支前动员准备'一二三'" [Preparation for Maritime Combat Support-the-Front Mobilization "One-Two-Three"], 国防 [National Defense] 11 (2015), 50–51.

61. "常万全在苏调研全民国防教育 专程察看角斜红旗民兵团" [Chang Wanquan Inspects National Defense Education in Jiangsu Province, Special Visit to Jiaoxie Red Flag Militia Regiment], 中国江苏网 [China Jiangsu Net], May 16, 2017, http:// jsnews.jschina.com.cn/nt/a/201705/t20170516_509602.shtml; "角斜民兵团: '红旗精

神' 在革命热土传承" [Jiaoxie Militia Regiment: Inheriting the "Red Flag Spirit" on Revolutionary Soil], 江海晚报网 [Jianghai Evening News], August 5, 2016, http://www.jhwb.com.cn/content/2016-08/05/content_2476022.htm; 章晓丽 [Zhang Xiaoli], "响应祖国号召 当好海防 '前哨'" [Answering the Call of the Motherland, Serving as a "Forward Outpost" in Maritime Defense], 新华日报 [Xinhua Daily], May 22, 2017, http://www.jsdpc.gov.cn/jmrh/gfjy/dxp/201707/t20170704_428996.html.

62. 宫玉聪 [Gong Yucong], "上海市国防动员训练又出新招" [New Tactics in Shanghai City's National Defense Mobilization Training], 中国民兵 [China's Militia] 2 (2018), 13.

63. 陈青松 [Chen Qingsong], "加强和改进海上民兵应急分队建设之我见" [My Opinions on Strengthening and Improving Maritime Militia Emergency Response Detachment Construction], 国防 [National Defense], no. 12 (2014), 35–36.

64. 陈青松, 周扁 [Chen Qingsong and Zhou Pian], "紧盯使命任务抓好海上民兵建设" [A Mission-Focused Grasp of Maritime Militia Construction], *National Defense* 3 (2016).

65. Wang He, "Maritime Militia Helicopter Rescue Detachment."

66. 唐社教 [Tang Shejiao], "紧贴实战需求 坚持任务牵引 深化推进海上民兵侦察力量建设" [Keeping the Demands of Actual Combat in Mind and Sticking to the Mission-Driven Principle to Further Promote the Building of the Maritime Militia Reconnaissance Force], 国防 [National Defense] 1 (2018), 49–50.

67. "Mobilization Chief of Staff Comes Out from behind the Desk."

68. Tang Shejiao, "Keeping the Demands of Actual Combat in Mind," 49–50.

69. 张莉 [Zhang Li], "加强海上侦察分队建设初探" [Preliminary Thoughts on Strengthening the Building of Maritime Reconnaissance Elements], 国防 [National Defense] 4 (2018), 57–58; Feng Wenping, "Building a Maritime Militia Reconnaissance and Intelligence System," 43–45; 姚淮宁 [Yao Huaining], "着眼形式任务 遵循特点规律 积极探索海上民兵侦察情报建设新模式" [Actively Exploring New Models for Facilitating Work on Maritime Militia Reconnaissance and Intelligence in View of the New Situation and Missions in Accordance with Characteristics and General Laws], 国防 [National Defense] 1 (2018), 46–47.

70. "海天一体战场通用态势图构建" [Construction of Sea and Space Battlefield Versatile Situation Picture], 装备学院学报 [Journal of Equipment Academy] 28, no. 2 (April 2017), 46–51. The primary author is from "91746 部队." Units numbered in the series 91XXX through 92XXX are PLA Navy units.

71. "关于做好2014年度民兵组织整顿和兵役登记工作的通知" [Notice on the Completion of 2014 Militia Reorganization and Military Service Registration Work], issued by Tingjiang Township, May 12, 2014.

72. "解放军动员演练遇尴尬: 海上民兵无纪律未到齐" [An Embarrassment for PLA Exercises: Lacking Maritime Militia Discipline and Attendance], 解放军报 [PLA Daily], December 1, 2015.

73. "闻令而动 国防后备力量掀起训练热潮" [Orders to Move, a Surge in Training of National Defense Reserve Forces], 中国军网 [China Military Online], January 4, 2018, http://www.81.cn/jmywyl/2018-01/04/content_7894738.htm; 李峰 [Li Feng], "回首这一年, 感受军改带来的新变化" [Looking Back on This Year and the New Changes Brought About by Military Reform], 国防部网 [Ministry of National Defense of the People's Republic of China], December 21, 2016, http://www.mod.gov.cn/mobilization/2016-12/21/content_4767360_5.htm.

74. 石江龙 [Shi Jianglong], "2650艘渔船分享1.94亿燃油补贴" [2,650 Fishing Vessels Receive 194 Million in Fuel Subsidies], http://paper.oeeee.com/nis/201311/29/145728.html; "台山市委书记张磊获得广州军区第七届 '国防之星'殊荣" [Taishan City Committee Secretary Zhang Lei Receives Guangzhou Military Region's Seventh "National Defense Celebrity" Distinction], June 16, 2015, http://news.tsbtv.tv/2015/0616/39266.shtml; "省军区司令员台山调研海上民兵建设工作" [Provincial

Military District Commander Investigates Tanshan's Maritime Militia Work], *Taishan Station*, November 27, 2013, http://www.jmtv.cn/news/a/e/2013-11-27/1385552619943 .shtml.

75. Erickson and Kennedy, *From Frontier to Frontline*.

76. 周厚江 [Zhou Houjiang], "加强海上侦察分队建设初探" [Preliminary Thoughts on Strengthening the Building of Maritime Reconnaissance Elements], 国防 [National Defense] 4 (2018), 57–58.

BIBLIOGRAPHY

Andrew, Martin, and Carlo Kopp. "Advances in PLAN Carrier Aviation." *Air Power Australia*, April 10, 2010 (updated January 2014). www.ausairpower.net/APA -PLAN-CV.html#mozTocId658924.

Asia Times Staff. "After Beijing's Criticism, Mattis Says, 'Steady Drumbeat' of FONOPS to Continue." *Asia Times*, May 31, 2018. http://www.atimes.com/article/after -beijings-criticism-mattis-says-steady-drumbeat-of-fonops-to-continue.

Association of Southeast Asian Nations. "Declaration on the Code of Conduct of Parties in the South China Sea." November 4, 2002. https://asean.org/?static _post=declaration-on-the-conduct-of-parties-in-the-south-china-sea-2.

Axe, David. "China Just Deployed Its Deadly 'Carrier Killer' Missiles in a Very Slick Way." *National Interest*, January 14, 2019.

———. "China: We Won't Use Nuclear Weapons First in a War." *National Interest*, July 24, 2019.

Bader, Jeffery A. *Obama and China's Rise: An Insider's Account of America's Asia Strategy.* Washington, DC: Brookings Institution Press, 2012.

Bader, Jeffery A., Kenneth Lieberthal, and Michael McDevitt. "Keeping the South China Sea in Perspective." *Brookings Foreign Policy Brief,* September 2, 2014.

Barr, David. "This Piece of Chinese Military Hardware Could Change the Military Balance of Power in Asia." *National Interest*, November 6, 2017.

Batongbacal, Jay L. "How to Reinvigorate the U.S.-Philippine Alliance." *Diplomat*, May 2019.

Baveria, Aileen S. P. *Bilateral Confidence Building with China in Relation to the South China Seas Dispute: A Philippine Perspective.* Ottawa, ON: Government of Canada, Department of Foreign Affairs and International Trade, February 2001. https:// www.researchgate.net/publication/265157899_Bilateral_Confidence_Building _with_China_in_Relation_to_the_South_China_Seas_Dispute_A_Philippine _Perspective.

Becker, Jeffery, and Erica Downs. "China's Djibouti Military Base the First of Many." *East Asia Forum*, June 27, 2018.

Beckhausen, Robert. "She Doesn't Look It, but This Chinese Coast Guard Vessel Is One Mean Ship." *War Is Boring*, June 1, 2016.

Beckman, Robert. "The UN Convention on the Law of the Sea and the Maritime Disputes in the South China Sea." *American Journal of International Law* 107, no.1 (January 2013).

Bickers, Robert. *The Scramble for China: Foreign Devils in the Qing Empire, 1832–1914.* London: Penguin Books, 2011.

Bickford, Thomas, Fred Vellucci Jr., and Heidi Holz. *China as a Maritime Challenge: The Strategic Dimension.* CNA Research Memorandum D0023549.A3/1. Alexandria, VA: Center for Naval Analyses, rev. October 2010.

———. "Haiyang Qiangguo: China as a Maritime Power." Delivered at the "China as a Maritime Power Conference," July 2015. https://apps.dtic.mil/dtic/tr/fulltext /u2/1014584.pdf.

Biddle, Stephen, and Ivan Oelrich. "Future Warfare in the Western Pacific: Chinese Anti-Access/Area Denial, U.S. Air Sea Battle, and Command of the Commons in East Asia." *International Security* 41 (Summer 2016).

Blanchard, Ben. "China Hints More Bases on Way after Djibouti." *CANMUA Net*, March 8, 2016.

Blasko, Dennis. *The Chinese Army Today: Tradition and Transformation for the 21st Century.* London: Routledge, 2006.

———. "PLA Weaknesses and Xi's Concerns about PLA Capabilities." Testimony before the U.S.-China Economic and Security Review Commission, Washington, DC, February 7, 2019.

Bush, Richard C. "Beijing's Goal with Taiwan Is Unification: Why Can't It Get There?" *Order from Chaos* (Brookings Institution blog), January 7, 2019.

———. "8 Key Things to Notice from Xi Jinping's New Year Speech on Taiwan." *Order from Chaos* (Brookings Institution blog), January 7, 2019. https://www.brookings .edu/blog/.

———. "Thoughts on the Taiwan Relations Act." *Brookings Op-Ed*, April 21, 2009. https:// www.brookings.edu/opinions/thoughts-on-the-taiwan-relations-act.

———. *Untying the Knot: Making Peace in the Taiwan Strait.* Washington, DC: Brookings Institution, 2005.

———. "What Xi Jinping Said about Taiwan at the 19th Party Congress." *Order from Chaos* (Brookings Institution blog), October 19, 2017. https://www.brookings.edu/blog/.

Bussert, James C. "China Debuts Aegis Destroyers." *Signal,* July 2005.

Bussert, James C., and Bruce Elleman. *People's Liberation Army Navy: Combat System Technology, 1949–2010.* Annapolis, MD: Naval Institute Press, 2011.

Campbell, Kurt M., and Ely Ratner. "The China Reckoning: How Beijing Defied American Expectations." *Foreign Affairs* 97, no. 2 (March/April 2018).

Capaccio, Tony. "China's New Missiles May Create a 'No-Go Zone' for U.S. Fleet." *Bloomberg,* November 17, 2009.

Carlson, Christopher P. "Essay: Inside the Design of China's Yuan-Class Submarine." *USNI News,* August 31, 2015. http://news.usni.org/.

Carolla, Mark A. "The Indian Ocean Squadron." In *The Soviet Navy: Strengths and Liabilities,* ed. Bruce Watson and Susan Watson. Boulder, CO: Westview, 1986.

Carter, Ashton. "A Regional Security Architecture Where Everyone Rises." International Institute for Strategic Studies, Shangri-La Dialogue, Singapore, May 30, 2015. http://www.defense.gov/Speeches/Speech.aspx?SpeechID=1945.

Chai, Tommy. "The Problem with Xi's 40th Anniversary Message to Taiwan." *Foreign Brief: Geopolitical Risk Analysis,* January 12, 2019. https://www.foreignbrief.com /asia-pacific/china/the-problem-with-xis-40th-anniversary-message-to-taiwan/.

Chan, Minnie. "China Is Working on a New Fighter Jet for Aircraft Carriers to Replace Its J-15s." *South China Morning Post,* updated July 5, 2018. https://www.scmp.com /news/china/diplomacy-defence/article/2153803/china-working-new-fighter-jet -aircraft-carriers-replace.

Chang, Teh-Kuang. "China's Claim of Sovereignty over Spratly and Paracel Islands: A Historical and Legal Perspective." *Case Western Reserve Journal of International Law* 23, issue 3 (1991).

Chase, Michael, Kristen A. Gunness, et al. *Emerging Trends in China's Development of Unmanned Systems.* Santa Monica, CA: RAND, 2015.

Chen, Stephen. "China's Underwater Surveillance Network Puts Targets in Focus along the Maritime Silk Road." *South China Morning Post,* January 1, 2018.

Cheng, Dean. "China's 'Core' Maritime Interests: Security and Economic Factors." Testimony before the Subcommittee on Asia of the Committee on Foreign Affairs, U.S. House of Representatives, Washington, DC, February 28, 2017.

Chin, Jeremy. "China's PLANAF Acquires New H-6J Bomber." *CSIS Missile Defense Project,* October 13, 2018.

China Power Team. "How Does China's First Aircraft Carrier Stack Up?" *China Power,* updated June 28, 2018. https://chinapower.csis.org/aircraft-carrier.

———. "What Do We Know (So Far) about China's Second Aircraft Carrier?" *China Power,* updated June 29, 2018. https://chinapower.csis.org/china-aircraft-carrier-type-001a.

Chung, Chris C. P. "Drawing the U-Shaped Line: China's Claim in the South China Sea, 1946–1974." *Modern China,* August 11, 2015.

Clark, Stephen. "Long March, Soyuz and Falcon Topped 2019's Launch Leaderboard." *Spaceflight Now,* January 2, 2020.

Cliff, Roger. "The Development of China's Air Force Capabilities." RAND document delivered in testimony before the U.S.-China Economic and Security Review Commission, Washington, DC, May 20, 2010.

Clinton, Hillary R. Remarks at press availability, July 23, 2010, Hanoi, Vietnam. http://www.state.gov/secretary/rm/2010/07/145095.htm.

Cohen, Warren I. *America's Response to China: A History of Sino-American Relations.* 5th ed. New York: Columbia University Press, 2000.

Cole, Bernard D. "China's Navy Expands Its Replenishment-At-Sea Capability." *Interpreter,* August 26, 2015.

———. *The Great Wall at Sea: China's Navy in the Twenty-First Century.* 2nd ed. Annapolis, MD: Naval Institute Press, 2010.

———. *Oil for the Lamps of China: Beijing's 21st Century Search for Energy.* McNair Paper 57. Washington, DC: National Defense University Press, 2002.

Collins, Gabriel, and Andrew Erickson. "China Deploys World's First Long-Range, Land-Based 'Carrier Killer': DF-21D Anti-Ship Ballistic Missile (ASBM) Reaches 'Initial Operational Capability' (IOC)." *China Sign Post,* December 26, 2010.

Collins, Gabriel, and Michael C. Grubb. *A Comprehensive Survey of China's Dynamic Shipbuilding Industry.* China Maritime Study 1. Newport, RI: Naval War College Press for the China Maritime Studies Institute, August 2008.

Contact Group on Piracy off the Coast of Somalia. "The PLA Navy of China Contributions to Counter Piracy." *Capturing Lessons Learned: An Authorized Posting from the PLA Navy,* January 2, 2016. http://www.lessonsfrompiracy.net /files/2016/01/PLA-Navys-Escort-Mission.pdf.

Cook, Damon. "China's Most Important South China Sea Military Base." *Diplomat,* March 9, 2017.

Couronne, Ivan. "In Space, the U.S. Sees a Rival in China." Phys.org, January 6, 2019. https://phys.org/.

Cropsey, Seth. "Transcript: The Rise of China's Navy: A Discussion with Captain James Fanell." Hudson Institute, Washington, DC, May 21, 2019.

CSIS Asia Maritime Transparency Initiative. "Spratly Islands Island Tracker." Center for Strategic and International Studies. https://amti.csis.org/island-tracker/spratlysvn.

CSIS Missile Defense Project. *Missile Threat.* Washington, DC: Center for Strategic and International Studies, modified June 15, 2018.

Deputy Chief of Naval Operations for Warfare Systems (N-9). *Report to Congress on the Annual Long Range Plan for the Construction of Naval Vessels for Fiscal Year 2019.* Washington, DC: Office of the Chief of Naval Operations, February2018. http://www.secnav.navy.mil/.

Dimbleby, Jonathan. *The Battle of the Atlantic: How the Allies Won the War.* Oxford, U.K.: Oxford University Press, 2016.

Director of Naval Intelligence. *The People's Liberation Army Navy: A Modern Navy with Chinese Characteristics.* Washington, DC: Office of the Chief of Naval Operations, August 2009.

———. *The PLA Navy: New Capabilities and Missions for the 21st Century.* Washington, DC: Office of the Chief of Naval Operations, 2015.

———. *Understanding Soviet Naval Developments.* 5th ed. Washington, DC: Office of the Chief of Naval Operations, April 1985.

————. *Understanding Soviet Naval Developments.* 6th ed. Washington, DC: Office of the Chief of Naval Operations, July 1991.

Dismukes, Newton, and James McConnell, eds. *Soviet Naval Diplomacy.* New York: Pergamon Books, 1979.

Dong Zhaohui. "China's Logistic Hub in Djibouti to Stabilize Region, Protect Interests." *Global Times,* March 15, 2016.

Drifte, Reinhard. "The Japan-China Confrontation Over the Senkaku/Diaoyu Islands: Between 'Shelving' and 'Dispute Escalation.'" *Asia-Pacific Journal* 12, issue 30, no. 3 (July 27, 2014).

Dryer, Edward L. *Zheng He: China and the Oceans in the Early Ming Dynasty, 1405–1433.* Library of World Biography. New York: Pearson Longman, 2007.

Duchatel, Mathieu, and Alexandre Sheldon Duplaix. *Blue China: Navigating the Maritime Silk Road to Europe.* Policy Brief. London: European Council on Foreign Relations, April 23, 2018.

Dutton, Peter, ed. *Military Activities in the EEZ: A U.S.-China Dialogue on Security and International Law.* China Maritime Study 7. Newport, RI: Naval War College Press for the China Maritime Studies Institute, December 2010.

————. "Three Disputes and Three Objectives: China in the South China Sea." *Naval War College Review* 64, no. 4 (Autumn 2011).

Dyer, Geoff. *The Contest of the Century: The New Era of Competition with China and How America Can Win.* New York: Knopf, 2014.

Dyer, Geoff, and Demetri Sevastopulo. "US Strategists Face Dilemma over Chinese Claim in South China Sea." *Financial Times,* July 9, 2014.

Dzurek, Daniel J. "China Occupies Mischief Reef in Latest Spratly Gambit." (Durham University, U.K.) *International Boundary Unit Research Unit (IRBU) Boundary and Security Bulletin* (April 1995).

Easton, Ian. *The Chinese Invasion Threat: Taiwan's Defense and American Strategy in Asia.* Arlington, VA: Project 20149 Institute, 2017.

Elleman, Bruce A. *High Seas Buffer: The Taiwan Patrol Force, 1950–1979.* Newport Paper 38. Newport, RI: Naval War College Press, 2013.

Erickson, Andrew. "Lengthening Chinese Airstrips May Pave Way for South China Sea ADIZ." *National Interest,* June 29, 2015.

Erickson, Andrew, and Lyle Goldstein. "Gunboats for China's New 'Grand Canals'? Probing the Intersection of Beijing's Naval and Oil Security Policies." *Naval War College Review* 62, no. 2 (Spring 2009). https://digital-commons.usnwc.edu/nwc -review/vol62/iss2/6.

————. "Studying History to Guide China's Rise as a Maritime Great Power." *Harvard Asia Quarterly* 12, nos. 3–4 (Winter 2010).

Erickson, Andrew, and Austin Strange. "China and the International Anti-Piracy Effort." *Diplomat,* November 1, 2013.

Erickson, Andrew, and Conor M. Kennedy. *From Frontier to Frontline: Tanmen Maritime Militia's Leading Role Part 2.* Washington, DC: Center for International Maritime Security, May 17, 2016.

Evans, David C., and Mark R. Peattie. *Kaigun: Strategy, Tactics and Technology in the Imperial Japanese Navy, 1887–1941.* Annapolis, MD: Naval Institute Press, 1997.

Fanell, James E. "Asia Rising: China's Global Naval Strategy and Expanding Force Structure." *Naval War College Review* 72, no. 1 (Winter 2019).

Finkelstein, David M. "Breaking the Paradigm: Drivers behind the PLA's Current Period of Reform." In *Chairman Xi Remakes the PLA: Assessing Chinese Military Reforms,* ed. Phillip Saunders et al. Washington, DC: National Defense University Press, 2019.

————. "China's National Military Strategy: An Overview of the 'Military Strategic Guidelines.'" In *Rightsizing the People's Liberation Army: Exploring the Contours of China's Military,* ed. Roy Kamphausen and Andrew Scobell. Carlisle, PA: U.S. Army War College, 2007.

Fonbuena, Carmela. "Duterte Reaffirms EDCA, US Ties in Meeting with Trump." *Rappler,* November 14, 2017. https://www.rappler.com/nation/188459-duterte -trump-edca-military-ties-asean-summit-2017-philippines.

Forbes, Andrew. "Western Pacific Naval Symposium." In *Australian Maritime Issues 2006: SPC-A Annual.* Papers in Australian Maritime Affairs 19, 2006, ed. Andrew Forbes and Michelle Lovi. Canberra: Australian Department of Defense, 2007.

Fravel, M. Taylor. *Active Defense: China's Military Strategy since 1949.* Princeton, NJ: Princeton University Press, 2019.

———. "China's Strategy in the South China Sea." *Contemporary Southeast Asia* 33, no. 3 (2011).

———. "Shifts in Warfare and Party Unity: Explaining China's Changes in Military Strategy." *International Security* 42, no. 3 (Winter 2017).

———. *Strong Borders, Secure Nation: Cooperation and Conflict in China's Territorial Disputes.* Princeton, NJ: Princeton University Press, 2008.

———. Testimony before the U.S.-China Economic and Security Review Commission Hearing on "A World Class Military: Assessing China's Global Military Ambitions." Washington, DC, June 20, 2019.

Fravel, M. Taylor, and Christopher P. Twomey. "Projecting Strategy: The Myth of Counter Intervention." *Washington Quarterly* 37, no. 4 (Winter 2015).

"Full Text of Hu Jintao's Report to the 18th Party Congress." *Embassy of the People's Republic of China in the United States of America,* November 11, 2012. http://www .china-embassy.org/eng/zt/18th_CPC_National_Congress_Eng/t992917.htm.

Gady, Franz-Stefan. "China Kicks-Off Construction of New Supercarrier." *Diplomat,* January 5, 2018.

———. "China Launches New Guided Missile Destroyer." *Diplomat,* June 30, 2017.

———. "China's 1st Carrier Strike Group Reaches Initial Operational Capability." *Diplomat,* June 5, 2018.

———. "China's Navy Commissions 41st Type-056/056A Stealth Warship." *Diplomat,* June 13, 2018.

———. "New Variant of China's Ch-5 Combat Drone Boasts Extended Range and Endurance." *Diplomat,* April 5, 2018.

Gao, Charlie. "China's Torpedoes Are Built to Kill (But Just How Good Are They?)." *National Interest,* March 10, 2018.

———. "Why the F-15, F-16, Su-27 and other 'Old' Fighter Jets Simply Won't Go Away." *National Interest* (blog), August 22, 2018. https://nationalinterest.org/blog/buzz /why-f-15-f-16-su-27-and-other-old-fighter-jets-simply-wont-go-away-29522.

Garafola, Christina L., and Timothy L. Heath. *The Chinese Air Force's First Steps toward Becoming an Expeditionary Air Force.* Santa Monica, CA: RAND Project Air Force, 2017.

Gertz, Bill. "Chinese Sub Stalked U.S. Fleet." *Washington Times,* November 13, 2006.

———. "PACOM: China Anti-Ship Ballistic Missile Tests a Signal to US, World." *Washington Free Beacon,* July 19, 2019.

———. "Pentagon Warns of Conflict over Chinese Buildup on Disputed Island." *Washington Free Beacon,* April 29, 2016.

Ghosh, P. K. "Game Changers? Chinese Submarines in the Indian Ocean." *Diplomat,* July 6, 2015.

———. "Shared Awareness and Deconfliction: Can the Success Story Be Applied to Southeast Asia?" *Indo-Pacific Defense Forum,* February 13, 2016. https:// ipdefenseforum.com/.

Glaser, Bonnie. *China's Maritime Rights Protection Leading Small Group: Shrouded in Secrecy.* Washington, DC: CSIS Asia Maritime Transparency Initiative, September 11, 2015.

———. "Is China Proselytizing Its Path to Success?" *East Asia Forum,* January 11, 2018.

———. "Statement before the House Foreign Affairs Committee, 'Beijing as an Emerging Power in the South China Sea.'" Washington, DC, September 12, 2012.

Goldstein, Lyle J. "China Prepares to Ramp Up Its Shipbuilding Process." *National Interest,* April 2, 2017.

———. "China's YJ-18 Supersonic Anti-Ship Cruise Missile: America's Nightmare." *National Interest,* June 1, 2015.

———. "Chinese Fisheries Enforcement: Environmental and Strategic Implications." *Marine Policy* 40, July 2013.

———. *Five Dragons Stirring Up the Sea: Challenge and Opportunity in China's Improving Maritime Enforcement Capabilities.* China Maritime Study 5. Newport, RI: Naval War College Press for the China Maritime Studies Institute, 2010.

Green, Michael J. *By More than Providence: Grand Strategy and American Power in the Asia Pacific since 1783.* New York: Columbia University Press, 2017.

Green, Michael J., et al. *Countering Coercion in Maritime Asia: The Theory and Practice of Grey Zone Deterrence.* Lanham, MD: Rowman & Littlefield for the Center for Strategic and International Studies, May 2017. e-book.

Grossman, Derek, et al. *China's Long-Range Bomber Flights.* Santa Monica, CA: RAND, 2018.

Hackett, James, ed. *The Military Balance 2019.* London: Arundel House for the International Institute for Strategic Studies, February 2019.

Hagen, Jeff. "Potential Effects of Chinese Aerospace Capabilities on U.S. Air Force Operations." Testimony before the U.S.-China Economic and Security Review Commission, Washington, DC, May 20, 2010.

Hagt, Eric, and Matthew Durwin. "China's Antiship Ballistic Missile: Developments and Missing Links." *Naval War College Review* 62, no. 4 (Autumn 2009).

Hammes, T. X. *Offshore Control: A Proposed Strategy for an Unlikely Conflict.* Strategic Forum 278. Washington, DC: National Defense University Press, June 2012.

Hara, Kimie. "The San Francisco Peace Treaty and Frontier Problems in the Regional Order in East Asia: A Sixty-Year Perspective." *Asia-Pacific Journal* 10, issue 17, no. 1, April 23, 2012.

Harris, Harry. "Statement of Admiral Harry B. Harris Jr., U.S. Navy Commander, U.S. Pacific Command, before the House Armed Services Committee on U.S. Pacific Command Posture," February 14, 2018. Washington, DC. https://docs.house.gov.

Hartnett, Daniel, and Fredric Vellucci. "Toward a Maritime Security Strategy: An Analysis of Chinese Views since the Early 1990s." In *The Chinese Navy: Expanding Capabilities, Evolving Roles,* ed. Philipp C. Saunders et al. Washington, DC: National Defense University Press, 2011.

———. *China's 2012 Defense White Paper: Panel Discussion Report.* CNA China Studies, CCP-2013-U-005876 Final. Alexandria, VA: Center for Naval Analyses, September 2013.

Hattendorf, John B., Jr. *The Evolution of the U.S. Navy's Maritime Strategy, 1977–1986.* Newport Paper 19. Newport, RI: Naval War College Press, 2004.

———, ed. *Sixteenth International Sea Power Symposium: Report of Proceedings.* Naval War College, Newport, RI, 2012.

Hayton, Bill. "The Modern Origins of China's Claims in in the South China Sea." *Modern China,* May 4, 2018.

———. *South China Sea: The Struggle for Power in Asia.* New Haven, CT: Yale University Press, 2014.

Heath, Timothy, and Andrew Erickson. "Is China Pursuing Counter-Intervention?" *Washington Quarterly* 38, no. 3 (Spring 2015).

Heginbotham, Eric, et al. *The U.S. China Scorecard: Forces, Geography, and the Evolving Balance of Power, 1996–2017.* Santa Monica, CA: RAND, 2015.

Henry, Caleb. "TeleSAT Says Ideal LEO Constellation Is 292 Satellites, but Could Be 512." *Spacenews,* September 11, 2018. https://spacenews.com/.

Hewitt, Duncan. "China Sees New Aircraft Carrier as Symbol of Its Growing Power." *Daily Beast,* August 26, 2016.

Heydarian, Richard Javad. "China Rolls Out Red Carpet for Rodrigo Duterte." *Al Jazeera*, October 27, 2016.

———. "Deciphering Rodrigo Duterte's China Triangulation." *National Interest*, October 31, 2016.

Hirschberger, Sarah. *Assessing China's Naval Power: Technological Innovation, Economic Constraints, and Strategic Implications*, Heidelberg: Springer-Verlag, 2015.

Holmes, James, and Toshi Yoshihara. "Small Stick Diplomacy in the South China Sea." *National Interest*, April 23, 2012.

Hoyler, Marshall. "China's 'Antiaccess' Ballistic Missiles and U.S. Active Defense." *Naval War College Review* 63, no. 1 (Winter 2010).

Hsu, Stacy. "Over 80% Reject 'Two Systems,' Poll Finds." *Taipei Times*, January 10, 2019. http://www.taipeitimes.com/News/front/archives/2019/01/10/2003707656.

Hu Jintao. "Renqing Xinshiji Xinjieduan Wojun Lishi Shiming" [Understand the New Historic Missions of Our Military in the New Period of the New Century], Speech to an expanded meeting of the Central Military Commission, Jiangxi Province, December 24, 2004. http://gfjy.jiangxi.gov.cn/yl.asp?idid=11349.htm (no longer posted).

Huang Li. *Sword Pointed at the Gulf of Aden: The PLAN's Far Seas Shining Sword*. Guangzhou, PRC: Zhongshan University Press, 2009.

Huang Panyue, ed. "Navy's Carrier-Borne Jet Force Takes Off to a Higher Level." *China Military*, September 17, 2018. http://eng.chinamil.com.cn/view/2018 -09/17/content_9284305.htm.

———. "PLA Navy Ends Era of Supply Ship Troika in Its Escort Missions." *China Military Online*, August 9, 2018. http://eng.chinamil.com.cn/view/2018-08/09 /content_9247256.htm.

———. "Role of Aircraft Carrier *Liaoning* Shifts from Training to Combat: Executive Officer." *China Military*, April 25, 2019. eng.chinamil.com.cn/view/2019-04/25 /content_9488581.htm.

———. "28th Chinese Naval Escort Task Force Ends Friendly Visit to Cameroon." *China Military Online*, June 14, 2018. eng.chinamil.com.cn/view/2018-06/14 /content_8062519.htm.

"The Important Political Decision to Ensure That the Party Has Absolute Leadership over the PAP." *People's Daily*, February 28, 2017. http://opinion.people.com.cn /n1/2017/1228/c1003-29732631.html.

Information Office of the State Council of the PRC. *China's National Defense in 2004*, December 2004. http://english.people.com.cn/whitepaper/defense2004.

Jane's, by IHS Markit. Content preview: "Undersea Dragon: Chinese ASW Capabilities Advance," 2017. https://www.janes.com/images/assets/911/72911/Undersea _dragon_Chinese_ASW_capabilities_advance.pdf.

Japan Ministry of Defense. *Defense of Japan 2018: Japan Defense White Paper*, March 2018, 21. https://www.mod.go.jp/e/publ/w_paper/2018.html.

Jiang, Steven. "China Will Not Give Up 'Any Inch of Territory' in the Pacific Xi Tells Mattis." *CNN*, June 28, 2018.

Jiang Zemin. "Report to the 14th Party Congress." *Beijing Review*, March 29, 2011, www.bjreview.com.cn/document/txt/2011–03/29/content_363504.htm.

Jiao Bofeng, Hou Rui, and Yu Qizheng. "Crisscrossing the Four Seas and Making Its Might Known Everywhere: The 'Qiandaohu' Open-Sea Fleet Replenishment Ship." *People's Navy (Renmin Haijun)*, September 16, 2010.

Joe, Rick. "Chinese Anti-Submarine Warfare: Aviation Platforms, Strategy and Doctrine." *Diplomat*, October 16, 2018.

———. "The Chinese Navy's Growing Anti-Submarine Warfare Capabilities." *Diplomat*, September 12, 2018.

———. "PLA Navy Projects to Watch in Next 5 Years." *Diplomat*, August 7, 2018.

———. "Pondering China's Future Nuclear Submarine Production." *Diplomat*, January 23, 2019.

————. "Predicting the Chinese Navy of 2030." *Diplomat,* February 13, 2019.

Johnson, Christopher, Scott Kennedy, and Mingdu Qiu. "Xi's Signature Governance Innovation: The Rise of Leading Small Groups." *CSIS Commentary,* October 17, 2017.

Johnston, Alastair Iain. "The Failure of the 'Failure of Engagement' with China." *Washington Quarterly* (Summer 2019).

Judt, Tony. *Postwar: A History of Europe since 1945.* London: Penguin Books, 2005.

Jukes, Geoffrey. "Soviet Naval Policy in the Indian Ocean." In *Soviet Naval Policy: Objectives and Constraints,* ed. Michael MccGwire et al. Halifax, NS: Center for Foreign Policy Studies, Dalhousie University, 1975.

Kalman, Brian. "Military Analysis: The Type-052D Class Guided Missile Destroyer." *South Front,* May 1, 2016. https://southfront.org/military-analysis-type-052d -class-guided-missile-destroyer.

Kardon, Isaac. "China's Maritime Rights and Interests: Organizing to Become a Maritime Power." Paper for the "China as a 'Maritime Power'" Conference, July 2015, Center for Naval Analyses, Alexandria, VA.

Karotkin, Jesse L. Testimony before Hearing on "Trends in China's Naval Modernization." U.S.-China Economic and Security Review Commission, Washington, DC, January 30, 2014.

Kaufman, Alison. *China's Participation in Anti-Piracy Operations off the Horn of Africa: A Conference Report.* CNA China Study D0020835.A1 Final (Alexandria, VA: Center for Naval Analyses, July 2009).

Kausikan, Bilihari. "ASEAN-China Relations: Building a Common Destiny." *American Interest,* September 23, 2014.

Kefu, Liu. "Push Forward the Construction of Maritime Power with Threefold Efforts." *Zhongguo Haiyangbao,* September 17, 2013.

Kelly, James F. "Naval Deployments in the Indian Ocean." *U.S. Naval Institute Proceedings* 109/5/963 (May 1983).

Kelly, Terrence K., David Gompert, and Duncan Long. *Smarter Power, Strategic Partners.* Vol. 1. Santa Monica, CA: RAND, 2016.

Kennedy, Conor M., and Andrew S. Erickson. *China's Third Sea Force, the People's Armed Forces Maritime Militia: Tethered to the PLA.* China Maritime Report 1. Newport, RI: Naval War College, China Maritime Studies Institute, March 2017.

————. *Riding a New Wave of Professionalization and Militarization: Sansha City's Maritime Militia.* Washington, DC: Center for International Maritime Security, September 1, 2016.

Koda, Yoji. "A New Carrier Race?" *Naval War College Review* 64, no. 3 (Summer 2011).

Krepinevich, Andrew, Barry Watts, and Robert Work. *Meeting the Anti-Access and Area Denial Challenge.* Washington, DC: Center for Strategic and Budgetary Assessments, 2003.

Lambert, Andrew. *Seapower States: Maritime Culture, Continental Empires and the Conflict That Made the Modern World.* New Haven, CT: Yale University Press, 2018.

Lampton, David Michael. *Same Bed, Different Dreams: Managing U.S.-China Relations.* Berkeley: University of California Press, 2001.

Landler, Mark. "Offering to Aid Talks, U.S. Challenges China on Disputed Islands." *New York Times,* July 23, 2010.

Lee, John. "China Comes to Djibouti: Why Washington Should be Worried." *Foreign Affairs Snapshot,* April 23, 2015.

Lena, Karen. "Pompeo Assures Philippines of US Protection in Event of Sea Conflict." *Reuters,* March 1, 2019.

Lendon, Brad. "Ballistic Missiles Can Hit Moving Ships, China Says, but Experts Remain Skeptical." *CNN,* January 29, 2019.

Li, Nan, and Christopher Weuve. "China's Aircraft Carrier Ambitions: An Update." *Naval War College Review* 63, no. 1 (Winter 2010).

Li Jianguo. "Keeping the Seas Safe." *Beijing Review*, March 22, 2007. http://www.bjreview.com/print/txt/2007–03/19/content_59601_2.htm.

Li Jie. "China's Navy Still Has Far to Go." *China Daily*, August 8, 2009. www.chinadaily.com.cn/opinion/2009–08/14/content_8568918.htm.

Li Xuanliang and Mei Shixiong. "At a CMC Meeting on the Reform of Policies and Institutions, Xi Jinping Stresses That It Is Necessary to Have a Clear Understanding of the Importance and Urgency of Pushing Forward Reform on Military Policies and Institutions and Build a Socialist System of Military Policies and Institutions with Chinese Characteristics." Xinhua Domestic Service in Chinese, November 14, 2018.

Lin, Jeffrey, and P. W. Singer. "China Is Building the World's Largest Nuclear Submarine Facility." *Popular Science*, May 1, 2017.

Liu Cigui. "Some Considerations on Building China into a Maritime Power" *(Guanyu Jianshe Haiyang Qiangguo De Ruogan Sikao)*. State Oceanic Administration, November 26, 2012. http://www.soa.gov.cn/xw/ldhd/lyx/201212/t2012 1204_19016.html.

———. "Striving to Realize the Historical Leap from Being a Great Maritime Country to Being a Great Maritime Power." *Jingji Ribao Online*, November 2012.

Liu Huaqing, *Memoir of Liu Huaqing*. Beijing: People's Liberation Army Navy Press, 2004.

Liu Xuanzun. "China Develops Y-20 Variants to Perform Aerial Refueling Mission: Military Insider." *Global Times*, November 26, 2018. https://thaimilitaryand asianregion.blogspot.com/2018/12/y-20-aerial-refueling-variant-is-now.html.

Lovell, Julia. *The Opium War: Drugs, Dreams, and the Making of China*. London: Picador, 2011.

Mahan, Alfred Thayer. *The Influence of Sea Power upon History, 1660–1783*. Boston: Little, Brown, 1890. Repr. London: Methuen, 1965.

Majumdar, Dave. "China's New Amphibious Assault Ship: A Big Waste of Time?" *National Interest*, March 31, 2017.

Mallory, Tabitha Grace. "Preparing for the Ocean Century: China's Changing Political Institutions for Governance and Maritime Development." *Issues & Studies* 51, no. 2 (June 2015): 111–38.

Marolda, Edward J. "Asian Warm-Up to the Cold War." *Naval History* 25, no. 5 (October 2011).

Martinson, Ryan D. *The Arming of China's Maritime Frontier*. China Maritime Study 2. Newport, RI: Naval War College Press for the China Maritime Studies Institute, 2017.

———. "China's Second Navy." U.S. Naval Institute *Proceedings* (April 2015).

———. *Echelon Defense: The Role of Sea Power in Chinese Maritime Dispute Strategy*. China Maritime Study 15. Newport, RI: Naval War College Press for the China Maritime Studies Institute, February 2018.

———. *"Jinglue Haiyang:* The Naval Implications of Xi Jinping's New Strategic Concept." *Jamestown Foundation China Brief* 15, issue 1 (January 9, 2015).

———. "Reality Check: China's Military Power Threatens America—The U.S. Can't Just Wish Away China's A2/AD Capabilities." *National Interest*, March 4, 2015.

Martinson, Ryan D., and Takuya Shimodaira. "Curing China's Elephantiasis of the Fleet." *Jamestown Foundation China Brief* 15, issue 10 (May 15, 2015).

Mattis, James. *Summary of the 2018 National Defense Strategy of the United States of America*, n.d. https://dod.defense.gov/Portals/1/Documents/pubs/2018-National-Defense-Strategy-Summary.pdf.

———. "US Leadership and the Challenges of Indo-Pacific Security." *Shangri-La Dialogue*, June 2, 2018. https://www.iiss.org/events/shangri-la-dialogue/shangri-la-dialogue-2018.

Mazzetti, Mark, and Thom Shanker. "Russian Subs Patrolling off East Coast of US." *New York Times*, August 5, 2009. https://www.nytimes.com/2009/08/05/world/05patrol.html.

McCarthy, Kerry. "Reef Wars." *Time,* March 8, 1999. http://content.time.com/time/world
    /article/0,8599,2054240,00.html.
McDevitt, Michael A. "America's New Security Strategy and Its Military Dimension."
    Global Asia 7 (Winter 2012).
———. ed. *Becoming a Great "Maritime Power": A Chinese Dream.* Alexandria, VA: Center
    for Naval Analyses, June 2016. https://www.cna.org/CNA_files/PDF/IRM
    -2016-U-013646.pdf. (Available only online.)
———. "The Modern PLA Navy Destroyer Force: Impressive Progress in Achieving a Far
    Seas Capability." In *China's Evolving Surface Fleet,* ed. Peter A. Dutton and Ryan
    D. Martinson. China Maritime Study 14. Newport, R.I.: Naval War College Press
    for the China Maritime Studies Institute, 2017.
———. "PLA Naval Exercises with International Partners." In *Learning by Doing: The PLA
    Trains at Home and Abroad,* ed. Roy Kamphausen, David Lai, and Travis Tanner.
    Carlisle, PA: Strategic Studies Institute, U.S. Army War College, November 30, 2012.
———. *The South China Sea: Assessing U.S. Policy and Options for the Future.* CNA
    Occasional Paper. Alexandria, VA, November 2014. https://www.cna.org
    /CNA_files/PDF/IOP-2014-U-009109.pdf. (Available only online.)
———. "Whither Sino-U.S. Relations: Maritime Disputes in the East China and South
    China Seas." In *U.S.-China Relations: Manageable Differences or Major Crisis?,*
    ed. Rorry Daniels and Juliet Lee. New York: National Committee on American
    Foreign Policy, 2018. https://www.ncafp.org/2016/wp-content/uploads/2018/11
    /NCAFP-2018-Edited-Volume_US-China-Relations.pdf.
McDougall, Walter A. *Let the Sea Make a Noise: A History of the North Pacific from Magellan
    to MacArthur.* New York: Perennial, 2004.
McFadden, Christopher. "Ten of the Deadliest Attack Submarines in the World."
    Interesting Engineering, March 2, 2017.
Memorandum of Understanding between the Department of Defense of the United
    States of America and the Ministry of National Defense of the People's Republic
    of China Regarding the Rules of Behavior for Safety of Air and Maritime
    Encounters. Signed November 9, 2014. archive.defense.gov/pubs/141112
    _MemorandumOfUnderstandingRegardingRules.pdf.
Military Strategy Research Department of the Academy of Military Science. *The Science of
    Military Strategy.* Beijing: Academy of Military Science Press, 2013.
Miller, Alice. "How to Read Xi Jinping's 19th Party Congress Political Report." Hoover
    Institution *China Leadership Monitor,* issue 53 (Spring 2017).
Milner, Marc. *The Battle of the Atlantic.* Stroud, U.K.: Tempus, 2003.
Mirski, Sean. "Stranglehold: Context, Conduct and Consequences of an American
    Blockade of China." *Journal of Strategic Studies* 36, no. 3 (2013).
Mitter, Rana. *Forgotten Ally: China's World War II, 1937–1945.* Boston: Houghton Mifflin
    Harcourt, 2013.
Mizokami, Kyle. "Why China and Pakistan Should Fear India's *Arihant* Class of
    Submarine." *National Interest,* January 22, 2017.
Monaghan, Angela. "China Surpasses US as World's Largest Trading Nation." *Guardian,*
    January 10, 2014.
Morris, Lyle. "China Welcomes Its Newest Armed Force: The Coast Guard." *War on the
    Rocks,* April 4, 2018.
Morrison, Wayne M. *China's Economic Rise: History, Trends, Challenges and Implications for the
    United States.* Washington, DC: Congressional Research Service, February 5, 2018.
Muller, David G., Jr. *China as a Maritime Power.* Lexington, VA: Rockbridge Books, 2016.
Mulvenon, James. "The Cult of Xi and the Rise of the CMC Chairman Responsibility
    System." Hoover Institution *China Leadership Monitor,* issue 55 (Winter 2018).
Newdick, Thomas. "China's Got an Aircraft Carrier: What about the Air Wing?" *War Is
    Boring,* March 3, 2014. https://medium.com/war-is-boring/chinas-got-an-aircraft
    -carrier-what-about-the-air-wing-c95283bc0279.

Oberdorfer, Don. "The Superpowers and the Ogaden War." *Washington Post*, March 5, 1978.

O'Connor, Sean. *PLA Ballistic Missiles*. Technical Report APA-TR-2010-0802. N.p.: Air Power Institute Australia, updated January 27, 2014. http://www.ausairpower.net /APA-PLA-Ballistic-Missiles.html.

Office of Naval Intelligence.*The PLA Navy: New Capabilities and Missions for the 21st Century*, https://fas.org/nuke/guide/china/plan-2015.pdf.

———. *The Russian Navy 2015: A Historic Transition*. https://www.oni.navy.mil/.

Office of the Chairman of the Joint Chiefs of Staff. *Joint Doctrine for Military Operations Other than War*. Joint Publication 3-07. Washington, DC, June 16, 1995.

O'Rourke, Ronald. *China Naval Modernization: Implications for U.S. Navy Capabilities— Background and Issues for Congress*. CRS Report for Congress, Order Code RL 33153. Washington, DC: Congressional Research Service, updated May 12, 2018.

———. *Navy Ford (CVN-78) Class Aircraft Carrier Program*. RS 20643. Washington, DC: Congressional Research Service, July 24, 2019. https://fas.org/sgp/crs/weapons /RS20643.pdf.

Paine, S. C. M. *The Sino-Japanese War of 1894–1895: Perceptions, Power, and Primacy*. New York: Cambridge University Press, 2003.

Palmer, Michael. *Guardians of the Gulf: A History of America's Expanding Role in the Persian Gulf, 1883–1992*. New York: Simon & Schuster, 1992.

Pandit, Rajat. "Chinese Submarine in Karachi, India Alarmed." *Times of India*, June 27, 2015. http://timesofindia.indiatimes.com/india/Chinese-submarine-in-Karachi -India-alarmed/articleshow/47845930.cms.

Parello-Plesner, Jonas, and Mathieu Duchatel. *China's Strong Arm: Protecting Citizens and Assets Abroad*. Adelphi Series. London: Routledge for the International Institute for Strategic Studies, May 2015.

Park, Yoon Jung. "One Million Chinese in Africa." *SAIS Perspectives*, May 12, 2016. http:// www.saisperspectives.com/.

Pedrozo, Raul. "Preserving Navigational Rights and Freedoms: The Right to Conduct Military Activities in China's Exclusive Economic Zone." *Chinese Journal of International Law* 9 (2010).

Pence, Michael R. "Remarks by Vice President Pence on the Administration's Policy toward China," October 4, 2018. https://www.whitehouse.gov/.

Peng Guangqian and Yang Youzhi, eds. *The Science of Military Strategy*. Beijing: Military Science Publishing House, Academy of Military Science of the People's Liberation Army, 2005.

Perlez, Jane. "U.S. Admiral's Bluntness Rattles China, and Washington." *New York Times*, May 6, 2016.

Permanent Court of Arbitration Press Release (*The Republic of the Philippines v. the People's Republic of China*), The Hague, July 12, 2016. https://pca-cpa.org /wp-content/uploads/sites/175/2016/07/PH-CN-20160712-Press-Release -No-11-English.pdf.

Phillips, Stephen E., ed. *Foreign Relations of the United States, 1969–1976*, Vol. XVII, *China, 1969–1972*. Washington, DC: U.S. Government Printing Office, 2006.

"PLA Navy Awards Commemorative Badge for Major Mission Performance." *PLA Daily*, December 29, 2011. http://eng.mod.gov.cn/DefenseNews?2011-12/29 /content_4332515.htm.

Poling, Gregory. *Recent Trends in the South China Sea and U.S. Policy*. A Report of the Sumitro Chair in Southeast Asian Studies. Washington, DC: Center for Strategic and International Studies, July 2014.

———. "South China Sea Code of Conduct Still a Speck on the Horizon." *East Asia Forum*, September 6, 2018.

Poling, Gregory B., and Conor Cronin. "The Dangers of Allowing U.S.-Philippine Defense Cooperation to Languish." *War on the Rocks*, May 17, 2018.

Pollpeter, Kevin. Testimony before the U.S.-China Economic and Security Review
    Commission Hearing on "China in Space: Strategic Competition," Washington,
    DC, April 25, 2019.
Pomfret, John. "Engagement with China Is Failing: Time for 'Constructive Vigilance.'"
    Washington Post, November 28, 2018.
Qing Hong. "Research Summary on the Construction of Marine Food System." *Marine
    Sciences* 39, no. 1 (2015).
Remnek, Richard B. "Soviet Access to Overseas Naval Support Facilities: A Military and
    Political Analysis." In *The Sources of Soviet Naval Conduct*, ed. Philip S. Gillette
    and Willard C. Frank. Lexington, MA: Lexington Books, D. C. Heath, 1990.
Rhoads, Edward J. M. *Manchus and Han: Ethnic Relations and Political Power in Late Qing and
    Early Republican China, 1861–1928*. Seattle: University of Washington Press, 2000.
Riu Zhao, Stephen Hynes, and Guang Shaun He. "Defining and Quantifying China's
    Ocean Economy." *Marine Policy* 43 (2014).
Roach, J. Ashley. "China's Shifting Sands in the Spratlys." American Society of
    International Law *Insights* 19, issue 54 (July 15, 2015). https://www.asil.org
    /insights/volume/19/issue/15/chinas-shifting-sands-spratlys.
———. *Malaysia and Brunei: An Analysis of Their Claims in the South China Sea*. CNA
    Occasional Paper. Alexandria, VA: Center for Naval Analyses, August 2014.
    https://www.cna.org/sites/default/files/research/IOP-2014-U-008434.pdf.
Roblin, Sebastian. "China's H-6 Bomber: Everything You Wanted to Know about Beijing's
    'B-52' Circling Taiwan." *National Interest*, December 18, 2016.
Rogoway, Tyler. "China's Type 055 Super Destroyer Is a Reality Check for the US and Its
    Allies." *The Drive: The War Zone*, June 28, 2017.
Roscoe, Theodore. *United States Submarine Operations in World War II*. 6th printing.
    Annapolis, MD: Naval Institute Press, 1958.
Rosen, Mark E. *Philippine Claims in the South China Sea: A Legal Analysis*. CNA Occasional
    Paper. Alexandria, VA: Center for Naval Analyses, August 2014. https://www.cna
    .org/sites/default/files/research/IOP-2014-U-008435.pdf.
Rupprecht, Andreas. *Modern Chinese Warplanes: Chinese Air Force—Aircraft and Units*.
    Houston, TX: Harpia, 2018.
———. *Modern Chinese Warplanes: Chinese Naval Aviation—Aircraft and Units*. Houston,
    TX: Harpia, 2018.
Samuels, Merwyn S. *Contest for the South China Sea*. New York: Methuen, 1982.
Saunders, Phillip, et al., eds. *Chairman Xi Remakes the PLA: Assessing Chinese Military
    Reforms*. Washington, DC: National Defense University Press, 2019.
Scobel, Andrew, and Cortez Cooper. "What Is Driving Asian Aircraft Carrier
    Programmes? The Case of China." In *Emerging Strategic Trends in Asia*, ed. Uttam
    Kumar. New Delhi: Institute for Defense Studies and Analyses, 2015.
Scobel, Andrew, Michael McMahon, and Cortez Cooper III. "China's Aircraft Carrier
    Program: Drivers, Developments, Implications." *Naval War College Review* 68,
    no. 4 (Autumn 2015).
Scott, Richard. "China-Owned Ships: A Rapid Rise to Become One of the World's
    Largest Fleets." *International Shipping News*. Reprinted in *Hellenic Shipping News*,
    March 17, 2015. https://www.hellenicshippingnews.com/china-owned-ships-a
    -rapid-rise-to-become-one-of-the-worlds-largest-fleets.
Seidel, Jaime. "Fatal Crashes Compel China to Speed-Up Carrier Stealth Fighter Project."
    News Corp Australia Network, July 6, 2018.
Shahryar Pasandideh. "Less Visible Aspects of Chinese Military Modernization."
    Diplomat, September 21, 2018.
Shambaugh, David. "A Matter of Time: Taiwan's Eroding Military Advantage."
    Washington Quarterly (Spring 2000).
Shear, David. Assistant Secretary of Defense for Asian and Pacific Security Affairs,
    "Statement before the Senate Committee on Foreign Relations," Washington, DC,

May 13, 2015. http://www.foreign.senate.gov/imo/media/doc/051315_Shear
_Testimony.pdf.

Shlapak, David A., David T. Orletsky, and Barry Wilson. *Dire Strait? Military Aspects
of China-Taiwan Confrontation and Options for U.S. Policy.* Santa Monica, CA:
RAND, 2000.

Singh, Abhijit. "Countering China's Submarine Presence in the Indian Ocean." *Lowy
Interpreter,* May 24, 2017.

Speller, Ian. *Understanding Naval Warfare.* New York: Routledge, 2014.

Stashwick, Steven. "Unsafe Incident between US and Chinese Warships during FONOP."
Diplomat, October 2, 2018.

State Council Information Office. *China's Military Strategy.* Beijing, May 2015.

———. *The Diversified Employment of China's Armed Forces.* Beijing, April 2013.

State Council of the People's Republic of China. *China's National Defense in the New Era.*
Beijing, July 2019.

Stires, Hunter. "Exclusive: CNO Announces the Return of Vertical Launch System At-Sea
Reloading." *National Interest,* July 5, 2017.

Storey, Ian. "China's Malacca Dilemma." *Jamestown Foundation China Brief* 6, issue 8
(April 12, 2006).

Suettinger, Robert. *Beyond Tiananmen: The Politics of U.S.-China Relations, 1989–2000.*
Washington, DC: Brookings Institution Press, 2003.

Sutirtho Patranobis. "China Takes Credit [for] Rescuing Ship in Gulf of Aden, Silent [on]
India's Role." *Hindustan Times,* April 10, 2017.

Swaine, Michael. "Chinese Views of Foreign Policy in the 19th Party Congress." Hoover
Institution *China Leadership Monitor,* issue 55 (Winter 2018).

Swift, Scott. "A Fleet Must Be Able to Fight." U.S. Naval Institute *Proceedings* (May 2018).

Tan Shoulin and Zhang Daqiao. "Determination and Evaluation of Effective Homing
Range for Ballistic Missile Attacking Aircraft Carrier." *Information Command and
Control System and Simulation Technology* 28, no. 4 (August 2006).

Tangredi, Sam. *Anti-Access Warfare: Countering A2/AD Strategies.* Annapolis, MD: Naval
Institute Press, 2013.

———. "Fight Fire with Fire." U.S. Naval Institute *Proceedings* 143/8/1347 (August 2017).

Tanner, Murray Scott, and Peter W. MacKenzie. *China's Emerging National Security
Interests and Their Impact on the People's Liberation Army.* Quantico, VA: Marine
Corps University Press, 2015.

Tate, Andrew. "China Commissions Fourth ASW-Capable Type 056 Corvette." *IHS Jane's
Navy International.* http://www.janes.com/.

———. "China Increases Construction Rate of Amphibious Assault Ships." *Janes 360
Sea Platforms,* June 10, 2019. https://www.janes.com/article/89152/china
-increases-construction-rate-of-amphibious-assault-ships.

Text of the Taiwan Relations Act (Public Law 96-8, 22 U.S.C. 3301 et seq.) of January
1, 1979. https://www.ait.org.tw/our-relationship/policy-history/key-u-s-foreign-
policy-documents-region/taiwan-relations-act/.

Thayer, Carl A. "China and Vietnam Square Off in War of Attrition over Disputed
Waters." Asian Studies Institute of Australia *Asian Currents* (June 2014). https://
www.scribd.com/doc/231875269/Thayer-China-and-Vietnam-Squre-Off-in-War
-of-Attrition-Over-Disputed-Waters.

———. "China's New Wave of Aggressive Assertiveness in the South China Sea."
International Journal of China Studies (December 2011).

———. "Dead in the Water: The South China Sea Award, One Year Later." *Diplomat,* July
2017.

Till, Geoffrey. *Seapower: A Guide for the Twenty-First Century.* 3rd ed. New York:
Routledge, 2013.

Tobin, Liza. "Underway: Beijing's Strategy to Build China into a Maritime Great Power."
Naval War College Review 71, no. 2 (Spring 2018).

Toll, Ian W. *Pacific Crucible: War at Sea in the Pacific, 1941–1942.* New York: W. W. Norton, 2012.

Tweed, David. "China Seeks Great Power Status after Sea Retreat." *Bloomberg News,* July 3, 2014.

2016 Digest of US Practice in International Law. Diplomatic note of December 2016 regarding SCS arbitration. 519–520 state.gov/s/1. https://www.state.gov /wp-content/uploads/2019/05/2016-Digest-United-States.pdf.

"The Type 055 Class Destroyer." *Naval Technology* (June 2017). https://www.naval -technology.com/.

United Nations. "Structure, Ownership, and Registration of the World Fleet." In *Review of Maritime Transport.* New York, 2018. https://unctad.org/en/PublicationChapters /rmt2018ch2_en.pdf.

United Nations Security Council. Press release, "Security Council Condemns Acts of Piracy, Armed Robbery off Somalia's Coast, Authorizes for Six Months 'All Necessary Means' to Repress Such Acts," June 2, 2008. https://www.un.org/.

U.S. Air University. *PLA Aerospace Power: A Primer on Trends in China's Military Air, Space and Missile Force.* Maxwell Air Force Base, AL: China Aerospace Studies Institute, 2017. http://www.airuniversity.af.mil/.

U.S. Defense Intelligence Agency. *China Military Power: Modernizing a Force to Fight and Win,* January 2019. www.dia.mil/Military-Power-Publications.

U.S. Department of Defense. *Annual Report to Congress: Military and Security Developments Involving the People's Republic of China 2015.* Washington, DC, April 17, 2015.

———. *Annual Report to Congress: Military and Security Developments Involving the People's Republic of China 2017.* Washington, DC, May 15, 2017.

———. *Annual Report to Congress: Military and Security Developments Involving the People's Republic of China 2018.* Washington, DC: May 16, 2018.

———. *Annual Report to Congress: Military and Security Developments Involving the People's Republic of China 2019.* Washington, DC, May 2, 2019.

———. *Indo-Pacific Strategy Report: Preparedness, Partnership and Promoting a Networked Region.* Washington, DC, June 1, 2019.

———. *The Report of the 2001 Quadrennial Defense Review.* Washington, DC, September 30, 2001.

U.S. Department of State. *China: Maritime Claims in the South China Sea.* Limits in the Sea No. 143, December 5, 2014. https://2009-2017.state.gov/documents /organization/234936.pdf.

U.S. Energy Information Administration. "China Surpassed the United States as World's Largest Crude Oil Importer in 2017." *Today in Energy,* February 5, 2018.

———. "Contested Areas of South China Sea Likely Have Few Conventional Oil and Gas Resources." *Today in Energy,* April 3, 2013. https://www.eia.gov/.

U.S. Navy. "Fact File: Aegis Weapons System." Washington, DC, January 10, 2019. https://www.navy.mil/navydata/fact_display.asp?cid=2100&tid=200&ct=2.

U.S. Senate Armed Services Committee. "Advance Questions for Admiral Philip Davidson, USN, Expected Nominee for Commander, U.S. Pacific Command." Washington, DC, April 17, 2018.

U.S. Seventh Fleet, "Fact Sheet," n.d. [2018]. https://www.c7f.navy.mil/Portals/8/documen ts/7thFleetTwoPagerFactsheet.pdf?ver=2017-09-20-040335-223.

U.S.-China Security and Review Commission. *2018 Report to Congress of the U.S.-China Economic and Security Review Commission.* Washington, DC: Government Publishing Office, November 2018.

Viray, Patricia Lourdes. "China's Continued Blocking of Redd Bank Drilling Could Cost Philippine Development—Expert." *Philippine Star,* July 16, 2018, https://www .philstar.com/headlines/2018/07/16/1834042/chinas-continued-blocking-reed -bank-drilling-could-cost-philippine-development-expert.

Vuving, Alexander L. "South China Sea: Who Occupies What in the Spratlys?" *Diplomat*, May 6, 2016.

Wang, Hongying. *A Deeper Look at China's "Going Out" Policy*. Waterloo, ON: Centre for International Governance Innovation, March 8, 2016. https://www.cigionline.org /publications/deeper-look-chinas-going-out-policy.

Wang, Kevin. "Yemen Evacuation a Strategic Step Forward for China." *Diplomat*, April 10, 2015.

Weiss, Jessica Chen. "A World Safe for Autocrats: China's Rise and the Future of Global Politics." *Foreign Affairs*, July/August 2019.

Weng, Jonathan. "Chief Designer Talks about PLA Navy Replenishment Ship." Beijing *China Defense Mashup Report*, February 12, 2009.

White House. *National Security Strategy of the United States of America*. Washington, DC, December 2017. https://www.whitehouse. gov/wp-content/uploads/2017/12/NSS -Final-12-18-2017-0905.pdf.

Wood, Peter. "Snapshot: China's Eastern Theater Command." *Jamestown Foundation China Brief*, March 14, 2017. https://jamestown.org/program/snapshot-chinas-eastern -theater-command.

Xi Jinping. "Secure a Decisive Victory in Building a Moderately Prosperous Society in All Respects and Strive for the Great Success of Socialism with Chinese Characteristics for a New Era." Delivered at the 19th National Congress of the Communist Party of China, October 18, 2017. *Qiushi Journal* 10, no. 1, issue 34 (January–March 2018).

———. "Work Together to Build a 21st Century Maritime Silk Road" and "Promote the Silk Road Spirit, Strengthen China-Arab Cooperation." In *The Governance of China*. Beijing: Foreign Languages Press, 2014.

———. "Xi Jinping Stresses the Need to Show Greater Care about the Ocean, Understand More about the Ocean and Make Strategic Plans for the Use of the Ocean, Push Forward the Building of a Maritime Power and Continuously Make New Achievements at the Eighth Collective Study Session of the CPC Central Committee Political Bureau." Xinhua, July 31, 2013.

Xu Sheng. "Follow the Path of Maritime Power with Chinese Characteristics." *Qiushi Online: Organ of Central Committee of the Communist Party of China*, November 2013. http://www.qstheory.cn.

Yamaguchi, Shinsi. *Creating Facts on the Seas: China's Plan to Establish Sansha City*. Washington, DC: CSIS Asia Maritime Power Initiative, April 17, 2017. https:// amti.csis.org/chinas-plan-establish-sansha-city.

Yeo, Mike. "Taiwan Takes Delivery of First Locally Upgraded F-16." *Defense News*, October 22, 2018.

Yoshihara, Toshi. "The 1974 Paracels Sea Battle: A Campaign Appraisal." *Naval War College Review* 69, no. 2 (Spring 2016).

Yung, Christopher D., et al. *China's Out of Area Naval Operations: Case Studies, Trajectories, Obstacles and Potential Solutions*. INSS China Strategic Perspectives. Washington, DC: National Defense University Press, December 2010.

Zhang Hongzhou. "China's Fishing Industry." In *Securing the "Rice Bowl": China and Global Food Security*. Basingstoke, U.K.: Palgrave Macmillan, 2018.

———. "Security Implications of China's Rising Appetite for Seafood." *Asia Global Online*, June 28, 2018.

Zhao Lei. "New Rules Mean Ships Can Be Used by Military." *PLA Daily*, June 18, 2015. http://www.chinadaily.com.cn/china/2015-06/18/content_21036944.htm.

Zhao Yinan. "Li Vows to Protect Rights of Chinese Working Abroad." *China Daily*, May 5, 2014.

Zhibo Qiu. "The Civilianization of China's Military Presence in the South China Sea." *Diplomat*, January 21, 2017.

INDEX

Note: page numbers with *n*, *p*, or *t* indicate notes, photographs, or tables respectively.

ABOUT THE AUTHOR

Rear Adm. Michael A. McDevitt, USN (Ret.), had four at-sea commands during his thirty-four-year Navy career, including an aircraft carrier battle group. He began a thirty-year involvement with U.S. security policy and strategy in Asia when he was assigned to the Office of the Secretary of Defense in 1990 as director and then as Acting Deputy Assistant Secretary of Defense for East Asia. This professional interest continues to this day.